THE THERAPEUTIC LISTENER

The

Therapeutic   Listener

by
DAVID W. SHAVE, M.D.

ROBERT E. KRIEGER PUBLISHING COMPANY
HUNTINGTON, NEW YORK

First Edition 1974

Printed and Published by
Robert E. Krieger Publishing Co., Inc.
P.O. Box 542
Huntington, N.Y. 11743

© Copyright 1974 by
Robert E. Krieger Publishing Co., Inc.
ISBN No. 0-88275-116-6
Library of Congress Catalog Card Number 73-84419

Library of Congress Cataloging in Publication Data

Shave, David W   1931-
    The therapeutic listener.

    Includes bibliographical references.
    1. Psychotherapy. 2. Communication--Psychological
aspects. 3. Transference (Psychology) I. Title.
RC480.5.S446   616.8'914   73-84419
ISBN 0-88275-116-6

Printed in U.S.A. by
NOBLE OFFSET PRINTERS, INC.
New York, N.Y. 10003

To My Wife, Janice

TABLE OF CONTENTS

ACKNOWLEDGEMENTS

I wish to acknowledge my appreciation to those very *special* clients of mine, who through the years have helped me to understand the subtleties of communication. I wish also to acknowledge the help in preparing this manuscript of my dedicated and very able assistant, Mrs. Evelyn Chatham.

David W. Shave MD

INTRODUCTION

THE THERAPEUTIC LISTENER is a detailed study of the subtle communicative processes in interpersonal relationships. It proposes a theory of a latent *part object* inter-relating that is unconscious, but which is unquestionably shown to be universal to all object relationships. *Transference language* is described as the *latent content* underlying the verbalizations of an interpersonal relationship. These verbalizations make up a metaphorical *manifest content,* which is secondarily formed, and reflects its emotionally oriented part object basis. These manifest contents hide the subtle transference induced interaction in the "here and now" between the ambivalent parts of the speaker, and the parts he unconsciously perceives in his listener. It is this part object interaction that can make emotional uncomfortableness or can remove it. The *therapeutic listener* is any person who attempts to make another more comfortable through a listening process.

Under a reality oriented guise of being intellectual and logical, man is the most *emotional* animal. Continually operating in his interpersonal relationship sphere, under a veneer of reality, is this illogical and emotionally oriented *part object* inter-relating of a sometimes intense degree, that is always *primary* to his intellectual functioning. Man must therefore deal with not only the reality of Life, but this *unreality* as well. This book will attempt to specify that unreality and to show that it is inseparable from reality, and that it has a unique importance of its own. An emotionally-oriented part object theory of communication is introduced that adds an entirely new and fascinating dimension to the understanding of human behavior. And because it *is* part object oriented, it will be seen to encompass all other theories, which are *whole object* oriented.

Lastly, this book implies that there is a *far greater* need for therapeutic listeners in the mental health field, than a need for psychiatrists and that *anyone* at all can become more comfortable by involvement with a therapeutic listener. How this is done is shown in the following pages.

FOREWORD

At a large state hospital in Iowa, I first became interested in "Schizophrenia", that "illness" of which I had been duly warned by some medical school colleagues: "There'll be a lot of psychiatrists out of work when they eventually discover the organic cause of schizophrenia". But finding that organic cause has been, as the late Dr. Lawrence Kubie put it, "like looking for a *needle* in a haystack", in spite of the regularly occurring "break-throughs" periodically published in newspapers and psychiatric journals, that seem to imply a discovery of the biological origin of the "illness" as just around the corner. These "discoveries" have ranged from subtle EEG changes, complex genetic abnormalities, microphysiologic defects, biochemical derangements, pathological neuroanatomy, dietary insufficiencies, to even bee stings. Interpersonal relationship "discoveries" have been equally as exciting to read, ranging from "schizophrenogenic mothers", to the entire society being blamed as the ultimate locus of the "illness". Nothing, in all of medical history, has been so elusive as that "needle in the haystack", and nothing more ludicrous than the search and capture of this apparent Unicorn of Psychiatry.

As long as I worked within the confines of a state psychiatric hospital, I felt certain I knew what "schizophrenia" really was. I could see, as a psychiatrist-in-training, the "signs of schizophrenia" so readily at the weekly diagnostic intake conferences, even before the Clinical Director would diagnose the patients as such. "Schizophrenia", at that early stage of my career was an *unquestionable* entity. Patients were all diagnosed and one had simply to learn the categories of "mental illness", and their classifying "signs". The difference between the "schizophrenic" and the "normal" was as easily made in the confines of the state hospital, as categorizing a person as an "alcoholic", when he is lying intoxicated in a gutter. But I began to see those "soft signs" of the same "schizophrenic process" in those that were diagnosed as "neurotic", "character disorders", "homosexual", "drug addicts", and "alcoholics". I prided myself in being able to diagnose the "pseudoneurotic schizophrenic", the "ambulatory schizophrenic", the "border-line schizophrenic", and the "pre-schizophrenic". "Schizophrenia" seemed everywhere in that mental hospital, and not just in those that had been *diagnosed* as such. One had only to *listen* a little more carefully.

After completing my residency, I began a full-time private practice of "psycho-analytically oriented psychotherapy". What I again saw in those that came to see me, was the same "signs of schizophrenia", I had come to know so well during my residency training. There didn't seem to be any difference, except that many of those that came were prestigious members of the community, and often accomplished in their particular fields of endeavor. The difference between "psychiatric patients" and others in the community began to blur. No longer terming patients "schizophrenic", I found it more conducive to my practice to simply call them "my uncomfortable clients". And they often contrasted as being much *less* "schizophrenic-like", than those I came to learn about in the community that wouldn't ever see a psychiatrist under any condition. That guilt that I had previously felt was the "schizophrenic's very core" was now seen as an asset as much as a liability in the people I knew. What I thought was *limited* to "schizo-phrenia" seemed *everywhere* I looked. I could even see it — and often blatently so — in my medical colleagues. And alas, I finally could see it in my *ownself*! Where before I would start off each day determined to "stamp out mental illness . . . *whatever it is!*", I came to realize that in any such attempt, one always ends up stomping on his own foot!

Dr. David Freedman, a psychiatrist in Houston, Texas, in a letter to the Editor in the *American Journal of Psychiatry*, has facetiously proposed a "Society for the Abolition of the Noun 'Schizophrenia'." Others would like to go one step further, and propose a "Society for the Abolition of Psychiatry", for if what has been described as "schizophrenia" is an inseperable part of being human, then *why*, they ask, call it an *"illness"*. They propose that neurology take care of that which psychiatry has usurped from it, and leave the rest to psychology.

It is not difficult to understand Dr. Arnold Mandell asking the pertinent questions at a recent annual meeting of the American Psychiatric Association in Dallas, Texas: *"What* is Psychiatry? *Why* is Psychiatry? and *Should* there be a Psychiatry?" Dr. E. Fuller Torrey, a psychiatrist at the National Institute of Mental Health was stating that witch doctors and psychiatrists were really one behind their exterior mask and pipe. Psychiatry is going through an "adolescent identity crisis", but some see that *"new"* psychiatry headed toward *no psychiatry*! Dr. Ewald W. Busse, a past president of the American Psychiatric Association, has stated that the very future of psychiatry rests upon the ability to clarify the concept of "mental illness," and properly classify the great variety of psychiatric disorders. A purpose of THE THERAPEUTIC LISTENER is to show how utterly impossible this task really is.

Since "schizophrenia", and "psychiatry" itself, seem so nebulously defined, what about "psychotherapy"? Is it just so much gobledegook and snake oil that has been given an air of respectability because of psychiatry's alliance with the rest of the field of medicine? Dr. Leslie D. Krian, Director of the Psychiatric Consultation-Liason Service at Bellevue-New York University Medical Center has defined *psychotherapy* as "an interaction between two or more individuals". Now, if this is so, one can conclude there must be millions upon millions of psychotherapists on this earth, and millions upon millions of therapy patients. How does one know the *patients* from the *therapists,* one might ask, when everyone is therefore a potential therapist and everyone must be a potential therapy patient? Perhaps one should bill everyone he ever listens to. I am reminded here of one psychiatrist I know, that comes closest to this in refusing to talk to his patients. He told his nurse (a client of mine) when one of his shock patients asked to talk to him: "I'm not doing *psychotherapy* with her, I'm giving her shock treatment! I can only get paid by her insurance company for doing *one* or the *other!*" Of such foolishness, I have come to learn that psychiatry is made.

Just what the difference is in a *"schizophrenic"* seeing a *"psychiatrist"* for *"psychotherapy"*, and those involved in a process of *"therapeutic listening"*, I have tried to make clear.

CHAPTER 1

THE PART OBJECT MAKE-UP OF THE UNCONSCIOUS

What will be presented in this beginning chapter is a theory that the unconscious of people in general seems to function as though it is made up of different and separate *parts*. Each of these apparent parts seems to have feelings appropriate to that part which have been derived from past emotional experience on a *part* object basis. This is a *part* object relationship theory, as opposed to a theory of object relations, which implies that the unconscious perceives the objects of reality as *parts* and reacts to them on a *part to part* basis. This is in contrast to the object to object relating that is characteristic of the conscious. What has been described in the psychiatric literature[1][2] as characterizing "schizophrenic" thought processes will be shown as the probable way the unconscious "thinks." In later chapters, it will be demonstrated in detail, that *the language of the transference* is the language of the unconscious that reflects its part make-up.

The conscious deals with reality. But there is a much greater size to the unconscious that concerns itself with unrealities, past and present. The iceberg analogy may be used to illustrate that the conscious is comparable to that part of the iceberg *above* the water. This is the visible part — the part that is so obvious and so readily definable. The unconscious may be likened to the eight-ninths of the iceberg *below* the water, that supports, with its massiveness, the mere one-ninth above. This part is not visible, and it is not so readily definable. Its shape, its dimensions, and its characteristics can only be inferred. Its importance comes from the fact that it shores up and supports what is so impressive on the surface. Whatever is so note-worthy above must depend on what is below.

Not only is there a remarkable difference between the conscious and the unconscious in regard to size, relative importance and obviousness, but there is a most significant difference in the functioning characteristics of each. The conscious is reality-oriented. It is concerned with *whole* objects, where objects mean persons, entities or experiences. The object is perceived and considered by the conscious as a totality. People are responded to as totals. And one object is compared with another, on a whole object basis. The conscious accepts identity only upon the basis of identical "wholes" or "totals," and not as parts or part objects. It tends to "think" in a way that follows the four Aristotelian Laws of Logic.

1

These reality-oriented "Laws of Logic," first described by Aristotle, are (1) The Law of Identity where "A" is always "A" and never is "B." (2) The Law of Contradiction where "A" cannot be "A" and "not be A," at the same time and place. (3) The Law of the Excluded Middle where it is either "A" or "not A" and cannot be in the middle. (4) The Law of Sufficient Reason where everything must have a sufficient *cause*. The classical example of this type of thinking is: "Man is mortal; Socrates is a man; *Therefore Socrates is mortal.*"

But this type of cognition is not characteristic of the unconscious. In contrast to the Aristotelian logic of the conscious that fits reality so well, the unconscious has a manner of "thinking" quite different. This type of unconscious cognition has been termed "primary process thinking," and it has been associated in psychiatric literature, almost exclusively, with the descriptions of "schizophrenia." Because this is so, it is appropriate to review briefly what has been described of primary process thinking with respect to "schizophrenia". Although "schizophrenia" is a voluminous subject, where, in the past ten years alone, over ten thousand articles have been written concerning it, it is only the so called "schizophrenic thinking" that we are concerned with here, that we are presenting as characterizing the unconscious.

Descriptions of "schizophrenia" go back as far as earliest recorded history. But we might begin our very brief review with Kraepelin,[4] the great German nosologist, who gave the name *dementia praecox* to this "illness." In 1896 he had attempted to designate "mental illness" as a part of medicine and to bring order out of the chaos of psychiatric nomenclature at that time. He categorized the previously isolated, but well described psychoses into a single grouping. He characterized this group as having a seemingly early onset with an irreversible and down hill progression. He felt it had some undiscovered organic basis or origin and that it was essentially a dementing process in the brain, thus the name *dementia praecox*.

In 1911, Bleuler[5] attempted to reconcile the contemporary psychiatry of Kraepelin, which was based on organicity, and the unfolding psychoanalytic discoveries of Freud.[6] Bleuler could not accept the diagnostic implications of Kraepelin's *dementia praecox*, nor could he be sure of its organic basis. He felt that the uncertain etiology involved a *fractionation* of thought processes, such that the person seemed to be characterized by continually being "split" in his thinking. The individual seemed to show that he didn't think as a "whole" but that his thinking and his speech seemed to reflect a make-up of different parts. He gave the name "schizophrenia" to convey appropriately that instead of whole object thinking, or cognition based on totalities, there was an apparent "splitting" of the mind into parts, each of which seemed to have feelings, wishes and fears.

Bleuler knew that the "schizophrenic" process could come to a standstill at any stage and that it wasn't dementing. He knew that the symptoms, in many

2

cases, cleared up by themselves without any treatment whatsoever. He personally knew of people who were very successful prior to the onset of the "schizophrenic" process and who led very successful lives following an episode of this "illness". Bleuler was influenced by Freud's contemporary work on dreams, where findings showed the unconscious wishes, fears and conflicts seemed concealed to the dreamer and yet could be revealed to the analytically perceptive listener. Bleuler clearly recognized the marked similarity between the psychodynamic symbolism of the dream, as described by Freud, and "schizophrenic" symptomatology.

Bleuler felt that the apparent "splitting" of the "schizophrenic's" thinking into opposing, and often conflicting parts, was a pre-requisite condition for the "illness." He felt it was on this, and this alone, that the complicated symbolic behavior, both verbal and non-verbal, was based. It was Bleuler who originated the term "ambivalence" to apply to "schizophrenia" with its mixed feelings arising from the apparent different parts. But in his attempt to clarify "schizophrenia" as a distinctive entity, Bleuler left a rather ambivalent heritage as to exactly what he did feel about the "illness." In illustrating some of the characteristics of some of his colleagues, the "schizophrenia" that he had minutely dissected in an attempt to delineate it more clearly than had Kraepelin, seemed to dissolve from a clear-cut entity and meshed, instead, into a confusion with "normalcy."

Stierlin,[7] in a study of Bleuler's analytic approach to "schizophrenia," states that Bleuler put the "schizophrenic" disturbance and all its symptomatology into the panorama of everyday human experience. He felt that Bleuler humanized the concept of "schizophrenia" and linked it inseparably to the common human experience, leading the reader to see that the thinking and affectivity, or emotional make-up, were different from the "normal" experiences in terms of quantity but not in quality. In many cases one couldn't even be sure of this distinction between quantitative differences when the particular *situation* the individual found himself in seemed to make the crucial difference of an "illness" or not.

Bleuler's concept of "autistic thinking," described in regard to "schizophrenia," was similar to Freud's concept of "primary process cognition." This so called primary process thinking, Freud had felt, was the very basis of the dreaming process and was common to all people in general. According to Bleuler, the apparent distortions of thought in "schizophrenia" were not to be differentiated from that which occurs in dreams. This then linked what was characteristic of "schizophrenic thinking" with the phenomenon of the dream.

Meyer[8] was a turn of the century American psychiatrist who had been a pathologist and had initially attempted to take up the challenge of Kraepelin to find the organic or pathological basis of "schizophrenia." He gave up trying to find an organic pathology and, instead, postulated a non-organic basis for the "illness," implying that it was a "reaction" rather than an "illness." He

3

characterized "schizophrenia" as a "habit disorganization," emphasizing the significance of life experiences. He implied that a *conditioning process* in early life was the basis of the development later of patterns of "insufficient adaptation" to less than "normal" life situations. This seemed to infer that one had the ability to distinguish whether there were "normal" or "abnormal" life situations in making a diagnosis of 'schizophrenia."

Von Domarus,[9] like Freud and Bleuler before him, made a remarkable contribution to understanding the unconscious while concerned with "schizophrenia." He clarified Freud's primary process thinking with his formulation of the "Von Domarus Law." He indicated that the so called "normal" person, whom he termed a "logician," accepted identity only on the basis of identical whole objects in their *totality*. He felt that the "schizophrenic," or what he called the "paralogician," accepted an equating of two objects based upon a *common predicate* shared by the two objects. In other words, two different objects could be equated as identical with this type of thinking if they shared a single characteristic in common.

This markedly contrasted with the Aristotelian rules of logic. Von Domarus offered the following as a contrasting example of primary process thinking. "Socrates is a man. I am a man, and *therefore I am Socrates.*"

This identification is, of course, an erroneous one. But it well illustrates this predicate type of thinking supposedly characteristic of both the dream and "schizophrenia." As an additional example, Von Domarus cited a case of one of his "schizophrenic" patients in an insane asylum at the University of Bonn. This patient believed that "Jesus" and "a cigar box" were all identical. The paralogic reasoning of this person was analytically determined to involve the association that these very different entities or objects shared an identifying predicate in this person's thinking. Each one of these objects, according to the patient, involved the characteristic of encirclement. Jesus was thought of by the patient as a saint with a halo encircling his head. A package of cigars was thought of as being encircled by a tax band. A woman was thought of by the patient as being encircled by the sex glance of a man. This characteristic of *being encircled*, in this particular person's mind, was the equating predicate that then made "Jesus," a "cigar box" and a "woman" identical. For clarifying the non-Aristotelian primary process cognition of Freud's, Von Domarus deserves special credit.

According to this non-Aristotelian type of thinking, two or more different people, or situations, or experiences, or impressions can be *equated* if they share, in some way, a *perceived common predicate*. The objects equated, may be very different from each other, and to someone else, may have no discernible common characteristic at all. But if one does perceive an attribute, an aspect, a characteristic, or a trait that is commonly shared by each of these objects, then they can be equated as *identical* with each other and responded to in an appro-

4

priately similar manner. The common predicate utilized to make this identical equating may be quite unrealistically or autistically chosen. It is as though an object, perceived as being made up of parts "A, B and C," is equal, in its entirety, to another object that is made up of the perceived parts "C, D and E." Because each of these different objects contained the commonly shared part "C," they are both held as being *identical* in their totality.

This method of equating can become extremely complicated when one recognizes that the common equating predicate may be very autistically perceived by an individual who makes two or more objects identical which, to someone else, might appear entirely unrelated. Without knowing the predicate used to equate the different objects, this latter person might logically conclude such equating as preposterous. However, had this other person had the same experiences with each object, he might readily understand how the common predicate perceived in each object could possibly equate them.

It is made even *more* complicated by the fact that the equating can be made on the basis of a commonly shared predicate which involves a *lack* of a certain attribute, aspect, characteristic or trait shared in common by two or more objects. As an example, "A, B and C" may be thought of as being identical to "D, E and F," "G, H and I," and "J, K and L" because they all have the commonly shared attribute of lacking "M". They might be thought of as being equated if they all had the common characteristic of lacking an attribute called "N," or "O," or "P," etc. Thus it becomes evident that, with this type of primary process thinking, any two or more *different* objects or past experiences, or situations have the potential of being *identically* equated.

Von Domarus felt this non-Aristotelian logic, that characterizes primary process thinking, was employed predominately by "schizophrenics" and by primitive people. This use by primitive man can be illustrated, for instance, in the naming of an Indian whereby, if an Indian were perceived to have the quality of *running fast* like a deer, he would be thought of as being identical to a deer and would then be named "Running Deer." Others felt that children also tended to use this same type of illogic in much of their thinking. If, for instance, children are observed playing with baby-dolls, the dolls are reacted to as though being "real" babies with real needs. The children respond to the dolls as though they need to be held, cuddled, clothed, fed, washed, and talked to.

Arieti[10] felt that there was, in the "schizophrenic," an illogical identification between the symbol and the object symbolized. He described, as characteristic of primary process thinking, confusion between a *part* of an object and the *whole* object. He continued to say that the equating of objects in reality for the "schizophrenic" seemed to be on a *part object* basis. The bizarre composition of different objects and entities as seen in "schizophrenic" drawings and neologisms were, he felt, all due to an apparent *part* object perception. This, he further felt, could be interpreted by an application of the Von Domarus Law.

He proposed that all Freudian symbolism, particularly in the dream, as well as "schizophrenic" thinking, and the thinking of primitive man and of children, could be totally explained by this Von Domarus Law of predicate equating and this part object perception.

Storch[11] felt that the "schizophrenic's" thinking seemed to reflect an earlier level in "normal" psychological development. He characterized the "schizophrenic's" thought as being similar to an infant's where there is little or no differentiation between real acts and wishes. Wishing, in the "schizophrenic's" thinking is identically equated, according to Storch, with the actual act. The wish, or thought, becomes immediately equated with perceived reality. A feeling of being the center or the focus of reality, accompanied by a feeling of omnipotence similar to what the infant is speculated as having, is supposedly characteristic of a "schizophrenic." Reality, then, is perceived with a *self-reference.* Thus, events, situations, and experiences of reality are felt to occur *in relation* to the "schizophrenic."

Storch also felt that heterogeneous parts of different objects, experiences or situations could be fused together into a perceptual entity even though these parts belonged to different objects and were, perhaps, from different periods of Time. This was an elaboration of Freud's ego defenses of projection, condensation and displacement which he described in regard to the dreaming process and the development symbols. Any one of these unconsciously perceived parts of an object could become the substratum of an entire complex which could then be responded to as a separate object in itself. Parts of different objects could be symbolically concretized into a new entity and then reacted to as an actual object of reality.

Maher[12] objected to the idea that the Aristotelian laws of logic were representative of how normal people think in common place situations. He felt that all people, and not just "schizophrenics," children or primitive man, tend to think at times in a rather non-Aristotelian way very similar to primary process thinking. But the "schizophrenic" was erring only as a matter of *degree.* In other words, predicate equating generalizations, according to Storch, tended in the "schizophrenic," to differ only in degree from that of the "normal." He felt that as far as the "schizophrenic's" responding to an aspect or an attribute of an object, as equated with another object's aspect or attribute, the behavior was quite appropriate and realistic. But in responding to the attributes of the object not covered by the identifying predicate, the lack of discrimination became "schizophrenic." Maher gave, as a hypothetical example, a patient of his, whose reasoning was as follows: "General Eisenhower is a veteran. My therapist is a veteran. Therefore my therapist *is* General Eisenhower." This patient would then address his therapist as "General," saluting him whenever they met and standing at attention in his office. Maher makes the point that if the patient *did* meet General Eisenhower, the same behavior would be quite appropriate.

6

Forrest[13] stated that the symbolic concretization, as descriptive of the thought of "schizophrenics" or of the dream, was based entirely upon the Von Domarus principle of predicate equating but was also found in the roots of normal language. The development of the metaphor, he showed, has an implied primary process type of "illogic" derivation. In taking an example of one of Bleuler's patients who felt he "owned Algiers" and then felt he suffered from "neuralgiers," Forrest showed that this same sort of combining of like predicates similarly occurs in the etiologic history of "normal" language where there is often a blend of two quite different things. Forrest gives, as an example, the word *"smog"* which is neologistically derived from "smoke" and "fog," and *"slithy,"* derived from the combination of "slimy" and "lithe." He called attention to the fact that a figure of speech in normal language termed a "synecdoche" is an example of the part for a whole type of thinking where "50 sail" is understood for "50 ships"; or the *whole* for a *part,* in the example, "cut throat" being understood for assassin. He felt that the "schizophrenic" uses an act of "poiesis" in just the same way as does a poet whose poetic diction is normally *expected* by any reader of poetry. He implied that the "schizophrenic" and the poet both shared a common type of thinking, characterized by predicate equating and part object percepting. The search for a "schizophrenic" language, according to Forrest, is like the futile quest for a "poetic" language as an entity separate from "normal" language.

This idea of Forrest's that a "schizophrenic" language doesn't really exist is supported by the work of Lorenz[14] who cautioned against the tendency to generalize a "schizophrenic language." Lorenz has suggested that there are no distinct features of "schizophrenic" language that differentiate it from ordinary language. Sommer[15] also recognized the fallacy of an artificial dichotomy and very appropriately asked: "Is there a schizophrenic language?" It is interesting to note that, together, Ruesch and Bateson[16] have shown that most of the categories listed under "psychopathology" really involve nothing other than *disturbances of communication,* and that the various "abnormalities" of human behavior can be readily described in terms of communication. Ruesch and Bateson further felt that any therapy should aim at *improving* the communications system of the emotionally uncomfortable person. They correctly predicted that in the future, psychiatric thought would move closer toward a realization of the importance of communication.

Present day psychiatry is embroiled with the question of whether "schizophrenia" really exists at all, or whether it is just, at *best,* an exaggeration of the "norm." Szasz[17,18] has well described the "myth of mental illness," while Liefer,[19] Laing,[20] and Albee,[21] as well as an increasing number of psychiatrists and psychologists, imply that the "medical model" of "mental illness" is inappropriate and most erroneous. Kraepelin had put "mental illness" into the domain of medicine, but there are now many who would like to see it removed.

7

Claridge,[22] for instance, cites that of the hundreds of biochemical, physiological, and even psychological measurements which have been taken on "schizophrenics," in no case has the distribution of the scores indicated a clear qualitative difference from the general population average.

In fact, what had been earlier described as so characteristic of the thinking of "schizophrenics" shows itself within the medical terms that apparently reflect a primary process type of cognition which is often rather autistically determined. To name just a few, one might mention "saddle noses," "pistol shot heart sounds," "kissing ulcers," "urea frost," "water hammer pulses," buffalo humps," "moon facies," "pill roller tremors," "hobnail" and "nutmeg livers," "oat cell tumors," "strawberry gall-bladders," "hot cross bun heads," "milkmaid's legs," "scrotal tongues," "gargoylism," "alligator skins," "splinter hemorrhages," "St. Vitus Dances" and "pin," "tape" and "hair worms." If one were to take the Latin derivations of many medical conditions, one would see a similar type of "logic." Psychiatry itself is guilty of the same type of "thinking" that it has accused "schizophrenics" of. The Don Juan Syndrome, the Ulysses Syndrome, the Lazarus Complex, and the Oedipus complex should suffice as examples.

The illogical part object identification that is based on the Von Domarus principle of equating by like predicates is actually more a part of our language than many recognize. For instance, the naming of plants and animals seems to reflect a *necessity* to compare one object, or an aspect of that object, with an entirely unrelated object and then to equate the two from this part object identification. Literally, what is implied is a type of "schizophrenic" reasoning as: "To me, *this* object is just like *that* object," and thusly the object is named. As for examples, one has "Lady Slipper," "Queen Anne's Lace," "Indian Pipes," "Toadstools," for a token few of the plants; "Garter Snake," "Hammer-head," "Cardinal," "Sword-fish," "Portuguese-Man-O-War," and "Hermit crab" should illustrate the animals. Scientific nomenclature, too, reflects the same illogic origins. For instance, the finch *"Pipilo erythropthalmus"* is apparently named "scientifically" because it reminded a taxonomist of its red eye. It might have just as well been named something else by the learned taxonomists using an illogic that supposedly only "schizophrenics," Indians and small children used. They could have utilized the bird's common names, which also involve predicate equating. It is called a *"Towhee"* in one part of the country because of one of its calls, and it is *"Ground Robin,"* to others in another locale, because its red breast and black head make it look similar to a robin. The "fiddler crab" is a marine crab that may have looked like, or reminded some of a fiddle as it has one enormous claw as big as all the rest of its body. However, the marine taxonomist apparently felt it was similar to a fighter, and not a fiddle at all, for its scientific name is *"Uca pugliator."* It isn't the mere listing of words like these that is important, but, instead, it is the autistic, primary process cognition and

8

part-object identifications involved in supposedly *normal* language which needs to be emphasized.

Returning now to the subject of the unconscious of people in general, what has been initially described as characteristic of the thinking of "schizophrenia," or as characteristic of the dream and even of the roots of normal language, also characterizes the unconscious. Not unlike the faces of Eve, people in general seem to have an unconscious part object make-up by which the different and opposing ambivalent parts, at times, have a capacity to show themselves. These different parts that seem to make up the unconscious are not simple opposing parts. The ambivalence is not of a simple bi-polar type, but instead seems to be made up of a multiplicity of different parts which can be reflected into the verbalizations of an individual like a revolving diamond that kaleidoscopically reflects from each facet as it turns.

When a person is emotionally uncomfortable, there will be a tendency to show more of this kaleidoscopic ambivalence from a more *intense* part make-up of his unconscious. A person may recognize that there's one part of him that wants to do one thing while realizing that another part seemingly wants to do another thing. Each of these courses of action seems to be supported from a variety of different parts. For instance, a woman may want to go to the beach with a male friend, on one hand, and feel on the other, that she should stay home. She may want to go the beach because she likes certain things about the ride to the beach, the beach itself, or about this male friend; or because she doesn't want to stay at home and have to do certain unenjoyable things there that she'd have to do if she stayed; or because the male friend might feel she doesn't like him if she refused to go; or because she *should* go, having refused him a previous time he asked her. Her *wanting* to go is not just a bi-polar opposing feeling of *not wanting* to go.

An expression of a part that wants to stay home may be entirely different from a part that doesn't want to go to the beach. Each part that is expressed seems like a separate entity that can be expanded upon and developed and can further lead into an awareness of still other parts. Neither is there a simple presentation of a conscious part versus an unconscious part but rather, a *multiplicity* of underlying unconscious parts.

This is illustrated by the woman who becomes emotionally upset on the day her daughter is to go into the hospital for a tonsillectomy. She fears that something will go wrong in the surgery and that her daughter will die. No reassurance from the surgeon seems to allay her anxiety. And there is a reason for this. Since the daughter is emotionally dependent on her mother, and because dependency is so often a two way street, the mother, then, is *dependent*, in part, on her daughter. Somehow there is an equating of this daughter, on whom the mother is partially dependent, with those in the past on whom the mother was dependent who let her down and to whom she is unconsciously *angry*. Thus one can imply a part of

9

the woman *wants* her daughter to die (the unconscious *wish* behind the conscious *fear*), because a *part* of the daughter is perceived as likened to the emotionally significant people of the mother's past who have let her down. A part of the mother, one can further imply, may also *identify* with the daughter if that part that identifies with the daughter is a *guilt-laden* part. This suspected part, because it *is* guilt-laden is *deserving* to die. This part is brought to the fore by the impending operation. There may be still another part that "remembers," as it were, the past repetitive part object experiences for this woman, that convey the impression that whomever she loves always seems to die, go away, or somehow leaves her.

An emotionally uncomfortable man also seemingly implies this part make-up of his unconscious in remarking: "My parents say I'm building too big a house, that I won't be able to pay for it, and that I won't be able to keep it up on a yearly basis. They say I ought to be satisfied with a much smaller one. When they tell me this, it gets me all upset." One can suspicion that there is an unconscious part of him that does believe, as his parents do and that he *is* building too large a house, that he *won't* be able to pay for it, and that he *won't* be able to keep it up. If he didn't have this part within him, he shouldn't really care what anybody else might say, but because there *are* different, conflicting parts within himself, he is "upset".

One may sometimes see this same thing illustrated in those people who take offense at being called a derogatory name. The person who becomes upset when he is called, for instance, an S.O.B., is so because there is an unconscious part of him that does feel he is an S.O.B. When he *is* called an S.O.B., his ego defenses against this part becoming conscious are threatened, and he angrily reacts to deny it or to project to the person who called him this name. It isn't just that this part is unconscious — for one could give illustrations of unconscious parts within this individual that imply that he is not an S.O.B. — but that his unconscious is made up of many *different* parts which have their roots in *different* past emotional experiences.

Unconscious murderous, as well as suicidal, aspects of the unconscious are frequently simultaneously shown in individuals, who, for instance, "breakdown" when their best friend or buddy is killed in combat. The guilt-laden part of one's unconscious that is *suicidal,* and identifies with the death of the lost friend, represents one reason for the emotional turmoil. But on the other hand, aggressive and murderous impulses, from a part that unconsciously *wished* the buddy to die, are another reason. Such simultaneously occurring and grossly conflicting feelings *necessitate,* that for emotional confortableness, they remain unconscious. When they intrude their ambivalence into consciousness, emotional uncomfortableness results.

This same tendency to identify from parts within ourselves makes it possible for us to appreciate acts of valor and heroism on the battlefield. Perhaps it is because these acts are so daring with life, or so tempting of suicide. Perhaps it is because they can be identified with our own hidden, aggressive parts which would like to express anger as the hero did. Perhaps it is, too, because we can vicariously satisfy, in part, a need within ourselves for the recognition that such individuals obtain. What this all demonstrates is that there is a "multiple part" make-up within the unconscious of a person.

Manifestations of this apparent part make-up of the unconscious, characteristic of people in general, can be interestingly found in studies of human behavior. Take, for instance, a 5 year old boy who, in feeling the need to be better appreciated and more favorably recognized within his family, decides, on his own and unbeknown to his mother, to clean the fireplace "just like Daddy does." In his vigorous attempt to do so, soot flies about soiling the living room rug and furniture. His mother, who might not have been as supportive to him as she could have been during the past week — herself being frustrated by her husband's seeming lack of appreciation, perhaps — turns upon the boy with anger. Proceeding to berate and punish the boy, she takes out on him the anger which has arisen from her own frustration. This is, of course, difficult for the boy to emotionally understand, particularly since he is specifically frustrated and hurt in his attempt to feel *more* wanted and be *better* accepted. He ends up feeling more alone and rejected, and is more an outcast to his mother. He cries, in part, because he has been emotionally hurt; and he cries, in part, because he has "hurt" his mother in making her so unhappy by his need-prompted action with the fireplace. That same night, he wakes up from his sleep fearfully crying that there's a "big black spider" in his bed, terrified that it might kill him. He insists on sleeping in his mother's bed and, in doing so, feels more safe and secure. Ironically, though, he is, in part, sleeping with the "big, black spider" *herself!* That aspect of his mother that can make the boy feel that he is deserving to be "eaten up", as well as his own feeling that he deserves to die for making his mother so unhappy, is symbolically concretized into the conscious conception of the spider.

In order to illustrate further that the unconscious of people in general seems to be made up of different and often opposing parts, consider a few examples which may very well be quite personally familiar. Take first of all the behavior of people, who, upon learning of a terrible automobile accident nearby, throng to the site to observe the wreckage and the possible carnage. The outward behavior that leads a person to view the scene is a concretization of many unconscious motivations which seem to reflect an apparent part object make-up of the individual. We might speculate, for instance, that the scene of the violence gives a *sadistic* pleasure to unconscious aggressive drives so that the potential violence, within a part of the individual, may be vicariously identified with the violence viewed at the scene of the accident. But, too, there may also be an unconscious part of the person that identifies with the victims, thus engendering a *masochistic* pleasure in seeing death and destruction. This may be identified with a guilt-laden or a self-felt death-deserving aspect of the unconscious of the person, as though he feels, in part, that *he* ought to be killed in a similar destructive scene.

Note that these unconscious destructive and self-destructive wishes and fears are evident, not only in those who rush to the accident scene, but evident, too, in those who rush the other way to avoid viewing the scene. Those who go to help do so, in part, to help unconsciously identified and projected aspects of themselves which they unconsciously feel are in need of help, too.

In a manner similar to the example given of the automobile accident, destructive fires seem especially attractive to many people and seem to satisfy or gratify unconscious parts or wishes within the individual. Again, this may be shown, when a crowd quickly gathers below the suicidal person who seems about to jump to his death. There are many cases where the crowd has actually chanted "Jump, Jump" as though obtaining some vicarious pleasure in anticipating someone else's demise and, perhaps, in this way, the hopeful demise of this unacceptable, death-deserving aspect of themselves. Others may try desperately, and again for multiple unconscious reasons from the different parts of an individual's make-up, to save the jumper's life. Even after the suicide has taken place, people can be seen coming to view the site where it happened, again motivated by various aspects of their own unconscious self which identify with the suicide, rarely, if ever, for a single reason. Even though some people may remark the usual "Isn't it dreadful?," one cannot help but recognize a pleasurable aspect in viewing the violence. Both the vicarious masochistic and sadistic pleasures that so attract people may give the person recognition of a "There, but for the grace of God, go I" type of feeling.

To further illustrate the existence of the part make-up of the unconscious of people in general, consider the fear of being in a very high place. This is so common to people that many of the very high road bridges have attendants or police on hand to drive a car over if the driver is so incapacitated by unconscious suicidal parts that he is unable to do so himself. When such individuals find themselves standing in an exposed and very high place, for instance looking down from the top of a high building where there are no barriers to guard against plunging to one's death, other than the psychological barriers within one's self, they often become most anxious and fearful. These unconscious suicidal wishes are well known in psychiatry and are thought to arise from the hidden death-deserving parts associated with unconscious feelings of guilt. It is interesting to note that when the intoxicated man is found walking a high bridge rail, he is more blatantly suicidal than the sober person who even fears to go near the rail to peer over the side. But the intoxicated person precariously walking the bridge rail will usually find himself the center of attraction for those who seem to take a vicarious pleasure, from a part within, in *watching* such an act.

12

How people unconsciously identify with an external object, situation or experience, from a part within their unconscious, is shown in the remark: "I always get terribly upset on seeing smashed and crushed defenseless little animals on the highway." Aspects of this person's unconscious have apparently identified with the manifestations of the dead animal on the road. What might be so "upsetting" to this individual is that the sight of the animal's plight is equated with how an unconscious part of themselves feels, as though they, too, have been similarly treated. What is "upsetting" is that this particular sight threatens their unconscious attempt to deny this part recognition by the conscious.

But there are undoubtedly other reasons for becoming "upset" issuing from still other apparent parts of this person's unconscious. For instance what might also cause this to be "upsetting" is that there might be, co-existing together with the part already described, an unconscious part of themselves that would like to take a cruel destructive revenge on something that is equated with an object of the past or present which they loved, but which treated them in an emotionally hurtful way. Here, their defenses against their denied aggressive wishes are threatened. One can see in these two speculations of what is "upsetting" for this individual that there is an etiologic connection between the possible existence of these two different parts, and that each can make a symbolic equating with an aspect of the sight of the run-over animal on the highway.

Many people identify with the plight of suffering or mistreated animals as though attempting to rectify an unconscious projected part within themselves. They feel a "need" within themselves to actively participate in activities that help animals. There are those who take a very active role, for instance, in the beneficial programs of the humane societies and the anti-vivisectionists. Other people apparently identify with the unhappy plight of unfortunate children and actively participate in beneficial programs that help them. Their involvement supports their defenses against these apparent unconscious parts from becoming conscious. It is because there *is* a part of an individual, in so many cases, that apparently identifies, in part, with people whose lots in life are more unfortunate, that benevolent organizations can get the needed support for their endeavors. Even though one might never have had multiple sclerosis, tuberculosis, or cancer, one can *"feel,"* from an identifying part within themselves, for the person who *is* afflicted. It is an unconscious part that symbolically has been similarly "afflicted," but it is *in part* that the identification comes about. Again, it is the Von Domarus type of predicate equating that makes the symbolic identification possible. All charity work may be thought of as arising from a process of identifying, from a projected part of the unconscious of those who are involved in this type of beneficial work, with those that are benefited. There is something that always seems to be equating between the unconscious part of the individual helping and the person helped.

13

One cannot simply rationalize the apparent great interest of people in the front page with a simple "keeping up with the news and current events." That which is so eye-catching *is* so because it *does* offer an identification with the unconscious parts within the individual that *are* symbolically associated with what is read. *This* is what makes it so interestingly front page material! It is important to recognize that unconscious human behavior is not so simple, when engrossingly entertained by television violence, one is only identifying with the hero, or the heroine, or even the victim. That one *does* enjoy the plot almost *necessitates* the unconscious process of identifying, from somehow similar unconscious parts within one's self, with *all* the characters, both male and female, victim and aggressor, and with all the components of the violence. Who does what and to whom, in order to be fully appreciated, requires similarly equated unconscious parts within the viewer for that appreciation. What is read in a newspaper, or seen on television, is made "interesting" because of these unconscious parts.

For instance, suppose someone views a television drama that involves some type of execution. The viewer will identify, from a projected part within himself, not only with the executioner but also from still another unconscious part within, with the one who is executed or is threatened with execution. The understanding of a situation like this, as it is presented in the plot, *requires* a part make-up of the viewer's unconscious. The enjoyment of the plot involves an unconscious projection of these aspects, or parts of one's self, into what is so engrossing. Because it is so engrossing there must be involved an understanding of each of these different view-points.

Note in the above example, that what is so involving *is* so because there is *something* in what is viewed that is being symbolically equated with an unconscious *part* within the viewer. If an individual abhors a particular plot or situation offered for viewing on television, it would be because the viewing of this material threatens an attempt to keep this unconscious part denied. An individual who neither is engrossed by the same material, nor abhors it, has little if any parts within himself that can be symbolically equated.

One might feel offended if someone implies they have such an unconscious violent part within. But this is an example of the necessity of keeping certain things unconscious. That they are offensive is a good indication of the existence of an unconscious part. There may seem to be no logical reason to believe that one would kill someone whom they love. Yet the assassination of Robert Kennedy motivated thousands of people in America to turn in their privately owned guns to authorities. Some of these people felt a sense of unexplainable guilt, that was associated with the assassination, in owning a gun, supposedly to protect themselves or their loved ones. In San Francisco, a "St. Francis of the Guns" statue, dedicated in June of 1969, was made from over two thousand guns from that city alone that were turned in after the senator was assassinated.

On the other side of this same coin, publishers clamored for the assassin's biography, knowing full well the sales appeal to those who have an unconscious identification, in some way, with the assassination act. One can speculate that there is an identification, on a *part* basis, with the assassin as well as with the person assassinated. There is an identification with the people who tried to protect the senator, as well as with those who might have played a role in assisting, in some way, the assassin in his work. These part identifications may extend to the individual punished, to those who do the punishing, to those who suffer and grieve the most, and to any others who are emotionally involved in the act — in short, wherever an emotional symbolic equating is made from an unconscious part within.

The unconscious of an individual is primarily concerned with *emotions* while reality puts a premium on the non-emotional. The symbolic equating of objects, situations and experiences of the present reality with one's unconscious parts is often done on an emotional basis. Something that represents an emotional loss in the present can be equated with a part within which has experienced an emotional loss in the past. The emotionally reactive fervor, in regard to gun control, seems to give conclusive evidence of those various opposing unconscious parts within an individual that one can suspicion exist. Some of these parts may involve emotions that are suicidal, on one hand, and homicidal on the other. Those who feel the possession of a gun is necessary for the protection of themselves or of those they love may imply a hidden homicidal part of *themselves* which they would bitterly defend against consciously recognizing. Again, the emotional fervor expressed by people in regard to capital punishment is evidence, too, of these same unconscious feelings, associated with murderous and suicidal parts within themselves, which may not be recognizable at other times.

These unconscious parts may not be apparent except in those certain situations of reality where they then may become more noticeable, and even blatant. The violence of fires, accidents, drownings, shootings, rapings, suicides, and wars can be unconsciously equated with similarly equated parts within a person's unconscious. They may threaten the defenses of the ego to *keep* these parts of the unconscious, *unconscious*. They may, too, offer a vicarious pleasure toward acting out certain wishes or conflicts, within the unconscious. An individual, for instance, may not have shown his hidden part that was so violence-oriented unless some situation had arisen in reality. With respect to viewed or perceived violence, there is a "There, but for the Grace of God, go I" type of identification with different parts of that violence.

However, this same type of "There, but for the Grace of God, go I" type of equating is done just as readily in situations and experiences of viewed or perceived *love*. For instance, when one views a love scene on television or reads a romantic story, there are aspects of one's self that identify with not only the one who does the loving, but the one who is loved as well. Just as was the case in perceiving a violent act, different aspects of the act of love are identified with the unconscious parts within. If one can understand a love story, it is because he can make these necessary identifications from the projected unconscious parts within himself, that apparently are associated on a part object basis with past emotional experiences of a similarly perceived nature, but on a *part object basis*.

The story one is unconsciously identifying with doesn't even need to have human characters for the primary process type of equating to take place. This subtle unconscious identifying process, from parts within the unconscious, can take place even if the characters are made up of animals as in, for instance, the stories "Lassie", and "Bambi". One can even make unconscious identifications, from parts within one's self, with the myths of the Gods and Goddesses. These myths are themselves derived from projected part object human experiences. A vicarious type of emotional involvement is associated with what is projected, from the part within one's self, into that which is externally viewed or perceived.

Take, for instance, the popular children's story of "Snow White and the Seven Dwarfs." What is entertaining or, really, need-fulfilling involves a *part* identification from the unconscious aspects within the reader so that he literally sees a part of himself in each one of the characters. One may take a personal pleasure in identifying with the guiltless "Snow White" and emotionally re-experience, from the unconscious memories within, the mistreatment that the reader himself went through on a part object basis. He perceived, in part, the similarly equated experience that "Snow White" is described as going through. But the identifications don't stop at Snow White: they involve all the characters of the story. As for the Dwarfs, we all know what it is, at least in part, from our own past experiences, to feel "grumpy," "happy," "dopey," "sleepy," etc. There is, too, a guilt-laden aspect within us that is felt to be ugly and repulsive and which lets us understand the ugly, repulsive witch who seeks so unrealistically to be the fairest in the land. The very creation of a "Snow White" necessitates a projection of the self-felt evil and ugliness within to the witch. The conflicts of the unconscious, with its part make-up, are projected into this story. The identification is made from those who know at least in part from past part object perceptions, what it is like to be similarly maligned, plotted against, poorly recognized, mistreated and finally banished, but who yet secretively wish to find the happy ending where, as in Snow White, someone of significant importance will find them deserving of some royal recognition and love.

These unconsciously made identifications are not sexual ones. It isn't that girls identify with Snow White and boys with the Prince. People who are happy don't identify exclusively with the Dwarf named "Happy." The identifications are made on an unrealistic level that involves part objects. Part object levels are well *below* the level of any sexuality. They involve feelings that are other than sexual feelings, and the deepest feelings are *non*-sexual. Both boys and girls identify with the heroine, Snow White. And both boys and girls identify with the Witch. Both boys and girls identify, in part, with the timely and magic-imbued Prince, who emotionally signifies that which transcends anything that might be conveyed in a simple sex-role identification.

This non-sexual identification of the unconscious parts can be further exemplified, for instance, in a movie where a woman is raped, or where a woman must go through child-birth by herself, or, perhaps, where she loses her baby. Regardless of the sex of the viewer of this movie, or the reader of a novel with similar action, there is an identification where the equating is done apparently without regard to sexual identity or gender role. All people know, in part, what it is like to be attacked; all people know, in part, what it is like to go through a very trying experience alone; and everyone knows what it is like to lose forever something that they love. It is from these parts, which have been similarly experienced, that empathy comes and the understanding is reached.

Just because there is an identification, in part, one should not make a whole-object conclusion. These unconscious parts defy the simple analytic summations that are so often erroneously given by those who are not familiar with the part make-up of the unconscious. Thus, psychological testing and hypnotic "revelations" may be grossly misleading when they imply a whole object orientation. For instance, a person may enjoy murder stories, war stories, or books on violence but not be anymore violent or hostile than an individual who enjoys reading love and romance stories is necessarily romantic and loving. The person who likes to read books of violence may *not* be characterized by violence, and the individual who likes to read romantic stories, frequently *isn't* characterized by being romantic! The point to be made here is simply that there is a conglomeration of unconscious parts within an individual, and these parts may be recognizable from specific situations, particularly when they involve a high degree of emotionality. When someone says: "You are what you read," they incorrectly imply a totality. One may very well *be* this, but *in part!* One may have other parts that contradict or oppose what might seem, at first, to be so representative of the unconscious. One cannot simplify, by any single conclusion, what is uncon-scious. There is always a complexity in this part make-up of the unconscious.

Our appreciation, then, of books, plays, movies and television derives from the identifying process based upon an apparent part make-up of the unconscious. Whether the unconscious actually is made up of parts, is impossible to determine. But for all practical purposes, it *seems* this way and can be considered as such. To explain "likes" and "dislikes" on the basis of hidden parts within the unconscious, in regard to stories, is quite applicable. This also lends itself to explaining the apparent part make-up of the unconscious of the author as well. For instance, suppose an author writes a book about the American Indian. There is something, then, that motivates the author to *do* this about

17

this particular subject. Perhaps it is that there is a part within this author that *identifies* with the American Indian from a great number of predicate equating possibilities. The necessary interest for writing such a book comes from this unconscious part, or parts, within the author. His understanding of the plight of the Indian, perhaps, comes from a similar predicate-equated past experience of his own again, on a part object basis. If the book becomes a best seller, then there must be thousands of readers who *also* can make a similar equating from a part within themselves.

It is interesting to note the projections of the part make-up of the unconscious of any author in the formation of his characters. That an author is able to create these characters stems from those unconscious parts within himself. But to be able to create them exceptionally well takes *more* than just having a similarly equated part within. Take for instance, Hans Christian Andersen who wrote "The Ugly Duckling." He, himself, was a very sickly person. We might speculate that he knew quite personally what it was like to be an "ugly duckling" and that perhaps he conveys, in this story, his own unconscious wish to be a swan, which in fact he did become with his fame as a great story teller for children. But what he knew so well from his own past personal experiences that created that "ugly duckling" part within himself gave him the capacity to present the wish to others who likewise, but perhaps on a lesser scale, feel like "ugly ducklings" and seek to be beautiful "swans."

The early life of deprivation experienced by an author, such as a Dickens or a Poe, no doubt was an asset in his ability to create the characters of many popular stories. It is interesting to speculate that the early life history that creates these unconscious parts within an author, apparently so necessary for successful writing, involves a personal emotional uncomfortableness. This personal emotional uncomfortableness from the author's past, retained in his unconscious as a conflict that lends itself to the creation of plots and characterizations, may make for emotional uncomfortableness in his present. Perhaps this is why so many of the well-known and more popular authors have had personal lives associated with alcoholism, emotional turmoil, depression and suicide. What they experienced on a part object basis in their past, later becomes an asset as well as a liability in their lives. Perhaps they would have been *more* happy, but much *less* successful, had they experienced less of what it takes to be so creative. But the reader's appreciation of these characterizations and plots comes from his own similarly equated experiences, but perhaps to a lesser degree.

Those hidden parts of himself that an author unconsciously projects into his characterizations, along with his own unconscious wishes, fears, and conflicts, touch upon our own. These part object orientations are projected into whole object characterization and totalities that dramatically interact within some setting of reality. The memories of past perceptions of part experiences are projected into whole experiences that are necessary for a conscious understanding.

18

However, for the conscious to logically understand, the part object derived emotions *must* be expressed in a whole object orientation. Stories and plays, for instance, afford an expression of these part derived emotions, as well as an opportunity to appreciate the presentation of the conflicts created by the existence of these parts, for those who enjoy the stories, movies or plays.

An understanding of the apparent part make-up of the unconscious, as well as the apparent part object perception by the unconscious, is a necessity for the therapeutic listener. What the therapeutic listener hears will always either be from the part make-up of his client's unconscious or will represent a part object perception. All "third ear" listening will involve this same part make-up and part object perception that we have previously considered. What has been presented as occurring in anyone's unconscious make-up seems more exaggerated in the emotionally uncomfortable person. In a person who is emotionally uncomfortable, or who becomes emotionally uncomfortable, the part make-up of his unconscious and his apparent part object perceptions become more noticeable and more readily perceptible.

Any practitioner of medicine is quite familiar with the individuals who constantly seek out diagnostic tests, medical confirmations, hospitalizations and operations for what they believe is a hidden or undiagnosed potential fatal illness or condition that they have. This seems to imply that they feel, in part from a *guilt-laden* unconscious part of their unconscious, that they have a fatal process within them. But anyone who seeks a physical exam each year also has an unconscious part which feels in a similar way, but perhaps not to the degree of the individual who cannot accept a qualified physician's statement that no fatal process can be found. The person with a more guilt-laden and death-deserving unconscious part can rationalize his unacceptance of this medical report of no illness, by noting the many instances where physicians *have* missed a cancer, a heart condition, or a fatal process.

One will hear an emotionally uncomfortable person express, on one hand, that they feel *lucky* in having the husband that they do and that they feel they ought to appreciate him *more* than they do. But on the other hand, they may ambivalently express feelings that they are *unlucky* being married to whom they are and that they ought to be *more resentful* than they already are for the way they are treated. One may hear this person say, on one hand, that they want the therapeutic listener to know every little thing about them, but on the other hand, they wish he didn't know as much as they fear he does.

The therapeutic listener is continually being exposed to communicated presentations of this apparent part make-up of his clients. When a client begins: "You're really going to think I'm nuts when I tell you this . . .," the client indicates that there is a part of himself that feels he is nuts. This is similar to "I know you think I'm neurotic," where the client *himself* feels, in part, that he is neurotic. Or again, "I know you're thinking that this is all in my head, and I'm

19

just imagining these aches and pains," implies that the client himself feels, in part, his aches aren't real but only imagined. And finally, "I know you think I'm a stupid dummy. Well, let me tell you . . ." when no one but *himself* thinks he's a stupid dummy! And when another client states: "You're not going to con me into coming here for the rest of my life," the client seems to imply that there *is* a part of him who *does* want this, and that this part prompted his defensive statement. This is similar to the client who says: "I hate the part of me that likes to come here to see you." Here the part make-up is shown to be even conscious.

Sometimes there is only a fleeting awareness of these unconscious parts, as illustrated in the following remark made by a client who comes ten minutes late for her appointment with her therapeutic listener: "Why is it that I get lost everytime I come here? (Therapist: Perhaps you really don't want to come.) Why, Dr. Shave, I *do* want to come! I'd *never* lie to you! (Laughs) Oh, I might not tell you the *whole* truth — just part of it. But I'd never lie to you! Of course, I want to come — through it *is* a long way to get here, and it *does* interfere with my work."

At times, clients don't seem to be so aware of that part make-up of their unconscious. One will hear such statements as: "I just hate to be such a worry and a bother to my husband with my being sick this way. I feel so bad that he has to do *so much* for me." They seem to imply, to others, that another part of her rather enjoys what she is putting her husband through. One may hear a client complain that they feel, on one hand, that they must, should, or have to do something that, on the other hand, an obvious part of themselves *doesn't* want to do. It's as though one part wants to do one thing, and another part wants to do something opposed to this.

For instance, a person may recognize that they want to go to the movies, and recognize as well that they don't want to go. Each of these different positions can be supported as well as refuted. Wanting to go, or not wanting to go, can be quite different than the recognized parts of wanting to stay home and not wanting to stay home. The part that wants to stay home may be different than the part that doesn't want to go. Each part seems like a separate entity that can be expanded upon, developed and lead to still other parts. There is then not a simple presentation of a conscious part vs an unconscious part, but a *multiplicity* of parts.

Some clients may be quite well aware of their seemingly part make-up and may express this: "One part of me hates it when I act like a baby around you. Yet another part loves it and wants to be treated like a little child by you." Still another client summed up the emotional dilemma facing her in marriage which arose from her own ambivalence as "My whole problem is that I *love* the son-of-a-bitch!"

Other clients seem to recognize a multiplicity of parts within themselves. One woman did in remarking on her relationship with her employer: "There's a part of me that feels he has no right to tell me what to do and resents his doing it. But there's another part of me that knows he's doing this for my own good, and that he's concerned for me. There's a part of me that likes that close relationship he has with me and still another part that resents it. *One* part of me resents *another* part of me for wanting him to be concerned. I'm all mixed up!"

When a person is so emotionally distraught, he does appear "mixed up." Too many of the unconscious parts come to the fore. For a person who is emotionally comfortable, only one of these parts at a time presents itself to the conscious. But as a person becomes more uncomfortable, there may be more of these parts showing themselves so that the person appears "mixed up" in his thinking. If he becomes even more "mixed up," he may eventually "go to pieces." The "pieces" represent the part make-up of what was previously unconscious. No direct course of action can be taken, nor definite decision made, by such individuals since they seem torn between courses of action appropriate for each of their parts. This is well illustrated by the young woman who jumped in a suicidal attempt from one of the highest bridges on the East Coast . . . but did so wearing a life jacket, in full-view of noon-time traffic, and from the very lowest span of the bridge! Another woman shot herself in a suicidal attempt . . . but in her left hand and on the front lawn of the local general hospital!

In summary, what we have presented in this chapter is the concept that the unconscious is different from the conscious in its use of primary process thinking and its tendency to perceive parts of objects from its own make-up of parts within itself. This identification and projection of parts within the unconscious of an individual will be seen as an essential foundation for the utilization of the therapeutic listener.

NOTES

1. Cancro, R., ed.: *The Schizophrenic Syndrome: An Annual Revies,* New York, Brunner Mazel, 1971.
2. Bateson, G., Jackson, D.N., Haley, J., and Weakland, J.: "Toward a Theory of Schizophrenia," *Behav. Sci.* 1:251-264, 1956.
3. Zilboorg, G. and Henry, G.W.: *A History of Medical Psychology,* New York, Norton, 1941.
4. Kraepelin, E.: *Dementia Praecox and Paraphrenia,* Edinburgh, E. and Livingstone, S., 1919.
5. Bleuler, E.: *Dementia Praecox or the Group of Schizophrenias,* New York, Int. Univ., 1950.
6. Freud, S.: *The Ego and The Id,* Hogarth Press Ltd., London, 1925.

7. Stierlin, H.: "Bleuler's Concept of Schizophrenia: A Confusing Heritage," *Amer. J. Psychiat.* 123:8, Feb. 1967, pp. 996-1001.
8. Meyer, A.: *Psychobiology, A Science of Man,* Charles C. Thomas, Springfield, Ill., 1957.
9. Von Domarus, E.: "The Specific Laws of Logic in Schizophrenia. In: *Language and Thought in Schizophrenia,* J.S. Kasanin, ed., Berkeley, Univ. of Calif., 1944.
10. Arieti, S.: *Interpretation in Schizophrenia,* New York, Brunner, 1955.
11. Storch, A.: "The Primitive Archaic Forms of Inner Experience and Thought in Schizophrenia, New York, *J. Nerv. Ment. Dis. Pub.,* 1924.
12. Maher, B.A.: *Principles of Psychopathology,* New York, McGraw, 1966.
13. Forrest, D.V.: "Poiesis and the Language of Schizophrenia," *Psychiat.* 28:1-8, 1965.
14. Lorenz, M.: "Problems Posed By Schizophrenic Language," *Arch. Gen. Psychiat.,* Chicago, 4:603-610, 1961.
15. Sommer, R., DeWar, R., and Osmond, H.: "Is There a Schizophrenic Language?" *Arch. Gen. Psychiat.* 3:665-573, 1960.
16. Ruesch, J., and Bateson, G.: *Communications, The Social Matrix of Psychiatry,* New York, Norton, 1951.
17. Szasz, T.S.: *The Myth of Mental Illness,* New York, Hoebner and Harper, 1961.
18. Szasz, T.S.: *The Manufacture of Madness: A Comparative Study of the Inquisition and The Mental Health Movement,* New York, Harper and Row, 1970.
19. Liefer, R.: *In The Name of Mental Health: The Social Functions of Psychiatry,* New York, Science House, 1969.
20. Laing, R.D.: *The Politics of Experience,* Pantheon, New York, 1967.
21. Albee, G.: "Emerging Concepts of Mental Illness and Models of Treatment: The Psychological Point of View," *Amer. J. Psychiat.* 125:7, 870-876.
22. Claridge, G.: *Psychiatric News,* Vol. 2, No. 20, page 25, October 18, 1972.

CHAPTER 2

THE CONCERN OF THE UNCONSCIOUS

If the conscious is concerned with reality, then the unconscious must be concerned with *unrealities*. In order to understand these unrealities, one must first go back to the earliest days of a person's life to speculate on what is occurring before there is an unconscious and before reality is recognized.

Prior to birth, the fetus is protected from uncomfortableness within his mother's womb. The amniotic fluid acts as an enveloping cushion against jarring stimuli, provides a uniformity of temperature, and offers a serenity that will never be reduplicated again in life. Food is continually brought through the mother's blood stream, and wastes are comfortably removed by the same route. The mother and her unborn baby are physiologically one. However, this tranquillity ends at birth, when, with a shock-like transition, the infant is expelled into the external world, crying, completely helpless, and totally dependent on its mother. If he were able to comprehend reality at that moment, it would not be at all pleasant.

At this early stage, the infant's central nervous system is not fully developed, and perceptive abilities are poor. Most of the infant's time is spent in sleep, but he does awaken at intervals with the feelings of uncomfortableness from the physiological need to be mothered. This waking period of uncomfortableness, brought about by hunger and other unpleasant stimuli, is followed by feeding and by mothering, after which he returns to sleep. The infant perceives very little of reality, but when he *does* so, it is with an initial *uncomfortableness*. While the hunger is being removed by the feeding process, the infant apparently has a need to be held, warmed, cuddled and made the very center of the mothering one's attention. This *need* to be the center of attention is *necessitated* by the infant's dependent state, and the various acts of mothering gratify this need. These important *accessory* actions of the mothering one, associated with the removal of the physiological hunger need, may be conceptualized as the *"good breast."*

The effect of the "good breast" becomes recognized as *pleasurable* in that it gratifies an *emotional* need while removing the noxious stimuli of reality and returns the infant to a state of sleep. When periodically the infant is aroused from his sleep by the uncomfortableness of his hunger need, the "good breast" eventually comes to give a relief from this uncomfortableness and offers, in doing so, a *pleasurable experience* by gratifying the emotional need. The feeding experience becomes equated with a removal of the feelings of uncomfortableness and, at the same time, gratifies the need to be the center of attention of a mothering person — what we have termed the emotional need for the "good breast".[1][2] The person who *does* the "mothering" has been termed the *primary object.* This is the first person whom the infant meets in a beginning world of interpersonal relationships, which *must* develop for him as time goes on. Since the infant at this early stage has poor perceptive abilities, he doesn't perceive the primary object as a *whole* object. One can speculate that the infant perceives only the *act* of "mothering," and this can be termed the *primary experience.* Physiologically, the infant is totally dependent on this primary experience to satisfy his hunger need as well as his accompanying *emotional* need to be the center of attention.

The infant ego begins to form when, with longer periods of wakefulness, perceptions of reality increase. The ego develops needs of its own that are associated with the feeding process and with dependency. The ego's first concern is with having the emotional and physiological needs met. Through the act of being "mothered," the ego perceives that the infant is the center of attention and that the gratification of his "emotional" need is pleasurable. The feeding experience and the associated emotional feelings of belonging, of not being alone, and of being the center of attention represent the primary pleasure of life. The fulfillment of both physiological *and* emotional needs becomes a necessity for a comfortable existence. This feeding pleasure is the antecedent of all later pleasures. The pleasurable experience of feeding, both emotional and physiological, is *anticipated* during the delay between experiencing the oral (meaning associated with feeding) dependency need and the satisfaction of this need. The delay is associated, in time, with memories of previous feedings at the "good breast." The pleasure of gratifying the oral dependency need is phantasized during the delay *before* the "good breast" appears. This is a time of wishful and magical thinking, for the ego, in which it escapes the uncomfortableness of the delay by phantasy.

The repetition of the experiencing of uncomfortableness, followed by a gratification of the oral needs, seems to *condition* the infant to *expect* that the "good breast" will come when he experiences uncomfortableness and the oral need. This enhances a feeling of *omnipotence* on the part of the infant. If he perceives anything at this early stage of neurological development, it is only a vague awareness that he is, at first, hungry and uncomfortable and, that by wishing and phantasizing, the "good breast" magically appears. It is as though the infant, in this omnipotence, can call forth the "good breast" by simply *wishing* for it.[4] In other words, as the infant lies wet, cold, hungry, alone and uncomfortable, he can magically bring forth the "good breast" by merely wishing and phantasizing his *incorporation* of it.

24

It is during the delay between the wakening from sleep with the experiencing of the oral need and the moment that the "good breast" eventually comes, that ego functions begin and the unconscious is formed. It can be also speculated that during this delay the infant is wishing for the comforts of the "good breast" of the primary experience. The ego begins to draw upon the incorporated memories of past pleasurable feeding experiences, phantasizing upon them to remove the uncomfortableness. As the infant grows in size, his time spent awake increases. His need to be emotionally mothered also increases, even after the physiological hunger need has been satisfied. The emotional satisfaction of feeding is remembered as pleasurable by the developing ego and is utilized to withstand the uncomfortableness of delay and deprivation.

The mouth, at this early stage of psychological development, has been described as a primary *erogenous* zone in that the infant experiences much of the pleasures of feeding and discovery through his mouth.[1,2] He communicates his pleasure in oral gratification, by his mouth, and his displeasure by crying during the delay before the "good breast" appears. The infant seems to look for a pleasurable gratification of his oral dependency needs through his mouth. He puts his mouth on anything he can and tries to incorporate it. One can speculate that much of reality is first experienced through the oral cavity. We shall see that the mouth retains its position as an erogenous zone but does so in an emotional unreality of interpersonal communication. Where the infant's mouth first "tasted" and tested reality, the mouth will continue to do so within the subtle communicative processes of interpersonal relationships. This gives all interpersonal communication a distinct emotional basis that began with the blatant orality of infancy and continues for the rest of an individual's life.[6]

Through a process called *oral incorporation,* the infantile ego "incorporates" the pleasurable aspects of the feeding process. The ego internalizes them, and makes them a part of the unconscious so that it can draw upon what has been incorporated during the inevitable delays before the "good breast" appears. The more the infant experiences the mothering of the "good breast," the more he has an opportunity to *orally incorporate* and to retain it as part of his unconscious so that it can later be utilized during uncomfortable delays. Reality is such that the "good breast" can't always be there the moment hunger is felt. Nor can it always be magically produced for that moment of need. There is an emotional necessity, then, for oral incorporation so that more of what is incorporated can be utilized later and vicariously *"fed"* upon within the unconscious until the "good breast" does appear in reality.[4 5 7]

What is being incorporated by the ego, for the unconscious, are the *emotional* aspects of dependency need gratification, which are first associated with the feeding process. This involves the feelings of being wanted, of being needed, of belonging, of being cared for, of being the center of attention, and of being of special importance to someone else. These "oral dependency needs" represent basic human desires, as well as the most important emotional needs that an individual has, or ever will have. They are the antecedents of later wanting to be recognized, wanting to be important, wanting to be looked up to, and wanting to be respected, honored and esteemed by "special" others within some reality-oriented context. Just how important these needs are is evident from the fact that nothing seems to *hurt* more, and nothing seems to make a person more *angry*, than when *frustrated* in the meeting of his oral needs.

The oral needs remain *paramount* in importance throughout an individual's life. They are the *basic* determinants of human behavior.[8] It is interesting to note that the oral dependency needs are evident in the various personality theories set forth by various writers in psychiatry. The goal of superiority or "catching up with brother" proposed by Adler[9] seems to be a reflection of the oral dependency need. Rank's proposed basic human need to overcome the *"separation anxiety from mother"* seems to reflect again this concern with orality. The need to escape the feeling of isolation and loneliness and to overcome the fears of death by entering into a relationship of *reciprocal dependence,* as theorized by Fromm,[11] likewise refers to this oral importance. Sullivan's[12] proposal that humans attempt to satisfy their emotional needs through *interpersonal processes* implies precisely what we will present here, on a part object basis. Finally, the aim of humans to achieve an *"inner independence,"* as suggested by Horney, will be readily seen to involve the psychological attempts to deal with the problem of oral needs in the face of guilt.

Man apparently has a need to continually seek to satisfy his oral dependency needs, long after there is any *physiological* need for the "good breast." Though his need to feel important, wanted, recognized, needed, and cared for may take a multiplicity of pathways in a reality (that may be highly individualized), man must satisfy the need to be emotionally comfortable. He may seek to gratify his oral dependency needs by obtaining some personally conceived level of recognized achievement or success. But in no matter what endeavor he may make, the orality is always there. It is, of course, more *hidden* by these reality oriented methods of gratifying the oral needs than when the physiologic dependency, in the primary experience, was so obvious.

How important these oral dependency needs become in a human life seems well illustrated in man's religions. God, for instance, seems primarily a "good breast" in his relationship to man. And He too, apparently shares with man the same oral need to be a focus of concern and a center of attention. That need to feel *needed* is, in everyone, always oral. One need only peruse some of the great hymns of the Christian religion to see the reflections of man's expressed oral need. One can even take the popular songs of the day to see the same reflections of the oral dependency needs in these, where the need to feel wanted, to feel needed, and to belong specifically to someone else seems well illustrated. Though there may be a reality focus to the opposite sex, there is underneath an expression of the need for oral dependency gratification. Indeed, one can find more on orality in a church hymnal and more on the problems and dilemmas of this orality in the popular songs than one can find in a standard textbook of psychiatry. When for instance, Buck Owens sings "I don't care if the sun don't shine, I don't care if the fire don't burn, just as long as I know that you love me," one has an insight into how important is this underlying need for oral dependency gratification. And one can become exceedingly more angry with things far less important than the sun not shining and the fire not burning when feeling unloved and uncared for. In fact, even with the sun shining brightly and the fire burning warmly, life may simply not be worth living for many. if they do not feel that their oral dependency needs can be gratified. Many of the favorite old time songs reflect this need to belong to someone special and the accompanying problems that it often presents. "You always hurt the one you love" could very well be the theme song of an emotionally uncomfortable person because of his oral problems. Some songs that on a reality basis are oriented toward a loved person, can be most appropriate for the therapeutic listener: "Just because you seem to understand, dear, every single thing I say and do", and "You stay there until I get there. We'll work it out together. We'll have a little walk and have a little talk. You'll feel a whole lot better!"

That feeling of *being important* is first enhanced through the relationship of the infant with his primary object. Feelings of self-worth, of self-confidence and acceptableness to others come about through oral incorporation in the infantile stage of development. That feeling that "everything is going to be all right" likewise comes through an oral incorporation of the "good breast" and all that goes along with the mothering process. The feeling of optimism, the feeling of omnipotence, and the feeling that there will be a gratification of human needs on an eternal level are enhanced by this same oral incorporative process that the infant first becomes involved with in his experiences at the breast. The perception of the self, as the very center of the universe, is enhanced by oral dependency need gratification. In spite of one's insignificance with regard to what one might know of the world about him, there is an importance in regard to his own self, in his perceptions of that world, that is enhanced by oral need gratification. What the person *emotionally* perceives, he does so in regard to his own self, which consequently becomes a reference point in considering the entirety of the universe.

It follows that the recognition of the insignificance of one's self compared to the rest of the world is enhanced by oral need *frustration*. This insignificance of one's self, in regard to what one knows of the reality of the universe, is brought about through a frustration of oral dependency needs. How little the actual facts of reality play, in regard to the development of these feelings, is illustrated in the perceptions of one's self, the feelings of self-importance or

27

of unimportance that are derived solely on the basis of oral need gratification or frustration.

What is seen to be so blatant, in regard to the oral dependency needs of the infant, is interestingly found again in old age. Here, the reality oriented methods of seeking a gratification of the oral dependency needs have often deteriorated, and the person, both physiologically and socially, is returned again to a more obvious state of oral dependence. It is not that the individual has been *less* orally dependent during the time between the stage when he leaves infancy and enters old age, but that his oral dependency needs have been *hidden* in reality. The unmet oral needs manifest themselves as feelings of being unwanted, unneeded, and unimportant, of no longer belonging, and of being left out. The interpersonal relationship sphere of many oldsters shrinks. Reality, again, as it did in infancy, *demands* a physical dependency in addition to the previously masked emotional dependency. The most pressing need for the geriatric patient is for an oral dependency type of relationship with someone else. A gratifying dependency relationship has often been shown to bring relief to the feelings of loneliness, sickness and depression that aged people often experience. It is interesting to note, because of its implied symbolic meaning, that many geriatric patients have been found to be most concerned about where they sit at the meal time table.

Returning again to the infant, we find that as he begins to grow, less of his waking time is spent with the physiological aspect of feeding and so more is available for the emotional aspect of this oral process. It can be speculated that, in this regard, he also becomes "mothered" by his father, who at this point is really an accessory mother. There may be aunts, uncles, grandmothers and grandfathers, who also gratify these emotional or oral dependency needs. Older siblings, neighbors, and family friends may aid in the gratification of the infant's oral dependency needs. What this represents then, is the beginning of an expanding sphere of interpersonal relationships that on a *part object basis* are unconsciously perceived as gratifying the oral dependency needs.[6] That this is done on a part object basis implies that other parts of these objects may *not* be oral need gratifying and may even be frustrating. But on a part object basis, the gratification of the oral dependency needs, first met by the primary object, are now being met by an increasing number of objects. There is then a *fractionation* of the original emotionally symbolic primary object into many different part-objects (below the level of reality). This process of fractionating the primary object will continue as the interpersonal relationship sphere expands. Play-mates, and later school chums, teachers and friends, will continue to gratify the oral dependency needs on a part object basis. Even pets may be oral need gratifying on a part object basis. Teddy bears, favorite dolls, stuffed animals, or the frequently seen blanket may be oral need gratifying when they become concretized as symbolic entities equated with the oral dependency need gratifying aspect of the primary object. Interpersonal relationship experiences in reality, on a part object basis, continue to present an opportunity for the child to gratify his oral dependency needs.

What is being proposed then, is that the oral dependency needs are gratified on a part object basis, through an unreality, within the interpersonal relationships that might be involved in his hobbies, social activities and religion, provide an opportunity to meet his oral depencency needs. The individual's interaction between the part make-up of his unconscious and the unconscious perceptions of the part objects in his interpersonal relationship sphere, continue to meet his oral dependency needs. What was communicated to the infant initially, through the mothering process, is now done through his communicative emotional interaction within the subtle part object relationships of his interpersonal relationships sphere. Interpersonal communication always involves this underlying attempt to meet oral dependency needs. It is as though an individual emotionally *feeds* from these part objects that are symbolic of the original emotionally significant primary object and its "good breast." The primary object, once so physiologically necessary and so emotionally significant to the infant, loses its emotional significance with the incursion of reality. It becomes diffused in the emotionality of a great many different part objects that supply what the primary object at one time did by itself. Perhaps, too, this is why the oral dependency needs of an adult become so hidden, in that the emotionally comfortable person is drawing a gratification of his oral needs from such a great many different part objects.

In order to examine the development of emotional uncomfortableness, with which the unconscious is concerned, let us return again to the small infant and his oral needs. It was noted that the "good breast" isn't always available when the infant experiences his hunger needs, because of reality. Because the infant must undergo this period of delay before the "good breast" appears, that caused the unconscious to form, oral incorporation takes on another aspect besides *preserving* the "good breast." A *"bad* breast" is speculated as being perceived by the hungry and emotionally deprived infant, that unlike the "good breast," *frustrates* the oral dependency needs.[1-7] As the "good breast" is loved or wanted for a gratification of the oral needs, the "bad breast" is hated because it frustrates the oral needs. The infant, experiencing the uncomfortableness of not having the "good breast," wishfully fantasized the pleasure of oral need gratification. When oral satisfaction did eventually come, he felt, in his omnipotence that it did so as a *result* of his wishful thinking.[4] The frustrated infant now wishes, during his emotionally uncomfortable delay, to destroy the "bad breast." He orally incorporates to *destroy* the hated "bad breast" that frustrates him in his attempt to have his oral dependency needs met. Thus his unconscious has a part that incorporates to preserve and a part that incorporates to destroy.

29

The greater the frustration of the infant's oral dependency needs, the greater is the tendency toward destructive fantasizes and wishes.[14,15] It is as though the infantile unconscious part thinks: "I wish to orally incorporate to *destroy* that which is so frustrating to me." And when the breast doesn't appear and the oral needs aren't met, it is as though the unconscious thinks: "I have *caused* it to be destroyed by my omnipotent wishful thinking." The unconscious wishful thinking that occurs during the delay before oral dependency gratification eventually comes creates the feeling within the infant ego that the oral dependency needs *themselves* have caused the "good breast" to disappear. Just as the omnipotence of the unconscious wish is reinforced by experiencing the "good breast," as though, "I have caused it to appear by my wishing," this same omnipotence enhances the feeling that when the "good breast" doesn't appear "I have caused it to *disappear* because of my destructive wishful thinking." In other words, the infantile omnipotence causes the infant to feel that his oral dependency needs are the very *cause* for the frustration. It is as though "If I didn't have these oral dependency needs, I wouldn't be experiencing the uncomfortableness I have now."

Freud[16] and others[1-7] have described this second part of their oral stage as ambivalent, in that there is both a desire to preserve *and* to destroy. The primary object then becomes both hated and loved at the same time. All feelings of love and hate in later life will reflect this early ambivalent relationship with the primary object. The first rule of human behavior is that one not bite the breast that gives the milk. Put another way, one should not bite the hand that feeds. When the infant is so emotionally dependent on so few objects, he must repress the anger *caused by frustration* of his oral dependency needs so as not to bite. From this repression of anger, from the frustration of oral needs, comes an unconscious sense of *guilt*. This unconscious guilt leads the infant ego to perceive a "bad me" aspect of itself that then feels it doesn't deserve to be fed.[12] When further oral frustration is experienced, accompanied by additional destructive fantasies associated with this aspect of oral incorporation, the resultant frustration is felt to have been *caused* by this "bad me."[12]

In the emotionally comfortable adult personality, the primary object or the "mothering one" on whom one was originally emotionally dependent, has been *fractionated* by the ongoing process of developing interpersonal relationships and the search for the "good breast." The developmental ambivalence is dispersed and displaced, for instance, into "likes" and "dislikes," "prejudices" and "preferences," and "loves" and "hatreds." It seems apparent the more comfortable a person is, the more sources he has for feeling needed, wanted, cared for and important to others. The more he has of ego acceptable and reality-oriented channels for the expression of anger arising from the frustration of his emotional needs, the more comfortable he is. But the more closely a person is emotionally involved with another object of reality, the more likely will be his concentration of love, as well as anger, and the more potentially uncomfortable he will be.

Depending upon the amount of unconsciously perceived oral need frustration, the resulting anger imbues the oral incorporative process with a self-felt destructive quality. The emotional feeding process then takes on, as stated above, a two-fold purpose that of preserving and that of destroying. The part that is involved with destructive wishful thinking, and the accompanying anger that is repressed, cause the development of *unconscious guilt* which becomes associated with the oral dependency needs. It is as though, *"I am to blame for the "good breast's" disappearance."* An oral incorporative guilt develops from the unconscious perception that the destructive fantasies, associated with the frustrated need, has by some omnipotent means caused the need to be frustrated. The oral dependency need *itself* is felt as the very origin of the frustration: "Because of my *need*, I have been *frustrated."* Or simply: *"I am guilty for having the need."*

Some psychiatrists[17] feel that there is a "depressed" or a "paranoid" position that the infant may take in regard to experienced frustration. This author[18] feels, instead, that oral incorporative guilt is *primal* and can be either *self-felt* or *projected.* When it is self-felt, the oral dependency needs are imbued with guilt, depending on how the unconscious ego handles it. When it is projected, instead of feeling *"I am to blame,"* there is a *"You are to blame for the frustration"* attitude.

To better illustrate this unconscious oral incorporative guilt, let us take the emotionally deprived infant. This infant is characterized by long delays before the "good breast" eventually appears. Reality-wise, we might imagine a home situation where the mother is forced by circumstances of reality, or by her own emotional problems, into doing other than caring exclusively for the infant. Perhaps she has other children to care for: perhaps she is not supported in her mothering role by her husband: perhaps there is sickness, hardships, divorce, death or a host of circumstances of reality which make it such that she or some other object cannot adequately meet the infant's needs. Perhaps too, this particular infant may be less-favored, disliked or even hated by the primary object. But through the omnipotent thinking of his infantile ego, the infant feels that he, *himself,* is the *cause* of the frustration he is experiencing. This unconscious feeling is repetitiously reinforced each time he is further frustrated, and he perceives this frustration as due to his guilt-laden oral needs. He feels his oral need rather than the primary object, is to blame. Perhaps there are psychological reasons hindering the mother from supplying the emotional "good breast" needed for the infant to develop with less of an unconscious oral incorporative guilt. Many times in reality, mother completely disappears through desertion, death or some other form of abandonment. When this is so, the emotionally deprived infant feels that he caused this disappearance. It is as though he feels "I have made the object go away because of my destructive oral needs." But the mothering one doesn't need to go away on a *whole* object basis. One can have this same

31

feeling engendered on a *part* object basis. The orally gratifying parts of the primary experience disappear while the objects of reality can still remain.

Those adults who are emotionally uncomfortable later in life often seem to have an early history that is repetitive in regard to a disappearing object, or part objects, on whom oral dependency gratification is sought. For instance, an infant may lose a mother through death, or lose a *part* of mother from the birth of a younger sibling, or from her sickness. Sometimes there is an infant who is taken over by the grandmother who, in turn, dies. This infant may then be given to another relative who again seems to disappear for one reason or another. The infant's emotionally depriving reality *reinforces*, through a conditioning process, the unconscious feeling that the oral dependency needs are the cause of the frustration of these needs. And this can subtly occur on a part object basis where the objects in reality remain, but their oral-need gratifying parts disappear. As an adult, they may remark, "Everyone that I get emotionally close to seems to go away." The markedly frustrated infant later develops a pronounced fear of his oral dependency needs. Where "love" is a synonym for oral dependency gratification, he has a *fear of loving, less his love destroy*. He fears any oral incorporation, because of its self-inflicted destructive aspects, and strives instead to somehow "go it alone." He develops then a secondary *"need" for independence*, seeking, thereby, to deny his oral dependency needs. But the oral dependency needs are an inseparable part of being human. They are inescapable. And one can function comfortably only to the extent that these needs *have been* met in the past and *are being* met in the present.

The "need" to be independent is a manifestation of the unconscious guilt applied to the oral need.[19] Though one part of the unconscious may desire dependency, a guilt-laden part of the unconscious is opposed to it. The person with more oral frustration, and who has repressed more of his anger, will have a proportionately larger unconscious part that abhors dependency. This person doesn't want to be dependent, for after all, this is where his emotional uncomfortableness arose earlier in life and repetitiously occurred in later life. He seeks to be independent at all costs. During later periods of increased oral need frustration, with increased repressed anger and hypertrophied guilt, this "need" to be independent enlarges. For the emotionally uncomfortable person, this fear of dependency becomes his *greatest* unconscious fear. Yet it is equally opposed by, an unconscious wish for dependency. While the conscious may fear death or punishment, the unconscious is most concerned about this dependency-independency conflict. The unconscious has, on one hand, the need for dependency, and on the other hand, the "need" for independence, which arises secondarily from the unconscious guilt.

The independency this person seeks is a cover-up for his unmet oral dependency needs. This person may *appear* quite independent, but when he experiences a period of oral need deprivation, he frequently shows that his independency is but a façade. During these times, he will also exhibit a great deal of anger, usually pent up within him, and he will manifest in his behavior the unconscious guilt. Many times, he can be heard to say later in life, "I'm a very independent person — I've *had* to be," thus implying that circumstances in early life frustrated his oral dependency needs. This "façade" of independency can be equated with his oral need frustration, regardless of any reality success that façade might have given him.

The person who *truly* is independent is so because he is *dependent* on a multiplicity of part objects for his oral dependency supplies. If for any reason, one part object may cease to be oral need gratifying, he can simply draw more heavily upon the other dependency sources. Because he is so dependent and so emotionally involved in such a broad sphere of part object relationships, there are more part objects available to bear an expression of anger when he is frustrated. Since he can comfortably express his anger, he doesn't have to deny it. He tends to have less anger to express because no object in his reality is too intensely emotionally significant as an oral dependency source. The question of independency for this person who is truly independent is never an *issue* as it is for the person who has a façade of independency that is only a *cover-up* for the unmet, guilt-laden oral dependency needs which he tries to hide.

It becomes ironic that the *only* way to a truly independent position is to *continue with dependency!* A "good" mother is one who adequately meets the oral dependency needs of her child while allowing him to emotionally increase his sphere of interpersonal relationships. But in order for her to do this, she must be emotionally comfortable herself. She must have had her *own* oral dependency needs adequately met so that she doesn't have an uncomfortable load of unconscious guilt that will hamper her ability to meet the oral needs of her children.

Ironically too, reality often puts a premium on a person who strives to be "independent" and "go it alone." In spite of frequent emotional uncomfortableness, he is often rewarded with success. His unconscious guilt drives him to better himself in some reality endeavor, and he may seek to accumulate something that becomes symbolic of his unmet oral dependency needs. Even though the artificial and defensive "need" to be independent is indicative of the potential emotional uncomfortableness of a person, there is a potential realistic value in this "façade" of independency. It becomes both an asset and a liability, depending on the circumstances of reality which that person may later find himself in. Comparatively, the person who is *truly* independent is drawing his emotional supplies from a great many part objects. He isn't so strongly driven in any line of endeavor to "make a name for himself" or to seek fame or fortune.

It is interesting to note that, as an example of the wisdom of reality, we are admonished to "trust in God." Perhaps this is because one learns so quickly in life that it may be folly to trust in anyone else. It is as though, knowing the frailties of humans and the reality of being disappointed in interpersonal relationships as acutely as do those with "independant" façades, one had better not trust in anything *less* than that which is Divine. Those who accumulate the most wealth or success are often those who will readily admit they do not trust other human beings. But in their lonely "independent" and anhedonic existence, they posess what is *emotionally necessary* to accumulate wealth or an outstanding level of success.

Maturity is not the state of being "independent" or being able to stand alone, for no man can really be independent of others, and no man stands alone for long. Emotional maturity is reached when there is a multiplicity of part objects from which an individual is drawing the gratification of his oral dependency needs. Emotional maturity represents a *dilution* of the previously concentrated oral dependency need ... not a denial or any *conscious* determination of simply having one's oral needs *diffusely* met, and not having a concentration of unmet oral dependency needs. Unfortunately, it is characteristic of life that there will always be frustrations and stresses. These cannot be avoided for they are a part of reality. Sickness and pain, for instance, are unconsciously perceived by the ego as *oral* need frustrations. Any physical pain or discomfort is emotionally symbolic and equated with the first uncomfortableness that the infant experienced when physiologic hunger and the oral need were one. When the infant was frustrated in his oral needs, he was physically as well as emotionally uncomfortable. This distinction between *physical* and *emotional* uncomfortableness is never made by the unconscious, and this probably has a bearing on why those who are emotionally uncomfortable as adults seek a physician for comfort. But any pain in later life is more endurable when the individual is supported by a great number of part objects. It is always less so when the individual feels so much alone. The immature person draws his emotional supplies from a relatively *few* emotionally significant part objects and, because of this, must repress his anger. If he were to express it, he would jeopardize his limited sources of oral supplies. When he further represses his anger, his guilt increases, and consequently, he becomes more emotionally uncomfortable.

Everyone must endure a degree of frustration of his oral dependency needs. Some will have more oral dependency frustration than others, depending upon the circumstances of their individual childhood experiences and situations. The individual who has experienced *less* oral frustration will be more emotionally comfortable later in life than the *more* frustrated individual in the same situation. This is an undisputable fact when one considers that to have less oral need frustration includes having less accidents, less physical pain, less sickness and disease, as well as less object and part object losses, and less of an inadequate primary experience. It follows that the person who is emotionally

34

comfortable later in life must also have an emotionally comfortable *situation* in life, as well as having enjoyed the oral need gratifying experiences earlier in life. This is so because the oral dependency needs have to be *continually* met on an ongoing basis in anyone's interpersonal relationship sphere, and they must involve a freedom from any physical pain or discomfort.

What is therefore implied is that the situation of reality contributes much to making an individual emotionally comfortable or emotionally uncomfortable. The emotionally mature and physically healthy individual has, as a result of his past and present reality, a relatively small concentration of oral needs, anger, or guilt. His oral dependency needs are diffusely associated among many emotionally significant part objects. This gives him a freedom in his interpersonal relationships while the emotionally immature person has a very restricted freedom in his interpersonal relationships. The immature person has an intensity of oral needs and often places a large demand on a single object for emotional support. In doing so, he frequently becomes emotionally frustrated and uncomfortable in his interpersonal relationships. This person tends to deny his unmet oral needs and attempts to control his anger and hide his guilt. Ironically, in attempting to do this, he often feels that he is being "mature."

Again, it becomes ironic that the emotionally immature person is characterized by having the greatest sensitivity in his interpersonal relationships, and the deepest and most passionate loves. He is capable of the greatest hatreds as well. The emotionally mature individual never has the need to be so deeply involved in either love or hate, in that his emotions diffuse into so many different emotionally significant part objects. Poets and writers who can describe these intensities of emotional feelings can do so possibly because they are emotionally immature. And we all can appreciate what they write because perhaps we, too, have, in part, the same emotional difficulties and immaturities. If we have these to a lesser degree, we can assume that we have had more of our oral dependency needs met in early childhood and, in the present, more part objects in the interpersonal relationship sphere from which we draw our oral supplies and express the anger arising from any frustration of our oral needs.

One is invariably frustrated, in part, in the gratification of his oral dependency needs, and there will invariably be some repressed anger. This repressed anger will manifest itself as guilt within the unconscious of the individual. Unconscious guilt, though, may be handled by the ego as being *self-felt* or *projected*. If it is projected, then the individual seems to take the stance that, *"I'm* not guilty, but *this* person is, or *this* situation is." An example of this guilt projection is any prejudice where the individual is projecting his guilt on a certain race or minority. The prejudiced individual has taken some of his unconscious guilt and rationalized it, in its projected form. He may receive support in doing this from others who might share his own prejudices. In every country, there will

35

always be a minority of people who are somehow different in appearance or behavior and, therefore, become the scapegoats for this projected guilt. When a person has an intense level of unconscious guilt that is projected predominately in this form, the prejudices become hatreds. In a lessened form, they may simply become dislikes. The unconscious guilt that is felt as originating with someone else represents the "he's to blame" or paranoid position. (Here "paranoid" refers to a more blatant projector of guilt.) For instance, when a client remarks, *"He* made me feel like an ass," or *"She* makes me sick," he is attributing this feeling, which is derived from his *own* unconscious guilt, to someone else. This, rather than his own unconscious guilt, he consciously feels is the very origin of his feelings of unacceptability. In doing this, he is able to unconsciously deny his guilt while allowing opportunity to express anger that otherwise would be turned inward and lead to increased uncomfortableness. Many marriages are characterized by having a "guilt-projector" and "guilt-acceptor" relationship that, in the extreme, may even take the form of a sadist-masochist relationship. One partner has a "need" to project his or her guilt for emotional comfortableness, and the other has a "need" to accept anger in order to assuage his or her guilt for emotional comfortableness.

It is erroneous to feel that the paranoid position is a regression to an earlier stage of emotional development where the infant felt omnipotent. At a stage of development where the infant feels omnipotent, he is at a *guilt-free,* pre-ambivalent stage of oral satisfaction. Ambivalence comes later when there is repressed anger and the formation of unconscious guilt. The infant knows only the "breast" as his world and feels he is the center of it. The paranoid position is taken when one projects unconscious guilt, so this is not at all similar to the omnipotent stage of infancy. The omnipotence of the paranoid is a *secondary* omnipotence that counter-acts the feelings of inferiority arising from unprojected guilt. The omnipotence of the paranoid does go back to the *ambivalent* stage, where wishful thinking is perceived as magically bringing about the destruction of the "good breast." It is always *guilt-derived,* and the guilt in the paranoid is always evident while the omnipotence of the infant comes from a *guilt-free* pre-ambivalent period.

This tendency to project guilt becomes an important means by which parents frustrate the oral needs of their children. The child, in his dependency state, becomes symbolically equated with the parent's own guilt-laden and denied dependency needs. The child becomes the object of the parents' projected guilt and is often talked to or treated in a manner that the parents wouldn't use with anyone else. And they can do this because the child is so emotionally dependent. The child seems to be a necessary object for the parents' projected guilt and expressed anger which allows *their* emotional position to be more comfortable. The parent has a target for expressed anger who is *trapped* in a dependency bind, so he *must* accept this anger because he has so few other interpersonal relationships to fall back on in contrast to the adult.

The analysts are erroneous when they simply attribute a child's feelings of rejection to "faulty bowel training." A parent can be far more devastating than being "castrating" when they frustrate a child in his oral needs. Deeper than any Freudian anal or oedipal expressions of rejection is the oral frustration that comes about when the guilt of the parent is projected to the child. It can begin *before* bowel training, and it can continue long *after* that stage. The child is taught to suppress his anger, to "respect his elders," or simply, "to accept the projected guilt and the expressed anger of the parent toward the child." Reality is on the parents' side, for "the child must *learn*." Perhaps this is emotionally symbolized in his bowel training, where he is taught that his "guilt" is unacceptable, and that he should control his "urges."

Many parents seem able to maintain only a degree of emotional comfortableness when they have this object toward whom they can direct their anger. Expressing anger towards the child keeps their unconscious guilt at a comfortable level. But in frustrating the oral needs of the child and not accepting anger in return, they give him a level of unconscious guilt similar to that which they themselves have. Thereby, they set the stage for this child to do the same thing, as an adult, with his children. If he's not a "guilt-projector" as an adult, he'll often marry one, so that either way, a child reaps what has been psychologically sown several generations earlier. It is for this reason that "schizophrenia" seems to "run" in families. Guilt from one generation is passed on to the next generation because of the paranoid position that the parents or emotionally significant relatives take in regard to projecting guilt to the children or to a particular child. The guilt-projector does well only because there is a dependency-bound object for the projection of guilt. It may be seen directly involving different generations, as a grandmother-grandson relationship, or grandfather-grandson, or any combination of relatives. The so-called "schizophrenogenic mother" is simply a more *blatant* guilt-projector. Sometimes, too, a whole constellation of family members seems to make one child the scape-goat for their projected guilt, so that he accumulates guilt from many different emotionally significant figures within the family, none of whom, alone, appears "schizophrenogenic.'

Many times the person who is the greatest guilt projector in a family constellation is the individual who has *reality* on his side, as evidenced by the high level of success he has attained which supports his guilt projection. He may project his guilt toward a child who ostentatiously manifests his own unmet oral needs. The display of oral dependency needs may be felt as most reprehensible for the guilt-projector who berates and chides the child for his obvious needs. "Stand on your own two feet, *I* did! Do it yourself, or you'll never amount to anything! Be independent, like I am; no one ever helped me!" He has his success in reality to "prove" he is *right* in what he has to say about anyone "amounting to something" in life. He "knows" what "help" is needed for the child when he begins to flounder emotionally. Since his success in reality is greater than anyone who professionally tries to help the child, their way, which will involve a meeting of the child's oral needs, is *wrong*. The "help" this parent feels his child needs is *more* guilt-projection, more "knuckling under," or, simply, more oral frustration. With a build-up of unconscious guilt, the child can become exquisitively *sensitive* to even the most subtly communicated oral frustration, particularly from a person who has a high emotional significance. Where a child with less unconscious guilt and with more secure sources of oral dependency may overlook these communications, the guilt-laden child is repetitively hurt emotionally.

In observing the parent-child relationships in certain families, it becomes most revealing to see how the guilt of the parent is so often projected to the child. When, for instance, a child spills his milk on the table the mother might respond, "You stupid thing!," projecting her guilt and anger to the child when her compensatory need for perfection and her need to keep her guilt "contained" is threatened by the child's act. The parent, because of her own emotional problems, often seems unable to accept the "childish" behavior of children and, so, holds the child to some perfect standard that she, herself, could never meet. One can readily see that it is the *projection of guilt* that is being conveyed to the child and little else. Yet reality supports this, as the mother might say, "How will he ever learn good table manners unless I *do* get after him!" This may very well be true, but it still involves guilt projection when the spilt milk symbolizes to the mother her own unconscious guilt. The true motivation of the mother's verbalization is *less* reality oriented than it is *unreality* oriented. When a parent screams at his child, "What's *wrong* with you — don't you know any better than to get out of the rain!," the child feels rejected in a situation where the child is out in the rain. Yet at another time, when the situation is reversed and the parent wants something done outside, he may scream, "What's *wrong* with you — a little rain never hurt anyone!" It isn't the reality of the situation, then, that makes a difference, for whether the child is in the rain or out of the rain, he is simply the object of projected guilt and expressed anger. These parents become veritable masters of the "put-down" and, in doing so, they plant guilt in their children.

Many more blatant examples of frustrating a child's oral dependency needs could be given. Because a parent is so much a source of concentrated oral dependency supply for the child, any oral rejection is significant and will have an accumulative effect. Since the child must be dependent upon his parents or parental surrogates, the parent is of extreme emotional significance. The oral rejection is perceived as more severe when coming from a figure of such emotionally high significance. Consider how a ten year old boy must feel when his father, who previously seemed so loving, comes home intoxicated and verbally, as well as physically, abuses him, projecting his own previously concealed guilt and anger to the child while the mother only watches. She needed her husband meek, passive and overly "nice" before, in order to accept her own projected guilt. Now, she is unable to take definitive action because of her unconscious guilt, which she verbalizes later, saying, "I couldn't have him arrested when he was beating the boy because then the whole neighborhood would know the boy's father was an alcoholic, and *that* wouldn't be good for a boy to have to face, so I've kept it all hidden."

Some parents seem "over-protective" in their frequent admonitions with regard to their children's safety. These admonitions convey an oral need frustrating expression of their own unconscious wishful thinking. They seem to convey to the child the feeling that no matter what he does is a potential hurt to himself or others. This type of "overprotection," which can always be well supported by reality, is not a meeting of the oral dependency needs for the child but is, instead, a compensation for the unconscious wishful thinking toward an object, that in its blatant dependency, is symbolic of the parents' own dependency upon a "loved" object that frustrated them. Yet in regard to their orally depriving admonitions, the parents have reality to back them up, since accidents, calamities and disasters do happen. But below the reality is the unreality of the parent keeping the child dependent and guilt-laden. This not so much meets the child's dependency needs as the parents', and it has the one-sided characteristic of making the child an object of projected guilt and expressed anger. This is a process that must be reversed through therapeutic listening.

An ironic outcome of this type of guilt-projecting relationship is the child who much later, as a client for therapy, remarks, "I never did talk with my parents much when I was growing up, as they always worried so about me." This implies that the child did not talk with the parents for fear that his parents would become upset. But the parents become upset with the problems of the child when their unconscious wishful thinking becomes too close to being revealed. The guilt-laden, emotionally uncomfortable parent creates a guilt-laden, emotionally uncomfortable child. In his relationship with that child, either by projection or by excessive worry or concern about the child, the oral needs are frustrated.

When a child has been subjected to guilt projecting parents, he will often show a distorted perception of his childhood. When the guilt-laden person is asked if he had a happy childhood, he will often reply: "Oh, yes, I had a very happy childhood. My parents were very good to me. In fact, they gave me *too much* (their guilt makes them feel that they really didn't *deserve* what they did receive). If they hadn't given me *so much*. I might be better able to cope with life now (an erroneous assumption). Now, I don't mean to imply I didn't get any beatings from them. I got plenty of them, but I deserved every one of them (i.e. because of my guilt). In fact, I got by without some that I know I should have gotten!" And when asked if they were close to their parents in growing up, they might remark, "Oh, yes, we were a *very* close family. In fact that's what I think the problem is — we were too close." But it's their guilt that makes them perceive this and blinds them to the fact that they *didn't* have a happy childhood in contrast to others, and that they *weren't* emotionally close as a family. They often support their positions by comparing themselves with more deprived childhoods rather than with childhoods of individuals who were genuinely close and happy.

Traditionally, the child is admonished to "honor his parents" and taught to "respect his elders." But a child is better able to do this when guilt-laden. And in this state, he is a better object for the projected guilt from a parent than a child who isn't so guilt-laden. Unfortunately, there has been little emphasis on the need to honor and respect children. There isn't the need for adults or parents to be respected so much as a definite need for parents to respect the oral dependency needs of their children. This is particularly important in the impressionable infantile years when oral dependency gratification is most intensely concentrated and most prone to be guilt engendering. The appreciation of the child in his developmental years is most in need of respect — not the parents', after their personalities have been formed. The best preventative in the mental health field has facetiously been expressed, with some truth, as, "having a happy childhood." What is apparently implied by this is to have an oral need gratifying childhood. But, interestingly enough, a guilt-laden child whose oral needs have not been adequately met often feels, because of his guilt, that he *did* have a happy childhood.

The term, "adequate mothering," must always be qualified adequate for what! The adequate mothering for producing a business tycoon must be different from what it takes to raise someone who is happy and contented in his work or his parental role. Whatever it must involve to produce a war hero, who posthumously receives the Congressional Medal of Honor, can be inferred to be distinctly different than that which is responsible for a soldier who consistently does his work well as part of a team. It is obvious that the quantities of ingredients in the "adequate mothering" which lay the foundation for a future Marine Corps General may not be the same as those necessary to produce a happy, adequate parent without aspirations for military "greatness" or "success." Though it is very well possible that from the same family there might be a great diversity in the lines of occupational endeavor among the children who do attain outstanding success, their "mothering" need not be at all similar. This is because there are differences in the "mothering" that each child in a family receives, due to differing circumstances of the family at a developmental stage that mothering is given, and because of a variety of different factors, as the sequence of births of the children, or interpersonal relationship factors outside the family that effect the child directly and indirectly. There is often a tendency to favor one particular child, by a parent, and often a tendency to project guilt to a certain child more so than to others in the family. Few studies, if any, have ever been done to assay the gratification of a child's oral dependency needs, and few, if any, to assay the projected guilt and the frustration of oral dependency that a child receives in growing up.

Even with the best of parents, an infant cannot have all of his oral dependency needs met. Perhaps if he were to remain as a very small infant with limited perceptions of reality, this might be possible. He would be simply feeding from the "good breast" whenever he was awakened by hunger, and then returning back to sleep. But as the infant grows, he spends less time asleep. He becomes more aware of reality with its unmet oral dependency needs, the uncomfortableness, and the realization of a lack of omnipotence. His perception of reality must be learned at the expense of his oral dependency gratification. As long as one can continually rely on the "good breast" with all it emotionally symbolizes, one can sustain the feeling of omnipotence which brings forth that "good breast." One can continue with the feeling that one's oral dependency needs can be met unequivocally on an eternal basis. Therefore, it is the increasing awareness of the *"bad* breast" that leads to an awareness of reality. The infant begins to learn that he and the "good breast" alone don't make up reality, and that the world does not center around him. Spitz[21] has postulated that much of the crying the infant does is a mourning of the loss of his fantasized central position in the universe. The perception of the self as the very center of the universe is enhanced by oral need gratification, while the recognition of the insignificance of one's self, compared to the rest of the world, is augmented by oral need frustration. The wisdom of reality that one begins to acquire so early in life comes about from this oral need frustration which must be reconciled within each person's unconscious.

That one must learn reality at the expense of oral dependency gratification is well illustrated by the child who may have parents who are consistently loving and caring. But the child has to learn, for instance, not to play in the street, and he must be "disciplined" if he does. He has to learn that he cannot play with matches or with fire, that he cannot stay up as late as he wants at night, that he has to wash his hands before meals, that he has to perform his bowel movements in specified places and at specified times. These are merely a few of the myriad of other demands of reality. If he isn't admonished by his parents on these regards, he will learn on his own, in perhaps an even *more* painful way. What this implies is the inescapable *necessity* of frustration in oral dependency need gratification in order to function in reality, and it further presupposes an inescapable degree of guilt in everyone. Even if one were born a king or a queen, one still couldn't possibly have a complete grat-

41

ification of their oral dependency needs. Reality causes everyone to grow old, to experience diseases and sickness, and to lose loved ones. It is this reality about which the unconscious is concerned, while attempting to ensure as much oral need gratification, anger expression, and guilt projection or compensation that can be comfortably allowed.

It is a recognition of reality by the developing ego of the infant that will sour the milk of oral dependency gratification and lead to a mistrust of whole objects. It is reality that first insisted we perceive the symbolic breast as a *whole* object, denying the *"bad* breast" to repress our anger, while focusing on the "good." Only in an unreality of part objects can the "good breast" exist, for it is never found long sustained in reality. Perhaps this is the reason man seeks the ultimate fulfillment of his oral dependency needs in some life after death, where he hopes he will be reunited with some reflection of that stage he enjoyed earlier in life when "reality" was just he and the emotionally nurturing, ever-caring "good breast."

The great religions of the world seem not only built from the human oral dependency need that is symbolic for the good and caring breast, but from oral guilt as well. One can logically understand the human desire to have an entity, which will gratify one's oral needs eternally, that derives itself from the oral need gratifying aspect of mother before she became too realistic, and from the oral need gratifying aspects of others before they, too, became too realistically recognized. But the concretized and symbolic aspects of these part object relationships become projected into a promised and hoped for eternally available source of oral supplies, gratifying emotional closeness, and freedom from all frustration. This requires an *unreality*, not a reality that anyone knows. Yet it is this same uncomfortable orality that necessitates the desired, but still feared, oral closeness to be relegated to the distant future. It is the orality that gives the person a feeling that *no one* should get too close *right now* — maybe later — but *not now*! A client in therapy has expressed this as, "One part of me wants God with me always (because of my unmet oral need), but there's another part of me that *doesn't* want to be [because of my guilt] so smothered with love, so carefully watched, so obligated and so much in the position to be judged that this closeness would bring."

In the formative years of childhood, the unconscious guilt that develops from the early frustration of the oral needs and from a repression of the anger can be termed *"personality core guilt."* We can call it this because the personality forms or molds itself in a very characteristic way depending on how this particular ego will attempt to meet the oral needs and how it will handle the guilt. The increase in unconscious guilt beyond that which is part of the personality formation, can simply be called the *"added unconscious guilt."* The concept we are presenting of a personality core guilt and an added unconscious guilt is somewhat similar to what Herron[22] had previously presented in trying to classify "schizophrenics" according to their pre-psychotic adjustment. He tried to categorize them as either "*process*," meaning chronic or long term, and "*reactive*" or tending to show a favorable prognosis when compared to the former. In attempting to categorize the "Unicorn," perhaps he was only seeing that some people have more *personality core* guilt than others, and that some people *add* an additional uncomfortable level of guilt, beyond their personality guilt that is more easily diminished than if it were in the personality core guilt form. In other words, two people, seen for the first time, may show equal evidence of an extremely uncomfortable level of unconscious guilt. Though their "psychiatric symptoms" may appear similar, the person whose guilt is predominately in the *added* form can be expected to have a very favorable prognosis, while the person whose guilt is predominately in the *personality core* form can be expected to have a very unfavorable prognosis. The person with the greater added guilt can be expected to more quickly enter a therapeutic listening relationship and more likely profit from it. The person with the greater personality core guilt will be less likely, first of all, to enter a therapeutic listening relationship, and, if he does, less likely to profit from it.

In summary, the unconscious is primarily concerned with the gratification of *guilt-laden* oral dependency needs. The dilemma of having unmet oral dependency *needs* on one hand and the resultant unconscious *guilt* on the other is the cause of a continual conflict for the unconscious. The therapeutic listener will deal with those who have emotional uncomfortableness arising from both an increase in their unmet oral needs and an increase in their unconscious guilt. Unconscious guilt can be categorized as either recently "added" or "personality core" guilt. In the next chapter, we shall examine some of many different manifestations of this unconscious guilt as it presents itself in relation to personality development and as so-called "psychiatric symptoms."

Bibliography

1. Fenichel, O.: *The Psychoanalytic Theory of Neurosis,* W.W. Norton and Co., New York, 1945.
2. Engle, G.: *Psychological Development in Health and Disease,* pp. 29-56, W.B. Saunders Company, Philadelphia.
3. Fairbairn, W.: *An Object Relations Theory of the Person,* pp. 1-59, Basic Books, Inc., New York, 1962.
4. Glover, E.: *Psychoanalysis,* pp. 22-32. Staples Press, New York, 1949.
5. Abraham, K.: *Selected Papers of Karl Abraham,* pp. 393-476, Hogarth Press Ltd., London, 1949.

6. Shave, D.W.: Paper presented in April of 1969 entitled "Orality in Communication" at the National Society for the Study of Communication in Cleveland, Ohio.

7. Shave, D.W.: "Oral Incorporative Guilt," *Internat. J. Neuropsychiat.* 5:1, pp. 438-446, 1965.

8. Bergler, E.: *The Basic Neurosis,* Grune & Stratton, Inc., New York, 1949.

9. Adler, A.: *Superiority and Social Interest,* H.L. Ansbacher and R.R. Ansbacher, Editors, Northwestern University Press, Evanston, Ill., 1964.

10. Rank, O.: *Will Therapy and Truth and Reality,* Alfred A. Knopf, New York, 1950.

11. Fromm, E.: *The Art of Loving,* Harper & Row, New York, 1956.

12. Sullivan, H.S.: "Therapeutic Investigation of Schizophrenia," *Psychiatry* 10(2):121, 1947.

13. Horney, K.: *Our Inner Conflicts,* W.W. Norton, New York, 1950.

14. Fromm-Reichmann, E.: *Psychoanalysis and Psychotherapy,* The University of Chicago Press, pp. 176-193, Chicago, 1960.

15. Roheim, G.: *Magic and Schizophrenia,* International Universities Press, Inc., New York, 1955.

16. Freud, S.: *The Ego and The Id,* Hogarth Press Ltd., London, 1925.

17. Klein, M.: *Our Adult World,* Basic Books, Inc., New York, 1963.

18. Shave, D.W.: "Guilt in Schizophrenia," *Internat. J. of Neuropsychiat.* 3:1, 1967.

19. Shave, D.W.: "Problems in Orality," *American J. of Psychotherapy* 22:1, pp. 82-95, 1968.

20. Federn, P.: *Ego Psychology and the Psychoses,* pp. 337-338, Basic Books, Inc., New York, 1952.

21. Spitz, R.: *The First Year of Life,* International Universities Press, New York, 1965.

22. Herron, W.G.: "The Process-reactive Classification of Schizophrenia," *Psychol. Bull.* 59:329-343, 1962.

CHAPTER 3

THE MANY FACES OF GUILT

We have seen in the previous chapters that emotional feelings are part object determined. The feelings of guilt, "shame" or "sin" are like wise part object determined on an accumulated basis. These feelings may not be reality oriented, because they are derived on an unconscious part-object basis, and must be rationalized. From a reality standpoint, many people who *ought* to feel guilty don't, while those having little, or no reason to feel guilty, often feel immensely so. Many people who seek professional help do so from intense feelings of guilt, while those people who are incarcerated for crimes against society, and who ought to feel a deep sense of guilt, very frequently don't feel guilty at all, but blame others instead. Whatever anyone attributes their feelings of "shame," "sin," or guilt in consciousness must be *whole* object oriented to be logical and, therefore, must be erroneous as to the true etiology. These reality-oriented rationalizations do not explain why one individual may feel guilt for committing a certain act and another individual may not feel guilty at all for committing exactly the same act. Or why an individual doesn't feel guilty upon committing an act he *should* feel guilty over, but then does so *much later*. The feeling of "sin" or guilt has little to do with the reality that the person is presenting as the "reason" for his feeling of "sin" or guilt. It is simply that the *level* of unconscious guilt, in its unprojected form, determines whether a person *feels* guilty, or whether he *doesn't* feel guilty. This seems to imply that there *is* something deeper, something unconscious that is the basis for the feelings of guilt. As has been stated earlier, all guilt, on the most basic level, arises from the repressed anger that occurs when the oral dependency needs are perceived, on a part object basis, as being frustrated.

The feelings of guilt are then concretized and placed in the conscious as metaphorical representations of the part object derived feelings of the unconscious guilt. An individual who feels guilty has an increased level of unconscious guilt which requires a reality rationalization. Each individual, in his own particular way, is directed by past conditioning processes to seek out a rationalization that is, in their conscious reasoning, most appropriate for their feelings. One has all of reality from which to draw the rationalizations for the unconscious feeling of guilt. The guilt derived feelings of inferiority, inadequacy, or unacceptableness may be manifested to others as problems in regard to "looks" (self-image or body image), family background, ethnic derivations, educational level, social status, financial trouble, age, sex, etc. These are all rationalizations, formulated by the unconscious ego, and unconsciously rationalized in a logical way, to be accepted by the conscious as the so-called "reasons" for the inferiority feelings. But behind the conscious rationalization are the timeliness of the unconscious and the accrued part object derivation of these guilt feelings.

Defense mechanisms other than rationalization may be utilized to deal with feelings of inferiority arising from the unconscious guilt. In what people have called "schizophrenia," one finds the most blatant examples of the ego's attempts to handle unconscious guilt. The so-called "hebephrenic" laughingly denies his guilt; the so-called paranoid projects his; and the "catatonic" is immobilized by immense self-felt guilt.[1] (For more on this interesting subject, see the author's article "Guilt in Schizophrenia" in the International Journal of Neuropsychiatry, Vol. 3 No. 1, January 1967.)

Compensation is a defense mechanism whereby the individual compensates, and may even greatly *over* compensate, for his feelings of inferiority. It is interest-to note how erroneous analysts have been in the past in attributing the origin of inferiority feelings to some aspect of reality, rather than to the unconscious guilt and unreality. For instance, some have speculated that Napoleon's driving need to be superior arose from underlying feelings of inferiority due to his diminutive stature. They support this with the fact that, characteristically, Napoleon would not allow others to stand in his presence unless he was on a horse, thus giving himself superior height. This explanation *does* seem logical — as any reason *should* be in reality — but it does *not* explain why an individual who *is* taller than average may *also* feel inferior! This individual unconsciously seeks a rationalization that, realistically, is logical for *his* situation in reality. Curiously enough, besides the people, who in their reality *shouldn't* feel inferior, but do, there are others, who in their reality *ought to* feel inferior, but don't! In light of this, one can only conclude that something *other than reality* is determining how a person feels.

Since a person seems to be made up of parts, there can be a guilt-laden part that may increase when the oral dependency needs are frustrated and the resulting anger repressed. During these times, the unconscious guilt increases in size, and an appropriate rationalization must be more arduously searched for. One's circumstances in life can be conducive to oral dependency need gratification at times, or they can be more frustrating. If more of the oral dependency needs are being met and if less anger is being repressed, the feeling of guilt decreases in size, and rationalizations of reality previously given, seem less important. During times in which less of the oral dependency needs are being met and more anger is being repressed, the unconscious guilt increases, and the rationalizations of reality become correspondingly more prominent. This is why, while the therapeutic listener can be attempting to gratify the client's oral dependency needs on a

46

rather uniform basis, the circumstances of reality involving his client's inter-personal relationship sphere outside of therapy may fluctuate with *more* or *less* oral need frustration, depending upon the circumstances of the client's reality.

When the unconscious guilt increases, certain things in a person's reality may become symbolic of this unconscious guilt. One client presented, grossly disturbed because the paint was peeling off her house, and her husband would do nothing about it. This somehow represented to her the exposure of increased unconscious guilt she was attempting to deny and her frustration in resolving guilt, which would require perceiving somebody emotionally significant doing someting about it. Another client was disturbed because the wall paper was coming off in one room, as though this, too, was symbolic of an uncovering of her increased unconscious guilt. Still another client became emotionally "upset" and sought "help" when her sewer pipes became clogged: "The maple tree roots got into the sewer pipes and the flushes didn't work right — my husband told me not to worry about it, but I couldn't get it off my mind, and it would keep me awake all night long thinking about it." Many housewives, when their unconscious guilt increases, will move furniture around, when the way the furniture was before, represented something too symbolic of the increased unconscious guilt. By changing the furniture around, they hope to magically remove the unconscious guilt. At other times, they will go to the beauty shop to have their hair re-done, buy a new hat or dress, or do something else that they feel will symbolically cover, re-arrange or, hopefully, magically remove the sense of guilt they unconsciously feel.

The unconscious guilt, and the manifestations or feelings derived from this guilt, can be rationalized in a great many different ways. However, it is important for the therapeutic listener to recognize that it *is* the unconscious guilt which makes a person feel guilty. Anything else that is consciously attributed as a source of guilt is simply a rationalization. A remembered experience, or an unforgotten act of either commission or omission is a whole object experience and, therefore, cannot be the basis for the part object derived guilt feelings. Whatever is presented as a logical possibility for the origin of one's guilt feelings, because it *is* logical, cannot be the real reason for the guilt. The real reason is *illogical*, because it *is* part object oriented or part experience oriented, and because it has been *accrued* over a period of time in the unconscious. Since everyone has unconscious guilt, everyone can usually find a reason for feeling guilty. There are always certain things, aspects or acts that one does not wish others to know about himself, even though people are human and, consequently, share all human characteristics. But what one feels guilty about will always be represented by a rationalization in one's conscious mind.

When a person's unconscious guilt increases, incremented by the more recent guilt from repressed anger, there is a greater need to rationalize this guilt and to seek a "logical" solution for it. For instance, a high school girl presented to a therapeutic listener with her unconscious guilt concretized in the fear that she might pass gas in the class room. This conscious fear prevented her from attending school, because "no one wants to be around a stinker." She had gone from one doctor to another, trying one treatment after the other, attempting to find a logical solution to her "gas problem," but no medicine and no reassurance helped. If this girl could be kept in a therapeutic transference, she would first begin to meet her emotional needs and then to express the previously repressed anger, thereby diminishing the unconscious guilt that was the basis of her problem. If she could do this in *any* of her interpersonal relationships, she would become more comfortable without the need for any "professional" help. It is interesting to note that his girl described several incidences of a boy in her class, who would "pass gas" in class, making the other members of the class laugh. According to him, it was an attempt to *meet* his oral needs, and apparently it was not associated with any guilt for him. Yet for her, who never did, it was.

The rationalization of guilt becomes a very *individualistic* thing, as in the above instance of the girl where the passing of gas was used as symbolic of her guilt that threatened to be exposed, as opposed to the boy who attempted, by this means, to meet his needs. One can describe a similar type of contrast in connection with a couple about to celebrate their fiftieth wedding anniversary. The husband wanted a picture of he and his wife in the paper, apparently to meet his oral dependency needs. But his wife was very much against this, apparently because this represented to her a reflection of her unconscious guilt. Again, one person may brag about his extra-marital affairs when they symbolize to him how much he's worth, or how important he is, as a concretized manifestation of his past part object oral gratification. But someone else may try to hide his extra-marital affairs when they apparently symbolize his unconscious guilt.

A person's unconscious guilt, which previously had been nebulous, may increase from oral need frustration and a repression of anger, and may then be concretized into a specific entity. This entity is then presented as the etiologic basis for the increased emotional uncomfortableness. For instance, a housewife, who had been increasingly frustrated in the gratification of her oral needs by a deteriorating marriage problem, suddenly becomes "upset" and seeks "psychiatric help". She gives as a reason for coming that she had "gone to pieces" after finding her husband masturbating one evening. One part of her apparently is angry that her husband was not seeking *her* for a gratification of his needs, projecting guilt to him and calling him "perverted." Another part of her apparently feels depressed when this act of his concretizes her increased feelings of inadequacy and unacceptableness. Her problems of increased unmet oral dependency needs, the anger from the frustration of these needs, and the increased level of guilt are all evident in her verbalizations of what she logically presents as the reason for her emotional uncomfortableness. By involving herself with a therapeutic listener, she meets her oral needs, ventilates her previously repressed anger, and diminishes the unconscious guilt. She can now emotionally establish a better marriage relationship than that before "I caught my husband".

Sometimes a particular incident of the past, in which there is good reason to feel guilty, is taken much later as the source of one's guilt feelings. For instance, an individual, some 30 years after his having been in the Navy during the Second World War, becomes involved in a life situation in which his unconscious guilt increases. He then feels that the basic cause of his unconscious guilt is that he was involved, as a member of a PT boat, in the slaughter of hundreds of helpless men. "They were husbands and fathers just like myself. (Cries) I can never live it down. I'm just a *murderer*, and that's all there is to it." The presentation of this is such, that from a logical standpoint, there is no solution, in that what is done is done. The presentation of the unconscious guilt isn't always done as a hoped for resolution, when severe as this, but as a statement of fact of how intensely the individual feels guilty. But the past can be made "right" through therapeutic listening, which allows the unconscious guilt to decrease.

There are many examples of how an individual, with recently increased unconscious guilt, will turn to the past, to seek a rationalization. For instance, a "debt" was recently paid to the Baltimore County school system by a repentent former pupil, who sent thirty dollars to the superintendent with the following letter: "enclosed are money orders covering the amount of damage to some of the games and toys that were in the Fort Howard Elementary School one day about ten years ago. Another boy and I threw some games around, and I think we took a couple of things too. This restitution act, please understand, is not done with the attitude that I have done something good of myself. It's only a response of what Jesus Christ has done for me through receiving His gift of salvation. It's wonderful!"

The Alaska Fish and Game Department received a cashier's check for seventy five dollars from an unidentified Seattle man, whose unconscious guilt increased and began to bother him to such a point, that it apparently necessitated his writing the following note, that he enclosed with the money: "While hunting in Alaska, I took some game in a manner which is not completely legal. This has bothered me to a great degree. While it is impossible to go back and change the event, I do feel that I can make some correction by sending you the amount that is enclosed."

How bizarre some of these examples of the feeling of intense guilt can be, is illustrated in the great number of people that inundate the police with calls, after a heinous crime has been committed, confessing that *they* did it and seeking to be punished. Besides the notoriety of the crime that becomes associated with their unmet oral need, and their unconscious wishful thinking associated with the violence of the crime, is the feeling of guilt and the "need" to be punished.. One client remarked after a "fire-bug" had set a house on fire that killed several small children: "Somehow I feel responsible for that tragic fire. I don't know why, but

I do. Maybe *I'm* the one that set that fire. Perhaps I'm a 'Dr. Jekyll and Mr. Hyde' type of person. I understand that split personalities are common. Maybe I did it, and can't recall it. Wouldn't one want to forget a thing like that ? I've heard of examples of amnesia where one totally forgets. I told my wife about my feelings, and she said: 'You're crazy!' Maybe I am! I told her I might have gotten up in my sleep, like a sleep-walker, and committed the crime, but she said: 'How the hell *could* you when you sleep with me all night!'' But Doctor, I've gotten up to go to the bathroom, and she didn't know I went.'' Even after the "fire-bug" was apprehended, this client *still* felt he was the actual culprit, and the police were holding the wrong man. "It is quite possible for the police to arrest an innocent person. In fact, I've heard of several cases myself.''

Sometimes it is not possible for an individual to adequately rationalize his illogic sense of unconscious guilt. The person feels guilty, but is at a loss to logically rationlize this feeling. These individuals know that they have no reason to feel as guilty as they do, but they are still at a loss to explain this intense feeling of guilt, and the accompanying "need" to be punished. At other times, they seem to pick out something from reality that seems to have very little realistic value as an explanation. For instance, They rationalize their illogic sense of guilt as coming from something they might have done when a person that they loved was dying. They imply, that if they weren't out seeking to gratify their own "selfish" oral needs, the death would have been avoided, as: "If I had only stayed with auntie that night, instead of going bowling with the girls, and having a good time, I might have called the doctor and she wouldn't have died.'' There is the implication here that the increased gratification of her oral needs has caused her to lose a loved object. And because of her "stolen pleasure," she feels she must now suffer. She attributes the intense sense of guilt to this particular "sin of omission," which in a way is rather illogical, in that the particular aunt had a fatal illness, and would have probably died had the person stayed home or not. One may often recognize, as in this case, the presence of an unconscious wish secondarily associated with a person's guilt feelings.

The psychiatric literature abounds in examples of guilt that are erroneously attributed to *whole object*, or whole experience derivations, at the expense of *part object* psychodynamics. Unconscious wishes, or incestuous desires can never be the *basic* cause of feelings of guilt, because they are whole object oriented, and do not imply the true part object derivations. It is only when the oral dependency needs are frustrated, and when the anger from this frustration is *repressed*, that the feeling of guilt comes about. But one *can* suffer sudden losses of oral gratification. If this loss is associated with a repression of the anger, the unconscious guilt rapidly increases. This sudden increase in guilt has been shown by the survivors of the recent catastrophic valley floods in Buffalo Creek, West Virginia. These people, having lost their sources of oral dependency gratification in the floods, rather suddenly developed increased unconscious guilt. A recent issue of *Time Magazine* (October 9, 1972) described some "typical" cases of this guilt, which they termed "survival guilt." Psychiatric symptoms" become evident with such a rise in unconscious guilt. For instance, a man lost his wife and children, and was then unable to sleep without a light burning. Darkness, for him, was an unbearable reminder of the moment when the electric power failed, just before the flood water struck his house. Another guilt-laden survivor lost two relatives, and then got cramps and vomiting whenever he tried to eat, with a resulting thirty pound weight loss. This was related to his having breakfast when the flood hit the valley. Still another survivor was a teenaged girl, who began behaving bizarrely, and eating so much that she gained almost fifty pounds. It is interesting to note that in this same article, there is mention of a *"listening therapy"* that was found to benefit those with this sudden increase in their guilt. This is the same guilt and the same *therapeutic listening* we are advocating here.

"Mental health professionals are not the only ones working to help valley residents with their emotional difficulties. To supplement these efforts, a three-man team of ministers trained in psychology goes from door to door, providing both religious solace and the same 'listening therapy' dispensed by the mental health aides. Ordinary medical doctors have been pressed into service, too, serving as listeners while they treat patients for physical ailments complicated by flood-inflicted traumas. One of these, pediatrician Mark Spurlock, has found that Buffalo Creek children have more nightmares now, and that 'asthmatics are wheezing more'. Among his patients is a child who comes in at intervals for allergy shots; his mother recounts the story of the flood on every visit. 'She doesn't even know she's told me before', Spurlock notes. But he never puts an end to her recital. 'Talking it out is the best thing in the world for her'."

Time Magazine (Jan. 15, 1973, page 53) again alluded to this "survival guilt", in an article entitled "Air Crash Survivors: The Troubled Aftermath". The guilt was described as an irrational feeling in those who have survived air crashes, concentration camps, atomic war, or natural disasters. These people apparently feel that they have somehow caused the death of others. But this so-called "survivor guilt" is nothing more than what has been previously described by this author as "oral incorporative guilt", (See "Oral Incorporative Guilt" in the *International Journal of Neuropsychiatry*, Vol. 1, No. 5, Sept. 1965 and "Problems in Orality" in the *American Journal of Psychotherapy*, Vol. 22, No. 1, Jan. 1968). We are now presenting it here as simply an increase in the unconscious guilt, due to the oral need frustration, that can come about by sudden decreases in sources of oral gratification, and the repression of the resulting anger. The guilt is consciously made referrable to the incident, which has precipitated a calamitous loss of part objects. The loss of part objects in an interpersonal relationship sphere, may not be so sudden, or so related to a particular disaster, as in "survivor guilt". But it is still the very same guilt that can accrue from part object losses and the repression of anger. Where the guilt and resulting depression may seem *logical* following a disaster, it is *not* so logically evident in, for instance, a so-called "endogenous depression". Here there seems to be no explanation for the depression since the objects of reality are still there. With the "endogenous depression" there has been instead an accruing loss of unconsciously perceived *part objects* for oral gratification, over a period of time.

The feeling that something is *wrong* with one's self also represents unconscious guilt, on a deeper level, that is self-felt. This, sometimes rather than being concretized, takes a nebulous form, where the individual seems to sense that something is amiss about himself, but is unable to make it anymore specific. When he seeks help, he will frequently ask: "Doctor, what's *wrong* with me anyway? You're not telling me, and I want to know." Sometimes this is projected, as though coming from other people, in which case the client will remark: " There's *nothing* wrong with me - people (including *you*, as well as others) *think* there is!" They might feel that they have some *fatal illness* that is undetected, and may go from one doctor to the other, and even one university hospital or clinic to another, seeking confirmation of what they "know" to be so, but feel that it is just "undiagnosed", or "undiscovered". They are *sure* that they have some type of cancer, or maybe some heart disease, when there is a guilt-laden aspect of themselves that feels as though they *deserve* to die. During times when the unconscious guilt is markedly increased, these fears, worries or over-concern about a specific aspect of their physical health, also increase. While many people simply feel that for some unknown reason, they are going to die young,and will never reach old age. At times there may be an attempt to concretize this nebulous feeling that something is wrong with the individual. For instance, many people suffer from a feeling of a "bad odor" about themselves that *they* can smell, yet others can't. Ann Landers, the well known newspaper columnist has recently shown how prevelant this feeling is, and at what great lengths people will go to futilely rid themselves of it. How intense it might be is illustrated in the woman that entered a state hospital wearing a gas mask, and a sack of camphor around her neck. Attempts to concretize this feeling of there being something "wrong" may take a great variety of different forms, one of which is exemplified in the virginal client that asks her therapist: "Do I have V.D."? Similar to the above is the frequently felt feeling that one has a "mental illness", which then prompts a feeling that they should see a psychiatrist. Others *fear* going to a psychiatrist, for fear, that their "mental illness" will be discovered. They may have a dread of mental hospitals, or even being around a "psychiatric patient", because of this fear within themselves that there might *be* something "mentally wrong" with themselves.

Closely akin to the feeling that something is "wrong" is the feeling the individual is *"different"* in some way from others. This can be manifested in a great number of ways that are rationalized in reality. Sometimes this feeling of being "different" is presented as *sexually* rationalized, and given a homosexual explanation, or a transexual explanation. Yet others, who also feel so alienated from people in general, present other rationalizations that *aren't* sexual, but involve other realistic categories that they feel are the basis for their being "different". They often seek to hide their self-felt "differences", while others try to accept them, but feel that others don't accept them. But the feeling of "being different", however it is rationalized or projected, is always guilt derived.

The need to seek *perfection*, in whatever one's definition of "perfection" might be, is guilt derived. Even though, reality-wise, there can never be perfection in anything, a standard of perfection is construed by an individual that counteracts their feeling of *imperfection* from the unconscious guilt. The "puritanical" morals, the need to be a "better Christian", and other perfection-seeking endeavors are derived from the unconscious guilt. "I expect too much perfection in myself", represents the statement often heard of the client in the *depressed* position. However, in the *projected* position, the individual feels *other* people expect too much of him, as though *they* have set up unattainable standards of perfection.

The feeling of *obligation* derives itself from unconscious guilt. The feeling that a person has to *do* for others, and that they shouldn't let others do for them, is a reflection of the unconscious guilt. It's the unconscious guilt that gives the feeling that a person has to make sure that the others are comfortable, *at their own expense*. But because they have unmet oral dependency needs themselves, and because they have repressed anger, they often do this for others, while ambivalently *resenting* it. They have to please others, and yet the same guilt makes them feel that no matter what they do, doesn't *really* please the other person. Since the guilt blocks a *perception* of oral need gratification, no matter what they do, in attempting to please someone else, is always taken as a rejection, or a "put-down".

There has already been mention that unconscious guilt gives a person the feeling that they are inferior, inadequate or worthless. The unconscious guilt is the basis of the inferiority complex. The person may attempt to rationalize this, in some concretized way, or he may be unable to put his finger on exactly why it is that he feels so inferior or inadequate. There may be no logical or rational reason for these feelings of inferiority, but they still can be felt as *very* intense. A person can be a "beauty queen", but still feel that her beauty is only "skin deep," and that underneath there is an "ugliness" that she, herself, is so much aware. She may have the feeling that others can also see this, and no amount of reassurance is helpful. One's conception of their body image is a reflection of this unconscious guilt. Sometimes the feeling can be *projected*, and presented as: "I'm ashamed to bring anyone over to my house, because of my *parents* - they are so uneducated, ignorant and poor." Either self-felt or projected, it tends to isolate the person from gratifying interpersonal relationships. In either position of being self-felt or projected, it can always be rationalized in reality. In the self-felt form, a person can even perceive himself as likened to a hungry beast or monster to be avoided. One

53

client remarked, on beginning a therapy session: "Well, here I am again, up from the swamp, rotten to the core and lower than a snake's belly.' Another client told of her fear of looking in the mirror, always avoiding a reflection of herself, and always being able to justify this fear to see her ugliness.

As an example of the projection of guilt to others, consider the following excerpt of a previously suicidal housewife in talking of her neighbor, "Bonnie", to whom she is alienated, and who is an implied aspect of her own self in this communication. "I just can't stand that girl. She gives me the creeps to be around her (shutters). I avoid her as much as possible, and everyone else does the same. No one wants to be around her. She's not pretty, though she acts at times as though she were. And that only makes her worse as she's actually ugly. She's simply repulsive! *Anyone* can see that once they get to know her. If I were like her, I would go out and commit suicide (laughs). Bonnie is a complete bore, and people know it. If they're stuck with her, they try and hide their real feelings about her. She's a beast to be around - in fact we all call her 'Bonnie the Beast'. (Pause) In a way, I feel sorry for her. She can't help the way she is."

There is a manipulative benefit of this unconscious guilt. Even in childhood, a mother will often utilize the guilt that she has given the child, into manipulating them into doing certain things. When a mother remarks: "Why do you *do* this to me?", she can often play upon the guilt of the child to get them to do something, or not do something from the guilt-derived fear of "hurting" the mother, or making her unhappy. People that are emotionally involved with each other frequently use guilt to manipulate the other. The prevalence of suicidal gestures, in regard to a young housewife, gives evidence of this manipulative value of guilt. Almost invariably, the first person trying to visit her in the hospital is the husband, who previously was frustrating her oral need gratification. In a marriage that is characterized by the husband projecting his guilt to the wife, and attempting to meet his oral dependency needs outside of the marriage, a suicidal gesture is frequently effective in getting the husband to return to his wife, when his unconscious guilt is played upon. Many times when marriage problems increase, an older housewife will undergo a surgical operation, or a hospitalization, with the husband then returning to the wife, when his guilt is manipulated in this often highly effective way.

The guilt gives the person the feeling that their *demands* for oral gratification are *excessive,*which almost necessitates a suicidal gesture. Even though a client may describe a situation representing obvious oral need deprivation, the guilt gives them the feeling that they should simply *accept* this, or that they themselves have *caused* it, and that they should be *satisfied,* count their many "blessings", and "cope" with their lot in life. They might refer to the analogy of the man that "complained his shoes were too tight, until he met a man that had no feet." Yet they are too much aware of others, who metaphorically, have "whole closets full of shoes - and even some to give away." They may even imply that they haven't been exposed in life to *enough* hardships and deprivations, "so as to harden me up so I can take these trying times like others do." They ask "Why can't I be *thankful* for what I have, and forget my troubles." This guilt derived feeling that their oral needs are *excessive* may be expressed in the frequently heard implications that they are talking too much. It's the guilt that makes them feel so burdensome, and so unimportant whenever they do talk. But not only do they feel that they talk too much with respect to oral need gratification, but to anger expression as well. They imply that they are smothering their emotionally significant person to death, sometimes perceiving that he wants to get away from them, and feeling as though they are a "jailwarden" or perhaps an "Army sergeant" to the object on whom they are so intensely dependent. "I should be *happy* about being unhappy" seems to be the "solution" that their guilt presents in regard to their unmet oral needs. When they *don't* feel good, because of unmet oral needs, they seem to say to themselves: "I *should* feel good because I don't *deserve* anything better, and I should *accept* my position of oral need deprivation."

They literally feel they *don't deserve* what they know they don't have, and yet ambivalently want. The feeling of being "thankful" and "grateful", for what little they perceive they do have, is derived from the unconscious guilt. Ironically, it is the persons that have been *most* deprived in their emotional lives that ofen *do* feel the most *grateful* toward the very person that frustrated them the most, in their attempts at oral need gratification. The frustrating mother of one client was described as: "Mother was a perfect angel. God bless her and rest her soul! Since my father was an alcoholic and left her, Mother had to work so hard in the shirt factory to support us. Sure, we got plenty of beatings, but there wasn't a one we didn't deserve. In fact, I got by without plenty I *should* have had! I don't know how she put up with me. She was more of a sister to me. (Suddenly appears anxious) I mean, she was a mother too - don't get me wrong! I was just that close to her. (Pause) Maybe I was *too* close. Perhaps that's why I still can't get over her death even now."

This same thing is shown in the alcoholic client that so frequently presents denying any difficulties in his marriage, when it becomes quite obvious that his wife is a projector of guilt to her husband. He feels he has a "wonderful" wife, because his guilt makes him feel that he doesn't deserve anything *better*. He might remark: "Sure, my marriage has had ups and downs, but all the downs I can honestly say have been due to me and my drinking." He implies that he has a better wife than he deserves, the same way the guilt-laden child, that has been deprived in its oral gratification, feels that it had parents that were *better* than what he deserved. These people, like we all do, utilize reality to only affirm what is unconsciously felt. This is so much a reflection of the unconscious guilt, in either its projected or self-felt form.

A frequent manifestation of the unconscious guilt is a feeling of *dirtiness*. That psychosexual level described by Freud, called the "anal stage", concerns itself, specifically, with this unconscious guilt. According to the psychoanalysts, this is the stage that the child goes through when it is being bowel trained, and these analysts attribute many emotional difficulties to problems arising from bowel training. The analysts can give many examples that *logically* seem to be symbolic of the unconscious concern with the bowel training. However, in going deeper on a psychodynamically *part object* basis, one can see that the "anal stage" really concerns itself with the unconscious guilt of *oral* frustration. The need to keep guilt hidden, and the ego's attempt to "clean up," in regard to this guilt, has an *oral* basis. All that is involved in Freudian "anality," concerning dirt, uncleanliness, and bowel movements, and all its symbolism is a reflection of the *oral* unconscious guilt. The unconscious guilt of some people may manifest itself by a pre-occupation with their bowel movements, the condition of their toilets, the cleanliness of their houses or their appearance. Sometimes the "anal" person is described as a somewhat hostile person, tending to be strict, miserly, scrupulous, moralistic, a "collector" or an organizer, but these are symbolic of the unconscious guilt on the oral level. He may compensate for this feeling of dirtiness in a myriad of different ways, as for instance, in being overly-clean. Many housewives, when their unconscious guilt increases, spend their time cleaning, particularly the bathroom and the kitchen. Most of what has been described as "anal" by the analysts of human behavior, turns out to be "oral" on closer scrutiny.

Sensitivity to others, or a concern as to how one's verbalizations or behavior will be taken by others is another face of the unconscious guilt. Many people, who are laden with unconscious guilt, present themselves as particularly "nice" or "sensitive", and as such, are very much acceptable to others. But because of the individual's unconscious guilt, they, themselves, don't *feel* so. They are uncomfortable with people, and their sensitivity, which can be an asset in many situations, is a liability in others or even in the same situation. They are too quick to see a rejection, a criticism or a condemnation in their interpersonal relationships. Although they are always afraid of hurting the feelings of others, they, all too often, are hurt themselves. Many times an individual may be attracted toward someone, who initially appears so "nice." But upon getting to know this individual — and unfortunately, many times *after* the marriage ceremony — they find out that this "nice" person has the demanding and troublesome accompanying unmet oral needs that may appear as a "bottomless pit," as well as the repressed anger behind the guilt that made him initially *appear* so "nice." The heavily guilt-laden individual will often show this sensitivity in his initial visit to a therapeutic listener. If for instance, a guilt-laden young female client is asked: "Are you married?", she may respond as: "No — what's wrong with that! I just haven't *felt* like getting married. I suppose you're going to attach some *psychological* significance to that! Well, I'm *not* a lesbian, if *that's* what you're thinking!"

The level of the unconscious guilt greatly affects the *perception* of verbal and non-verbal messages, of the behavior of others, and of reality in general. It can grossly distort the perceptions of one's interpersonal relationships. The ergasia, or "twisted thinking" first described as characteristic of "schizophrenia" by Meyer, is a manifestation of the perception-distorting effect of high levels of unconscious guilt. The perceived verbal and non-verbal communications of others are "twisted" to signify rejections, abandonments, condemnations and criticisms. When the unconscious guilt is at an uncomfortable level, interpersonal relationships are not oral need gratifying, but instead, become oral need frustrating. This is shown in the remark: "I don't know why I don't have any friends at all - just acquaintances. God knows *I* treat people right. But I don't like the way people walk all over *me*!" Or, again, as as: "I've *always* tried to get along with *everyone*. I greet *everyone* as a friend, and have *never* tried to hurt a single person. So why should they do this to me? Why should they talk behind my back, and try to get me fired from my job?" This person feels that he is being more than fair in his behavior to others, but he is perceiving an unfairness in the reaction of others to him. Not only does his guilt distort perceptions, so that they are perceived as oral need frustrating, but in doing so, he becomes alienated from others. When a client remarks: "I get so *damn tired* of looking out for everyone else, and getting back nothing, but a 'to hell with you' type of response!", he is reflecting this distortion and resulting alienation in his interpersonal relationship that is due to his level of unconscious guilt. He perceives a "no one seems to care whether I live or die" attitude from those that are emotionally significant to him. In projecting the difficulty to others, in his interpersonal relationship sphere, he perceives it as emanating from *them*, and not from his *own* unconscious guilt. Because of his unconscious guilt that makes him feel so "displeasing", he has a "need" to be always pleasing others, but sees in turn, only rejections, when others who have less guilt apparently don't have this "need" to please him. He will go out of his way to do things for others, but will still perceive himself as being *selfish*, and *self-centered*. No matter what outstanding success he might achieve in reality, he still perceives himself as a failure, and perceive others as feeling likewise about him. No matter what another person can do for this guilt-laden individual to meet his oral needs, it will be perceived as an oral frustration.

When a client remarks: "I'm not doing anything at home to please anybody. (Therapist: Are you supposed to?) Well, everybody seems to think so!", there is the implication that the problem arises from others. This person may talk about an object in his interpersonal relationship sphere as: "My husband wanted me to fit into a mold", or "Dad is always letting me know I never quite measure up", or "They expected more of me than they did of my brothers", without realizing that these expectations arise from his *own* unconscious guilt. This is so, regardless of whether the object in reality might, in fact, *want* the person to fit into a mold, or to meet unattainable expectations. But a less guilt-laden individual is less bothered, if he is at all, while the guilt-laden individual is trapped in the situation by his dependency and his "need" to please. It is his own guilt that blocks a perception of "measuring up," and it is his own guilt that makes him feel he could have always done *more* than he did, no matter how hard he tried to please.

A client may be heard to remark: "According to Bill, I'm not supposed to have any friends of my own. I'm supposed to just stay at home, and work all day long. He doesn't want me to have any pleasures, and on top of that, he even tells me I'm lazy." This is not a communication of a "schizophrenic", but what one can hear so frequently expressed by anyone that has an uncomfortable level of unconscious guilt, and who projects the difficulty arising from his own guilt to others. "People (or a specific emotionally significant person) treat me like I was *dirt*" is again a reflection of the unconscious guilt that can alienatingly distort perceptions in interpersonal relationships. This is often more emphatically expressed as: "I get tired of being crapped on!" When this client involves himself in a therapeutic listening relationship, he may perceive such involvement as being motivated solely because the therapist is interested in his money. No matter what anyone can do for the guilt-laden individual, the behavior is perceived as an oral need frustration. Their own guilt makes them unconsciously feel they *are* lazy, that they *shouldn't* have any pleasure or friends, and that they *deserve* to be "crapped upon." If the unconscious guilt is self-felt, it may be expressed as *"I'm* weird..." and then this feeling is rationalized. When the guilt is projected, it becomes *"He's* weird...", or *"He* thinks I'm weird...", and then these feelings are rationalized. "I'm not important to others", "He's not important to others", or "He thinks (or "others think") that I'm not important" represent projected guilt that can be expanded with rationalizations.

Nothing is more disastrous in one's interpersonal relationship sphere than an added increment of unconscious guilt. Perceptions of oral gratification become more difficult as the guilt increases, while perceptions of oral rejection are more easily made. Guilt always put the "fly in the ointment" of pleasurable interpersonal relationships. The lonely but guilt-laden housewife doesn't appreciate her husband phoning her during the day. "He only calls me when he needs something. He *never* calls unless he wants me to do an errand for him!" She angrily implies that she is only being *used,* but it is her unconscious guilt that also makes her feel that she *deserves* being used. Even when her husband calls with no errand for her, she may still perceive it as a rejection. "He didn't have any reason to call me. He just wanted to see what I was doing. Well, I don't like people checking on me, and I told him so!" If a neighbor should drop in, she would be upset and angry if her house is perceived by herself as unready for company. "I don't like anyone dropping in like that and finding the house a filthy mess. They'll think I'm disorganized, and not able to function like some *neurotic!*" But had the house been orderly and cleaned, she might have remarked: "I don't like her dropping in like that, and finding the house so perfect. She'll think I have nothing to do but keep the house immaculate like some *neurotic!*" Feeling as though others find her an "unacceptable neurotic" no matter what her situation is, she will tend to withdraw from others. Her interpersonal relationship sphere shrinks, which is due to, and which enhances, a build-up of unconscious guilt.

This distortion of the perceptions of reality by guilt can be so unrealistic that even when the attractive, but guilt-laden girl wins a beauty contest, she may remark: "Being attractive is a real disadvantage to me, because I can't tell how a person *really* thinks about me. I have the feeling that the only reason they seem to like me and accept me is just because of the way I *look* — I wish I *wasn't* so attractive." And yet, one can surmise that if she wasn't as attractive, she would be just as uncomfortable, but would now rationalize her unconscious guilt as due to some physical defect. The saying "Love is blind" is well known and refers to how one can be blind to reality when involved in an intense oral need gratifying relationship. But guilt is just as blinding! No matter how much someone tries to tell a guilt-laden person, that reality is otherwise, he will continue to feel an oral rejection, and will perceive, as well, that his "someone" is misunderstanding, if he can't perceive the oral rejection too. The guilt-laden husband will often describe his wife as "cold and unloving", and may add "The only time she's nice to me is when she wants something," or "The only time she kisses me is in saying 'good-by' — she's hoping she won't have to see me again." Nothing this wife can do, with the level of perception-distorting guilt he has, that could convince him that she does love him. One client was asked by the therapist just what his wife *could* do to lead him to feel his wife did care. He quickly replied: "She could kiss me like she used to — those were kisses I could *easily* tell she really cared!" But this perception will depend solely upon the *level* of his unconscious guilt.

The perception of oral frustration, that arises from the unconscious guilt, and that *promotes* oral frustration, is illustrated in the lonely client that comes for professional help, remarking: "I've just been so disgusted with men — they all seem to think that just because I'm an unmarried school teacher that I'm going to be wanting to go to bed. So they all try every way possible to get me in bed. That just turns me off. Then I met Bill, and he seemed real nice at first. He didn't even kiss me until our third date. He's *never* tried to take me to bed in the month we've been going together. But that's just it — it makes me wonder if I've got 'B.O.', or maybe he thinks I've got syphilis or something? And if that's the way he feels, then I don't want to see him anymore!" This implies that no matter what the man she is dating does, or doesn't do, it will be perceived as a rejection. This client later remarked to her therapeutic listener: "You're staring at me — what's wrong with me?" At still another time, she remarked: "You're not looking at me — what's wrong with me?" It is always the level of the unconscious guilt that determines whether perceptions that are being made are to be interpreted as oral need *gratifying*, or oral need *frustrating*. How difficult the perception of that which is oral need gratifying is made, by someone so much in need of this perception, is shown by this same client who remarked: "I want someone to notice me", implying she wanted her oral needs met. But everytime a person was perceived as "noticing" her, it didn't meet her oral need, but instead was perceived as "seeing" her *guilt!*

The depressed client is one that is involved in the throes of a high level of *unprojected* unconscious guilt. These individuals show very clearly the distortion of their perceptions. They will often go for professional help, chastisizing themselves for their inability to "cope" with their life situation, seeing only that they need to adjust to the situation, that to someone else may be seen as *blatantly* oral need depriving. One often hears them remark: "All I do is cry, and I have absolutely *no reason* to cry." But to someone else, who learns intimately of their emotional situation, one may recognize that they have *good* reason to cry, and may even be impressed that they haven't cried *more*. One will often hear the remark: "I have no reason to be depressed", when they seem so blind to the depressing emotional situation they are in. One depressed woman, who could see "no reason in the world" to feel depressed, described her husband as "he couldn't be any *nicer* to me", when her guilt made her feel he *shouldn't* be as nice as she perceived him to be. But to the social worker, who interviewed her husband, he made the impression of being harshly dominating, guilt-projecting, and not at all understanding of his wife's emotional needs. This woman had a mother, who lived with her, and who manipulated her daughter with "spells of heart trouble". How blind the client was to this manipulation is evident in her remark about the mother: "Mother knows how her spells upset me, and she tries to keep them from me. I feel so sorry for my mother, and what I'm putting her through." But it's her own guilt that makes her feel she *deserves* to be uncomfortable, and with "twisted" thinking, implies that she is concerned *more* with the uncomfortableness of her mother and her husband, than she is with her own uncomfortableness. This client, out of all her sisters, thought the most of her mother, and was most attentive to her. However, she also felt the mother thought the least of her, and would frequently be shown this. The feeling that her mother thought less of her was derived from her unconscious guilt, but the reality of the emotional past behind this perception is that the mother probably *did* slight this daughter, and because of this, laid the foundation for the unconscious guilt, which when increased, now prevents the client from seeing the psychodynamics involved. She only feels now that she *is* depressed, that she *shouldn't* be, and that her depression is upsetting to both her husband and her mother. Her guilt makes her feel she is a troublesome burden to the very ones she loves, which, at this point, may well be true in reality, because of the severity of her depressed condition.

There are some interesting aspects to unconscious guilt affecting the perception of reality. Anyone's perception of reality must always be in the light of their unmet oral dependency needs, and their unconscious guilt. One's reality is perceived through the unreality of one's unconscious emotional feelings. For instance, clients often feel they don't have an inferiority *complex*, but believe instead they *are* inferior. They feel inferior with such an intensity that they *know*

60

they are so, and one can no more change their belief than one can talk a "paranoid" out of his delusions. The level of unconscious guilt determines what they "*know* to be true."

Similar to the distortion of reality by self-felt guilt, one can project their guilt in a paranoid fashion to an object or situation in reality that may, or may not be deserving of blame and condemnation. One woman, who often projected her guilt, felt the water in her home was poisoned. It *was*, and was due to the chemicals her husband was putting on the lawn to kill the weeds, that drained into her well. Another guilt-laden individual felt his mother had heart disease, and imminently close to death. He was told she didn't by her family doctor, but he continued to worry. She *did* have heart disease and very shortly did die of a coronary. Whether one's guilt is self-felt or projected, it is part of an emotional unreality that isn't to be separated from one's reality. The unreality is always an inseparable part of perceived reality. And reality may often involve other people's unconscious guilt as well. For instance, one guilt-laden person would get up and change her seat, thinking that others would find her unacceptable to sit beside. But her act of moving her seat, led others to feel that it was because of *them*, and *their* guilt that the change of seating was necessary.

Unconscious guilt can give a person the feeling of *not being acceptable* to others. It may present as a *contaminating sense of unacceptableness* that leads a person to feel as though they are "poisoning" everyone that they come in contact with, and particularly those that are emotionally significant to them. One client put it as feeling like a "crock of old rottening garbage that nobody wants to be around." They feel as though they are a *burden* to others, that they are a detriment, that they are unwanted, and that other people would be better off if they weren't around. This is sometimes rationalized as deriving itself from the fact that they were an "unplanned for baby", or that they were "adopted." They often remark: "Everyone would be better off if I never had been born." (Note the fallacy derived from explanations of a whole object orientation, in regard to whether one should tell, or not tell, a child he is adopted, or whether one should tell, or not tell, if there is a Santa Claus, in believing there is a psychological importance either way).

The guilt may take the form of a self-felt feeling of *"sinfulness"*, and be so intense that they not feel acceptable even to God. They may not be able to involve themselves in any church activity, and may spend their time, alone, praying for forgiveness. Yet they may still not feel "forgiven." Some may become involved in increased church attendance, and "religiousity", while others may be found sitting in the church alone, feeling unworthy to be with others. Still others may feel so "sinful" that they change religions, often to a more ritualistic, or demanding type of religion, in an effort to relieve themselves of this uncomfortable feeling. Yet no matter how hard the person prays, or no matter how many times he attends a church, he may still not be able to find the relief from the feeling that he is the very *worst* sinner that has ever lived, the most *wicked* person in the world, or the person most suitable for *Hell*.

The "need" to *worry* is another manifestation of the unconscious guilt. It is only human for parents to worry about the possibility of an accident when, for instance, their child goes on a field trip. But being this "human" is a manifestation of the unconscious guilt. And when one's unconscious guilt increases, there is an increased tendency to worry. One can reach such a point that they seem at a loss to being able to control their worries. They become obsessed with worry and may become insomniac. As one guilt-laden client remarked: "If I can't find something bad to worry about, then I'll make up things that aren't even realistic." But one can usually find in reality enough logical things to worry about. One can always worry realistically about the possibility of a nuclear war, one's ultimate death, the eventual death of loved ones, or the inevitable possibility of sickness, disease or accidents. Though these are realistic possibilities, the worry about them always comes from the unconscious guilt — not from reality — and in a person that has more of this guilt, there is more of a "need" to worry. A person can worry about the mistakes of the past, worry about his present lot in life, or worry about the future. Associated with the need to worry are feelings of *insecurity,* for the guilt-laden person is an insecure person. When his unconscious guilt diminishes in size, he becomes less worried, and is less insecure.

Another aspect of the unconscious guilt that may manifest itself, is that of expecting the worst to happen — some catastrophe, disaster — or a calamity. This feeling of impending harm, or even doom to themselves or to loved ones, is a direct reflection of the unconscious guilt. Many people are afraid of taking an airplane ride, for fear that if they were to do so, the plane would surely crash. If they are in a crowd of people where some calamitous thing might happen to an individual, they feel that *they* are the ones that it would happen to. *Pessimism* and a defeatist attitude represent the unconscious guilt, which can become very burdensome, and even incapacitating when the unconscious guilt increases. But it is interesting to note though that the opposite, or optimism, or expecting the best, derives itself from part object derived oral gratification, and is involved in those that buy lottery tickets, in the hopes that they are the ones that will be the lucky winners. The same is true of horse racing, or in any other type of betting. The "set" of the unconscious guilt may manifest itself in one way, while the "set" of the oral dependency gratification may manifest itself in still another way. In other words, a person may be afraid to take an airplane ride, as a manifestation of his guilt, but still be an enthusiast of lotteries or horse racing, as a manifestation of his oral need gratification.

An interesting presentation of the unconscious guilt is the feeling that if an individual likes an object, or enjoys a particular thing, that it will surely cease to exist, disappear or somehow be taken away from them. This goes back to their earliest attempts to meet their oral dependency needs from the "good breast," which repetitively resulted in a disappearance of that "good breast," each time they attempted to emotionally feed from it. As though through a conditioning process, whenever they attempted to intensely meet their oral needs, they were rejected, abandoned or somehow let down. They become *afraid* to do anything that might be enjoyable, or that might give them pleasure, for fear of destroying that particular object that can provide oral need gratification, or that they will have a painful price to pay for their pleasure. This is humorously exemplified in a cartoon that shows a man and wife watching TV, with the man remarking: "I'll give you a darn good reason why this show won't last — I *like* it!"

The unconscious guilt can make an individual *anhedonic*. He can't experience any pleasure when extremely guilt-laden, for to do so, is symbolically equated with the pleasure of oral dependency gratification that is so guilt imbued, by the conditioning processes of his past. He *must* work, and he develops a perverted "pleasure" in finding himself "happy" only when he is working or accomplishing something. The unconscious guilt continues to drive him to work harder and harder, and where, in may many cases, no accomplishment seems to be able to remove the unconscious sense of guilt, and the act of accomplishing may even add to his guilt. This seems well shown in the person who attempts to satisfy his feelings of insecurity, his feelings of inferiority, and his "need" to work, with financial gain. With his anhedonia, and his compulsion to work, he may make one fortune after the other, but never be satisfied with himself, feeling instead, he could have accomplished more, and that because of this, he is a failure. Others may find it difficult to understand his feelings of dis-satisfaction with himself, in light of his obvious accomplishments in the financial world. It has been conservatively said that in the U.S. alone, there are over a hundred suicides a year by millionaires.

This anhedonia, or the inability to experience pleasure, and the "need" to work, do have a redeeming value in reality. Even though "successful" in reality, these people are still emotionally uncomfortable. These individuals, who have guilt that expresses itself this way, are often *overly-conscientious* in regard to their jobs. They worry about the loss of their job, worry about how people feel that they are doing in their work, even, when to others, they appear to be doing *more* than anyone else, and may even be doing outstanding work. When this is projected, they feel as though the job, itself, *requires* this anhedonia and over-work. They never seem to be able to work *enough*, to give them that feeling of security that can only be reached by a diminution of their guilt. As one woman expressed it "I *can't* take it easy, as I feel I *have* to work to pay for all the medical, hospital, and the disability insurances I keep up, trying to get things in order in case I might suddenly become ill." It's the unconscious guilt that makes her feel that there *is* some impending disaster for which she *has* to prepare herself. Reality-wise, there *is* a chance that such a disaster might happen, and this type of individual *would* be prepared. Another person felt that he couldn't meet girlfriends because of the town in which he lived was "unfriendly". He then rationalized his anhedonia as

"Since I can't find any girlfriends, I might just as well spend my time working." The more he worked though, the less exposure he had of meeting others of the opposite sex that could have met his oral dependency needs, and the more depressed he became.

Running one's self ragged with things they feel they *ought* to, or *need* to, *should* or *must* do is guilt derived. When a person asks for "pep" pills, they are reflecting this unconscious guilt that makes them feel that they *ought* to accomplish *still more* than what they are. They can't slow down and continually push themselves. "I don't work hard — it's *easy* work — I should be doing *more*" is the remark of a depressed person already working 3 different jobs on a 7 days a week basis. A sense of worth is apparently derived, but only in part, from what they can accomplish in regard to work, (but note that a feeling of increased self-worth can come about from either *added* oral need gratification, or by *decreasing* the unconscious guilt — and one way of decreasing the guilt is by assuaging it), while another part may resent the "need" to work, and may interpret it as an oral need *frustration*. But in spite of their driving "need" to work, they often consider themselves *lazy*, and will remark: "I could very easily sit around and do nothing if I'd just let myself." This isn't true because they *couldn't* do it — at least comfortably — because of their guilt. They have the fear that if they did lose control that they would do nothing, and would be *worth* nothing, and this would be too uncomfortably symbolic of their guilt. When they come into therapeutic listening depressed, they often ask: "What should I do to *work* on, between now and when I see you again", as though feeling that they *ought* to be "working" at something, making some type of a strenuous effort, and implying that nothing is being accomplished since they *aren't* doing this. They can't accept "doing nothing", or "resting up", or in any way, meeting their oral dependency needs. Anthing pleasurable, or oral need gratifying, evokes the feeling that they will destroy that which is symbolic of the little oral dependency they are deriving. What they seem to ask for is more hard work, more suffering, more oral deprivation, and more anhedonia to *assuage* their guilt. When this guilt-laden, they appear repulsed by anything that is oral need gratifying, including emotionally gratifying communicative involvement. It's the guilt that makes a person desperately try to do what they, *in part*, obviously don't want to do. They feel ambivalently, on one hand, that they're doing too *much*, and, on the other, that they're *not doing enough*, and that they shouldn't even *ask* for help.

Many times, there is evidence in human behavior that the unconscious guilt is being assuaged by long and hard work in some difficult and dangerous task, or daring feat of courage and heroism. These attempts at assuaging the guilt are frequently accompanied by the desire for oral need gratification, such as outstanding recognition, or a position of importance, often accompanies the anhedonia of guilt. At times, the intense feeling of guilt is sought to be assuaged by shock treatment, and even by psychosurgery. If the person can avoid the onus of psychiatric treatment, he may seek out some form of general surgery. Through a hospitalization, and particularly involving surgery, oral dependency needs can be met in a way that is acceptable to the family, and to friends, while the guilt is being assuaged. Frequently family psychodynamics can be manipulated through the hospitalization. A woman, who had previously been unable to "slow down", because of the uncomfortable level of her unconscious guilt, conveniently developed "female problems." Taking the advice of her gynecologist, who felt her emotional problems were *secondary* to her physical problems, she underwent a hysterectomy. Having assuaged her guilt through the operation, and being forced into *accepting* oral dependency gratification in the recuperative period — now with the active support of her family — she finally was able to "slow down." But it is because her guilt was now at a much *lower level*. She rationalized this as: "My doctor told me I shouldn't do anything at all for the next six weeks. He doesn't even want me to touch the housework, and doesn't want me to go back to work at the factory for at least two months." Her gynecologist's predictions were true and she gratefully remarked: "I feel 100% better now — I'm so glad I had the operation — I only wish I didn't wait as long as I did." The reason she *did* wait was because of the previous high level of unconscious guilt that made her fear the outcome of the operation. One can suspicion that in a majority of general surgical cases, and regardless of the reality of the situation that may "require surgery," there is the unreality of a "need" to assuage guilt. Reality and unreality are not separable entities. The irrefutable truth is that every "hypochondriac" is going to die of some physical problem sometime. A pathologist could take anyone, and if he could perform an autopsy, would find some illness, physical aberration, pathologic process, or some organic abnormality. No one technically has "no physical illness". And some surgeons will readily admit to a personal axiom that leads to a highly successful practice: "every person that comes to you has at least three problems for which you can operate...Your job is to find them!" Who can ever say that a patient *shouldn't* be diagnostically worked up, or perhaps even surgically explored, when his own doctor, or another doctor, feels there *is* a question, even if slight, of some physical pathology? Hysterectomies and gastrectomies may appear as symbolic *removals* of a physical part of the body that seem most equated for the guilt-laden oral needs. But any type of surgery may be guilt-assuaging, and one can often hear later reflections of both the oral need for recognition, and the guilt as: "The doctor said it was the very *worst* case he ever saw! I mean I nearly died! Ten pints of blood! I shouldn't even be alive today. I was seven hours in surgery!" It is as though these people imply: "I have *suffered*, so I *deserve* now to have a few of my oral needs met." Much in reality can offer opportunities to assuage guilt, in fact one can say that reality is conveniently guilt-assuaging.

An accident or illness can often assuage enough guilt, and offer oral need gratification, to allow the person to function more emotionally comfortable afterwards. For instance, a couple that had been involved in marriage difficulties from increased guilt may separate. But on the advent of some illness, operation or accident for one, they become reunited again, when the unconscious wishful thought for one is apparently enacted in reality, and plays upon the person's unconscious guilt. One frequently hears of a depressed person, who upon getting involved in an accident, feels no longer depressed, when he assuages his guilt, and is captivated in a situation where he must accept oral need gratification. One is familiar too with the depressed housewife, whose husband's patience runs thin, and "gives her Hell!" Where previously she couldn't do the housework, she now is able to do the work and appears less depressed. This husband will often later remark: "She didn't need any psychiatric treatment! All she needed was a kick in the ass!" And it appears as though he's right! Sometimes, though, when a husband physically abuses his guilt-laden wife, who previously was ill-treated, he often assuages enough of her guilt that she, at least temporarily, feels more sure of her position, because of less unconscious guilt, more able to express anger, and more confident in herself. She may have her husband arrested and jailed, or if he's an alcoholic, perhaps committed. But then the guilt increases on her part when she has lost her object for oral dependency gratification, and guilt projection. She feels sorry for her husband, will take him back, and cycle begins anew. But guilt that can be assuaged, like the guilt that seems to dissolve in alcohol, is usually the *added* unconscious guilt, and is rarely the personality *core* guilt.

Being worried and insecure may be an uncomfortable emotional situation, but there are circumstances of reality, where to *be* so concerned about worrisome possibilities, can be an asset. People who are worried about their health, for instance, may take steps to ensure good health. People that are worried about the possibility of fire, or of some accident, may take the necessary steps that then prevent or decrease that possibility of happening. There are occupations in reality that seem to demand, or may reward a person that is worrisome and overly-conscientious. In fact, one can take all the many different faces of the unconscious guilt, as they present themselves, and envision situations in reality, where to be this way, is definitely an asset.

Needing to clean up something, straighten out things, or put things in order, can, from a reality point of view, be *highly* advantageous. At the same time though, it is still a reflection of one's unconscious guilt. People with high levels of "core" unconscious guilt may manifest this in obsessive compulsive behavior, and a pre-occupation with cleanliness, orderliness, and organization. But when their unconscious guilt increases, there is an often irrational, unrealistic or fanatical behavior on their part that doesn't fit with their circumstances in life. But the circumstances in life determine so much, the degree that a person is comfortable with his level of guilt. A person with the same amount of unconscious guilt that manifests itself in this way may be quite comfortable in a situation where such pre-occupation and over-concern are necessary, and very uncomfortable where it is orally unrewarding.

The conscious feeling of being important, of being cared for, of being favorably recognized is a concretized conglomeration of unconscious part object perceived feelings of the past that are then rationalized into an individualistic reality-oriented way. This may involve everything that may range from the desire to *become* a president to unfortunately, *shooting* a president. The desire to be, or the knowledge that one has the "greatest", the "prettiest", the "most", the "first", the "last", the "only", the "best", the "most difficult", etc., etc. is only an expression of the same oral need we have seen before, but placed in an individualistic metaphorical framework of personal significance, representing an unconscious concretization of part object perceptions that counters the feelings of worthlessness derived from the unconscious guilt. The framework that one seeks to find the answer to one's need to be important, or to be favorably looked upon by others, may differ markedly from someone else's. But whether one seeks a high military position, a political office, an honored place of esteem in the arts and sciences, great financial, or even spiritual wealth or any other position of recognized success, the uncomfortable orality can still be seen, and seen as *inseparably* from that which seemed *necessary* to produce the level of success. The driving force is the unmet oral needs and the oral guilt working together.

It isn't an incidental factor that the business tycoon had such an early life of oral deprivation, for it involved so intimately the very motivation for his ceaseless striving, to cover his guilt-derived feelings of inadequacy, inferiority, and his insecurity with one fortune upon another. His "psychopathologies" may show at times, but these cannot be considered "liabilities" for they are, simultaneously, the very "assets" of his success. The feelings of the unfulfilled oral need, the anhedonic manifestation of the guilt, and the anger seem a necessary part of whatever it takes to be successful in an endeavor. Yet all too often, even the level of success attained isn't enough to satisfy the guilt-blocked insatiable oral need, so that for an example, the alcoholism, or the suicide, of this "successful" person may seem to some quite difficult to understand. But it is no more difficult to understand than the understanding of how he *attained* such a success-oriented personality coming from the orally deprived childhood he had where his siblings might have become "failures", or how his own children are now such "failures", or why his wife must see a psychiatrist, when she suddenly experiences a psychotic upwelling of intense anger, intense needs, and guilt from being too long, too "independent" of others. It is difficult at times to tell the saints from the sinners, or the "mental patients" from anyone else, (and the differentiation may depend more on the *times* than anything else) when the desire to be recognized as a manifestation of unmet oral needs is accompanied by the need to assuage the oral guilt for having these needs. This tendency to assuage and to compensate the underlying guilt, at the same time one seeks to have their oral needs met, is not only the essence of outstanding feats of heroism and endurance, but also the very same unconscious motivation of similar not-so-evident emotionally uncomfortable people, who turn up on the surgical wards for the same unconscious goals. The guilt from oral needs that cannot be met more directly are assuaged with the partial gastrectomies, the sub-mucosal resections, the hysterectomies, the vitamin injections, the allergy shots, etc., etc. Hospitals are over-crowded with emotionally uncomfortable people, who are there under a guise of a medically oriented reality.

In reading the biographies of successful men, one may have the feeling that it's impossible "to tell the players without a score card", and that the whole "game" is unfairly "rigged" by circumstances of fate. That underlying problem that manifested itself with "incurable alcoholism" caused one person, in a particular situation, to be forced to resign from the Army as "unfit for military service". Yet that same underlying "problem" must have been the basis for those very characteristics, which under just the right circumstances of fate, and another enlistment, led to his being the most effective Union general. He was able to get the war won when other generals, with less of a "problem", couldn't do it, and went on to become the 18th President of the United States. The heroes that we all look up to, that set our country free, may have become so, from a projection of their inner emotional conflicts that sought to free themselves from an unconscious face of guilt. Always accompanying this guilt is, of course, the oral need that drives them to seek the lime-light, or the heroes' role. The anger from the unmet oral needs can often be utilized in fights for freedom or in struggles toward some lofty and worthy goal in reality. Success in reality requires the unmet oral needs, the anger and the guilt. It is as though reality appropriately lends itself for the expression of the emotional conflicts within an individual. One can often find a cause, in reality, or an endeavor in which to meet one's oral needs, to express one's anger and to assuage, or compensate one's guilt.

It is necessary to emphasize again that in many situations in reality, the unconscious guilt may represent a definitely required asset. The feelings of inferiority are *best* compensated by success and achievement. This feeling of inferiority, compensated by success, is supported by many guilt-laden individual's tendencies toward anhendonia. These people have a "need" for perfectionism, for hard work, and deprivation. Their guilt-derived ability to suffer, the anhedonia, and their fear of dependency are ironically what is *necessary* to be an acclaimed outstanding success in reality, no matter what one's field of endeavor might be. If a person were emotionally comfortable, and didn't have those guilt derived feelings of inferiority and worthlessness, he wouldn't have a need to try and "better" himself. The great accomplishments of the human race all have motivations in not only a desire to gratify the oral dependency needs, but to assuage and to compensate the underlying guilt.

68

Wanting to be punished, psychiatrists have labelled as being "masochistic," or "abnormal," through their erroneous application of the medical model to human behavior. But the same unconscious guilt, and often to the same degree in one set of circumstances in reality makes a "psychiatric patient" out of one individual, and an acclaimed "success" out of another. That same guilt-derived ability to take "punishment" and to be so accepting of deprivation, is what has been *necessary* for the great feats of determination, courage and endurance in exploration, in the sciences, in the military and in any other aspect of reality. The unmet oral needs that drive a person to seek his individually chosen "limelight," accompanied by his driving unconscious guilt can lead him to the heights of success, or to the nearest psychiatrist — and the difference depends not in the quantity of unmet oral needs or the quantity of the unconscious guilt, but so often in the *circumstances* of reality. The road to the very greatest heights of outstanding success, or to the state mental hospital *is the very same road!* The person who stands alone to face his particular depriving reality by himself, without wanting help and refusing all help offered, we have admired. This is that admirable substance truly "great" men have. But the person who does this very thing best is found in a corner of a back ward of a state hospital. And the biggest impediment toward becoming an outstanding "success" in life, no matter what one's endeavor, ironically, is to have a truly happy childhood. In such a childhood, one's oral dependency needs have been sufficiently met, and one accrues a comfortable amount of personality core guilt. Therefore, if one were to eradicate the very roots of "mental illness", one would be eradicating the very roots of "success", as well! The very essence of what "successful" people are emotionally made, is the very essence of so-called "mental illness". Just as one has heard the expression: "Show me a hero, and I'll show you a bum!", one can now add: "Show me an outstandingly *successful* person, and I'll show you an emotionally *uncomfortable* person!"

What little understanding Psychiatry has shown in recognizing the identical role of guilt, in the so-called "mentally ill" and the "successful" individual is illustrated in a recent issue of the American Journal of Psychiatry. As words of wisdom, this illustrious journal of the American Psychiatric Association gave the following for its readers: "No man that ever *became* a success, *thought* he was." We know that it's his guilt that made him think he *wasn't* a success, while the same guilt *made* him a success. But one should no more be presenting this for psychiatrists (who, as a group, have one of the highest suicide rates in the country) to emulate, than the case of a college girl, who sees a psychiatrist because she's always worried she's going to fail in college, but who consistently gets the highest grades in her class.

In the preceeding, we have seen metaphorically expressed manifestations of the many faces of this universal primary guilt that can show itself in the emotionally comfortable and the uncomfortable. We have seen that this primordial guilt is not only handled by the personality of the individual, but that it can increase, and as such produce an added level of emotional uncomfortableness, the so-called "psychiatric symptoms", that then may cause an individual to seek, in some type of interpersonal relationship of reality, a diminution of the guilt, as a type of solution. It is well to remember that the level of unconscious guilt can *increase* or *decrease* in between the sessions of therapeutic listening, *independent* of what goes on in therapy, due to the circumstances of one's reality, which can help meet the oral dependency needs, or aid in the expression of anger, as well as frustrate the individual more in his attempts to meet his oral needs or to express his anger. The therapeutic transference is just one of the many types of transference relationships that any individual has in his interpersonal relationships. The more "therapeutic" are his relationships, the more comfortable he is. The therapeutic relationship though, because it *is* therapeutic, should be consistently emotionally gratifying, as well as accepting of the client's projected guilt and anger.

CHAPTER 4

THE PHENOMENON OF THE TRANSFERENCE

There is little reason to review the often conflicting definitions of *transference* found in psychiatric literature, that all erroneously involve a whole object orientation. We have already emphasized in the first chapter the part object orientation of the unconscious. Since the transference is an *unconscious* phenomenon, any definition based on *whole* objects must be considered as erroneous. Transference cannot be simply defined as an emotional re-enactment in the *present*, of an earlier relationship with an emotionally significant figure of the *past*. Neither can it be defined as a transferring of earlier infantile and childish relations, associated with a parent or a parental figure, to an object of the present. Because the transference is *not* whole object oriented, it cannot be the simple reproduction of forgotten or repressed experiences of early childhood. Since the transference is *unconscious*, it is a product of a part object oriented *unreality* that is not so logically explained as what is implied in the definitions involving whole objects, or total experiences, of the *past* in relation to a whole object, or a total experience of the *present*.

It is, though, historically interesting to note that in 1891, Adolf Breuer, the early co-worker of Freud, while preparing with Freud their *Studies on Hysteria*, was heard to remark of their newly discovered transference phenomenon: "I believe that *this* is the most important thing we two have to give to the world." For this recognition, Breuer deserves far more credit than he has been given, particularly when many Freudian analysts have considered the transference as only a "contaminant" of psychoanalysis, or of any form of psychotherapy, without realizing it is the very *essence* of any psychotherapeutic endeavor.

When Breuer arrived at a house on Liechtensteinstrass in Vienna in 1880, he thought he had come to treat a young girl for cough. He very quickly recognized though, that his patient was suffering from what was then called "hysteria." By talking about her problems, she became more comfortable. In that way, Breuer stumbled almost accidentally on a method of treatment that his patient referred to as her "talking cure." It might better have been termed a "talking and listening cure," for it was his *listening*, as much as her talking, that effected a "cure." Rather than any contaminant that simply can't be avoided, the transference is the emotionally resolving phenomenon that can

71

be found in any therapeutic endeavor in reality, from quackery to religion, that can bring about a degree of emotional comfortableness. But in like fashion, within anyone's interpersonal relationships, it is the subtle phenomenon that can bring about degrees of emotional uncomfortableness as well.

Freud, the father of psychoanalysis, began his interests in the unconscious while studying hypnosis under the great French neurologist, Charcot. He later discovered he could dispense with hypnosis altogether. This was fortunate, for he was not a good hypnotist. He found that by letting his client talk at random while he listened, the client would, after a while, overcome his emotional difficulties, and seemed then to be able to recognize logical and reality-oriented causes of his previous emotional uncomfortableness, with intellectual hindsight. Freud, like later classical psychoanalysts, attributed the client's attaining this emotional comfortableness as solely dependent upon this intellectual hindsight, which was then termed "insight." His new method of the "talking cure" was based on "free associations" where the client was instructed to say whatever came to mind or was given words upon which to "free associate." This method of analyzing and interpreting, in regard to whole objects of the client's past and present, led to the beginning of psychoanalysis. But, as will be seen, psychoanalysis can be dispensed with just as easily as Freud did with hypnosis, and still obtain the same end results.

Freud was rather organically minded in regard to his early orientation of the unconscious. He tended to view his "talking cure" as a type of catharsis, involving the expression of "psychic energy," from the verbal motor responses of the brain. He never did fully appreciate the importance of the transference as the emotionally resolving ingredient of psychoanalysis, but emphasized instead the intellectualized insights the analyst and the client would later develop. It was the intellectual hindsight that seemed to be effecting the change from emotional uncomfortableness to emotional comfortableness. He failed to realize that what was dynamically occurring within the transference, while the client talked, and while the analyst listened, was an emotionally resolving unconscious interaction between the two. The proposition, implied by Freud, is that the "insight" brings about emotional comfortableness. What is undoubtedly correct, instead, is that emotional uncomfortableness can *only* be resolved by an emotional process, and not an intellectual process. It might seem, reality-wise, and particularly within the context of a psychoanalytic situation, that it is the intellectual process that brought about the change. The subtle emotionality that is made possible by the transference, and *not* the analytic intellectualizations, gives the relationship its emotional conflict resolving potential. What we are implying here is that a talking and listening process, coupled with the naturally occurring transference phenomenon is the true cause for the change. This involves an unconscious, illogical and an unrealistic process that stays veiled by logical reasoning and reality concern. It is still this emotional relationship of a person, coming to another for help, of talking out one's conscious problems, and of having somebody else, who is *special*, and who *listens*, that effects the change from uncomfortableness to emotional comfortableness.

The feeling that someone cares enough *to listen* in the present — and this need only be an unconscious *part* object perception — is the necessary pre-requuisite to expressing the angry feelings to him that will decrease the unconscious guilt. It is as though by an illogic and magical process afforded by the transference that *"undoes"* or *"makes right"* all the personally perceived injustices of the past. This isn't then, a simple catharsis. It isn't a simple expression of "dammed up" verbal motor energy. Instead, it involves an unconscious phenomenon that is taking place in the "here and now," within the immediate relationship between the person talking and his listener, that has imbued the listener with a quality that equates him, on a part object basis, with the emotionally significant parts of people in the talker's past. It is these people in the emotional past that have attempted to meet his needs, but have *frustrated* him, *angered* him, and have *made* him emotionally uncomfortable. The transference makes the listener of the "here and now" equated with those people of the past. It is the relationship of the "here and now" that can rectify the "wrongs" of the past, within an unreality, that differs from reality where "what is past *is* past," or just "water over the dam." Nothing is "past" in the unconscious, and no water ever goes over the dam. And it is because of the transference that the part objects of the past, the part objects of the present, and the unconsciously perceived part objects of the "here and now" are equated as *one* and the *same*! Freud[8] felt that the transference was represented by the client seeing in his analyst the return, or "reincarnation," of some important figure out of the emotional past of the client. He felt the client consequently transferred onto the analyst the feelings and the emotional reactions that were associated with that earlier relationship. He noted the way clients seemed to have a tendency to *repetitively* relate to others, as a reflection of an earlier past emotional relationship, so that he came to view the transference as a "repetition neurosis." He pointed out that past emotional experiences were revived and applied, as though through a "false connection," to the analyst. He described transference reactions as merely "reprints," or new impressions of the old, and continuing this analogy, he felt that analysis alone offered a "revised edition," and not just a republishing or a simple reprinting.

A definition of the transference must involve the concept of part objects and part perceptions. The transference phenomenon, in this light, becomes marvelously more complex than a simple whole object oriented definition implied in "reprinting." The unconsciously recognized specific "parts" of the emotionally significant objects of the past are *equated* to certain aspects of the unconsciously recognized part objects of the listener. What is transferred then, in the transference, is illogical, highly ambivalent, frequently shifting feelings, that were associated with those emotionally significant past *part objects*, but which produce something *different* than anything past. It isn't that the analyst is viewed as a "mother" figure, or a "father" figure, or that the emotional feelings stem from any one single past emotional relationship, but from *all* past emotional relationships. The transference is an unconscious phenomenon that involves the illogic predicate equating based on the Von Domarus principle. Chapter Two shows how this type of equating can make any object identical to any other, if it shares at least one common aspect or characteristic. Since the unconscious doesn't recognize the concept of time, the transference phenomenon can involve feelings associated with all the part objects of the distant past and with the immediate present as well. And emotionally significant people in a person's emotional life involve a lot more than parental figures. Even when a client in a psychotherapeutic endeavor does remark spontaneously: "You remind me of my father," the client is only responding to a *part* perceived aspect of the listener, and is presenting this on a *whole* object basis. It would be erroneous to infer that this means that the client, *in toto*, is relating to the listener, as a child to her father, for she might just as well have remarked: "You remind me of my husband," or "You remind me of my son," or even "You remind me of my neighbor." Part object perceptions have to be rationalized on a whole object basis. They have to be explained in metaphor, or analogy, in that an unreality of perceptions on a part object basis cannot really be expressed as such in a conscious oriented to logic. In defining the transference, one is faced with the same.

In order to illustrate the formation of the transference as a new entity different from anything in the past, consider the stirring song, "The Battle Hymn of the Republic," that has become so much an emotionally touching hymn of great religious faith. Written during the time of the Civil War, the part object impressions and those part experiences of this intense struggle that were well known, and often intimately felt by so many at that time, were captured by the author. The feelings associated with a great moving mass of determined and dedicated soldiers were crystallized into the formation of something even *more* awe-inspiring than any of those past impressions, that could be understood so well by those, who knew from their own experiences, what was being presented on a level above reality. The author's impressions of the Union Army on the move were molded into something that in it's totality was *different* from those part object experiences from which it was made. In the common reality of that war the Union Army wasn't always victorious, nor was it always glorious. It suffered many defeats and humiliations, and leadership was often poor. It was no more dedicated and no more determined than the army that it fought. There never was a "trumpet that had never called retreat" in either army, but there *were* experiences enough to hopefully *envision* such a trumpet. An army that could be undefeated was not

74

a part of any reality on either side at the time Julia Ward Howe wrote her hymn. But enough part object experiences could be drawn upon and concretized into the formation of something far greater than anything reality could produce. There were enough experiences and impressions from *parts* of that war to envision an always glorious and always victorious army that was *totally* determined and dedicated. By taking the emotional parts of the reality of the Union's war that *were* glorious, the conception of a still *greater* glorious army was produced. Yet, those reality parts, of which it is made, are still evident, but having been separated from their inglorious parts, they are fashioned into something that becomes most awe-inspiring and transcends reality. With the rolling of battle drums, the measured cadence of thousands of marching feet, and the vision of a terribly powerful army force, an entity beyond anything in reality is produced that can transcend, in emotionality, the feeling of being victorious on a battlefield. "I have seen Him in the watch-fires of a hundred circling camps," "writ in burnished rows of steel," and encapsulated other part object perceptions of that war's experiences and impressions give this entity of unreality a most realistic character.

To illustrate in a different way how the synthesis of something that in it's entirety is new and different from any of it's part objects that go into the make-up of it, consider, for instance, a person's conception of hell. This non-terrestrial place may be made a familiar entity, seemingly very real, and having a considerable personal emotional impact and significance. It is created by a construction of past part object experiences, past impressions and bits and pieces of past knowledge of "hellish" terrestrial experiences that become fused into the concept of a new entity that has characteristics of its own. It becomes unique, different, and quite separate from any of its parts. One can understand the meaning, the feelings, or the experiences, of this newly created entity because of those past experiences that the individual might have had. He can envision a new and different *total* entity by his past familiarity with its parts.

In a similar manner, one might have used for an analogy the synthesis of heaven from earthly "heavenly" experiences one might have encountered on a part object basis. The creation of an entity of unreality can become unquestionably real. Those "heavenly" past part experiences from the reality of an individual, where oral dependency gratification appeared free from ambivalence, where pleasure was free of guilt, and where the feeling of a very special "togetherness" seemed uncontaminated by any orally frustrating aspect of reality are utilized to envision the perfect "heavenly" totality. These experiences lend a realness to the unreality that is formed. And what is produced is uniquely personal, and individualistically appropriate for the present in its entirety. It is different from any past whole experience. It transcends even the sum of all its parts by this whole object envisioning or wishful thinking. But note that the development of these entities, like the nature of the transference, must be intimate, very personal and very much unlike any other individual's conception because of those past experiences and those unconscious wishes upon which the entity is created.

In just this same way, the therapeutic transference is formed in an unreality, not a reality. And it is done so by granting oral dependency, and becomes more intense, the more dependency is granted. Anyone that *listens*, while someone else talks, becomes an object on whom a transference will be formed, because dependency needs are met through listening. The listener becomes an entity of an unreality, made up of a conglomerate of emotionally significant past part object relationships, that when concretized, as in the *Battle Hymn of the Republic*, can attain an awesome emotional significance and potential. That emotional potential, like the hymn, can be greater than the sum of all its parts. Unlike the Aristotelian logic of reality, where the whole can *not* be greater than its parts, this entity of unreality, created by the unconscious from certain bits and pieces of past part object relationships, can be *immensely* greater than the *sum* of its component parts. Where a past object of the individual may have met some of his oral dependency needs and frustrated others, enough part object experiences of oral dependency gratification have been experienced to hopefully *wish* for a relationship of pure oral need gratification. This unconscious wish for pure oral need gratification can find a phantasized fulfillment in an object, as the therapeutic listener is, when the object isn't really known in reality. Seen only as the "listening one," the perception that he can fulfill the unconscious wish for pure oral need gratification is very readily made. This unconscious perception, as the hoped for fulfillment of an intense need, is transferred to the object granting oral dependency gratification in the very "here and now."

This person, more unreal than real, granting oral dependency, is equated by this perceived aspect with *all* the part objects of the past, who did likewise. *Added* to this are the *phantasized* perceptions of still greater and more perfect oral need gratification. Transference involves more than the concept of "transferring." It involves this phantasized perception of perfect oral need fulfillment. What is probably present in all transferences of object relationships becomes intensified in a therapeutic transference where the "listening one" is only known in this role of reality. The therapeutic listener becomes then, an object of an unreality, and imbued with immense emotional significance that far transcends any object of the individual's past. It is the unreality that makes him such. Yet, he can appear so realistic from the reality of perceived discernible characteristics, just as in the Battle Hymn, there are parts, aspects or characteristics that remind the individual of its realism from his own past experiences and impressions. All the past part objects that are equated with a certain percieved part or aspect of this transference object, *and* the phantasized perceptions, give the object what in reality could never be attained. The transference object, and particularly the therapeutic listener, has the capacity, then, of being viewed as appearing real. On the extreme of one side, he appears as the greatest of *"good* breasts." But as the extreme on the other side, he can become the greatest of *"bad* breasts." Even though the individual may know very little of the actual reality, or "humanness" of the transference object, he feels as though he knows it well — even most intimately so. The feeling that someone especially cares, that someone is genuinely concerned, or that someone feels the person is uniquely important, must transcend the rationality of past daily life, and the logical fact of an orally frustrating reality that no one does anything for anybody without some price, and some gain for themselves.

To illustrate how easily, and how illogically transferences *are* formed, consider a traveler in a distant country. Even though the traveler may be with friends and acquaintances, he is away from his home situation, and as such, may be experiencing some added frustration and a diminution of his normal sources of oral supplies. This is not to imply he is necessarily emotionally uncomfortable, but there is an oral need lack that is present. With unmet oral dependency needs, he is more susceptible to forming an intense transference relationship, which he may very well do, when this traveler meets another person from America. If the traveler is, for instance, from Texas, we might anticipate an even *greater* transference response, if the person he meets is *also* from Texas. He may greet this person in an illogical and unrealistic way ... as though he's meeting a long lost friend. "It's damn good to meet a fellow Texan!", he may exclaim, then continue to respond emotionally as though this newly met person was emotionally significant to him. This newly met person symbolizes, in part, a concretization of the traveler's oral need gratifying associations of home and his phantasized perceptions of oral need fulfillment. This imbues the person with a phantasized potential of meeting more of the oral dependency needs here in the moment. Had the situation occurred at home, where his oral dependency needs were being met, and where there was *less* of a need, this same individual would have walked right on by anyone that would simply say "I'm from Texas too!." Reality-wise, Texas is a big state, and realistically, one doesn't get emotionally involved with everyone in their state, and probably not even with everyone in their hometown. It is the perception of "something in common" in a time of *oral need* that seems to initiate an intense transference phenomenon.

Friends of the teenager met at summer camp can become imbued in a similar manner with an intense transference relationship. Away from his usual oral need gratifying sphere of object relationships, this teenager has an increased need for oral gratification. Not necessarily "home-sick," he may meet someone whom he finds has something in common with him. It may not be that this acquaintance is from his home-town, but there are enough other possibilities that provide that "something," that on a reality level, brings the two together. The reality introduces them to each other, brings them together, and sustains the relationship, while inseparably the factors of an unreality begin to enter the relationship. As they talk more with each other, and spend more time with each other, there are more oral dependency needs being mutually met. Phantasized perceptions of more perfect oral gratification may be involved. At the end of summer camp, and during the following months, the relationship with this summer camp friend is looked forward to with great anticipation. Army buddies, too, become emotionally significant from similar oral need frustrating situations, and the emotional significance may be retained long after they separate. This may be to the distress of the later wife, who fails to see the "logic" of such a relationship that she may feel threatens her own. She may be jealous of the emotional impact of a visiting "ole Army buddy" on her husband, and resent the planned Army unit reunion. One can see the same thing with old college classmates, or with those of any other situation where there is oral dependency need frustration, and then oral dependency need gratification from one object that then becomes imbued with an immense emotional significance. One can speculate that the same thing is also involved in a frustrated husband's affinity to a neighborhood bar, and to a particular drinking "cronie." Frustrated in oral dependency gratification, he may periodically seek the perception that someone is listening specifically to him, and is intensely grat- ~~the perception that someone is litening specifically to him, and is intensely grat-~~ ifying his oral needs. Out of similar situations that are *oral need frustrating*, come those that seek out the therapeutic listener. They may feel like an alien in a foreign land, feel as though they've been through something as bad as any war experience, and feel more lonely than a teenager at summer camp, the girl at college, or the person who frequents the bar. But within whatever reality-orientation that might be appropriate for the relationship between themselves and the professional from which they seek help, they will *talk* while the other *listens*. In just this way, the transference can become most intense.

One can become most impressed with the apparent major unconscious concern of the client with the "here and now" unreality of the transference, even while the client verbalizes about his reality *outside* of the client-listener situation. The therapeutic listener may not only see the reflection of past interpersonal relationship problems mirrored in the reality problems that his client is verbalizing, but may also recognize a subtle part object interrelating within the transference, between the client and himself. What is produced then is a "psychodrama" that is almost totally unconscious on the part of the client, between his ambivalent "parts," and the "parts" that are unconsciously perceived in the listener. This on-going drama encapsulates the emotional conflicts, and dilemmas that led the individual to his emotional problem in reality, prior to his seeking professional help. In other words, it reduplicates the problem in reality, but at the same time reflects the distantly past emotional conflicts and dilemmas that the individual has had in life.The past, the present, and the "here and now" are all brought together by the transference phenomenon. All that is emotionally significant, in past and present, become fused within this unreality of the "here and now," into a *one-ness*, as only the unconscious can do with its primary process predicate equating, and its disregard for time. It is as though the unconscious of the client thinks: "I perceive an aspect of this listener, here, meets my oral needs; just as my wife does, at times; just like my best buddy did, before he let me down; just like my favorite aunt did, before she died; just like my father did, before he went away; just like my mother did, before my brother was born — so therefore this listener *is* my wife; he *is* my buddy; he *is* my aunt; he *is* my father; and he *is* my mother! And when I talk of someone in the past or present, this listener, *here*, is that *very same person!*" The transference may become most ambivalent when the unconscious begins to later think: "I perceive an aspect of this listener, here, *frustrates* my oral needs just as my wife does; just as my buddy did; just as my aunt did; just as my father did; and just as my mother did — so therefore this listener *is* each of these. And no matter whom, in the past or present, that I might angrily talk about, this listener, *here*, is that *very same person!*"

Sometimes the therapeutic listener will hear direct evidence being verbalized that indicates the presence of an intense transference in the relationship, as: "You're as frustrating as my husband," or "That's just what John told me," or "My mother was exactly like that," and "You remind me of my boss." This may not be so directly expressed, but may be implied. This is illustrated in the client verbalizing about her husband as: "He's so inhuman, so cold, frigid, uncaring and so indifferent to my needs. It's as though he doesn't have a feeling in him! I thought a human being is supposed to have some warmth, somewhere, but he doesn't seem to have any! I mean, I'm sure you *must* have some warm feelings for your *wife*, don't you?" The therapeutic listener will often be tended invitations of a personal nature, befitting a close relative, or a dear friend. These must be handled in a way that will enhance the unreality of the transference, in that it is the unreality, and *not* the reality that has made him so significant. Non-verbal evidence is often seen from the emotional reactions of the client, such as warm smiling, or laughter in the session, indicating the therapeutic listener is being viewed as a very emotionally significant figure. The client often comes dressed as though for church, a date, or some other important meeting, with appropriate make-up and hair-do. The therapeutic listener often receives remembrance gifts, mementos, notes and letters, and "special" Christmas and Valentine cards. The client's behavior, when by chance encountering the therapeutic listener outside his office, belies an extreme emotional significance that can't be explained except through the transference phenomenon. He has become someone special — especially loved, and in time, especially hated. He has attained through the transference the potential of becoming to his client "all things" past and present. No one in his position in reality can achieve the emotional significance that one can attain in a transference, regardless of his position in reality. One of the impressive manifestations of the transference, where reality is at a minimum, is shown in the person that comes one or two times to a psychotherapist before encountering too much emotional resistance to continue her appointments further. The person discontinues, but then for months regularly mails long and detailed daily notes of everything the person has been doing and thinking. The wished-for emotional closeness is phantasized and perceived as *real,* but· the reality of it all is kept at a distance. The therapist can become the *very greatest* to the client in regard to emotional significance. But this greatness involves everything between, and including, both a God and a devil position. Again, this emotional significance is enhanced when the relationship between client and therapeutic listener keeps the reality at a minimum, and the unreality of the transference at a maximum. When there is evidence that the listener is being viewed in a God-like fashion, one can accept the fact there is a potential, that this same listener will be viewed, in time, in a devil-like fashion as well.

Just as one man's hell may be another man's heaven, one person's transference reaction to an object may be as different as hell is to heaven, to another person's reaction to that same object. One's transference reaction toward an object may seem as though it is constructed as differently from another individual's transference reaction as the creation of the differences between a "hell," and a "heaven." Even within an on-going transference with one object, there is a dynamic and often shifting concretization of utilized past part objects and associated wishes that are being symbolically equated with the perceived parts of the object. The transference can totally change from moment to moment in its appearance. This is particularly shown where transferences tend to be intense, and where there is a continued on-going emotional involvement. An object may be unconsciously viewed as an immense "good breast," and later be viewed as an immense "bad breast." Or there may be evidence that the object is being kaleidoscopically viewed as a "good" *and* "bad breast" at the very same time!

Client-therapeutic listener relationships often do become most intense. This is so, because those that enter these relationships, do so from emotional uncomfortableness. They have an uncomfortable intensity of both a need for oral dependency gratification, as well as an intensity of anger from being previously frustrated. Such a transference always reflects a potential for being highly ambivalent. The therapeutic listener can be viewed in a range of possible perceptions that course from being seen as something equated to the devil on one hand, and something similar to the Divine on the other. There is a spectrum of relationships that can be easily detected through a study of an ongoing intense transference relationship where two people continue to be emotionally involved. Loving feelings associated with past part object relationships that were oral dependency need gratifying, are concretized and focused upon the listener, creating an almost God-like importance to him. Hostile or "negative" feelings, associated with unconsciously equated oral need frustrating past part objects and experiences can be reflected upon the listener, making him appear as the very devil himself.

The therapeutic listener may be *initially* viewed, in some cases, as "God-like," or "devil-like," even in the very first session. An individual coming into a therapeutic listening relationship, usually does so without such intensely shown *initial* transference relationships. In other words, one usually will not see evidence of the initial "God-like," or "devil-like," viewing of the therapeutic listener, unless the therapeutic listener has a reality-role (such as a physician's) that *induces* an intense transference, even before the client meets his listener. These "God" and "devil" positions will develop, though, in *any* transference, if it involves an intense meeting of oral dependency needs. Those that begin without a previously induced reality role transference tend, in time, first to show that they perceive a "God-like" image of the therapeutic listener as oral need gratification becomes intensified. Then later, as the transference becomes more ambivalent, a "devil-like" perception will become evident.

In 1909 Freud[9] correctly pointed out that the transference phenomenon arises spontaneously in *all* human relationships. He recognized that it wasn't *created* by psychoanalysis, as it was a part of any human relationship, but that it only *revealed* itself there. That this is so is undoubtedly due to the formal nature of this particular relationship, where the client is the focus of concern by an understanding, empathic and listening analyst. Since the analyst's verbalizations are usually at a minimum, there is more opportunity for the client's transference to intensify, and to become more evident than in some other type of relationship, where *both* people are verbalizing freely. In this formal analytic type of relationship, listening very carefully is paramount. This intensifies the transference and hastens its appearance. What undoubtedly occurs in any object relationship is less veiled in psychoanalysis, more apparent and more readily available for scrutiny. Another reason for the transference to be so obvious in this type of relationship, as opposed to other object relationships, is that the client is an individual who is emotionally uncomfortable and is coming for help. He has an intense need for oral dependency gratification. Or, put another way, he has more of a need to seek out the "good breast" in this particular relationship than the individual who is finding the "good breast" in a multiplicity of interpersonal relationships. Those with the most *need* will form the most intense transferences when they do get involved with an oral need gratifying object. The person with an intense need for oral gratification, because of his past frustrations, has more of a need to express his anger toward a person of emotional significance. And his guilt will give him the feeling there is something "wrong" with him. His oral need, his "need" to express anger, and his guilt that makes him feel the former two are representative that something is *wrong* with him, lead him into an analytic situation where his developing transference may become most blatant. But it is the same transference phenomenon, though less intensified, that one can find in all object relationships. The same transference phenomenon that makes the analytic relationship *therapeutic*, also makes it possible for the more emotionally comfortable person, in his interpersonal relationships, to continue to have his oral dependency needs met, to continue to express his anger for the frustration of his oral needs, and to continue to project his guilt. It is through the transference phenomenon, first identified with psychoanalysis, that object relationships, in part, can be emotionally gratifying — or they may be emotionally frustrating. The emotionally uncomfortable person searches, in part, for the "good breast," and the transference allows him to find it.

This search for the "good breast," in order to satisfy frustrated oral needs, becomes more intense the greater is the perceived frustration of the individual. This is so even on the back wards of a state hospital, where superficially, it might appear that these individuals do not form transferences. However, just the very opposite is true. These people *readily* form transferences, and may intensely do so with any one that they encounter. But their guilt, their repressed anger, and their past experiences with frustrated oral dependency is such that they avoid emotional involvement with everyone. It is for this reason that they don't talk with anyone, or will not relate in any way with anyone else. Because they have an intense oral need, which is being denied, they do have the potential of forming intense relationships, but give the appearance of not being able to form transferences. That they do form transferences is evident when they may suddenly go into a "catatonic panic," attacking anyone about them. The reason they can attack anyone so indiscriminately is because everyone, apparently, is a transference figure.

Those people with the most intense unmet oral dependency needs are the individuals who most intensely will form a transference relationship when they do so. One client, for instance, implies this when she remarked: "What's wrong with me anyway? I can't seem to have a *comfortable* relationship with anyone. I get so *emotionally* involved with anyone I befriend. It seems as though every time I get involved with anyone else it *always* ends up in an *intense* emotional relationship that I would have been better off if I *avoided*. But why is it that I have this undeniable need to have somebody care about me?" Another client refers to the same thing, but in regard to the therapist, when she remarks: "I can't come in here and talk to you like an adult the way I do to other people, but I have to relate like a little child!" This is not a "neurotic" *regression*, as the transference is erroneously described by analysts (and recently popularized by Berne,[13] and Harris[14]), but simply that the individual is more involved with intensely gratifying her oral needs with an emotionally significant figure. One can see the same thing between two intensely involved lovers, who may use "baby talk" with one another.

Besides the difficulties that the many faces of guilt may present, leading a person to seek "professional help," are the entanglements produced by an intense unmet and guilt-laden oral need. People may *seem* to be able to "get by" in life by denying their unmet oral needs, but it is in times of increased oral frustration (or times of an increased need for oral gratification) that they become emotionally involved with another person. For instance, a business executive, who complained his wife was sexually cold, came for professional help when he found himself involved with a young lady in a relationship that tapped into his previously denied oral need. He became emotionally entangled with his guilt and his anger (and hers as well) when she represented too much of an oral dependency granting object. In his initial session he complained: "I'm all wrought up. I can't sleep at night because of her, and all day long I can't get her off my mind. I'm not getting my work done, and I'm going through hell because of her. When I'm with her, it's like heaven, but she's married and so am I! I can't possibly have her. There's *no way*, whatsoever, in reality it can *ever* work out!" She symbolized the inaccessableness of his guilt-blocked oral need gratification. But what he unconsciously did in seeking professional help was to establish a transference relationship between himself and his therapeutic listener that began to meet his oral needs the same way this woman had. This relationship afforded him an opportunity to ventilate his anger from past frustration, which lowered his unconscious guilt, allowing him to gratify his oral needs in the part objects of his interpersonal relationships. The woman of reality became *less* of an emotional problem to him, as the therapeutic listener became *more* of one. The client had transferred the emotional problem he had with the woman that was equated with the emotional problems of his past, to the therapeutic listener. (And this is what we all do, but more subtly, in our object relationships.) He very quickly reached a point where he decided that the woman was "no good for him," and decided to see her less frequently, remarking: "Why should I bother myself with her! I don't *need* her the way I thought I did!" At this point, when he was much more emotionally comfortable, he began to cancel or skip his therapy sessions. He finally discontinued altogether, and was not heard from again, until a year later when he returned, remarking: "I've got the same damn problem I had last year, but this time with another woman!" He again continued just long enough to reduce the recently "added" guilt, before his personality "core" guilt demanded he discontinue the relationship.

83

The transference always involves, as its name implies, a *transferring* of the emotionality of past part objects, to the unconsciously perceived part objects within the object that one is emotionally involved in the present. Take, for instance, the young teacher who comes for professional help, relating: "Two years ago I was engaged to Norman and was ready to marry him when I found out that he was more interested in money. I broke off with him, because I didn't want to marry anyone like my father, who was only interested in going after the almighty dollar. He only measured people by how much they were worth in dollars and cents. (Apparently she feels, in part, because of her unconscious guilt, she isn't worth much.) I was doing real well until I met Robert six months ago. He appeared understanding, considerate, and seemed what I've always wanted in a husband. We became engaged and this past March, I bought him an Easter card that cost a dollar. Well, he told me I spent too much for the card. It was then that I first began to see a little of Norman in Robert. Lately, I've been seeing more and more of it. I have the feeling now that he's only interested in me because he knows I make a good salary. My mother was that way too. She had a habit of using people, just to get as much from them as possible. So I broke off with Robert. Now I'm wondering if it all isn't *me*! Maybe there's something wrong with *me* that I can't continue with an engagement." Needless to say, she quickly became emotionally "engaged" with her therapeutic listener, quickly became emotionally comfortable, but then suddenly discontinued, feeling that her therapeutic listener was only interested in her money, and was using her. She was not heard from again, until her denied unmet guilt-laden oral needs once more caused her uncomfortableness.

The therapeutic listener is one that utilizes the naturally occurring transference phenomenon to bring about a level of emotional comfortableness. He may do this in any guise at all of reality. What he accomplishes is a gratification of previously unmet guilt-laden oral dependency needs, a ventilation of previously repressed anger and a resulting diminution of the uncomfortable unconscious guilt. Any psychoanalysis, any psychotherapy, any counseling, or any object relationship at all essentially can do the very same thing! And a person can later look back over their relationship with a therapeutic listener, and remark as one client did: "I don't know how you helped me, because you never said a thing! But you somehow did, as no one else could!" Anyone can utilize the transference phenomenon, and make it *therapeutic* for the emotionally uncomfortable person, if he allows a gratification of the oral needs, if he allows the ventilation of anger and if he can keep the relationship on-going in some rationale of reality. The transference is formed from the need to seek out the "good breast," and because the unconscious ego has a wish to "*undo*" the emotionally traumatic events of the past. This tendency toward repetitive reliving, in part, of the emotionality of the past, with the ob-

84

jects of the present, is the very essence of the therapeutic aspect of the therapeutic transference. Since the unconscious doesn't differentiate between the emotionally significant part objects of the past, with the emotionally significant part objects of the present, there is afforded the opportunity to "make right" the past and the present, with the part objects of the "here and now." If one felt he was slighted by an emotionally significant person in the past, he can ventilate his anger to the emotionally significant part object of the very "here and now" that is equated with that object of the past. *This* is what makes the transference *therapeutic*, and nothing else! All that is reality oriented is superficiality.

It is most erroneous for the psychoanalysts to propose as some do[15] [16] that the working relationship between the client and his analyst is a "new" relationship. No object relationship can ever be "new," except the relationship of the infant with his primary object, for all relationships in reality will entail inseparable transference factors. The analysts propose to break what they call "the repetitive emotional reliving of a client's object relationships," by getting him to realize that the present relationship, between himself and his analyst is not an emotionally *past* relationship with respect to reality. Their "working alliance," as they call it, has a purpose of supposedly separating the transference (as if anyone could!), which they call a *contaminant*, from the "real" relationship. It is as though the analyst is able to get his client to realize: "Look, you're responding to *me* as though I'm your *father*. I'm *not* your father; I am your *analyst*! Therefore, your responses to me have been *inappropriate*." The client is encouraged to separate the *"unreal"* from the *"real"* in his responses to his analyst. But this is totally impossible, for a part of every reality-oriented relationship is always the unreality oriented transference. They are inseparable! But both the client and his analyst may, in time, feel they *have* accomplished their purpose in changing the client's behavior from what they call "neurotic and inappropriate" to "non-neurotic and appropriate." Actually, it is *only* because the transference has become *less intense*! What has *caused* it to become less intense is *not* any intellectualization about the relationship, but the fact that the client's oral dependency needs are more *adequately* and more *diffusely* met. However, the client will continue to have an unreality associated with everyone of his object relationships, but the unreality is less noticeable. It had been more noticeable before, because of the intensity of oral dependency in the client-analyst relationship, and prior to that, because of the intensity of oral dependency on so few a number of part objects.

The therapeutic listener, essentially, is unconsciously perceived as the "good breast," but may also be simultaneously perceived as the "bad breast" as well. He accepts the client, cares for him, comforts him and nourishes him in a *subtle* emotional process, that on the reality level would be intolerable. The

85

therapeutic listener does this on the unreality level from the listening process itself. The process of listening in interpersonal relationships meets oral dependency needs, for the person that is talking has his mouth open as a reflection of the first time he did so — to *gratify* his oral needs, and to *ventilate* his anger. The need to talk is a reflection of the earliest oral need gratification. Just as one fed off the primary object, one continues to feed from all his later object relationships. An individual emotionally "eats" his way through his life's object relationships. The more a person has been frustrated in the gratification of his oral needs in the past, the more he has a need to talk to someone in order to get emotional support and ventilate his anger. (He may often deny this need though.) But a part of this unreality of his emotional life is reality. What he talks about is reality, and what he consciously perceives of himself and others is reality.

This reality of which he is consciously concerned is inseparable from the unreality of his emotions that is derived from past, present and "here and now." For instance, a woman may enter a professional relationship to talk about her reality problems with another person, male or female. The relationship between herself and the professional may seem initially devoid of anything emotional. (Actually it is not devoid, because there are emotional factors associated with why she involved herself with this particular professional.) But with a continuation of this relationship, with further oral need gratification, and an intensification of the transference phenomenon, it soon becomes highly emotional. She may even find herself *sexually* attracted toward this professional. However, this is not to say that the transference is sexual in any way. It is reality that may make it so. The woman who lives in reality may interpret the emotionality of the transference as sexual, when, in fact, it is a *part* object oriented *orality*. Any sexuality that is present represents the reality overlay to this orality.

To illustrate how the orally oriented transference may become imbued with a reality oriented sexuality, take the case of the orally frustrated married secretary. She has reached a point where she does not have her oral needs adequately met in the relationship with her husband, nor in any of her other relationships. She now focuses upon her "bad marriage" as the *cause* of her uncomfortableness. By chance, in her work, she becomes associated in a casual relationship with a male, who is also orally frustrated, and may share, in common with her, a "bad marriage." They both have a need to talk. And although they may begin by talking about non-emotional things, the more time they spend together talking, the more intense the transference relationship becomes between them. They begin to become *emotionally* involved, and very shortly may become sexually involved as well. What attracted them to each other was a commonly-shared *oral* need, not a sexual need. It is the *oral* need that makes a person so emotionally uncomfortable, and it is the gratification of the

86

oral need that makes a person comfortable. One can speculate that this woman could have continued her relationship with the man she met, *without* the sexual involvement. Many relationships that involve intense transference reactions are characterized by being *without* a sexual involvement. (Perhaps the best examples of most intense, but completely *sex-free* transferences involve religions and patriotism.) But where orality deals with part objects, and sexuality with the reality of whole object relationships, it is only logical that persons feel as though their uncomfortableness is sexual in origin, and that a resolution must involve sexuality. This erroneous, but reality-oriented thinking characterizes the analysts who look upon the transference as being sexually oriented. To them, the transference figure is a "mother," or a "father" figure, associated with incestuous wishes, rather than the *oral* wishes and the orality that is actually involved.

Any object relationship may be "therapeutic" if it allows a diminution of the unconscious guilt. (One might question the term "therapeutic" if the diminution of guilt is derived from a guilt-assuaging process as the medieval practice of treating the "mentally ill" by burnings, bakings and beatings, or the modern day carry-over of shock treatment — all of which are highly effective in diminishing guilt.) It is unfortunate that there hasn't been more of a utilization of "therapeutic listeners" for those that might not have found as much of the "good breast" in their earlier lives, or for those whose circumstances in reality are particularly orally frustrating, such that they can profit by such a relationship. The "medical model" orientation of present day psychiatry is a detriment toward the utilization of therapeutic listening and the transference phenomenon. The "medical model" involves the assumption that a person is "sick" if he needs help. To feel oneself as sick, or having something "wrong" implies a desire to get "well" as soon as possible and doesn't imply a prolonged relationship. For a relationship to be "therapeutic" it must be *ongoing*, and it should extend *beyond* the time a person has reached an emotionally comfortable state. There is an inescapable onus, too, about seeing a psychiatrist that is oral need frustrating. It must be in *spite* of this onus for a psychiatrist to meet his client's oral needs. Reality-wise, it isn't necessary for anyone that is emotionally uncomfortable to resolve his uncomfortableness with a physician of any sort, let alone a psychiatrist. Since any object relationship can be "therapeutic," it is possible to utilize non-medical personnel for therapeutic listening, and leave physicians to practice medicine. If a person can present a reality rationale for becoming professionally involved with an emotionally uncomfortable person on an on-going basis, he will attain the same position of emotional significance that any physician can attain. The greatest challenge in the mental health field lies in this utilization of non-medical therapeutic listening.

Any person can find himself in the role of the "therapeutic listener," if he is having someone *talk* about his problems to him. Through the act of *listening*, the individual becomes a transference figure that transcends the reality of his position in life. It becomes ironic that even a highly trained graduate student, or a very skilled , technician, or a financially successful business man involved in a transference relationship, seems to view his transference figure as "all-knowing." He may talk about his reality-oriented problems as though in reality, his listener is quite familiar with those technical and specialized reality problems. By the act of listening, which meets oral dependency needs, the transference can become very intense, so that reality is transcended, and the client may feel the therapist is all understanding. But it is an *emotional* understanding, primarily. If there is a reality understanding as well, this is even better. But the therapeutic listener need not say anything, but only listen to have his client feel, in time, he is even wiser than he is, and anyone else he knows of. What the emotionally uncomfortable person does, in entering any reality oriented object relationship, for whatever emotionally uncomfortable reasons, is to purchase a therapeutic transference. The analytically oriented psychiatrist "sells" his client a transference that comes so readily from his position as a physician. The quack as a "healer" does exactly the same thing. Oral support is afforded by this transference. The business executive may, for instance, remark: "I'd like to come in on a weekly basis to talk over these troublesome business problems I have that are getting me down. I can't talk to anyone else. My wife doesn't want to hear them, and there's no one else I can turn to. I have to make some pretty difficult decisions in my business, and I need advice and help." Reality-wise, his business acumen is far greater than his therapeutic listener's — and is probably greater than his listener's will ever be! But this client doen't really want advice, just as no one really wants advice. What he seeks is an emotional comfortableness, which he'll attain through the therapeutic transference relationship. When he is comfortable enough, less ambivalent, and his guilt diminished, he'll make his own decisions. He'll know himself the correct course of action to take in business, but, ironically, he may feel as though his listener made it for him. Whether the client is involved in business, nuclear physics, or any of the highly specialized fields of reality, the therapeutic listener can be of immense help, but on an emotional level that is afforded by the therapeutic transference. Therefore it is *not* by emphasizing the *reality*, as the analysts imply, that the professional relationship is most therapeutic, but by emphasizing the *unreality* and making use of the transference that any accomplishment is really made!

The beginning therapist is often advised not to "play God." But this isn't a choice he really has, for his client himself will *make* a "God" of him. The therapeutic listener becomes imbued with a God-like image that is afforded by the transference. Some clients may appear angry when they view the therapist as God-like. Yet it is their *own* unmet oral needs, that are now being gratified within the transference, that makes the therapeutic listener *appear* so omniscient and omnipotent. Many physicians unfortunately *do* act God-like, and they do so, perhaps, from being exposed to the transference reactions of their patients, such that they begin to feel in reality they are what an unreality has made them. This is shown for instance in their higher than average flying fatalities, and their tendency to take greater than average business risks. This is also evident from those who give advice that is reality oriented, but involves more than medicine, and act as though they are authorities on all of Life. Ironically, those, that often know real life and humanity best are the very ones that the medical professional has called "mentally ill"! The physician, an authority in medicine, is not necessarily an authority in all the problems of life. Physicians, medically knowledgeable in sexual anatomy and sexual physiology, are often deficient in their knowledge of sexual behavior (as has been shown in many studies). But their own belief that they *are* is enhanced by their patients, who, in feeling that doctors know "how sex works," turn to them for help for their unconscious emotional problems with *oral* needs and *oral* guilt. These oral problems are metaphorically manifested in their sexual problems. The knowledgeable therapeutic listener is an authority only in the *unreality,* and he over-steps his bounds if he acts as an authority in reality. All the answers to reality problems can never be found in any one human being. It is only through an intense transference reaction that one might *think* he can find all those answers from a single object — but that object will be more unreal than real.

The reality-role of a person may lend itself to a ready-made transference relationship. Those people, who are sought-out for professional help, when there is any type of uncomfortableness present, are ready-made transference figures. These include, among many others, physicians, teachers, clergy, political figures, outstandingly successful business men and people of renown. But it is *particularly* so for physicians. Physical uncomfortableness is always associated with emotional uncomfortableness, and there is a tendency for those, who are attempting to *deny* an intensity of guilt-laden oral needs, to translate this emotional uncomfortableness into physical problems. Perhaps it is for this reason that the early work on transference phenomenon was done by physicians, in that they were in a position to become more aware of its presence. The whole field of medicine has always been inseparably intertwined with transference interaction and the need for oral gratification in the face of guilt. (Note what is orally implied in the word *"nurse,"* and ask any nurse if it isn't the oral needs their patients seem to emphasize most in their relationships with them.) Yet, from a reality standpoint, it *shouldn't* be. The physician is a highly trained technician that ought to be able to practice his profession separate from these transference factors. Airline pilots do, where for instance, the life or death of those entrusted to them is solely within their hands. They are financially rewarded as a direct result of their *technical* skill — the way physicians ought to be. The physician in private practice especially isn't. He isn't as much rewarded for his technical skill as he is for his skill in utilizing the transference, though he may call this his "bedside manner," or simply his manner of helping the uncomfortable. These physicians, like many quacks, may have the largest practices because they are capitalizing on the transference phenomenon. The "art" of medicine that we all miss in the old-time country doctor involves more of a transference utilization and oral need gratification than it does of medical knowledge. People have preferences for certain physicians (like people have preferences for certain quacks), and they may have dislikes for others. What often seems to make the difference between a preferred or a disliked physician, is his ability to utilize the transferences of his patients, that is afforded by his role in reality, to gratify their guilt-laden oral needs. The American Medical Association has always fought quackery, perhaps, as it has sometimes been said, more because it is so much a *financial* threat to medicine that anything else. And some quacks do become notoriously proficient at practicing that "art" of medicine. But in accepting psychiatry as a specialty of medicine, one permits a highly skilled person to forsake his highly learned skills and practice instead, the very essence of quackery — the utilization of intense transferences. The psychiatrist, as a therapeutic listener, becomes a quack, with a genuine medical degree! This is like requiring a person to become skilled at flying a Boeing 707, but then permitting him to do nothing more than sit and listen to anxious passengers talk — or else sitting *alone* with an empty seat when the passenger that bought a ticket doesn't even show up!

The sometimes popular dislike for military physicians is a good example where transference factors may be minimally utilized. The military physician isn't interested in building his practice. He often doesn't want a large following of patients. He practices his medicine with a minimum of cultivating the transferences, or meeting the guilt-laden oral dependency needs of his patients. The opposite may be true of many in private practice, who, like many quacks, are often better capable of meeting the emotional needs of their patients under a guise of reality than many psychiatrists are. The transference reactions of these medically-oriented relationships are often intense, and often transcend the logic of reality. It is not unusual that one will hear a patient say of a physician, who may have a well-known alcoholic or drug problem, "I'd rather have Dr. Brown *drunk* as my doctor than any other damn doctor in town!" The epitome of this was recently shown where a doctor in a small town in Michigan was exposed as being a fraud with no medical school training at all. Upon his exposure and removal from the community, hundreds of people who previously had been his satisfied patients, wrote in to ask that he be allowed to continue in the capacity of their physician because he was so well liked and "such a good doctor." The exposure of medical falsehoods in quackery seems to make little difference to the vast number of people that will still seek out various forms of quackery as an answer to their uncomfortableness.

NOTES

1. Fairbairn, W.: *An Object-Relations Theory of the Personality*, Basic Books, Inc., New York, 1962.
2. Fenichel, O.: *The Psychoanalytic Theory of Neurosis*, W.W. Norton and Co., New York, 1945.
3. Greenson, R.R.: *The Techniques and Practice of Psychoanalysis*, Vol. 1, International Universities Press, New York, 1967.
4. Lowenstein, R.M.: "Developments in the Theory of Transference In The Last Fifty Years," *Int. J. Psychoanal.*, 1969, Vol. 50, 583-588.
5. Orr, D. W.: "Transference and Countertransference: A Historical Survey", *J. Am. Psychoanal. Assn. 1954* Vol. 2, 621-670.
6. Sandler, J.: Holder, A.: Kawenoka, M.: Kennedy, H. E.: Neurath, L.: "Notes On Some Theoretical and Clinical Aspects of Transference," *Int. J. Psychoanal.*, 1969, Vol. 50, 633-645.
7. Calef, V.; Harley, M.; Blum, H.P.; Loewald, H.W.; Weinshel, E.M. "Panel Discussion on Current Concepts of the Transference Neurosis," *J. Amer. Psychoanal. Assn.* 1971 Vol. 19, 22-97.
8. Freud, S.: *Studies on Hysteria*, 1895, S.E. 2.
9. Freud, S.: *The Dynamics of Transference*, S.E. 12.
10. Freud, S.: *Five Lectures on Psychoanalysis*, S.E. 11, 1909.
11. Hoffer, W.: "Transference and Transference Neurosis," *Int. J. Psychoanal.*, Vol. 37, 377-379.
12. Greenson, R.R. and Wexler, M.: "The Non-transference Relationship In the Psychoanalytic Situation," *Int. J. Psychoanal.* 1969 Vol. 50, 27-39.
13. Berne, E.: *Games People Play*, 1964, Grove Press, Inc., New York.
14. Harris, T.: *I'm Okay, You're O.K.*, 1969, Harper & Row, New York.
15. Nunberg, E.: "Transference and Reality," *Int. J. Psychoanal.*, 1951 Vol. 32, 1-9.
16. Bibring, E.: "The Conception of the Repetition Compulsion, *Psychoanal. Q.*, 1943, Vol. 12, 486-519.
17. Greenson, R.R.: "The Working Alliance and the Transference Neurosis," *Psychoanal. Q.*, 1965, Vol. 34, 155-181.

CHAPTER 5

THE NATURE OF TRANSFERENCE LANGUAGE

Transference language, simply defined, is the unconcscious implied language of an individual within a transference. As a *product* of the transference, it shares the former's characteristics of being oriented to an unreality, and not reality; to being part object oriented, and not whole object oriented; to having no regard to time, making no distinction between the past and the present; and to operating under primary process cognition, with that Von Domarus type of predicate equating. Like the transference, it is continuously on-going, and not an isolated phenomenon in time. It is dynamic, often highly ambivalent, and never static. Like both the dream and the transference, it is unconsciously formed and any conscious volition has no part whatsoever in it's production. One has no conscious control over its formation, its presentation or the nature of its implications. Latent implications that can be made in tactful communication, or diplomacy, are not transference language, which remains unconsciously determined, and usually is unrecognizable to the individual, though he may have a fleeting awareness of "having said more" in a transference relationship.

Interpersonal communication has a marked similiarity with what is known of the dream phenomenon. Both seem not only analogous, but also seem somehow intimately related in some unknown way. They both may be suspicioned to be a part of the same unconscious parent phenomenon. Like the dream, communication has a *manifest* content, and a *latent* content. Transference language, strictly speaking, is the *latent* content of interpersonal communication. The manifest content is oriented toward reality, which acts as a disguise or cover-up for the emotionally-laden latent content. The manifest content provides a logical veneer of reality, which gives to it an erroneous appearance of primal importance to convey the illogical latent content, which is actually primal. It operates under secondary process thinking and Aristotelian logic. It is both whole object and time oriented. The manifest content tends to be *less* emotionally oriented, while the latent content is *need* oriented and *more* emotional.

The verbalization of the manifest content of interpersonal communication is anologous to the dramatization of the manifest content of the dream. The manifest content of both is made up of complex inter-related symbols. In both, the dream latent content and the latent content of communication is projected into the manifest content. The emotional conflicts that are part object oriented, that are under primary process cognition, and that have no regard for time, are screened by an unconscious ego function. If there is a "dream censor" that does this screening, as we have been told there is, then there must also be a "language censor" too. This "censor," whether in the dream or in interpersonal communication, prevents emotional conflicts that are too threatening to come up into the manifest content. Not only can one say that these conflicts are "too threatening," but that the conflicts of the latent content "don't make any sense," and would be rejected by the conscious, in that they are part object oriented, both from the unconscious part make-up of the individual, and from what he perceives in his part object relationships. This, alone, would make a necessity for keeping them out of the conscious. The conflicts "don't make sense" too, because of the disregard for time, where object relationships of the distant past are viewed the same as the object relationships of the present, and the very "here and now."

Not only is there a censoring function of the unconscious ego in both the dream and in interpersonal communication, but there is an ego "work." If this is called *dream elaboration*, then in communication, one might term this similar "work" *language elaboration*. The ego's language-work, like dream-work, takes the latent content and through displacement, condensation, symbolization and projection creates the manifest content. Part objects of the latent content are concretized into whole object symbolization. Part object experiences are given whole object oriented dramatizations or verbalizations of whole object concern, that then convey in anology what is of concern in the latent content. The conflicts of the latent content, in both the dream and in interpersonal communication, are projected up into the manifest content, so that there is something produced that tends to "make sense," and then appears as the foremost concern of the conscious. In both the dream and communication, then, there is a manifest content that tends to be whole object oriented, and appears as the real and focal issue, when in fact it isn't.

For instance, suppose a person recalls that they had an anxiety-laden dream that raccoons were getting into the rubbish barrels, tipping them over and spreading around the rubbish. The dramatization of this manifest content that is recalled is that there was whatever the "raccoons" symbolized in their part object condensation, getting into whatever the "rubbish" symbolized. Something then is getting into something else, normally containered or properly disposed of, that it shouldn't. On the manifest content level, this is an anxiety-filled dream of raccoons and rubbish barrels. But on the latent content level, the theme is the same, but it is on a *part* object basis. Through dream work, the latent theme is elaborated, disguised, dramatized and presented as a dynamic interaction of whole objects.

Dreams tend to serve as a defense against anxiety, with the dreaming process being hypothesized as a means of handling the anxiety from unconscious latent conflicts. Dream deprivation is known to produce increased anxiety. If severe enough, it may cause an ego disorganized state. Dreaming apparently is a necessary process, probably resolving anxiety on a regular basis. Isolating a person from interpersonal relationship contact can also produce a similar degree of anxiety, emotional uncomfortableness, and, if severe enough, even ego disorganization. If a nightmare that arouses an individual up from his sleep represents a "dream failure," then *communication breakdown* must represent a similarly originating *language* failure, with the same unconscious factors involved in each. (One can hypothesize an increased build-up of unconscious guilt as due to each of these.) Interpersonal communication seems to be as necessary as the dreaming process for maintaining emotional comfortableness. It is interesting to note that individuals residing on the back wards of state mental hospitals are most characteristically withdrawn from interpersonal relationships, and communicate little, if at all, with other people.

It has been shown that all people dream just as all people communicate. All interpersonal relationships will involve, to a matter of degree, transference relationships. Therefore, all interpersonal relationships will have, to a matter of degree, transference language. Where there is *less* of a transference present, there will be *less* of a noticeable transference language. In other words, the degree of transference language will depend upon the degree of transference within an interpersonal relationship. Where there is a less intense transference, there will be a less intense transference language. Where an object is being utilized *more* intensely for oral dependency gratification or anger expression, there will be, to the same degree, a *more* intense and a more noticeable transference language.

The make-up of the manifest content is an on-going allegorical drama in the dream, and an allegorical verbalization in spontaneous interpersonal communication that is, on its most *basic* level, orally oriented. The meaning or interpretation of these allegories in both the dream's and interpersonal communication's manifest content lies in the entire dream acted out or the entire verbalization presented, and not in the particular dream symbol or a specific word. What is being conveyed is done so by the action, the plot, the drama or the on-going interaction. It is erroneous to pick out a particular dream symbol, out of context, and assign to it a specific meaning. One is taking it out of it's relationship with other symbols where the meaning is only made through these relationships with other associated symbols. It is likewise erroneous to define the dream symbol, in that the symbol has a part object derivation which cannot be ignored. The dream symbol may be formed from a condensation of equated part objects from different objects from different periods of time. This would make it impossible to assign a whole object derivation to any dream symbol, when the derivation is from part object perceptions of such a variety of objects. Most erroneous is the presentation by analysts of universal symbolizations in dreams, as though implying, when two individuals dream of a particular dream symbol, or whole object in the manifest content, that it means a particular thing, just because that

94

object appears in the dream. There is no universality of symbols, and a symbol may mean different things in context at different times, to the same individual, depending on how it is used in the dream drama.

In communication, the meaning of a word, as a symbol, comes from how it is used in the *entire* presented verbalization, so that it, too, would be erroneous to assign to it a specific symbolic meaning. The word, as a symbol in the manifest content of communication has a part object and a very individualistic derivation. Meaning comes from the story told, the joke remembered, and the verbalizations expressed of a particular thought or past experience, which only then conveys the meaning. The unconscious part object derivations become condensed into a particular consciously recognized whole object or whole experience, which then interacts with other complex symbolic condensations. For instance, if a person angrily talks about his "inconsiderate neighbor," then one can speculate that this whole object — the inconsiderate neighbor — is a concretization of an unconsciously perceived aspect of the listener that is, in turn, equated with aspects of emotionally significant people of the past, of this individual, that were also perceived as "inconsiderate." What is being verbalized as a theme about this neighbor is analogous to what has been perceived in the past in regard to the "inconsiderate" aspects of past emotionally significant people, and to the perceived "inconsiderate" aspects of the listener. The meaning then comes from the interaction, or the analogy presented. The meaning of a specific symbol in the manifest content of communication is undefinable, except on a *part object basis.* To define it further would be getting into the confusing illogic of the unconscious.

In the dream, we know that the latent content is more primal than the manifest content. The manifest content is thought to be only the product of the unconscious ego's work in changing the latent content, or translating it into something that is acceptable for presentation as manifest content. The latent content is primal, both in importance and in formation. We are talking about an outcome, or a result, when we refer to the manifest content of the dream.

If the dream and interpersonal communication continue to be analogous, then one can be faced with a most startling conclusion. That is, the manifest content of communication, no matter how logical it may seem, no matter how appropriate or timely it is to reality, is still an *outcome,* or a *result* of something that is taking place on a deeper level. Even if the manifest content of communication appears to be devoid of emotion, there is an underlying unconscious emotionality that is subtly involved in this manifest content. There is an illogic, an unreality, and a timelessness that underlies the manifest content of interpersonal relationship communication. If the dream manifest content has been described as an awesome production of the unconscious ego, then the manifest content of communication must then be even more so. How quickly the manifest content of interpersonal communication is formed is perhaps the most remarkable and most impressive feat of the unconscious ego. The seemingly effortless rapidity of its action, its exquisite sensitiveness, its evaluative ability and its acuity transcend anything that can be produced by conscious cerebration. The marvel of the human mind is not just in the conscious application of mental functioning, but in this remarkable unconscious formation of manifest content in interpersonal communication, under a disguise of reality-oriented conscious application.

Like the manifest dream, where the dreamer is always present in disguised forms, as projected, dissociated aspects of himself, in relation to aspects of his emotionally significant objects, the manifest content of spontaneous interpersonal communication also contains projected, disassociated and disguised aspects of the speaker, in relation to unconsciously perceived aspects of his listener. Where various aspects of the dreamer appear simultaneously in the manifest content of the dream, so too do various aspects of the listener in his manifest content of his interpersonal communication. When Freud described the dream as the "Royal Road To The Unconscious" he apparently recognized only one small area of that road. It is the understanding of *any* recall or, in other words, *any* verbalization that is the Royal Road. The reader must recognize that what a person *"remembers"* of his dream's manifest content (dream recall), and *tells* to someone else, is not the same as the dream manifest content. Dream recall is not dream manifest content, no more than what one "recalls" they said the day before, or what they recall they said even longer ago, is the same as the manifest content of that previous communication. Recall is what one remembers sometime later of a previous manifest content. This "remembering" comes under unconscious emotional factors, whereby certain things are brought into the conscious because there's a particular *importance* to them to be remembered, in regard to what is going on at the moment, while others are "forgotten," or do not come up into the conscious. There is then a "screening" and an evaluating action of the unconscious ego that makes any "recall" so different from an actual past manifest content, whether it is from a dream or from interpersonal communication.

When an individual relates his dream to someone else, then his telling of the dream comes directly under the transference effect of that interpersonal relationship. This dream recall may be quite different from the actual dream manifest content, and different too, than if he simply recalled it to himself. There is no way of determining dream latent content. There is no way even of determining, for sure, dream manifest content. Dream studies deal only in *dream recall . . ,* what is remembered by a person of their dream manifest content, *to* another person, who is always an *important* person. Whenever there is, in any way, a communication of "recall" to another human being, there will be a transference effect. Verbalized dream recall then, is really a part of transference language. It comes under the transference phenomenon and represents the manifest content of interpersonal communication. When a person recalls a dream's manifest content to someone else, his recalling is manifest content of communication. Dream recall then is no different than any other recall, whether it is of distantly past events, or what happened on the way to the analyst's office. There is no more psychological significance connected with one recall than another recall. A recall of a dream can theoretically be just as emotionally apropos as a recall of some past event. The transference language *of the moment,* between speaker and listener, is the only important recall *at that moment.* Verbalizations in interpersonal relationships are the Royal Roads To The Unconscious, regardless of the nature toward which the manifest content orients itself.

Verbalizations that are spontaneously made convey a metaphorical manifest content that has something to do with the unconscious perceptions of that individual and his relationship with his listener. Even when a person spontaneously volunteers information about the past, what he brings up is metaphorically appropriate for what is going on, within that particular transference relationship, at that very *moment.* There is a "here and now" appropriateness to what is being latently conveyed within the manifest content. Although the manifest content may be oriented toward what has happened during the "other twenty-three hours," what has happened in the distant past, or what one is concerned about in his present, or even the distant future, what he is metaphorically *conveying* is what he unconsciously perceives in the very "here and now" of the *immediate* transference relationship.

If the above is so, there is a very interesting set of *part* object psychodynamics involved. What is so emotionally upsetting, for this individual, about his present situation, is a reflection of the distantly past emotional problems of the individual. In other words, his past emotional conflicts and problems are reflected into the present emotional difficulty that he is verbalizing upon. Yet at the very same time, what he is verbalizing on, is a metaphorical manifestation of what he unconsciously perceives, at the very moment, of the "here and now" situation between himself and his transference listener. The past, the present, and the "here and now" are made *one* within the immediate transference relationship. Here is the very key toward a continual resolving of emotional difficulties by anyone in his own interpersonal relationship sphere.

In the production of dream manifest content, the latent content with its conflicts, wishes and fears is projected up from its part object derivations into a manifest content dramatization for partial *resolving.* In other words, the dream's manifest content, with it's actions and dramatizations works out, in a way that is perhaps similar to a Moreno psychodrama, a solution to the conflict. It is probably not that any solution is made in any one night, but the dramatizations add, little by little, toward an ongoing process of resolution. Perhaps this is the necessity for dreaming on a regular basis. And perhaps this is a reason for dreams, or dream-themes to re-occur.

In a similar way, one can speculate that the manifest content of interpersonal relationship communication provides the same opportunity toward a presentation and resolution of the underlying latent conflicts, wishes and fears. Again, a single and final solution is not had by any one particular verbalization of a manifest content, but by continually verbalizing in interpersonal relationships, a solution is worked *toward*. Certain verbalized manifest contents "recur," particularly in the emotionally uncomfortable, just like certain dreams seem to recur. This is putting an analytic focus on the simple statement "a person likes to talk about certain things." In other words, both the dream's manifest content, and the manifest content of the interpersonal relationship communication can be emotionally conflict resolving. Deprivation of either apparently can be anxiety producing.

One can speculate a greater importance to the manifest content of interpersonal communication than any dream manifest content. The dream manifest content is an *intra*psychic pheonomenon. It is a phenomenon that occurs within a single individual. The manifest content of communication is *inter*psychic, as well as being *intra*psychic. It has to involve two or more people. There is an interpersonal relationship involvement that is *immediately* taking place with the formation of any manifest content of communication that adds an increase in complexity over the intrapsychic dream. With the manifest content of the dream, there is no other person that the unconscious ego has to be perceiving, assimilating, evaluating and contending with at the very moment. The unconscious ego, in the dream, doesn't have to be concerned with the immediacy of a reality situation that is so necessary in the production of manifest content of communication. The reality orientation of the manifest content of the dream can be less carefully done than the reality appropriateness in the formation of communication manifest content. This would make the production of a manifest content of a dream relatively easier than the production by the unconscious ego of communication manifest content. As an added point to consider, in the greater importance of interpersonal communication manifest content, is that the dream latent content concerns itself with *past* and probably present interpersonal relationships. In other words, there is an *inter*psychic concern of the unconscious ego in presenting a dream manifest content, even though it is, essentially, an *intra*psychic process. The manifest content of communication, however, is not only past and present oriented, but more complexly *here and now* oriented as well, adding still another dimension to its symbolization.

Analysts, as well as clients themselves, have been erroneous in concluding the nature of the latent content of the dream from recall of dream manifest content. When a client, for instance, recalls: "I dreamt big pieces of my skin were coming off, leaving ugly looking sores that I was afraid others would see. It was all very frightening and I awoke very anxious. (Long thoughtful pause.) I think that this dream somehow goes back to my mother, and is connected to her having had psoriasis. She had a hideous case of psoriasis (shudders) she was always trying to hide, that was so ugly and repulsive. My dream must have something to do with a hidden fear of getting psoriasis from my mother and probably explains why I never was able to get close to my mother." Within her recalled manifest content of the dream, she is correct only in deducing that the origin of the dream symbolization and dramatization is her mother's psoriasis. This may very well be the origin of the *symbols* of the manifest content, but it is *not* the *latent meaning* of the symbols. It is where the symbolization *derives* itself, and not what the symbolization *latently stands for*. They are not the same, although there may be a predicate equated similarity. If the dream analyst asks her for further associations in regard to her mother's psoriasis, attempting to uncover conflicts, wishes and fears associated with this, he can erroneously conclude that the latent content of the dream was oriented about the client's mother's psoriasis. But verbalizations about the origins and the speculation of the development of the dream recall, in regard to the dream manifest content, do not represent an investigation into the latent content of the dream. It is, instead, an investigation into the possible *origins* of the *symbolization*, and not the latent meaning.

In this particular dream, one can be sure that the client isn't really *emotionally* concerned at all with her mother's psoriasis, but what this *symbolically* represents to her *now*. Interpreting this on its probable latent content level, this client, in referring to the "ugly looking sores" is latently equating her mother's psoriasis with her own nebulous, part object derived, unconscious sense of guilt, that she, herself, tries to hide from others, and prefers to keep covered up. She doesn't have a fear of getting psoriasis *unconsciously*, though this may very well be a *conscious* fear, but has a fear of exposing her self-felt sense of contaminating guilt, which, though part object derived, is well concretized in the fear of psoriasis. Her "uncovered" fear of psoriasis and the recall of a problem with her mother is appropriate, reality-oriented, understandable, logical and "makes sense" to others. But what is unconscious in a dream's latent content is *unconscious* for a reason, and no intellectualization nor psychoanalytic manipulation can make what is unconscious, conscious. Under the transference phenomenon, between this client and her analyst, the fear is that her guilt will be "uncovered" *to him*. But there is a "need" to keep this unconscious, and this would be borne out by the fact that if this were proposed to her, it would undoubtedly be denied, called "unrealistic" and felt to be entirely "inappropriate." That this is done is more of a "proof" that one is dealing with *unconscious* matters than a client's ability to talk about it in an *accepting* way.

The dream analysts are correct in believing one can learn of the conflicts of the dream latent content by continuing to listen to presentations of what a person "remembers" or recalls of their dream manifest content. They are erroneous if they attempt to explain these unconscious problems with psychodynamics based on whole objects or whole object experiences. They can be grossly misled if they don't recognize that subtle transference reaction between that person and themselves. They can be further misled if they don't analyze, at least to themselves, their client's problems, to the deeper *oral* level where all emotional conflicts have their basis.

99

In analyzing the latent content of communication, one can take the manifest content of a person's various verbalizations and eventually recognize what is being latently conveyed by comparing one manifest content with another. An individual will often verbalize one manifest content with a particular reality orientation, and then say the same thing latently, but with a still different reality orientation to the manifest content. These manifest contents may appear superficially unrelated and may even appear "loose," but the latent communication, or the transference language remains very much related. Just as one doesn't dream the same dream manifest content over and over, one doesn't verbally present the same manifest content over and over either. But like what the dream analysts attempt to do, one can compare the manifest contents and discover the latent content problem that the individual is facing. By continued listening, a transference figure, or a therapeutic listener, can tell what is being presented as the emotional problem between speaker and listener, and what is being hopefully resolved. We shall see later that *no* interpretations are necessary for resolvement in that the process, just like the dreaming process itself, requires *no* dream analysts for its effectiveness. That is, if one continues to dream, it is possible to resolve one's emotional conflicts to a more comfortable level, just as people have been resolving their emotional problems in communicative interaction for years before there were any analysts. And if one who is emotionally *uncomfortable* continues to verbalize to a transference figure, this person too can become emotionally *comfortable*, without the interpretations of any analyst or psychiatrist.

The manifest content of communication, then, is metaphorical and allegorical. Whatever is being presented as a reality concern is only superficial to a deeper unreality concern between that individual and the transference figure who listens. The unconscious ego is continually allegorizing in the formation of the manifest content of communication. All that is spontaneously brought forth by an individual verbalizing in a transference relationship is allegorical, no matter how reality oriented, how factual, or how appropriate that manifest content is. It will always have a basis in an unreality that underlies what is being verbalized. The allegory that makes up the manifest content is made up of metaphors, so that communication is both metaphorical and allegorical.

Manifest content tends to be reality oriented like the manifest dream. It can be factual, scientific, and unquestionably correct. But it is still a manifest content to a latent content. Why it *is* spontaneously brought up by a person within a transference situation has something emotionally to do with that situation. The motivation behind the spontaneously mentioned verbalization comes from the latent transference interaction between the speaker and his listener. For instance when a client in therapy asks: "Nick wanted to know if I was making any progress as he doesn't think so. He says he doesn't think you know what you're doing," she, *herself*, wants to know, in part. Perhaps Nick *does* want to know about progress in reality. But *she* does too, *in part*, within the unreality of her relationship with the therapist. By presenting it as Nick's question, she has the safety of emotional distance. She can say things that her unconscious ambivalence could not logically present more directly.

When a client queries: "My husband wanted me to ask you if I needed to get out more," she, *herself*, wants to know, but she presents it in regard to reality as her *husband* wanting to know. She may then go on to present different aspects of her own ambivalence as: "*I* don't think I need to get out any more than I am, but my *husband* does." She is presenting aspects of her own ambivalence, as well as unconsciously perceived aspects of the therapist, implying, she feels, *he* wants her out more.

When a client comes in for her therapy session, leaving her two children out in the waiting room, and remarks several times during the session: "I'm so worried my children will tear apart your office," she is latently concerned about a self-felt potentially destructive and poorly controlled aspect of *herself* that could "tear apart" the therapist's office. Reality-wise, her children are destructive, but her worry is reality oriented on the conscious manifest content level, and unreality oriented on the underlying latent content level.

An individual's unconscious ego has all of reality from which to draw his analogies and his allegories for his part object derived unconscious conflicts, wishes and fears. This reality doesn't even have to be correctly perceived to be utilized. The reality may be purposefully viewed from an opposing standpoint. But what is presented in the manifest content of communication conveys what is being perceived latently of the "here and now" relationship between speaker and listener. The transference language can be strong enough, that even when subject matter is brought up by the listener, it will be utilized by the client to convey his latent feelings. For instance, if a therapist were to say, when his client walks in the office: "I see the sun's out and we're going to have a nice day." The therapist, in his spontaneous remark is conveying a latent message of acceptance to his client. The client may respond: "Yes, I'm real *glad* to see the sun; it's going to be *good* for my garden." However, another client might have responded to this with: "The sun's raising *hell* with my white house paint," or "It's drying up my lawn." One gets the feeling that this client views the therapist a little differently than the first.

It is interesting to note that the metaphor is a well-known figure of speech, which consists of comparing one whole object by an attribute, an aspect, or a part of another object and then inferring a whole object equating. It is an emphatic *comparison* between two quite different objects or experiences that is apparently made with a primary process type of Von Domarus predicate equating. The color of the sun and one's envisioned lustre of a golden chariot are likened, and become metaphorical, and illogically equated, when one says: "The sun, a golden chariot, rides across the sky." The type of "thinking" that can create, or can accept such metaphors is the very type of cognition that psychiatrists have told us is supposed

101

to be a unique characteristic of "schizophrenia." It is the same Von Domarus predicate equating that is characteristic of primary process thinking, not the secondary process thinking (or Aristotelian) of the conscious. The golden chariot and an aspect of the sun can have an autistically perceived shared characteristic or aspect, and therefore held to be equated.

This apparently acceptable primary process thinking involves every metaphor, whether it is a recognized figure of speech or whether it is the unconsciously created metaphors of the manifest content of communication. The manifest content of communication, like the manifest dream, is analogical. If some people have likened the dream to "schizophrenia" because of its predominance in each of primary process cognition and timelessness, further saying that everyone is "schizophrenic" in their sleep, then one can conclude we must all be "schizophrenic" while communicating as well! A better conclusion would be that we use primary process cognition more than previously recognized, and that perhaps "schizophrenia" doesn't exist at all, but has only been the elusive unicorn in psychiatry! What has been attributed to "schizophrenia," and what has been described of the dream, is essentially the very same thing that is subtly involved as well in interpersonal communication.

The use of the primary process oriented metaphor is not just an incidental part of communication. People who have been outstanding for their oratorical abilities have been those who frequently utilize the metaphor the most. The articulate individual makes use of the metaphor because it does, most succinctly, convey meanings. The metaphor presents a "common meeting ground" of understanding between the speaker and his listener by presenting something that the listener is well aware of from his own past experiences and then equating it with something else that is trying to be conveyed. The metaphor presents a "common meeting ground" for the listener, in that what is presented, is an experience or familiar entity that has been shared, in part, by the listener. When a person talks about something that his listener has experienced, at least in part, or knows intimately of, there is a mutual experience that is called forth that two or more people can come together on. The listener may have the feeling that he is "tuned in" to the person talking. This is why people get together when they have common interests, such as hobbies, or current affairs, whether in their own living rooms, the neighborhood bar, the PTA meeting, group therapy session, etc. What is talked about is mutually understood. For instance, one wife might say to another: "Don't get Fred and John talking about politics — they'll be at it all night." When the metaphors are carefully chosen, they can convey meaning and feelings like nothing else can in conscious communication.

When the listener can understand the metaphors and analogies that are being presented, he is better able to grasp the meaning that the other is attempting to convey. Since feelings are so difficult to communicate, presenting them in metaphor facilitates understanding. And these metaphors don't even have to be reality-oriented to convey meaning. They may be entirely unrealistic, and even autistically determined. Yet the meaning is perfectly clear, and it's usage fully accepted, even though it is autistic, is not reality-oriented and represents blatant primary process thinking. The meaning seems to be quite emphatically made, though quite unrealistic, in "scarcer than hens' teeth," "busier than a one-armed paper-hanger," and "finer than frog's hair." Though these expressions are actually similes, the metaphor that drops the "like" or "than" is just as readily accepted in conscious speech. Some people with no awareness of the unconscious metaphorical aspect of communication feel that the spoken word may even involve a metaphorical *necessity*. Those that understand transference language realize it *is* a necessity.

Both the expressive characteristics of the *conscious metaphor*, as well as the *unconscious* metaphorical make-up of the manifest content of communication, is well shown in the following excerpt of a client involved in an intense transference relationship with his therapist. The different people of whom he speaks are either a metaphorical aspect of himself, or an unconsciously perceived aspect of the therapist. The situation of concern in this excerpt mirrors the identical metaphorically presented concern for the "here and now" transference relationship. "I'd be as crooked as a dog's hind leg if I said I wasn't worried about this trip (a reference to the therapeutic transference) that I have to take. It's not my cup of tea at all, but something that's a part of my work I can't weasel out of. And you can bet I've tried to. The kingpin is going along, so we're going to have to watch our P's and Q's. He used to be a neighbor of mine, but he's gone right up to the top of the heap. He's the top banana in my bunch right now. His role is sort of an oddball one with me though, because he's actually too busy with a lot of other projects to be totally concerned with what goes on in my sandbox. He's there if someone has to toss him the ball for an end run. He'll point out the paths to take, if asked, but the actual clearing of them is up to us. (Here "us" refers to certain unconscious aspects of himself as well as aspects of the therapist.) He keeps careful track of the time schedule, and will blow the whistle to end a play (a reference perhaps to the ending of a therapy session) whenever he wants to. He's not one to pour money down the drain in some picayune endeavor. What he grabs hold of he'll do with a bulldog grip until the job is wrapped up. That's what I like about him. There's a couple of other engineers (i.e. other metaphorical aspects of himself) that are going along too. In fact, there may even be a few more before the show gets on the road. Jim's (one unconscious aspect of himself) going. He's the one we call the 'swinger' (laughs warmly). He's always out to enjoy himself and any situation he's in. He loves people and doesn't give a tinker's dam about his work. He can't speak German at all, but he sure can communicate when he wants to — particularly when he meets a broad (a reference to an unconsciously perceived aspect of the therapist with certain specific implications quite different from those previously implied). He's promised to show us a good time while we're

103

there. (Smiles and therapist returns it.) Then there's Pete (a metaphorical presentation of an aspect of himself that is different from what was previously implied in "Jim"), who if you throw him a curved ball, you can bet he's going to strike out. Why he is even going along is beyond me, but I guess the company (therapist) has hopes for him. Anything that just bumps his apple tree will cause all his apples to come tumbling down. He's going to get a lot of bumps too, because the electrical circuitry is all in his bailiwick. I'm most worried about him, as we have such a tight schedule, and so much depends on him that he can spoil everything if he gets in a stew. He won't be able to just run back to the showers, like he usually does, and worry about it for a few days, if his game isn't going right. It's not going to be played according to Hoyle anyway. I'd hate to see him go belly up when things don't turn out as expected. I'm just glad the boss (therapist) is going to be there so we can fall back on him if necessary."

Verbs, adverbs, pronouns, nouns and their qualifying adjectives build characterizations of the unconsciously perceived aspects of the transference situation, and are presented for resolution. When a person spontaneously talks of his interpersonal relationships, his present or his past reality, he inadvertently conveys by metaphorical implication what he unconsciously perceives of the "here and now" transference situation between himself and his listener. This can become exceedingly complicated when described objects, experiences and situations of reality are interrelated into analogies and allegories that reflect what is unconsciously being perceived of the part object oriented transference problems of the moment. One *is* concerned with reality, and with what a speaker is presenting. But his reality concern reflects not only the distant emotional concerns that *require* that he *be* so concerned in the present, but also *this* is what is being transferred into the transference relationship of the moment as the unreality concern. All that is verbalized becomes metaphorical for the immediate underlying transference relationship. Under a guise, or veneer of reality, there is the unreality of the transference that is being continuously projected into manifest content, from its part object latentcy.

A teenaged client complexly, and most dynamically, presents different unconscious aspects of *herself* in relation to different unconsciously perceived aspects of her *therapist* when she relates: "I don't like Jeff (therapist). I just use him because he'll take me anywhere I want to go. He doesn't try to make out with me like that Frank (another aspect of the therapist) does. I hate to be around him, in fact I can't stand him. (Snears.) Well, Jeff took me over to Donna's (an aspect of herself) house and she was on the phone talking to Bill (still another aspect of the therapist) . . . you know, the guy I was telling you about last week that got his head smashed in a car accident last month. His jaw is all wired up so he can't say anything except 'Mhmm' (laughs). (Note how one could erroneously conclude her affect was inappropriate if ignorant of the latent message). I don't know how long Donna was talking to him, but her grandmother (a still different unconscioulsy perceived aspect of the therapist) was having a fit because of the phone bill she was running up. She was trying to get Donna off the phone, but Donna was trying to get Bill to get Jimmy (a perceived aspect of the therapist the client feels frustrated in reaching) to come to the phone. She told him I was there, but Jimmy won't have anything to do with me. Jimmy's still blaming me for his getting busted by the 'narc' (the therapist with certain other perceived characteristics equated with a narcotic agent) when I left a 'roach' on the floor of his car. I'm going to kill myself if I don't get to see Jimmy. God! I can't live without him. But if Donna's grandmother didn't louse things up, Frank and Judy (a combination of an aspect of the client and an aspect of the therapist that could be enlarged upon to convey certain other unconscious perceptions of the transference) did. They had to come over and mess things all up. Judy used to go with Jimmy and she wanted to talk to him when she found out that Bill had Jimmy there. She ruins everything! Damn her! I wish she'd get out of my life and stay out! She's no friend of mine at all. Why Donna goes around with her is beyond me. As soon as she came in, she started in. 'Give me the phone. Give it here. *I'll* talk to him!' I told Donna to hang up, and since her grandmother was getting real nasty about it all at that point, Donna did hang it up. And Jeff and I just walked out."

The extent to which all interpersonal communication is metaphorical is difficult for the inexperienced therapeutic listener to fully appreciate, but perhaps it can be clarifed with the following. Suppose an after-dinner speaker begins with: "I feel like the little boy that . . ." and then goes on to give, in analogy, his own particular feelings and impressions in an easily perceived way. This same after-dinner speaker may later on mention: "This reminds me of a story . . ." where the story again represents in analogy what he is trying to convey. It doesn't seem too much to infer that the speaker is still talking latently about *his* feelings, *his* impressions, *his* concerns, *his* fears and *his* wishes, if he simply left off the introductory "I feel like the . . ." and the "This reminds me of a story." When one accepts that the superfluous introductory phrases *can* be left off, one may then be able to accept that all spontaneous interpersonal communication is metaphorical, analogous and allegorical. What a person spontaneously chooses to talk about, inevitably conveys a latent communication about the transference relationship of the moment.

This is shown by the woman who remarks in therapy: "I hate being involved in this weekly Sunday School class. How I ever got involved I'll never know! It's supposed to be such an uplifting experience, and so meaningful, but frankly, I don't get a damn thing out of it. I think the reason I detest it the most is because of this one woman in the class (she, *herself*, in metaphor) that can't seem to keep her big mouth shut. Everytime she opens it, everyone (meaning both she and the therapist) can see how stupid she really is. And what bugs me is that she thinks she's great! She tries to get the class to focus all their attention on her, and she does everything possible to be the main attraction. Everybody's sick of her. She spoils it for all the rest. If she wasn't there, maybe I'd get something from the class (but this woman, since it's so important a part of the client, herself, *must* always be there, and she's there in the transference as well). I may just quit, but I did tell my mother (i.e. the therapist) I'd give it a try."

This personal reference to the speaker and his listener, is again shown by a client in therapy, who conveys how he, *himself,* feels in not trusting the therapist — with perhaps some reality basis, in that the therapist *is* the author. The client comes into the office and, as he seats himself, the therapist says: "Before we begin I should tell you I will not be here for therapy two weeks from today, as I will be presenting a paper in Cleveland, but I will be here as usual the following week." Client: "Oh! (Pause) Okay. I was planning to be out of town myself then, so it'll work out fine. (Pause) You will be here next week? (Therapist acknowledges with a nod he will be.) You're giving a paper? (Long thoughtful pause and then becomes anxious.) Now, don't tell them about me! (Laughs anxiously.) I'm just joking. (Pause.) This reminds me of a joke about the little boy, who, on going to his first confession, said to the Father: 'Don't tell *anyone* what I just said. *Promise* me you won't tell *anyone* what I told you!' The priest assured him of the confidentiality of the confession, but during the next Sunday's sermon when the priest began: 'Once there was a person who . . .', whereupon the boy leaped to his feet, angrily shouting: 'Liar! You *promised* you wouldn't tell anyone!' "

Emotionally close interpersonal relationships are characterized by this self-referring communicative quality when mutual needs, feelings, fears and wishes are being expressed within a manifest content of commonly shared past experiences. There is a sharing of experiences, impressions and opinions behind the manifest content's metaphors and analogies which are being unconsciously utilized to express the ambivalent deeper feelings that have been equated by the Von Domarus phenomenon previously mentioned. But more than simply presenting a "common meeting ground" for communicative endeavors, the metaphors afford an opportunity for the latent content of the transference language to express the various and often conflicting and opposing aspects or parts of one's self.

What is metaphorically being presented within the manifest content becomes a framework for the subtle communicative interplay between the speaker and the listener within the transference relationship. There is a continual psychodrama taking place in any talking and listening relationship, particularly when it is continued on an ongoing basis. This psychodrama is made up of the different aspects of the part object make-up of a person when he spontaneously verbalizes in regard to his own ambivalence, and the unconsciously perceived part object make-up of the listener. Into the manifest content, there are projected these perceived aspects of this relationship no matter what an individual may spontaneously choose to verbalize upon. It is as though the speaker is continually saying: "This is how I see *myself,* in relation to *you,* in *this* situation." Or: "This is *my* emotional problem that I have had in the past, that I am having in the present, and that I am *transferring* into this relationship between *you* and *me*, and that *we* must resolve together."

Metaphorical presentation in the manifest content of communication affords a safety in distance, not only from the ambivalence within the individual's own unconscious, but also the ambivalence of the unconsciously viewed listener. The part object make-up of the ambivalent unconscious, and the ambivalently perceived transference, demand a metaphorical expression that gives a necessary distance from opposing facets of the ambivalence, and a logical presentation in the manifest content. By utilizing metaphors, one is able to express a part object feeling or impression to someone else, and still be able to fall back on an "I didn't say that!" type of defense. For instance, the politican may say "I'm not going to stand up here and say my opponent is dishonest — *others* may, but *I'm* not." But what he actually doesn't say in reality, he still implies. And what one couldn't say directly from his unconscious, one, like that politician, can still convey a latent metaphorical message to his listener that can be readily denied in reality if ever confronted.

As an example of the interpersonal distance afforded by the metaphor, two people meet on the street, each of whom may suspicion the other of having an "It's none of your damn business" feeling. Fearing a hostile rejection, if personal things were broached too directly, one may greet the other with the following non-direct, open-ended, and metaphorical inquiry: "Well, how are things in Memphis?" This allows the other to present what he unconsciously feels safe in presenting to the other, who, if he comes from Chattanooga, may then be asked in return: "Well, how are things in Chattanooga?" This affords the other the same distance and the same opportunity to present, in metaphor, how things are going for *him*, on a latent and implied basis. If he volunteers that things are "all fouled up," the other can assume that the person feels, at least in part, that things are "all fouled up" with him *personally*. Further verbalizations would bear this out. What is brought forth, when done so, in a spontaneously verbalized fashion, *does* reflect a personal communication of unconsciously perceived aspects of himself.

There is a definite practical "value" in utilizing metaphorical presentations for various aspects of how one feels himself. One can "get away" with saying certain things, by implication, that he might not have been able to do otherwise if expressed more directly. Take for instance a realtor, who had been told by his client that his home should be sold at $25,000 and no less. He comes back to the client after having seen a prospective buyer with the following "testing" type of inquiry, which in a safe manner reflects, with conscious tact, or else unconsciously, his own feelings. "A Mr. Green came by to look at your house. He felt it was a good buy at $24,000, but I *told* him the price was very firm, and that you would *not* accept anything less. He felt that because it didn't have central air

107

conditioning that $24,000 was a more appropriate price. I told him that I'd mention it to you." The realtor then is able to not only "test" the client in regard to a possible lower price, but avoids the position of being the direct object of any expressed anger in regard to the possible rejection of the previously determined price.

This same type of informative metaphorical communication that hides latent implications is readily apparent in the first verbalizations of a person who enters someone else's house, as: "Oh, I just *hate* that type of panelling. I wouldn't have that in my house." The other person may quickly recognize the implication that she, herself, at least in part, is not welcomed in the other's house either. While a remark as: "I would *love* to have that panelling in my house" can be taken as a latent invitation.

On an intrapersonal basis, a person may convey on one hand that he is worthless, no good and a burden to others, while on the other express anger that he isn't recognized as being important or as having some value. He may express anger that his needs *aren't* being met, and then express evidence of his guilt that makes him feel his needs *shouldn't* be met. When a person feels ambivalent, the metaphor is particularly appropriate for expressing facets of this ambivalence. To express this ambivalence directly would not be logical. For instance, it is not logical to say that one wants their oral needs met and one doesn't want their oral needs met at the same time. Neither is it logical to say that one wants to express anger for the frustration of past unmet oral needs, and not want to express anger, at the very same time. By utilizing various metaphors and analogies, the different opposing aspects of this intrapsychic unconscious ambivalence can be presented for a hoped for resolution. This is similar to the way that the ambivalence within the latent content of the dream is projected up into the manifest content of the dream in the metaphorical make-up of the dream's manifest content, but is still hidden from the dreamer.

A woman who was unable to relate any more of her early childhood than a very guarded: "Oh, I had a happy childhood — same as anyone else," conveys a lot more than what she would consciously admit to of her own past oral deprivation and rejection in her analogy of her dog, "Lady." "Yes, I live out on the island with 'Lady.' We don't get many visitors as it's rather inaccessible (and so is she) out there except when the tide is up, and you can get a boat over the bars (analogous to the difficulty of the therapist in getting emotionally close to her). I hope you can come over and visit sometime. I like to talk to people who have an interest in dogs. You can always find me anywhere you can find Lady and vice versa. We're always together. She was a stray, and I don't know how she ended up on the island. I wish she could tell me how, but of course she can't. I know she had been treated terribly, probably beaten, and was underfed, if not outright starved. People can be so cruel to dumb animals like that. There ought to be a law against such neglect. (Therapist: Yaa.) You can tell that she's been hurt in the past; she's very meek and painfully shy, and so terrified of strange people. Unless she's gotten to know you, she'll hide under the house with her tail between her legs. You won't see her at all as she's so timid and passive. She's afraid even now, and will stay in the background even around people she knows. (Therapist: She's had it pretty rough!) Yes, she has and I bet she could tell you about it if she only could. It's made her so she's not like other dogs. She's never running around playfully, or barking, and making a lot of noise like most dogs. And she's petrified of thunderstorms . . . (laughs) I'm that way too. I guess she's a lot like me."

A therapeutic listener was able to establish a working relationship with a teen-aged, previously withdrawn, girl, who seemed to require that the manifest content be "light and lively." In her fifth session, she came in remarking: "I've been feeling a lot better this past week. (Smiles warmly.) It seems as though I've been more happy!" (Therapist: Are you getting less beatings at home than before?) (Laughs.) "I don't get any beatings. I never did, and you know it. (Laughs.) I just feel better! That's all! So quit trying to analyze it. You're always trying to make something out of nothing. Can't a person feel happy without getting his head shrunk? (Therapist: Well, you must be in love . . . you've got a boyfriend!) I *do not* have a boyfriend either. And I don't want a boyfriend! I'd rather take a beating than get all the trouble of having a boyfriend. Boyfriends! Bah! (Laughs and then pauses.) But my aunt has one! She's got a *good* one. (Both client and therapist laugh.) I was down to visit her last weekend, and she really looks nice. There's a big change in her. She's the one I told you about last time that they nearly took away to the gooney-bin. (Laughs.) She had it pretty rough growing up because her mother died when she was little. (This client's mother has not died, but the "dead mother" analogy has an appropriateness.) Some people (latently referring to herself) can get the rottenest luck! Her husband died, and then she had a boyfriend, and he died too. Now she's got this new boyfriend. (Therapist: I hope he doesn't look like he's going to die!) No, he doesn't! He's pretty healthy-looking to me, and lots of fun to be with. I think it's done a lot for my aunt, and actually he's just what she needed, instead of any gooney-bin and psychiatrists!"

Sometimes the metaphor, or the analogy, is inadvertently unveiled to the chagrin of the speaker. This undisguised transference language that comes into the manifest content is what has been called a "Freudian slip." The person is presenting material from their unconscious in their manifest content that should have remained unconscious to the speaker. While unconscious material is presented in analogy for resolution in the manifest content, there is a need for distance from the problems of one's own unconscious. To suddenly remove this distance creates embarrassment. This is illustrated in the client who had been referred for psychotherapy, but who steadfastly denied any emotional problems, and who could see no reason at all why her family physician thought a psychiatric consultation was necessary. "There's *nothing* wrong with me at all except this female trouble I've had for years. That's the *only* problem I've got. I thought the hysterectomy would take care of it, but it hasn't. In fact, it's worse. But why should a woman with a long standing gynecological problem see a psychiatrist? You see I *never* was *normal* (suddenly becomes flustered). I mean normal in regard to my periods!"

However, many times the implied or latent part object derived message, even if it is unconscious, is perceived by the listener, who may take offense to it. Take for example two people conversing in a bar, where one begins to make disparaging remarks about California to another person who is known to be from that state. This second person may recognize a personal derogatory message conveyed in the metaphorical remarks about California that seem to apply to him. This person, apparently, unconsciously equates himself with California. A bar fight may then follow with the second individual remarking: "No two bit punk can talk to me of California that way!" when this person has a recognition that the metaphorical implication is to he, himself. After the fight, one might hear bystanders remark "They were just talking about *California,* and the next thing I knew they were fighting!"

This illustrates that there is an implied meaning in the remark made, the joke told, and the story remembered that can convey a personal reference to the listener. Where an individual has less guilt, and is less sensitive, he can accept the inuendo, and accept the anger conveyed in the metaphor, with continued verbalization. With more guilt, he may resort to withdrawal, or to retaliatory anger. When, for instance, a husband comes home from work, and makes a remark about the waiting dinner as: "Don't tell me I'm having *that* again!" or in some way makes a derogatory remark about the *dinner,* the wife may become angry because she may have perceived a latent implication to *herself* . . . because *she* unconsciously feels that *he* feels the same way about an aspect of *herself* that is similar on a part object basis and thus equated to what has been expressed about the dinner. The remark is taken as conveying a personal condemnation or unacceptableness from which she takes offense. This may not have been *consciously* intended by the husband. Unconsciously, and *in part,* it *was* intended! The covering effect of the metaphor is unvieled. People often *do* make remarks in a rather obvious "if the shoe fits, wear it" type of way. And many times, too the speaker will unconsciously make his remarks as specifically applicable to the listener as Cinderella's glass slipper!

But depending upon the amount of one's unconscious guilt, one may "overread" or place too much of a personal emphasis upon latent part object implications of others. Even though there may actually *be* a hostile or condemning implication, a person with less unconscious guilt will unconsciously "overlook" it, or may unconsciously accept it, and even support it. With less unconscious guilt, he can continue the communicative exchange. With a high level of unconscious guilt, there may be a communication breakdown. There is a tendency then for all of us to be somewhat "paranoid" in regard to our "third ear listening." The so called "ideas of reference" that supposedly are "schizophrenic" are found as part of any unconscious ego's functioning in "reading" transference language. In any interpersonal communicative interacting, each unconscious ego may be envisioned as saying: *"He's talking about me,"* in regard to the other's communications. But with too much unconscious guilt, one can become too hypersensitive in regard to perceived communication. One emotionally uncomfortable woman, for instance, remarked: "When I was growing up, I *always* looked for hidden meanings in everything I heard. When someone would talk to me, I would always hope that they would imply something *nice* or *complimentary* to me. But I would always get the feeling, instead, they were *condemning* me, or *criticizing* me, or saying something *bad* about me. Even today, I always catch myself asking 'What's the person *really* saying about *me*'?"

This woman is simply more aware of a process in communication that is usually more subtle and more metaphorically veiled. But what this woman has an awareness of, the therapeutic listener must always keep in mind. It becomes important for anyone most effectively dealing with close interpersonal relationships to always ask himself this same question: "What is the person *really* saying about *me* in regard to *our* relationship?"

One can take verbalized statements from any transference relationship and readily detect the latent message that is being conveyed. One can see the oral dilemma of what is being presented from the "part" make-up of the speaker in regard to certain unconscious parts of the listener. This is shown in the following recorded statements: "Sometimes I'm mad because he leaves me . . . other times I wish he'd get the hell out of my life and stay out!" or "It's all over as far as I'm concerned — if he's going to make me this upset, I might as well end it — I don't want any part of it" and "If I tell my mother off, like I've been wanting to for years, she'll stop babysitting for me, and right now I need her for that, as the children are too young to stay by themselves."

A therapeutic listener can become suddenly startled with a sudden awareness to transference language with its personally oriented communications. For instance, one client realized that she seemed to possess an ambivalent make-up of parts that was making her so emotionally uncomfortable, remarking: "I've come to the conclusion that there's a part of me that's a *swinger* . . . I mean one that would like to throw morals, customs and all sense of decency aside, and then there's another part that's a little *child* and wants to be treated as such, and still another part that *resents* being treated as a child, and still another part that's a grown mature *woman*, and expects to be treated just that way." The therapist, understanding what she was saying, began to summarize it as: "That's right! There are many parts of your unconscious, each with their own particular make-up and each with their own particular expectation for being treated. Some of these parts are opposing, and this is what makes you so uncomfortable." The client listened during this, and then, after a brief pause, added: "Yes, and there's a part of me that *hates* to be lectured to." It's right here that the listener is suddenly struck with the appropriateness of her remark to her "here and now" relationship with him. It is *so* appropriate that it is almost unbelievable that she doesn't have some conscious awareness that she is talking, in part, about her listener. For she doesn't, and she immediately goes on to expand this remark, talking of her *husband's* tendency to lecture her. Her emotional relationship with the listener remains unconscious, as it should be.

A therapeutic listener can be suddenly taken aback by the uncanny knowledge that a client seems to show about the transference phenomenon and its language. Verbalizations made in the manifest content seem so fitting of how the client is feeling at the moment about his listener that one is astounded by the client's unawareness of the appropriateness of what he has just said. This is shown in the excerpt of a bachelor engineer involved in psychotherapy about his recently acquired girlfriend. "Sure, she has a profession, but how she ever got to be a nurse, God only knows. She doesn't do any nursing work at all. Apparently all she does is sit at a desk and look important. And for that she gets *paid*. The place she works at *requires* a registered nurse, but doesn't require her to do any nursing. I don't think she could do anything else. It's unbelievable how stupid she is! Talking to her is like talking to a brick wall. It's a chore to get a message through to her. I'll tell her something, and by the look on her face, I can see I've lost her. She hasn't got the message at all, and doesn't even have the faintest idea what I'm trying to tell her. (Laughs.) So I'll begin again, and present the same thing another way in hopes she'll get the message this time,. She'll *still* have that blank look on her face! After I've gone through presenting what I wanted to tell her in a variety of different ways, her face will show a little glimmer of enlightenment, before she eventually gives out with that 'Oh! Now I get it!' look. It's a blessing she doesn't see anyone that *needs* to see a nurse!"

So many times a therapist, in attempting to follow the psychodynamics of the interpersonal relationships involved in the manifest content of his client will not recognize until later that the client has actually been conveying her latent impressions of the transference situation. When he reads over his notes, he discovers how appropriately expressed were the client's verbalizations to metaphorically imply what she is emotionally working through with the therapist. But this post therapy-session recognition may be quite adequate, for if the therapist is understanding of the manifest content, and is appropriately supportive, his own latent interaction appropriateness will naturally follow. He is a better *therapeutic listener*, though, if he recognizes it *during* therapy.

CHAPTER 6

GRATIFYING THE ORAL NEEDS THROUGH COMMUNICATIVE PROCESSES

We have been presenting a theory of human relatedness that is based on part objects. This theory proposes that the all-important oral dependency needs are subtly met in the interpersonal communicative processes from unconsciously perceived part objects. These part objects that allow oral gratification continue the emotional relationship of the primary experience. The infant had first explored the reality around him by erogenously mouthing whatever he found. That search for the "good breast" by the exploring infant seeking emotional gratification is continued by the adult through his interpersonal communication. But reality will make it more difficult to see. It was reality that frustrated the infant's oral need gratification with increasing perceptions of the "bad breast." The infant's search for the emotionally satisfying "good breast," becomes more of a necessity, as reality becomes more clearly recognized. The very *motivation* for expanding the sphere of interpersonal relationships by the growing infant is this search for the "good breast." Because reality becomes more obviously frustrating on a whole object basis, the insatiable oral needs demand a gratification for emotional comfortableness and happiness on a part object basis. The "mouthing" of the adult is still erogenous, and the oral need gratification is still the goal, but the process becomes hidden in reality concerns and orientations.

Each emotionally significant object that is added to the enlarging sphere of interpersonal relationships is imbued with a reverberating circuitry of trans- ference that interrelates this object with past and present part objects. We are already familiar with how a part of the object of the "here and now" can be equated with part objects of the present and the distant past. The emotionality of interactions between a perceived part in the object, and a part of the object *perceiving*, is conveyed in the latent transference language that is uniquely concerned with oral need gratification. One's interpersonal communication becomes metaphorical with a pervasive characteristic of having a *self-reference*, not unlike what has been described of the "schizophrenic's" ideas of reference. The metaphors are formed by an unconscious process involving identification and projection in regard to those unconsciously perceived aspects of the listener and the unconscious aspects of the speaker. Reality becomes a cover-up for the subtle emotional process of oral need gratification through interpersonal com- munication.

113

An excessive level of unconscious guilt will tend to block the perception of oral gratification in one's object relationships. It is necessary for the therapeutic listener to understand that because of this guilt, an individual may appear to be involved in his object relationships, but may still not be perceiving oral gratification. The withdrawal (that on a whole object basis is termed "schizoid") may occur on a part object basis. The part objects, from which the oral dependency needs were previously gratified, may decrease in number, or may cease to exist at all, while object relationships are maintained. Those part objects that were once orally gratifying may even be viewed as orally frustrating. This places the individual, still involved in object relationships, in a *more* uncomfortable position than the schizoid individual, who simply withdraws from his object relationships. The psychodynamic explanation of the so-called endogenous depression can be easily formulated under a theory of human relatedness that is based on part objects. Since any explanation on a whole object basis may be obviously inadequate, it is only "logical" that many researchers turn to a biochemical, or an "orthomolecular" theory.

Explanations by a person for why he is feeling so emotionally uncomfortable are always difficult because of the ambivalence of his unconscious parts, and his part object perceptions. The depressed or emotionally uncomfortable person who is perceiving part object rejections often finds himself at a loss to explain this to someone else. Reality, with its whole object orientation, can easily refute the part object perceptions. For instance, a person may perceive from his own guilt-derived sensitivity that he is being unfavorably talked about. With this exquisite sensitivity, he picks up the inuendos of condemnation and the nuances of non-acceptance from his friends. If he were to confront these people with what he has perceived and felt so deeply, they would realistically respond with an emphatic: "Now, nobody said that about you!" A person, who has perceived, *in part*, an oral rejection, may find it difficult to justify this on a whole object basis. The other person might counter with: "Did I *ever* let you down?" where the answer is an unquestionable "No." But on that illogical part object level, where a small part of the object may gain a sizable emotional significance when equated in timelessness with other frustrating parts of objects in the past, the answer is "Yes." An attempt to explain these part object perceptions, directly, to someone else would result in a reply as: "You're *wrong* to feel that way!," or worse, "You're crazy!"

The client that feels his parents always disapproved of everything he ever did would hardly be able to substantiate this feeling with reality. If he were to confront his parents with the statement that they *were* disapproving of him, they would quickly refute it, and would probably tell him they *never* disapproved of him in the way he feels, or that they never said he couldn't measure up to their expectations. And reality-wise they may be correct! However, in the unreality of transference language, they can be very wrong! To illustrate how this feeling of being disapproved of, or of not measuring up, can be conveyed, consider the re-

114

mark from the same client: "It seemed as though every friend I ever had, my parents ran down." If this client *did* have his parents speak disparagingly of his friends, there may have been an identification of a guilt-laden part of the client with his friends. A rejection of the friends, by the parents, on the reality level is then *simultaneously* a rejection, *in part*, of the client too. Here guilt isn't being ostentatiously projected to the child by the parent, as we saw in Chapter Three, but projected *indirectly*, yet still perceived as an oral rejection by the child. The unconscious of the parent undoubtedly equated the unacceptable friends with a part of their child made unacceptable too by their projected guilt. In their communications to the child regarding his friends, their derogatory remarks about the friends are latently meant to be for this unacceptable part of the child. This communication of rejection that can't be justified in reality is readily perceived by the child. From just such part object communications the message of being dis-approved of is repetitively amplified.

Since an increased level of guilt is usually derived from part object perceived rejections and abandonments, whatever explanation the person might give to himself, or to others, for his unhappiness will be a whole object oriented concreti-zation. It may seem realistic and logical — but it is still incorrect as the true cause. Anyone's intellectualization for his unhappiness is a rationalization and a meta-phorical, or analogic conceptualization of these part object experiences. And regardless of whatever guise the rationalizations of reality might take, the individual is basically seeking, in wanting to be happy, a more comfortable level of guilt, in order that more of his oral needs can be met within his interpersonal relationships. The reasons verbalized as an explanation for one's unhappiness are metaphorical simply because one's oral dependency needs aren't being adequate-ly met on a part object basis.

Conversely, any verbalized explanation of what can make one happy in reality becomes a metaphorical presentation for the desired oral need gratification. It is this *lack* of oral need gratification that makes up that "missing something" that so many unhappy people come to recognize is absent from their lives. No matter what might be conjured up as an answer in reality to fill this void, they feel within themselves, will be negated by some other aspect of reality. They know there must be a lack of something to explain their unhappiness, but they can't seem to identify or capture it in the reality world of objects. They learn that no equivalent of reality success can substitute for the unmet oral needs if they are blocked by guilt. As we saw in Chapter Three, nothing on a whole object basis can remove the feelings of failure or inferiority *derived* from guilt. Though they may search for it in various endeavors, and may think they're found it, they will realize in time that it has escaped them again. That elusive "Bluebird of Happiness" is the unmet oral needs that are made ungratifiable by the level of the unconscious guilt. Whatever they thought was the answer becomes apparent in time it isn't. The "Bluebird of Happiness" has to be found in the part objects on one's interpersonal relationships sphere, that are permitted to be perceived as orally gratifying, by a low enough level of unconscious guilt.

An unhappy person may enter a continuing relationship, attributing for instance, his unhappiness to his marriage. He may think he's found the answer when he meets another woman that seems to accept his confidences, and to understand him. She may give him a feeling of trust he never felt he had before, or that feeling of being especially cared for that he feels he's never had. She may convey the feeling he is the very center of her emotional life with all her thoughts and wishes revolving about him. Yet, even at this point, where he feels he's finally found the answer, he may recognize, in the light of reality, the illogic of his feelings in knowing she's already been through several affairs like this before, that she really *can't* be trusted as he would *like* to believe she can, and that he's no different than all the others in the past with whom she's been emotionally involved. Perhaps she initially *did* love him, and he her, but it was only because then they really didn't know each other. So even "love" itself doesn't seem to be the continuing answer in reality for that missing "something" in the guilt-laden individual. One may come to realize that this resulting disappointment and depression from a search for love isn't just anger turned inward, but an anger at *themselves*, for having the apparent *need* for someone else that one wishes they *didn't* have, in that it invariably leads to such frustrating circumstances of reality. One may realize too, that the depression involves, once again, the uncomfortable feeling that doesn't lend itself well to whole object explanations, that nobody really cares about them, and that people only seem to try to use them. That sense of deep loneliness and emptiness is still there, and often more so now than it was before. Nothing in reality seems to be the answer for the nebulous guilt blocked oral needs that produces the unhappiness. Nothing in a reality of whole objects seems to fill the void. It is here that suicide may seem the only "solution" possible in reality. And for many people, on that *reality* basis, it is.

The same search for a continuing unconscious perception of oral dependency need gratification, on a part object basis, will be transferred into the therapeutic relationship. Even here, it will defy a logical, or reality oriented explanation. Clients may have a fleeting awareness of the emotional significance of their therapeutic listener. They may have an awareness that they want to be cared for, totally and completely in an infantile way, by the therapist. But the reality of even this relationship can lead them to conclude: "How in the hell can I expect *you* to care so much for *me*... I know you're just practicing your profession; I know you see a lot of other people just like myself; and I know you *shouldn't* get as emotionally involved with me as I want, as it would mean that you, *yourself*, would be potentially emotionally uncomfortable and would be with me!" They might be as aware, as the knowing therapeutic listener is, that there can be *no* solution to this missing "something" in reality, that no object of reality, no experience, or no involvement of any type, on a whole object basis, can provide the

116

sought-for answer. No amount of analysis of their emotional problem, no intel-lectualization of their dilemma, and no advice, even though logical and practical, can possibly be the answer. The answer lies in the illogic of an emotionality of part objects. When a client asks: "Why don't you analyze me now — after all my talking you must know me well enough to draw a few analytical conclusions," they are seeking more of an acceptance that their own unconscious guilt won't let them accept, even if the therapist were to verbalize it. On the one hand, they are wishfully hoping for a confirmation of a *total* acceptance, while on the other hand, it's their guilt that makes them feel they should only receive a condemna-tion and a rejection. It's as though the client is saying: "Show me how much you think of me, as I want to hear it directly from you. But I can't believe any of it, not only because of my *guilt*, but also because of what I *know* of reality."

No simple solution, then, is found in the gratification of oral dependency needs from any need gratifying object of reality. If one thinks he's found a solution in a single object, a single experience, or involvement in reality, he will only be frus-trated again because of the *reality* of that object or experience. Because of the transference of an emotional *unreality* as well, the object of the present reality will be imbued with what was so frustrating in the past objects of that individual's life. The solution is most complex. It is *non-reality* oriented and involves the illogical and the unconscious. The complexity of the dilemma of the underlying orality can't be fully appreciated by any study of human behavior that is oriented toward whole object relationships, or that seeks to understand the problems of any reality without a concern for the latent unreality reflecting the distant past. With such an understanding, one knows why the perception of a "good breast" is no guarantee at all that there will be gratification for the orally hungry person, and why he feels that to "give in" to the "good breast" is a "weakness." One understands the dilemma of such a person in wanting someone to care so inti-mately about them, but who feels, when exposed to such a person, that he is only prying, questioning or grilling them. One knows that continued oral dependency gratification is *always* in the face of guilt that will tend to block that gratification. One knows what a client is referring to when he says: "I feel you're my *Dutch uncle* on one hand, and a *parole officer* on the other." The immensity of subtle part object relationships, continually being mirrored in interpersonal communica-tion, will go unnoticed in any psychotherapy, psychoanalysis, or client-profession-al relationship, unless one realizes that his client is seeking that missing "some-thing" — the gratification of his guilt-laden oral needs — in every one of his emo-tional involvements including the immediate one.

Only within the unreality of a world of part objects can one find the sought-for solution to the void of unmet oral dependency needs. One must psychologically grow, and emotionally mature in a process that is just the very opposite from "E Pluribus Unum" (from many, one). From the single object of the primary experience, one must go to a multiplicity of part objects from which to draw that oral need gratification. The therapeutic listener has the potential of being unconsciously perceived as a multiplicity of part objects that will be later reflected by an increasing sphere of interpersonal relationships in the reality of the client. Only this is how the oral needs can be met, and can *continue* to be met, and where the meeting of the oral needs will eventually become *less* of a problem to the individual. The therapeutic listener fosters the process of going from *one* to *many*, by *utilizing* the unreality afforded by the transference. The client, in turn, will attain a feeling of trust, a feeling of being uniquely important, a feeling of being wanted, needed and cared for, of not being alone, and of somehow finding that "something" that is associated with these oral feelings. He does so in a way that transcends any reality, and will resist being *negated* by any logic, or by any reality.

The person who does have a high level of unconscious guilt has also a high level of potential anger, as well as a concentration of those unmet oral needs. Because of the ambivalence that this situation creates, a listening silence is the best rule to follow for the therapeutic listener. Questions though, can be asked of the client in regard to the rationalizations being presented by the client that clarify the problem he is metaphorically presenting. Questions such as these, that concern themselves with the reality situation, are always appropriate, in that the therapist is staying within the manifest content. Though what the client is presenting is whole object oriented, or logical to reality, it is still metaphorical and is always *appropriate* to the part object oriented latent content. In the therapist's listening, in his questioning, and in his occasional paraphrasing that conveys an interest, a concern and an understanding, the client's oral dependency needs will begin to be met. (Note that it is not necessary for there to be a conscious recognition of oral dependency need gratification on the part of the therapist for there to be the ambivalent expression of subtle anger that will diminish the unconscious guilt, in that a therapist that has no knowledge of transference language will naturally *stay* within the reality of any manifest content.)

It is necessary here to emphasize the importance of just listening in the meeting of the oral needs. Many times, verbalizations on the part of the therapist may be quite supportive or effective, but at other times they may not be. Some knowledge of what the client is latently implying, as well as his *level of guilt* in regard to his oral needs, is necessary in being sure that any verbalization by the therapist will be taken as supportive. It is risky using verbalizations, when the client is so ambivalent. And particularly so when often even a simple paraphrasing of what the client has just said will be *denied* by the client because of his ambivalence. For instance, a client remarked: "My husband beats the children," and the therapist responded: "He tends to be overly harsh with those he loves." Whereupon the client, who metaphorically was presenting her guilt-laden self in this analogy, remarks: "*No*, not at all! — He only does it when they really *need* it." When a therapist verbalizes, and attempts to vigorously support a single aspect of the manifest content of a client, he can lose sight of the other aspects too quickly. The *"I* feel" verbalizations of a manifest content are of no more importance, and should receive no more support, than the *"he* feels" or *"she* feels" verbalizations. In the same manifest content they are *all* aspects of the client. One is continually dealing with ambivalence in regard to the uncomfortable individual with increased levels of recently added unconscious guilt.

Evidence that emotional support, or oral dependency need gratification, *is* taking place with a client, is sometimes shown where a client will make a remark as:: "I should have *listened* to you — I found out that you were *right* all along." When in fact the therapist did *not* advise, or counsel, or even verbally imply that his client was right or wrong. It was the act of *listening* by the therapist that unconsciously was perceived by the client as emotionally supportive. This is similarly shown where a client unconsciously perceives oral gratification from the listening process, and remarks: "My husband (meaning an aspect of herself) says you just tell me what I *want* to hear (implying latently that the therapist gives her oral gratification, which she *wants*, but her guilt makes her feel she *shouldn't* have). Reality-wise, the therapist doesn't tell her anything. He only *listens*, but this listening is perceived as *active verbal support.*

That emotional support, or the meeting of the oral dependency needs, is enhanced by just the act of listening is well illustrated when a person, who, for instance, has a severe alcoholic problem, and comes, forced into therapy, by his relatives. He involves himself for only 5 or 6 sessions, during which time he ventilates anger and projects his guilt. The wife now feels threatened in that her husband is doing so well with less dependency on her. And now with decreased guilt, he is less accepting of her usual projected guilt and anger. She demands to see the therapist, and if by chance she does reach him, she projects her guilt and anger to *both* the therapist and her husband. Even though the therapist may not have verbalized at all to her husband, other than a "good morning," and a "let us continue next time," at the close of the session the wife will angrily question: "What I'd like to know is why *you* told Donald — ," or "How is it that *you* feel that he is right (and I'm wrong) in his — ." She may go on to say: "He said, *you* said — — ," which does sound familiar, only because the client, alone, was verbalizing this, and the therapist was only listening. She implies, as her husband felt, that the therapist actively verbalized his support for her husband's projections of guilt toward her, which she obviously resents, when this makes her own guilt too uncomfortable, or too much in the focus. The important point to recognize here is that the "simple" act of listening seems subtly to convey to the person verbalizing a *"he's on my side"* type of feeling. There is a latent oral dependency gratification that is afforded by the listening process.

We have seen that a recognition of reality tends to frustrate the oral needs. One can never return to the sublime emotional state of the infant where the world consisted only of the oral need on his part, and the "good breast" of the primary experience. This was a stage in which one was completely guilt free — a stage one can never attain again in reality. One must look to some future hope or promise *beyond reality* for the same guilt free union with the "good breast." It is the mobilized guilt and anger that will usually prevent any *continuing* massive oral dependency gratification from a single object in reality. If it *does* take place in the guilt-laden individual on a continuing basis, it has to be subtle and part object oriented. It should not be openly verbalized, or confirmed by the therapist. Statements by the therapist such as: "I care for you," or "You are important to me" are utterly trite, nonsensical, and *at best*, worthless. They may very well lead the client to wonder what the therapist is covering up, in his own mind, that necessitates him to say this. One best conveys that the other person *is* important by the very process of *listening* to him. The listener subtly conveys an "I'm with you" type of communication that can't be denied in reality, because it isn't explicit in reality. Reality-wise, the client can't really be sure that the listener *is* "with him" and therefore cannot bring forth the arguments based on the reality of the past, where individuals had *seemed* as though they were "with him", but in fact were *against* him. Finally his own ambivalence is such that it would make it almost impossible for anyone, on a reality basis, to *be* "with him," when there are so many different "hims"! It is made more difficult too, to verbalize oral dependency support when the words of the past deceived, confused and often hurt this individual. And too, dependency has always entrapped him in the past, so that if he now does accept oral dependency gratification, he'll more likely do it if it is subtle, and if he himself can set the emotional distance.

At times, it can become most clear that the client doesn't want anyone "with him." In the following excerpt of a client that admits to suicidal ruminations, "Linda" (his wife) is metaphorical of the unconsciously perceived *caring* aspect of the therapist that apparently is unwanted. "Some mangy cat," and "some old dog" are metaphorical for the guilt-laden aspect of himself, that deserve, he feels, to be "thrown out." "Linda is the type of person that if she finds some stray mangy cat, she'll bring it home with her and care for it, which makes me mad as I'd like to throw the damn thing out. She's doing that now with some old dog she found going down the wrong way on the highway. I wouldn't give a damn if the dog got himself run over and killed! But Linda's got to bring it home, so now we've got that to contend with. If she wasn't this way, I wouldn't have half the problems I've got."

The acceptance of oral dependency need gratification, other than at that infantile level, is usually ambivalent — if not initially in a relationship, it soon becomes this. It does seem less so, though, in the early phase of many therapeutic relationships, where the therapeutic listener is viewed as the wished for "good breast." At this point, it seems as though the therapist can do nothing wrong, and precedes the ambivalent stage when anger is expressed. How confusing this

120

ambivalence can become is shown in one client's remarks: "I get tired of people not listening to me. I want someone to listen to *me* (pause). I don't mean that I want someone to listen *just* to me — I want them to listen to *others* — (pause) but that's just it, they're *not* listening to me, they're listening *too much* to others and not enough to *me*. (Sighs.) I don't know what I'm trying to say, except that I want someone to listen to me (i.e., to meet my oral needs), and I don't want someone to listen to me (i.e., because of my guilt)."

Because the client does feel ambivalent in regard to accepting gratification of his oral needs, the therapeutic listener should not rush in to support the verbalized aspect of the ambivalence that indicates that the client is accepting, or wants to accept, oral need gratification. There seems to be a stage in the client-therapist relationship where, after a period of oral need acceptance, the client will begin to feel the braking action of their guilt, which puts a damper on any further oral "feeding." At this point they ask, within some manifest content: "Do you think I'm asking too much?" Just because the client has to *ask* this, should be evidence enough that they ambivalently feel, on the one hand, that they *are* asking too much, and on the other hand, their unmet needs lead them to feel that they're *not* asking too much. Rather than to give the more logically and reality oriented reply: "You're not asking too much," it is more therapeutic to simply ask: "Well, how do *you* feel about it?" To rush in, impatiently offering support to only one side of the ambivalence, will be met by opposition from another side. By phrasing a question that will get the client to verbalize further, in order that the therapeutic listener can continue to listen, will resolve this ambivalence, in time, in an *emotional* way, which is the *only* way that it *can* be done.

How guilt tends to block oral need gratification will frequently be shown where the guilt is projected, in some metaphorical conceptualization of the problem, as though it is arising not from the client, but from someone else. For instance, one client remarked: "Barbara (a *less* guilt-laden aspect of herself) thinks I'm working too hard in the office, and she wants me to slow down. That's because she likes to sit and talk (i.e. meet her oral needs), and I (a *more* guilt-laden aspect of herself) don't have time for that. I know that there's so much work that has to be done, and so little time to do it. I just don't feel comfortable unless I'm busy at it (a reference to her guilt-derived anhedonia). As long as I keep busy, and don't have time to really think about myself, I do all right. (Note that this client has reduced her *added* unconscious guilt and is functioning well — but her *personality core* guilt is still evident in her anhedonia, and her difficulty in accepting further oral need gratification.) Barbara isn't that way. She could sit and talk all day long, and it wouldn't bother her a bit. I'm not like Barbara (but she *is*, in one unconscious aspect of herself — and that's why Barbara, in reality, *bothers* her). Barbara seems to be able to get away with being like that. If I just sat around and talked, I'd be immediately fired from my job, with my luck. I don't see how Barbara does it. And more importantly, why the boss (therapist) lets her. I couldn't

121

get away with it. (Pause.) My doctor (a perceived aspect of the therapist that is opposite of what was connoted in "boss" above) has put me on a diet. (Therapist: Put you on a diet?) Yes, he says I'm getting too fat, and he wants me to cut down on what I've been eating. I seem to love all the foods (implying that which is especially oral need gratifying) that are not best for me. He's put me on a real low carbohydrate diet — you know, I'm not supposed to eat anything that's really good. (Laughs.) I cut out a cartoon that I'm going to mail to him that shows a woman sitting at a table with a surprised husband. The table is loaded down with all types of delicious food (an analogy for the unconsciously perceived therapeutic transference), and she's saying that the freezer broke down, so she and he have to eat up all the food. I guess that's what I'd *like* to do, but then I've got to do what the doctor wants."

The resistance to oral need gratification that comes about because of the level of the unconscious guilt is often metaphorically presented in analogies involving dieting, giving up tranquilizers, stopping smoking, discontinuing active memberships in church, clubs, bowling team, or terminating relationships with certain individuals, including breaking an engagement, dropping a "steady" or getting a divorce. They may present analogies of dropping a course at college, quitting a business, or stopping some type of activity that offered the opportunity to be oral need gratifying. Presentation of stopping any thing that is pleasurable often aptly carries the reality that it is immoral, illegal, fattening or bad for one's health. An example of this is where a client says: "I've given up smoking at work . . . I use to take a break when I smoked . . . Now I work and get a lot more done . . . When I smoked, it just showed lack of control." Many times the dilemma of being caught between the *desire* for oral need gratification, and the *guilt* from the oral dependency needs, is presented as a fear of the possibility of having an affair, of having met a person that *wants* to have an affair, or of actually having an affair. In situations like this, the therapist must be extremely careful not to give verbalized support to any involvement that might not be in the client's best interest, in reality, but at the same time not act judgmental.

Sometimes the resistance to oral need gratification that arises from the unconscious guilt is expressed metaphorically as coming directly from the client and not from someone else as it is above. This will often show some interesting implications in regard to the client's earlier life as it does in the following: "I don't agree with the way my wife (i.e. the therapist) is trying to raise the children (his oral needs). I mean I was never raised that way! I don't understand her reason for letting them run all over the place. They get into everything (i.e. they get into his guilt) and that bothers me. I was never allowed to do that. I couldn't even go into the living room, and my mother (implying an oral need frustrating aspect of the therapist) never wanted me in the kitchen. My wife lets the children go where they want in the house. She likes to have them in the kitchen with her. I feel there's a place for children — where they can't be heard and preferably where they can't be seen, as well. I feel a lot more comfortable when they're controlled. That's for sure! (Pause.) Another thing that bothers me is that she'll keep them sitting at the table, even though they're not hungry. I don't see why they can't leave the table if they don't feel like eating. She'll go around to them saying: 'Eat your meat up; don't you want some more vegetables?; let me get you some more potatoes.' Then she always gives them sweet things, which I don't think is good for their teeth. If a person wants good strong teeth, they shouldn't eat sweets (and it *is* true that one does develop a better "bite" if he has less of the "good breast"). I will say that I owe it to *my* childhood, and the way that *I* was brought up, that *I've* got such good teeth."

It doesn't help the client to have it interpreted to him that his resistance to oral need gratification is due to an unconscious level of guilt. Since this guilt has unconsciously arisen from past emotional processes involving part objects, it can only be reduced in a similar unconscious fashion. Because it is unconscious and part object oriented, the therapeutic listener needs only to keep the relationship on-going for the process of guilt reduction to naturally take place. Questions on the part of the therapist that are appropriate for the manifest content being presented can frequently be oral need supportive. This can be illustrated, for instance, in the client, who during a therapy session, remarked: "I talked with my sales manager last week. (Therapist: "Dick was down?") Yes, he was — with all the people you see and have to remember, it surprises me you can even recall who my manager is!" (The therapist makes a habit of keeping track of the manifest content of each of his clients, in that each client's problem is being latently presented through metaphor and analogy, as well as being latently resolved.) In asking this question, the therapeutic listener conveys to the client that the therapist is very much "with him" in what he is presenting, and at the same time implies a significance to what is being presented in the face of the client's guilt-derived tendency to feel his verbalizations are trivia. The undeniable "I'm with you" type of feeling that is conveyed rests safely within a comfortable emotional distance that is set by the reality of the manifest content. If the therapist must verbalize, it is always more supportive if he either paraphrases what was just said by the client, or asks a reality oriented meaningful question that might allow the client then to expand the presentation of his feelings in what he is metaphorically presenting in regard to the latently perceived transference situation. To stay within the manifest content without implying anything different than what has been presented, or implied, by the client, is the safest road to take in regard to verbalizations of the therapist. It is often effective, at times, to take the *opposing* side of what has been presented or implied, and, still staying within the manifest content, ask a leading question. The apparent comprehension of the client's emotional problem, in all its ramifications, is often oral need gratifying to the client.

123

Through the listening process, the oral dependency needs of the client are met. And the client, in his metaphorical manifest content, will frequently show indications that there has been an oral incorporation of the symbolic "good breast" of the therapeutic listener. This is illustrated, for instance, in a previously depressed client who, after just a few sessions, remarks: "I have to go up to Baltimore, which I've been dreading as there are parts of that city that just aren't safe! I've always hated to be alone in that city, but now I've found out that Bill (the unconsciously perceived oral need gratifying aspect of the therapist) is going up there the same time that I'm going. So he and I are going up *together*. It turns out that what I was dreading I'm now looking forward to. We have such a good time together, as we seem to enjoy each other."

What was illustrated above, is shown again in the excerpt of a woman who became depressed following the sudden death of her husband. She came for six sessions of therapeutic listening, and then remarked: "Well, I've had a pretty good week. I've been getting along pretty good, but I've found out that I get along best if someone is with me. I didn't feel that way at first, as I didn't want anyone around me. But I've recently met this woman (therapist) that's got the same problem that I have, and we seem to understand each other. I think one has to go through losing a spouse before they can really know what it's like. No one else can possibly understand. (Therapist: Thats right.) She's been a big help to me, and I don't know what I would have done if I hadn't met her. I've been hating to go to my mother-in-law's (the therapist — perceived with different connotions), as she always gets to talking about the past, and bringing up stuff that I'd rather not hear about. I want to forget about all that morbid stuff, but she is always dwelling on the past, so I've been kind of keeping away from her as much as possible. This past week when I went to see her, I brought my friend over. It really helped to have her along, because instead of bringing up all this morbid stuff that she usually does, she didn't. We all enjoyed ourselves, and I was glad I had Nancy with me. (Smiles warmly at the therapist.) Nancy and I decided to go out to a church supper last Sunday. The food wasn't anything elaborate, but was just good home cooking, which I actually prefer. I haven't wanted to eat since Bill died, so I haven't had any home cooking. The neighbors brought over a lot at the time Bill died (note the oral psychodynamics of bringing, and eating food at a wake, as though symbolizing a *substitution* for the lost oral dependency gratification, and the underlying oral *significance* of the bread, in the Christian communion) but *they* ate it. I couldn't (bcause of her guilt). There was home cooked chicken and dumplings, candied sweet potatoes, and fresh strawberries for dessert. Oh, how I dearly love fresh strawberries. (Smiles warmly again at therapist.) I don't think I've eaten this much since before my husband passed away. It was so good. I understand we ate at the best church too, for one of those church suppers. I hear there are a couple of churches in town — but I don't want to say which ones they are — where I understand the food isn't very good. (This is *not* a latent

124

reference to her therapist's psychiatric colleagues — but a reference to other aspects of the therapeutic transference that she perceives in a bad light.) I actually know of a couple of people (she, herself) who got sick from the food. But this church I can highly recommend as the food was delicious. It reminded me a lot of home, when I was a little girl, sitting at the table with mother bringing on all that chicken and dumplings. (Pause.) I had to laugh when I was at the table because some members of the Happy Time Club were there (referring to perceived aspects of herself in relation to the therapist), and apparently they were dating. (Laughs warmly.) These were people in their sixties and seventies who had lost their spouses, and they were actually dating. Can you imagine that? I could hardly believe it! They acted like school kids on a date with their steadies. (Laughs warmly.) But I think it did me good to see them enjoying themselves like that. It gave me a lift, and I guess I needed that. There's no cure for loneliness like a human being. But don't get me wrong, I have no intention of getting involved with any male suitors. I've got one fellow (another perceived aspect of the therapist) that seems to think that's what I need. I'm managing to stay *away* from him, and let me tell *you*, I'm going to keep on. (Pause.) Things are going very well at work. I had a fellow (still another perceived aspect of the therapist) call me up, and he didn't say who he was. Just that alone would have upset me before. He asked if I was getting along all right and whether I needed any help. I told him 'none at all' (a denial of her oral need). I finally recognized his voice. (Laughs.) He's someone that works with me. He's happily married, so he's no threat to me. We must have talked for an hour about this and that. I know his wife quite well. ("Wife" is metaphorical for herself, in part, and this is well born out later in the manifest content when she elaborates on this woman's apparent shortcomings.) I really appreciated his asking about me, and I told him that I did appreciate his call. I've got some real nice co-workers. (Smiles warmly at therapist during a comfortable pause.) My little nieces and my nephews (metaphorical for the therapist with still different connotations) called last night, and they want me to come and visit them this June. I'm really looking forward to seeing them, as they're so much fun to be with."

Evidence that oral dependency gratification is being perceived may be metaphorically presented in either self-references, or references about other people that indicate increased self-esteem, self-confidence, feelings of security, and increased ability to express themselves. These metaphors and analogies indicate the client is involved emotionally with many people. Inanimate objects are described as less flawed, or worth more. A house may be described as coming along very nicely. Things are growing, increasing, multiplying, going up in value, etc. When a client does use the first person in presenting his feelings. opinions and impressions, it is well to remember he is only presenting one aspect of his ambivalent unconscious. There are many other facets of this ambivalence. and these are often presented as though arising from other people as: *"I enjoy* so much coming here to talk to you, but my *husband* is so much against it, and wants me to stop."

The analogies and metaphorical presentations of increased oral dependency gratification from the therapeutic listener are often verbalized in the manifest content in a variety of different ways. It may present itself as becoming more active in the church, joining a club or fraternal organization, spending more time in recreation, or becoming more and regularly involved in some extra-therapy interpersonal relationship, or with a group. Getting married, dating, going steady or palling around are often metaphorically used to conceptualize the drawing of more oral need gratification from the therapist, and may be presented as an observation of one's self, or about someone else. Sometimes it is presented not from a personal reference, but from a second person standpoint as: "The baby is eating more. I was so worried how *little* she was eating before, but now it seems as though she'll eat *anything.*" One client spent a session describing how her husband put up a bird feeder, and "how the squirrels have been eating twenty pounds of bird seed a month, much to my husband's dismay." She had previously mentioned, when more guilt-laden: "I hate myself for liking to come down here and talk." Second person presentations of increased oral gratification may involve, for instance, descriptions of how a student is doing better in school . . . "He really likes the teacher he's got this semester." If the client has been put on a mild tranquilizer by the family physician, she may remark that she is now taking it regularly, and may not show the "side effects," or the resistance, she initially had. There may be analogic presentations of a work situation where the implication is that the client is enjoying work, receiving more benefits, or getting a raise in pay.

Manifest content verbalizations presented from a second person standpoint, presented as an observation about some inanimate object or experience, can convey the confirmation of oral need gratification just as easily as if it were presented in the first person. For instance, a client may remark: "I met a person that lately has been going regularly to church that seems to have the same interests I do — we get a chance to spend some time with each other afterwards, and I find myself enjoying talking to him." This same communication might have been expressed as: "Annabelle is doing a lot better in school since she befriended another third grader during recess time. It's *just* the thing that was needed for her, as she felt so much alone before. She was always feeling left out, and that no one really cared about her. She felt at first she *had* to go to school because it was her duty and responsibility to go. Now she goes because she's learned that going to school can be *enjoyable.* She wants to have this little girl over after school, and I don't see why she can't."

What is conveyed in the analogies above might have been presented in a manifest content of still another client: "The new garage is coming along very nicely. I think it's going to be a real asset to the property, though at first I didn't think so.

The roof has been laid already, and they're starting to put the siding on. It's going to be so much easier on everyone in the family when the garage is finished. I think a lot of the conflicts were because we didn't *have* a garage. Now there will be more room for the children's toys, and a place for them to play on rainy days. My husband wants to set up a little workshop in it, as he loves to putter around with making things."

In the following excerpt, a client presents her unconscious perception of oral need gratification in a religious orientation: "When I felt that other people didn't accept me, I felt God didn't either. Then I met the minister's wife. She had meant a lot to me in just being able to talk, and to be myself around her. I use to feel, before, that people were pushing me away — like they didn't want me around. But she's helped me to accept myself. I can talk to her like I can't to anyone else. I think that just throwing things out in the open with her has helped me an awful lot. I even told her what I was feeling guilty about. And she accepted it when I couldn't accept it myself. I've got now where I can speak out and say what I really feel, while before I wouldn't. It's because *she* listens that I know *God* does. It's because of *her* that I've found God!"

As metaphorical evidence of increased oral dependency gratication, consider the following excerpt: "The garden is coming along very nicely. Two months ago I was ready to let the whole thing go to weeds. Nothing was going right (referring in the manifest content to her garden, but implying much more than this, *latently*). There wasn't enough rain, and what did come up, in such poor soil, either the rabbits (her destructive oral needs) ate it or it simply shrivelled up (a reference to the perceived paucity of guilt-free oral gratification). I had just about given up on it. But you should see it now. (Smiles warmly.) The marigolds are all in bloom, bushy and hardy. I never dreamed it would turn out so well. I think I owe a lot of the success with this garden to my husband. At first he didn't care whether I wanted a garden or not. It was 'Sure, you can have a garden — but *you* do all the work yourself.' I've done most of the weeding. But he's done a lot of the other things for it. He's fertilized it, watered it very regularly, sprayed it for bugs, edged it with a fence to keep the rabbits out, and clipped the dead blossoms to keep the flowers blooming. He says it's his way of relaxing. And I think he's telling the truth, as he never did like to work. (Laughs.) My neighbor (therapist) was over last week admiring it, and she's been wanting me to join the garden club. I have to laugh because I always thought I couldn't grow anything. It's been a real surprise to me, how well it's come along, and I think it's been a big boost to my ego and morale to know I can do a thing like this. I've really enjoyed it. It's been something I didn't really *have* to do. It was something that I just got interested in, little by little. I intend to keep on with it. I've already picked out a few plants for next year that I didn't dare get involved with this year, as I've heard that they are so difficult to grow in this climate, but I think I'll give them a try."

The following spontaneously presented manifest content conveys a latent statement of fact that oral need gratification is taking place within the therapeutic transference: "The class trip to Philadelphia turned out to be a big success. Before I went I was having a lot of second thoughts as to why I volunteered myself into taking the children (a latent reference to her oral needs) on that trip. But I was surprised how it all turned out. A couple of the teachers (i.e. therapist) told me later that they had heard how well I handled the children. Even the principal (the therapist with other connotations), who sat like a stone-faced old Buddha at the back of the bus, congratulated me. The children really did have a good time. They all sang together (latently referring to perceived mutual dependency with the therapist) on the way up and back, and I told them some stories too. I could sense there was a real togetherness there. I must say I worried about them at the museum. They climbed all over the statue of Ben Franklin (the therapist with still different connotations), which would have been blasphemy if I had done that as a child. I wasn't even allowed to talk in that museum back then. We took that togetherness we had on the bus right into that museum, and I think everybody got a lot more out of it. I talked about what the statues and the different things meant in history, and even the teachers were listening. I told them what the Liberty Bell represented, and how even though it was cracked, it meant so much more for being that way. I told them that crack stood for all that the bell went through in attaining what it symbolized in man's freedom to express himself. (Therapist: That's right.) I think I enjoyed myself as much as the children did. When the class bought me a little gift afterwards, it really surprised me. They didn't have to do it, but I guess they appreciated what I did."

Although one can give excerpts indicating "pure" oral need gratification, it is necessary to emphasize that the gratification or oral needs is usually ambivalent, and that a sequence of verbalizations will indicate this. The client may verbalize an analogy for an unconsciously perceived aspect of the therapeutic transference that indicates that oral gratification is taking place, but then present another analogy indicating that the therapist is being perceived not as the "good breast", but the "bad breast." Perhaps it is that one can never have a life situation, like the one of the guilt-free infant early in life, feeding off the "good breast." The transference, and the necessary projection of guilt, will make any "good breast" bad! Presentations may indicate oral need "feeding," but others will indicate that guilt projection and anger expression is taking place. There must be this perception of "bad breasts" that comes about through guilt projection for the guilt to be decreased, allowing still more oral need gratification. The following excerpt illustrates this ambivalence in oral need gratification within the therapeutic transference. "I'm really enjoying my driving class. At first, I was so leery of it, and felt sure that I wouldn't be able to continue with it, because I usually get so nervous and up-tight. On the last test, I got an 'A.' My instructor was real proud of me. She told me so. (Smiles warmly at therapist, and he returns it.) I can tell she thinks a lot of me, and of course, I think the world of her. (Smiles warmly again.) She told me that if I continued much longer in the class she was going to adopt me. (Laughs.) I wouldn't mind being her daughter either! She's so understanding, so patient and so consistent. She never gets angry, even when I make mistakes. She makes learning to drive so much fun. She's just the *opposite* from my father. (And here she introduces the opposing facet of her ambivalence.) I was out practicing driving with him the other day (a reference to therapy), and he was on me all the way. I like to take my time, and I don't like to be hurried. But he had to get me all upset, right in the middle of traffic, when I was trying to make a left hand turn: 'Go ahead! Go ahead! What are you waiting for? Do you want to get smashed in the rear! You've got the right of way! Get going!' That got me all shook up and I stalled the car in the middle of the on-coming lane. Then he really got on me. He said I was the worst driver he ever saw, and that if I was going to act that way, I shouldn't even have a license. He said that I was nothing but a typical woman driver. He always has to put me down. Whenever he's with me in a practice driving session, he's putting me down for something I'm not doing right. Even when he just looks at me, I can tell he's criticizing me. I wasn't even sitting right in the car, according to him, and we hadn't even begun to drive anywhere! I've never been able to do anything right to please him. Yet, I've got to have him with me, as the law requires that I have an adult with me in the car as long as I only have a learner's permit. And no one else in the family has a driver's license. (Therapist: You should have put him in the trunk then.) Why didn't I think of that! (Laughs warmly.) That's where he belongs. (Laughs again and then becomes serious.) Getting him into the trunk would be like belling the proverbial cat!"

As another example of the ambivalence in oral gratification, a client who previously was subject to anxiety attacks remarked: "I went to that damn dentist (a latent reference to the therapist) again last week. God, I hated to go! He wants me to have regular appointment with him so he can get all my teeth capped, and all my cavities filled (implying: "he's going to take care of my guilt"). I've come to the conclusion he thinks it's somehow unethical for him to simply pull the bad teeth and be done with them. He wants me to undergo all these dental procedures that will probably, I'm afraid, take the rest of my life to complete (the conscious fear, but the unconscious wish). I have a feeling he doesn't *ever* want to discharge me, but wants me to keep coming again and again. I was kidding him last week that if I kept on seeing him this often that the people in town will be thinking I'm having an affair with him! (Laughs warmly.) I do like him. He's very gentle, patient and seems to show a lot of interest in me. He's got one of those modern drills that doesn't hurt — at least, *he* doesn't think so. And all the time he's drilling out a cavity, he's talking to me about what I've been doing the past week. He knows me better now than my own mother! I think, if I let myself, I'd even *enjoy* going to see him. (Laughs.) That must show how *bad* off I am, if I'm *enjoying* going to a dentist. I keep asking myself: 'What makes you run back and forth to him when your teeth stopped aching a long time ago?' I wish Doctor Oakes would realize that if he pulled all my teeth he wouldn't have to bother with me and he could spend his time on somebody younger and prettier, instead of wasting it on some old hag like myself with a bunch of rotten teeth! My husband (she, herself) is having a fit about my going to him, too. It's costing me something every week, and I feel guilty about having money (guilt imbued oral dependency) spent on me. My husband calls him "Ole Call-again Oakes" and thinks he's just taking me for a ride for what he can get out of me. Sometimes I wonder, myself, what he's trying to accomplish. I told him that I didn't think my teeth were worth fixing up, but he insists on correcting my bite. My teeth never did come together (a latent reference to her past inability to express any anger), but that doesn't dismay him. I ought to just quit and go to another dentist, but I keep remembering that I haven't had a toothache since I first saw him, and I wouldn't want to have another like that last one I had that just about drove me right out of my mind!"

Another client, who was referred for psychotherapy because of a multiplicity of vague abdominal complaints that did not respond to one internist's regimen of diet and drugs, remarked: "My stomach has been a lot better since I went to see Doctor Williamson (therapist) last week. I only wish now that I had gone to see him before. He told me that I had a small hiatus hernia and couldn't understand at all why I was sent to a *psychiatrist*. Why the other doctors (guilt-imbued aspects of the therapist) didn't recognize this is beyond me. I just have no faith at all in *any* of the doctors in this town. They're not the least bit interested in their patient's uncomfortableness, but just how much money they can get out of them. They'll see you (here "you" means she, herself) for only a certain length of time, and then they show you the door and put you out. It doesn't make any difference to them whether they're made you comfortable or not, or whether they've even found out what the trouble is. It's ' out you go.' Doctor Williamson isn't like that at all. He explains everything to me. He made a little drawing for me to show how the wrong food (guilt-laden oral dependency) can back up into the esophagus and cause burning and discomfort. He said it could even cause pain like I had, though in most people apparently it doesn't (which *is* true, since most people have *less* guilt). He told me about some foods I should avoid, and certain actions like bending over. He thought I was doing entirely too much bending. He also said I should sleep on an extra pillow at night so that the stomach contents wouldn't have a chance to go up into the esophagus. He explained that with my sensitive esophagus I had better be very careful about not eating too much. (Therapist: One does have to be careful with a hiatus hernia.) He never seems hurried. He won't even answer the phone if it rings in the office when I'm with him (yet this same characteristic of the therapist is frequently used by clients expressing anger at the unavailability of the therapist). He pulled up a chair right beside me and seemed

130

so genuinely interested in me. I'm not going back to see that other internist ever again, but I'll keep on with Doctor Williamson.''

The opportunity for oral gratification is unconsciously perceived as being offered within the therapeutic transference, but because of the client's guilt it is largely refused. This seems well illustrated in metaphor and analogy by the following excerpt: "I went down to my folks' last week. I really didn't want to go, but since they *are* my parents I thought I should. My father (an unconscious aspect of she, herself, in metaphor that she attempts to deny) is getting worse. Each week I'm there I can see how bad off he really is. If I don't go down there, I somehow put it out of my mind. It's uncomfortable for me to see him the way he is. In fact, it's very upsetting. He doesn't even know who I am (a reference to her own psychological problem that arises from the intensity of her ambivalent feelings). I was Karen last week, but I didn't even bother to correct him. I used to say, when he'd get me mixed up with my sisters: 'No, Dad, I'm *not* Karen, I'm Mary Lou!' He'd say: 'Why of course! How could I make such a mistake!' He's so confused and disoriented! He's always having trouble finding the bathroom, and he'll go in circles before he ends up in the right place. Last week he didn't. He went out on the porch and urinated over the railing (perhaps a reference to unveiling her guilt in the previous session). I don't know what the neighbors (aspects of the therapist) must have thought about that. I just hate being associated with all that. I don't know how my mother (the therapist again in metaphor, but in a more accepting light than that conveyed in "neighbors") can put up with him, but she does. She never complains and takes it all in stride, like she's been used to it for years. She's always glad to see me, gives me a big hug and tells me I've been staying away entirely too much. She knows it isn't easy for me to come. She expects me down there at least twice a week, and can't seem to understand that as a school teacher I've got other things to do besides running down there. She's always baking up everything I love to eat. I try to tell her I'm on a diet, so I won't look as fat and ugly as I do (this client is, in fact, quite attractive). She's always trying to get me to eat something. It's 'Oh, Mary Lou, have some of this cake I just baked . . . I made it just for you!' It looks so good I can't resist. Then she has to run out the cookies, the home-made fudge, and all the other things I'm trying to stay clear of. I tell her 'Mother, *I'm not hungry!*', but she loads me up with more than enough to last a month! And if that's not enough, she'll give me a plate of food to take back to my apartment with me. 'Here, Mary Lou, take this along. I know you're not getting enough to eat in that lonely place of yours.' I either take the plate and dump it out on the way home, or else I give it to an old half-starved dog (herself, in metaphor) that lives next door that never seems to get enough to eat. I told her I throw away half the stuff she gives me, but she keeps right on. She'll search through her refrigerator looking for some food she thinks I can't resist. Her pantry is always filled. I'd hate for her to see *my* refrigerator. All I've got in it, right now, is the left-over roast she gave me last week, and my jar of peanut butter. I never was a big eater since I went away to college."

Another client presents her perception of offered oral dependency need gratification as: "I don't like Frank (her husband, but the therapist in metaphor) going with me to do the shopping. Whenever he's along, I always end up with groceries I never wanted at all. I'm trying to stay on a budget. I only get the bare essentials for the family, but he'll go up and down the aisles looking at all those exotic and too expensive foods that I try to avoid. When I go to the store, I try to get what I need and no more, then get out as quickly as possible. Not Frank — he wants to linger around the shelves examining all the different kinds of canned goods and wanting me to try this and that. He'll say: 'Say, look at this . . . I bet this is real good! Let's give it a try!' Frankly, what he has usually turns my stomach with just the thought of eating it. I never was much on trying new or different foods. I mean, I always ate because one was *supposed* to eat in order to live. Maybe that goes back to my childhood when we didn't have much in the way of food (note the latent implications here). Times were hard, and I often went to bed without anything to eat. Frank feels eating should be a pleasure. But I'm *afraid* to let myself go. Because I *didn't* have enough food as a child, I'm afraid I'll become a regular *glutton* now. I've seen too many people get fat and repulsive from eating too much. I watch very carefully what I eat, but with him bringing home the food like he does, it's getting more and more difficult to do."

Similar to the above, another housewife and mother of a teenager, presents her own unconscious problem of feared *uncontrolled* oral need gratification with the therapist: "I don't know what I'm going to do with Beth (she, herself in metaphor). She's in love — at least *she* thinks she is. She's found this boy (the therapist in metaphor) in her Algebra class that, according to her, is God's own gift to womanhood. He's all she can think about from the time she gets up in the morning to the time she goes to bed at night. For all I know, she probably dreams about him. He is a nice boy, I guess. He comes from a nice family, seems polite, and treats Beth with respect. But then one can be fooled by that type. (Therapist: That's right.) I don't mind her seeing him occasionally, but I don't want it to go any further than it is right now. He wants to take her out every Friday night (a latent reference to the expected regularity of therapy sessions), and I know she's old enough to be having dates and *should* be dating boys. But if she keeps on seeing him, the relationship is bound to deepen. You know that. I don't want her to be getting into the trouble I went through when I was her age. Yet I don't want to prevent her from having the fun she should have as a teenager. I missed all that with my having to get married at seventeen. I never had what I want her to have. (Therapist: I understand.) But how do I let her have this, *without* going through what I went through! As it is now, all she can talk about is how wonderful he is. Maybe I should let her date him regularly, and then she'll find out in time that he's *not* as wonderful as she *thinks* he is!"

Sometimes, oral need gratification is latently acknowledged as perceived, but with the implication that there is a reluctance to grant it, by the therapist. This represents a projection, by the client, of her own guilt-derived resistance to the therapist. This is illustrated by the client who complains about her husband: "He (therapist) gets on me because I bought myself a ball of yarn for $1.39 (analogy for this much oral need gratification). When I told him I was going shopping today, he said: 'What are you going shopping again for? You just went the other day!' Sure I went. But I didn't even buy anything for myself. I got Sharon (one small aspect of herself) a little dress that was on sale that she absolutely needed, but he was mad about that. He was mad last week because I bought an antique table for five dollars. It was the first thing I've bought for a year, and then I was going to fix it up for *him* to use as a smoking stand. *He* can buy a new camera, fishing rod, etc. That's all right. But I can't even buy a ball of yarn without his getting all upset over it (cries). I didn't think the purchase of a ball of yarn was being *that* extravagant. But apparently it is to him. And if it is, I'd rather go without it, than have to go through all he put me through. I guess I'm not supposed to get anything myself. I wanted the yarn; I was going to make myself a scarf. He says I'm being selfish. And *I don't know — maybe I am.*"

The following excerpt latently implies that the client knows that an opportunity for oral need gratification from the therapist *is* being offered, but like the previous client, she can't accept it because of her guilt. "I enjoyed having Billy Jo visit with me last week (a reference to the emotional closeness of the preceeding therapy session) . . . I haven't seen her since nursing school. But it kind of tired me out . . . not that she's any problem . . . don't get me wrong . . . but I felt a pressure when she was with me. (Pause.) She wanted us to get together again for a coming nursing school reunion. She thinks I'd have lots of fun seeing my old girl friends (note the implication here of that guilt-derived "can't win for losing" feeling). I've just accepted it. Our problems are financial ones right now. I'm always worried we don't have enough money to live on, yet Henry goes out and buys things for himself. (Sighs.) I wish I liked private duty. I cout get $30 per day (here the money apparently represents a metaphor, relating to the recognition of a possible increase in her oral need gratification, if she would accept "private duty" — a reference to the therapy situation). But private duty makes me feel so uncomfortable. I can't stand to spend my time with one person. (Squirms in chair.) I want to be able to leave a person and go on to the next one, like I do in general duty . . . but the pay (oral gratification) isn't anywhere as good. Whenever I have to sit with a person for any length of time, I feel the walls closing in on me. (Therapist: I understand it's not easy for you.) I just can't help it. (Long pause as she shifts frequently in her chair.) Henry wants to remodel the kitchen (perhaps a reference to ego reconstruction). It really does need doing over, but it's going to cost a lot more than what we both planned on (a latent reference to the amount of resistance from her guilt, and the immensity of her oral needs, which *she* feels, and what she feels, *the therapist* feels — thus the "we"). I don't know whether we should go ahead with it or not. If I *liked* private duty, and could do it, we could have the kitchen remodeled. But I *don't* and that's the problem!"

In the following excerpt, the latent implication is made that the therapist *is* granting oral dependency need gratification, but only half of what she asks. The client acknowledges getting some gratification, but projects the resistance to obtaining as much as she is asking to the therapist. Note that if she were less guilty, she could logically ask for more than she would actually need, and would, if her husband is as consistent as the way she presents him, get, then, an adequate amount. But the solution to her problem can't be solved in such a logical way. By continuing to let her "feed," within the therapeutic transference, she will eventually get enough of the "good breast" that she can express her anger and diminish the guilt that makes her feel, in part, that her demands are excessive. "He thinks I'm always wasting his hard-earned money (his granting oral need gratification) on myself. He begrudges every little bit of money he's ever given me. I asked him last month for a hundred dollars to pay the monthly living expenses. He only gave me fifty dollars. He's always been like that. I mean, if I told him I *had* to have fifty dollars for something I, or the children, absolutely needed, then he would give twenty five dollars. If I told him I *had* to have twenty five, then he'd give me exactly twelve dollars and fifty cents!"

Another client latently acknowledges the offering of oral need gratification by the therapist, but her unconscious guilt apparently blocks her from fully accepting it. She presents this as: "Sure, Dale has been a lot more attentive to me lately. He took me out to the movies last Friday night (a complex metaphor for an unconsciously perceived aspect of the therapeutic transference) which was the first time he's done that in the past three years (her involvement with the previously perceived aspect of the therapist that didn't allow a gratification of her oral needs may have seemed like "three years," but in reality was only six weeks). He's been helping me with the dishes at meal times and he even bought me a bouquet of flowers on Saturday. He calls me regularly at noontime, which he never did before, and asks me how things are going. I appreciate what he's been doing lately, but I don't think he really *means* it and I know it's not going to last. He's been this way before, and then slipped right back into his old ways again, just the minute I start accepting him as changed. I'd rather not have him like he is now if I know that I'm just going to be let down again, because then I'm *worse* off than if he *wasn't* this way! Do you understand? (Therapist: I see.) I think he's just doing it to make me forget all the trouble we've been through during the past year. He wants me to forget all that, and just go on as though it never even happened, so he can act the way he did before. I'm supposed to forgive him and forget. But I can't do it. I can't accept him playing the role of a good little husband when I know he doesn't mean it."

Once again, the "good breast" of the therapeutic transference is over-shadowed by reflections of the "bad breast" of the emotional past, for the guilt of the client puts a damper on the amount of oral need gratification now possible.

Here, a previously shy and withdrawn twenty year old male, who had to discontinue college, talks about his job in a feed mill, while simultaneously presenting his feelings about himself, the therapist and the therapeutic transference. "Before I started working there, I had trouble meeting people. I felt so self-conscious and so inadequate. But this job has helped me. I feel much less inadequate now, and it's because I've picked up some of my boss's mannerisms. He advocates a ready smile, a hearty handshake (the therapist doesn't shake his client's hand unless it is first offered by a client, but this analogy is appropriate for what is being presented in regard to "fake" friendliness), and a listening ear. He tries to get his customer to talk, in order to find out what his interests are . . . you know . . . something the customer might be interested in. He wants to get them talking about themselves, about their likes and dislikes, or about what they're involved in. He said he could tell how good a customer they are from how much they talk to him. He doesn't come right out and ask what they think of the company. He told me that if he did that, he wouldn't believe what they said anyway. He tries to find out from little things they say — you know, from inferences and implications. I know he thinks he puts out the finest feed in the state. (Laughs and therapist does too.) He seems like the friendly, talkative, easy-going business man, but he's shrewd. I know, because I've been noticing how he operates. He's always interested in the business. That's first and foremost with him. Even though he looks like he's enjoying small-talking about fishing, playing golf, putting in a new lawn, or anything else with a person who likes to do these things, he's still got an ear cocked for the business. His eye is always on how much feed he can sell, no matter what. I know, because sometimes he'll say, after a customer has left, when we're both alone: 'How'd I do?' Sometimes he'll say: 'That guy sure can talk an arm off me' (to make this a reflection of a castration problem is to miss entirely the implication of the client's self-felt immense, destructive, and guilt-laden *oral* needs). He does have customers like that, you know . . . ones that seem to take advantage of him. They'll just sit around and talk about anything, yet he won't let on that he's bored. He'll put up that false front, and he'll lay on his little techniques to give the person the feeling he really enjoys them. (Therapist: You mean you think he's a fake?) Well, not really . . . I mean I know from experience, from watching him, and from working right along with him, that he does use little techniques to establish and then to build a working relationship, but I don't think I would call it fakery. There is a little artificial acting on his part . . . you know, a little covering up of feelings on his part. I know he wouldn't be as successful as he is if he didn't. But he puts a wall up between him and me. I don't want to be like him, yet I'm taking on his ways. I want to be more genuine and more uncalculating. (Therapist: Sure.) I don't want to be using people, and I don't like people to use me. That's what I mean. When he tries to get the other person to talk, I know

135

what he's doing. For instance, I've seen him bring up a subject that he knows a person is interested in, and then use it to get the person to talk. That's the way, he says, he keeps his customers. For instance, if he knows the customer is a golfer, he'll greet him: 'How's that golf game going?' If the person likes to fish, he'll ask: 'How're they biting?' Then he goes on to ask all about the bait, where the fishing spots are, and so forth. According to him, one *has* to do it for the business. I say it's manipulating the customer. Most of the time the customers don't know he's doing it. It's a veneer, a cover-up — but it's not being *entirely* a fake. He *is* interested in golf, and he *is* interested in fishing, but I know it's all *secondary* to the business. Do you see what I mean? (Therapist: I understand.) Someday I'd like to disagree with him, but I don't think I could do it now. It would be too uncomfortable and I'm too dependent on him for a job. I'd like to be able to tell him directly that I don't like the way he manipulates other people's emotions. I'd like to tell him that anyone that friendly and that much interested in other people reminds me of the "Marcus Welby, M.D." type that seems so nice, so understanding and so much concerned with others, but is just a professional front that covers up what his wife (he, himself, in metaphor) is all too familiar with. I always turn Marcus Welby off whenever I can."

CHAPTER 7

UNCONSCIOUS GUILT AND THE BLOCKING OF ANGER EXPRESSION

In the preceeding chapter we have seen that guilt can block the gratification of the oral dependency needs. The individual fears orally gratifying relationships, and the oral needs become imbued with the connotation that they are *destructive* . . . destructive to the very object on whom dependency is being drawn. This unconscious feeling tends to promote a withdrawal from part object or object relationships that might have provided the needed extra oral gratification in the face of orally frustrating circumstances of life. The oral incorporative process is avoided so that the individual neither feeds off the unconsciously perceived "good breasts" of his interpersonal relationships, nor bites the frustrating "bad breasts" of these same interpersonal relationships. The unconscious guilt, not only blocks oral gratification then, but it will also block anger expression as well.

We saw earlier that the unconscious guilt may take the form of a primordial *personality core guilt*, which was formed in the developmental period of an individual's psychological growth, and the more recently *added unconscious guilt*. Both are due to oral need frustration, but one is from the distant past, and the other is of more recent origin. The personality core guilt is, of course, greater, the more there was a frustration of the oral needs earlier in life, with an inability to express the resulting anger. Guilt derives itself from this *repressed anger*. The ego defense mechanisms that make up the personality attempt to handle this guilt. In times of later stress and oral need frustration, there will be added unconscious guilt. This is because that earlier primordial guilt will cause the anger, from the recently perceived frustration, to be repressed.

The defense mechanisms become more strained with the addition of this more recently added unconscious guilt. Much of what has been termed *"psychiatric symptoms"* are simply the manifestations of this emotional uncomfortableness that arises from added guilt. Personalities, that tend in their make-ups to be paranoid, or projectors of guilt, become *more* so with the added guilt. Those that tended toward obsessive-compulsiveness as a manner of handling their primordial guilt become even more so with their additional guilt. Those that tended toward toward self-felt guilt have increasing feelings of inferiority, inadequacy and unacceptableness to others, and will manifest this in their verbal and non-verbal behavior. Fears of impending death, occult fatal illnesses, or pre-occupation with one's physical health increase as the unconscious guilt increases. The added guilt often manifests itself as exaggerations of the previous ways that the ego tended to use before in the handling of its primordial personality guilt. It is interesting to analyze the hallucinations and delusions of people admitted in a most emotionally uncomfortable state at psychiatric hospitals. They show most clearly the manifestations of this guilt and the attempts of the unconscious ego to handle it. These attempts usually represent intensities in the previous manner of handling the earlier guilt.

Those individuals with *more* personality core guilt will have *more* of a tendency to repress anger in times of later oral need frustration, and therefore will have *more* of a tendency to *add* unconscious guilt. Because of an excessive personality core guilt, individuals may not have a wide enough sphere of interpersonal relationships from which to draw oral need gratification from a great many part objects. Their oral need gratification is often only tenuously held, more concentrated in a small number of objects, and as such, they are more prone to frustration.

Opposed to the individual that undergoes more oral need frustration earlier in life, and has more of a personality core guilt to deal with, the individual with *less* personality core guilt is *less* likely to be adding unconscious guilt later in life. This is so because he has a wide enough sphere of part objects from which to draw oral need gratification, and a wide enough variety of part objects to project his guilt, and to express his anger from any oral need frustration that might arise. He is less likely, then, to be accruing added quantities of unconscious guilt in times of stress. Contrastingly, the person with increased unconscious guilt, when exposed to a continuation of oral need frustration, will continue to accrue the unconscious guilt, so that his so-called "psychiatric symptoms," or simply the signs of emotional uncomfortableness, can be quite pronounced, often unrealistic, and at times incapacitating.

For any human being, there can be circumstances in life that can be severely oral need frustrating, in spite of an individual having a small amount of personality core guilt. It is possible in reality that some tragedy or circumstance of fate may markedly decrease the part objects from which an adult individual is drawing his oral need gratificationl Oral need frustration need not be in the interpersonal relationship sphere. It may involve physical trauma, disease or physiologic or biochemical dysfunction where the discomfort or the pain is felt by the unconscious ego as a reflection of the initial uncomfortableness of life that arises from oral need frustration. There is much in the reality of life that *is* upsetting, or emotionally uncomfortable, and it is erroneous and indicative of emotional uncomfortableness to believe that to be "cool, calm, collected and coping", is the disposition for everyone to take. To be emotionally upset may be unavoidable for anyone; and may be due to any of the possibilities that the circumstances of fate and of life can provide. But the individual with less primordial personality core guilt can still withstand better these unfortunate, but often unavoidable, frustrating circumstances than the individual that begins life with a greater amount of personality core guilt. This latter individual has more difficulty in expressing anger from the more recent frustration of his oral needs. And this is because of the tendency of his unconscious guilt to *block* the externalization of anger. (Note though that it is possible for an individual to begin life with a large personality core guilt, but instead of encountering oral need frustrating situations, may find himself in circumstances of little stress, and may even find himself in a life situation where his core guilt is more definitely an asset for an endeavor toward "success" than a liability.)

The unconscious personality core guilt tends to make the individual feel inferior, inadequate, and unacceptable to others, regardless of any reality of his situation that may lead others to feel otherwise, and gives him the feeling that there's something somehow *wrong* with him. When unconscious guilt is added to his personality core guilt, those feelings can become greatly intensified. A person feeling that he is a "nobody," that he is "stupid," that he is "wrong," or that he is *"not right"* isn't an individual, even on a reality basis, that can express anger effectively in his interpersonal relationships. The unconscious guilt gives him the feeling the he is in error, and prevents an opportunity of arguing his position with anyone else. It is necessary to have a feeling of being "right," before one can effectively express anger about something in reality. Emotionally the anger is unexpressable. It must be repressed, and when it is internalized, it becomes transformed into an added quantity of unconscious guilt.

The outward appearance of two individuals may be deceiving in regard to the amount of repressed anger that each individual might have. Both individuals may appear quiet, easy-going and tolerant. One though, may be withholding his anger from recently perceived frustrated oral needs because of his guilt. He has ego defense mechanisms that are holding back, or preventing the externalization of this anger. However in times of certain increased levels of stress and frustration, this individual will show his "temper," uncontrollably expressing his anger, and then will feel guilty, on a conscious level, afterwards. His quiet appearance and tolerance is only a defensive façade. However, the other quiet individual may be having more of his oral dependency needs met. He has less of a *reason* to be angry, and less need to *express* any anger. He appears quiet, easy-going and tolerant, as the first individual did, but unlike the first, it is because this individual's oral needs are *being* met. The outward appearance of tolerance seems the same for each individual. Yet one is withholding more anger, and is increasing his unconscious guilt. This same individual begins to block more of his oral need gratifying part object relationships. Where both the *outward* appearance and behavior may be the same, one individual is creating a great *potential* for emotional uncomfortableness. The other isn't. When this other *does* perceive oral need frustration, he may, ironically, because of *less* personality core guilt, show his ability to express his anger. He may also in the face of an equally frustrating situation show no sign of anger because he is drawing *enough* oral supplies from other sources.

There is an irony, in regard to this problem, then, in that the quiet, easy-going, and tolerant individual may represent a person who is having his oral needs met, who has a fairly comfortable level of guilt and relatively little repressed anger. As such, he is a potentially *non-violent* individual. On the other hand, if there is a great amount of unconscious guilt, repressed anger and unmet oral needs, this other individual represents a potentially *violent* individual. This latter person's unconscious guilt tends not only to make him appear unassuming (but often a seeker of attention or publicity), but also makes him particularly quiet and non-expressive of any violence. This may be so to such an extent that he may be termed a "model" citizen in that he seems so opposed to self-centeredness, so tolerant and uncharacterized by anger expression. It is just this type of "outstanding" individual that has this guilt-laden personality that can "run amok" with great violence. The author has collected over the past several years a series of cases from newspaper articles that rather consistently show that the individual that *does* run amok *is* the quiet "model citizen" that previously was *exemplary* in his conformity, and his *lack* of anger expression. Characteristically, both his neighbors and his co-workers are always shocked by his sudden outburst of homicidal behavior in that his violence seems so alien to his outward personality. The person that does run amok does not have a personality that previous to the homicidal outburst of violence was characterized by frequent anger expression.

There has been little done in psychiatry to differentiate this individual from the individual that superficially appears much the same way, but *has* oral need gratification adequately taking place, is *not* perceiving oral need frustration and therfore has *little* repressed anger. If there were a way to assay the unconscious guilt, particularly in its added form, or to determine the extent of unmet oral dependency needs, one would have a means of differentiating the *most likely* potentially violent individual from the *least likely* when outward appearance seems so similar. Two of the criteria would be the ability to accept oral need gratification or pleasure, and the ability to express anger in oral need frustrating situations without a gross disruption of the interpersonal relationship sphere.

The individual that enters a therapeutic transference is one that has a concentration of unmet oral needs. He is seeking a gratification of his oral needs through the *transference phenomenon* that is set up in the therapeutic situation regardless of the reality orientation. The listener becomes an intense transference figure, if he is not already one by his role in reality, and becomes *more* symbolic of those that were emotionally significant to this individual in his distant emotional past and in his more recent present. But because of so much unmet oral needs, and because the listener is such a multisymbolic figure, there will come in time a secondary "need" to express anger toward that transference figure. The anger of frustrated oral dependency needs of past and present part objects is transferred to this figure. The unconscious guilt, though, will tend to block the expression of anger. However, with continued emotional support providing a deepening of the transference relationship, the more emotionally difficult it becomes for the client to withhold his anger. Whether the manifest content orientation of this relationship takes the form of regularly kept counselling encounters, a psychoanalytic relationship, or some form of psychotherapy, or quackery, there eventually comes a time when this emotional closeness and degree of oral dependency gratification seems to provoke a mobilization of the repressed anger behind the client's guilt. This will be true in *any* on-going interpersonal relationship where there is a regularity of frequent enough encounters, and where oral dependency needs are being increasingly met.

The client at first may seem to unconsciously attempt to deny, to prevent, or to thwart this mobilization of anger. Since this mobilization of anger begins with a projection of guilt, clients may seem to resist "seeing" in their therapist their projected guilt. They show a dislike to talk about others (which implies a reluctance to "talk about the therapist"), are afraid of "spreading gossip and rumors," and chastize themselves for even the thought, or idea, that their emotional uncomfortableness is anybody else's fault than their own. But it is an *inescapable* process of guilt projection and anger mobilization that will come about *naturally*, if the relationship can be continued. It is important to emphasize that it *is* a naturally occurring process that requires no work other than "simple" listening on the part of the therapist. The transference figure becomes that emotionally significant because of the degree to which he is meeting the oral dependency needs of his client. He becomes symbolic, in part, of those in the distant emotional past who were also oral dependency need gratifying part objects, but who frustrated the client. And he is symbolic, in part, of those in his present interpersonal relationship sphere who are oral need gratifying objects, but who also frustrate the client. Whether his reality oriented manifest content focuses upon the distant past interpersonal relationships, upon the present, or a combination of both, or upon his misfortune or ill-luck in circumstances of fate, the therapeutic listener, within the magic of the transference, becomes truly "all things" to his client. Through the illogic of unconscious mental functioning and that all important Von Domarus equating of like perceived predicates, the listener becomes the very part object toward which all the anger within the client is directed.

There are some types of "therapies" that attempt to get the individual to externalize his anger with no regard to the transference phenomenon. One can doubt whether meaningful anger expression is really possible, except in situations where the transference phenomenon *is* operable. In such cases no effort is necessary on the part of the therapist in his reality orientation to mobilize the anger. The therapist need only to be present, to *listen* and to continue his latent role of meeting oral dependency gratification, without a necessity of fostering, or

141

attempting to enhance in any way, anger expression. Anger expression will eventually come about on its own if the transference relationship is continued.

This is illustrated in the remark of a client: "I'd like to tell my father (a perceived aspect of the therapist) off as he's paid no attention at all to how high his stock in the company (the therapeutic transference) has gone up in the past few months. It's as though he doesn't really *care* that his stock has sky-rocketed. I don't think he even knows that he's worth *considerably* more than he was before. *I* looked it up *myself!* Now, I'd say that's pretty *poor* financial management on his part, wouldn't you?" Another client shows in her remark about her boy-friend, that what has made the therapist so "great" is the very reason for being angry: "Everything I seem to do is all right with him!" Still another client implies in a single sentence that he resents the position his own transference has given his listener: "Even Jesus Christ had to wipe his ass!"

There can be no short cut to this process. The transference figure must become, first of all, that *symbolic* for anger expression. This can only be done through oral dependency gratification. To get the client into this position, though, requires a skill on the part of the therapist no matter what role in reality he might be taking in regard to the manifest content. For the skill is applied to keeping the client involved *long enough* for the process to take place. The unconscious guilt of the client will tend to make him withdraw from intensifying his oral dependency gratification, and to withhold his anger in any way possible, and by any rationalization. He will attempt to withdraw from the relationship to gain emotional distance, or will discontinue completely the relationship. The therapist must therefore walk a fine line at this point, in that his client is viewing him kaleidoscopically, as both the object of his oral dependency gratification as well as the object toward which his anger is directed. Both positions will be opposed by the unconscious guilt.

Such an ambivalently held situation is possible only because of the transference phenomenon, and the perception of part objects by the unconscious. This places the unreality in a *supreme* position of impòrtance and relegates reality to a much lesser position. The unconscious language that is implied in this relationship is the transference language. Because it *is* metaphorical, it will show a continuation of oral dependency gratification as well as anger expression to the very same object in reality. It will also metaphorically show the opposition to both from the unconscious guilt. A person with less unconscious guilt, with less repressed anger, and with less oral dependency needs is not found involved in such an intense transference relationship. And ironically, neither is the *excessively* guilt-laden individual either! The more emotionally comfortable person that has his oral needs met diffusely doesn't have the capacity afforded by concentrated unmet oral dependency needs to *get* involved. He is not found in this relationship with such an intense transference taking place. Ironically, these other *excessively* guilt-laden individuals with intense concentrations of unmet oral needs also seem to lack

142

the capacity, *because* of the degree of guilt, to be involved in intense transferences. They act defensively when they have too much unconscious guilt and too
much repressed anger to the possibility of such involvement. Such an intense
relationship, that *could* be therapeutic, is feared. They will often show, too, a
necessity to avoid intense emotional involvement at all costs. The individual that
is involved in a transference process, though, is better off, in that he does have the
possibility of becoming emotionally comfortable by decreasing his unconscious
guilt through an externalization of his anger. But the differentiating of those people *not* involved in therapeutic transferences, and who *should* be, from those
who have no *need* to be, will again depend upon the development of a means to
assay unconscious guilt and unmet oral dependency needs. Psychiatry so far has
done nothing toward this endeavor.

An individual involved in a therapeutic transference, that has as its goal, a reduction of the unconscious guilt to a more emotionally comfortable level through
communicative processes, may involve himself just long enough to decrease this
added unconscious guilt that is producing his emotional uncomfortableness. He
enters the relationship, gains emotional support, then ventilates his anger, decreases his *added* guilt, and then discontinues. He is, though, left with a personality *core* guilt that will tend, in times of emotional stress and oral need frustration, to accrue the added unconscious guilt again. His *core* guilt will tend to block
anger expression as it does oral gratification in the ongoing interpersonal relationships. This individual, if he can luckily avoid many of the emotional stresses
of life, may do fairly well. He may do well too because he has ventilated his anger
to his objects *in reality.* Unlike the person who has received *shock* "treatment"
to reduce his guilt, he may cause these objects to shift their guilt projection *away*
from him and onto others. It becomes most difficult to get the guilt-laden individual to continue the relationship long enough for the therapeutic transference to
work on the personality core guilt after his *added* guilt has decreased. This core
guilt is defended by well-entrenched and time-proven ego defense mechanisms
that have been developed for the very survival of that ego. They are not at all
easily shifted or relinquished.

To diminish this unconscious *core* guilt involves, by necessity, a personality
change, as the defense mechanisms must change. While the reduction of the
added unconscious guilt produces a simple return from an emotionally uncomfortable state to a more comfortable one, this return may be enhanced by a brief
involvement in a professional therapeutic transference with the circumstances of
life remaining the same, or simply by a shift of the circumstances of life that
made the individual's situation in life so orally depriving. Removing the *added*
conscious guilt is often relatively easy. Removing the *core personality* guilt is
much more difficult and involves more than the mere alleviation of orally frustrating life situations. This is complicated with clients that have a large enough
unconscious core guilt that they seem consistently uncomfortable, and become

even *more* so when undergoing ego collapse from *added* unconscious guilt. Yet because of their continuing level of emotional uncomfortableness, they may be easier to keep therapeutically involved than an individual with less emotional uncomforatbleness because of his life circumstances of the moment. To keep any client involved in a therapeutic relationship is a most difficult task for any therapist regardless of his role in reality. What the therapist attempts to do in the unreality afforded by the transference is something that cannot be done in any reality. He allows the client to literally bite the breast that gives the milk, when both the need for the milk and the need to bite is being denied.

In each client there is often — if there isn't a rapid projection of guilt to the therapist and a quick expression of anger that terminates the relationship — a "honeymoon" in which the client verbalizes readily in his reality-oriented manifest content, and actively "feeds" upon the therapist. There comes a time though, when the "honeymoon" seems to be over, when the client becomes threatened by his own mobilized anger, and the relationship takes on an ambivalent nature. The therapist has to take a more formal position at this time in order to retain the client in the relationship. He must utilize fully the unreality of being "all things" given him by the transference. He must verbalize very little in the face of such ambivalence, allowing the client to keep a "safe" distance that seems so necessary for the client, not only from the ambivalent aspects of himself, but from the therapist if he is to continue. There may be long silences that seem motivated by this feeling: "I won't say *anything*; then you won't see how *guilty* or how orally *deprived*, or how *angry* I am." By allowing the individual to set his own emotional distance from his own intrapsychic ambivalence, and from the ambivalently perceived therapeutic listener, the relationship can be continued long enough to lower the personality core guilt. If the therapist is foolish enough to attempt to uncover the client's anger prematurely, it will be vigorously denied. The client will feel an oral frustration from such an attempt, perceiving the therapist as misunderstanding, and certainly not being helpful, emotionally supportive or simply oral need gratifying to the client.

It is in the best interests for an *ongoing* transference relationship that the anger as well as the oral dependency gratification from the therapist be *metaphorically* expressed. Though the relationship may tolerate a brief recognition on a conscious level that the listener *is* an object of oral need gratification, or a target for expressed anger,it is still better in the long run that this be predominately metaphorical. Since the client is caught in a predominately one-sided dependency relationship, the therapist may have a wide leeway as to what he can do or say, and *still* have it accepted by his client as part of the reality of the relationship. This leeway would include every form or technique of psychotherapy or quackery there is, and range, in fact, through every possible type of interpersonal relationship encounter. The reality of these non-verbal and verbal maneuvers may or may not jeopardize the ongoing transference relationship. But for therapists not involved in a "therapy" form of "laying on the hands," gadgetry, medical practice or religious ritual, but involved instead in a "talking and listening" relationship, a metaphorical presentation by the client for what is perceived of the therapist, and minimum verbalization by the therapist, is best. The unreality of the transference, like the Divine Transference, often seems best continued by silence or non-verbal support. It is only through this unreality that the listener can symbolically wear so many different and varied "hats" in his latent role in this relationship.

Although interpersonal relationship communication of emotionally comfortable people, and particularly emotionally *un*comfortable people, will show metaphorical evidence of oral need gratification and anger expression toward the listener, it is best shown in the more intense and more *formal* transference relationship where the listener doesn't introject a counter-transference language of his own. The metaphorical expression of anger is more readily seen and more easily followed with a non-verbalizing listener. In the following example, a client, in a therapeutic transference, is angry at her husband, Fred, in reality. In the unreality of the transference, Fred is the therapist in metaphor. "Nancy" represents the client's oral dependency needs, which the client perceives, the *therapist* feels as unacceptably gluttonous and worthy of condemnation, particularly her "hunger" following the therapist's week long absence. This is rather openly connoted in the analogy of "not having mashed potatoes for over a week." "I was so mad at Fred the other night at the dinner table (a latent reference to therapy). He had to get after Nancy while she was eating. It seems as though he can't leave her alone when she's eating, but has to find something wrong and bring it to her attention. He'll pick at her, make snide remarks and find some reason to put her down. (Note the father's guilt projection, and the daughter's oral rejection, in the reality of this.) He does everything possible to spoil her meal times. She's growing girl and needs food, particularly something she likes. So we had some mashed potatoes since she hadn't had any for over a week. But Fred had to keep after her with 'Watch out what you're eating — you're eating just like a pig,' or 'If you don't look out, you'll be as fat as Mable' (tearfully) until the first thing I noticed she wasn't eating at all. She just sat there with her head down crying. (Wipes away a tear with a kleenex from each eye.) Now she especially needs food (oral supplies). But why is he so against her eating? She can't help it if she's a growing girl. And she's so sensitive about her weight (guilt). I just couldn't stand his making fun of her by the way he was looking at her, and the things that he was saying that got her crying while she was trying to eat. I can take it *myself* from Fred, but I just hate to see Nancy crying that way at the table."

One client, like many others, seems to react to her first real expression of anger within the therapeutic transference relationship as though it was destructive. This is typical for the guilt-laden individual who unconsciously feels that when attempting to meet oral needs in past emotional experiences that this oral need gratification *was* destructive. They cannot seem to take much oral need gratification without the risk of exposing their guilt and the repressed anger behind this guilt. This is metaphorically expressed by a thirty-three year old teacher as having "blown a gasket" and "spoiled the food" in regard to the previous session which involved some mild anger expression. "Now I'm in real trouble — the referigerator isn't keeping cool at home, and the food is spoiling (a reference to the self-felt "spoiling" or her oral dependency on the therapist). I found out what the whole trouble is though. I guess I need a new one of those rubber rings that goes around the inside of the door — what do you call them? Oh, yes, gasket! I guess I need a new gasket. The one I have is pretty worn out from opening and closing the refrigerator door, and it's not been doing its job. Last week it just dropped right off the door, and I don't know how long the food was exposed to all the summer heat we've been having, particularly during the past couple of weeks. I'd hate to have the food spoil, as food is so expensive now. At least it is on my salary. So my husband will have to put a new gasket on for me so it won't come dropping off again when the refrigerator door is opened. I've asked him three times now to get me a gasket, but it doesn't seem to bother him at all. I really shouldn't blame him as he's not in the kitchen as much as I am. (Pause.) I'm going to get a new gasket *myself* as he doesn't show much inclination in getting one for me."

Many times in a therapeutic transference relationship clients seem to take one step forward as far as expressing their angry feelings, and then they seem to require taking two steps backwards because they feel so guilty in regard to the anger expression. The listener, utilizing the metaphor that is appropriate for the manifest content, can subtly support the client in this ambivalent expression of anger. He can subtly convey to the client that his anger is not destructive, even though it may seem to the client as though it is. This emotional support should not be vigorous though, in that it runs a risk of being oral need frustrating. Because, by the simple process of listening, anger expression will again be forthcoming, it doesn't need to be verbally supported at all, other than to keep the manifest content on-going. Furthermore, it is well to remember that it isn't really the anger expression that the client fears *most*, but oral dependency. Too vigorous support by the therapist may be perceived as an emotional moving in by the therapist. The client himself is best left to set his own emotional distance in both the meeting of his oral dependency needs *and* the expression of his anger. He will move in when he feels emotionally comfortable in doing so, and move away when emotional distance seems necessary, when he feels emotionally uncomfortable either from what is transpiring in the therapeutic transference, or is being transferred *into* this transference from the circumstances of his life situation *outside* of therapy.

The client will find it hard to see the constructive value of externalizing his angry feelings. They often verbalize this as: "What's the use of being *mad* — it never solves anything." They can utilize much of reality to support this feeling. After all, one is admonished in the Bible "to beat their swords into plough shares". For them, being angry seems to be equated with being unchristian, unacceptable, "bad," "abnormal", or even "insane". The *Robins Reader* is a small quarterly of "words of wisdom" published for the medical, dental and veterinary professions by the A.H. Robins Company of Richmond, Virginia. In one of their recent editions (No. 3 1972) an editorial entitled "Fruits of Anger" presents so well what the client, whose anger expression is blocked by guilt, feels and so often metaphorically presents:

"Boy, did I blow my top!" we heard a man say to another as we passed them on the street. We wondered, as we went on our way, what had made him so mad and just what 'blowing his top' had got him. For that matter, what does it get anybody?
Did you ever hear of a person who landed a better job, got a raise, made a new friend, or really helped anybody by losing his temper? The men in the laboratories tell us that anger produces a poison in the system that actually can be measured, one powerful enough to kill certain animals.
Nine times out of ten it is your pride that is responsible for your anger. Doesn't it seem pretty short-sighted to let your pride get you so steamed up? Horace, who could be rather blunt about such things, insisted that anger is nothing more or less than temporary insanity. Alexander Pope described it as an odd way in which a man takes revenge on himself for the faults of others. Only a 'mad' man would do anything like that."

(Note in the above that the "having one's feelings hurt," and the "blow to one's pride" are *oral* "put-downs" or *oral* need frustrations.)

People with unmet oral dependency needs seem, at times, to have learned all too well from their emotional past to "turn the other cheek" and to "walk the extra mile." They feel they *must* do this too, because they feel that *guilty*, but still simultaneously feel *more* resentful, and *more* angry for having to do it. When this person *does* give token vent to their repressed anger, they do so with a realistic fear that it might reach rage proportions if it is not controlled. They seem to experience the expression of even token anger as having a highly exaggerated affect, implying or rationalizing that it was destructive in the analogical presentation they give in their manifest content. As they become more emotionally supported in the transference, and anger is more readily expressed, they will often guiltily remark with self-condemning introspection so typical of the guilt-laden: "I'm like a cranky old self-centered demanding crab for saying that," or "I bet you think I'm just an ogre, and I wish I wasn't that way," or "I've got to learn to *control* my feelings, as I have a nasty mouth, and I have no right to complain the wa I do." It is their *guilt* that makes them feel they should gratefully accept, without complaint, resentment or bitterness, their oral need frustrating position in life, and that to want *more* oral dependency gratification is being selfish or self-centered. Sometimes they may metaphorically present their reluctance to express anger to the therapeutic listener as: "I'm always jumping on him. All he has to do is open his mouth, and I bite his head off." It is again their unconscious guilt that makes them remark: "I just sound like a nagging, bitchy old hag that ought to count her blessings and bear her cross like others do." They seem to seek a *contentment* with their own discontentment. They seek a "strength" and an ability to "cope" or to "adjust" to situations that upon very little scrutiny, are obviously so oral need depriving.. Neither wanting to gratify their oral needs, nor to express their anger, they seek to assuage their guilt by further oral need frustration or oral need deprivation. One will often hear them, in their therapy sessions, make the remark, following some anger expression: "I shouldn't be running my mouth this way — I wish you hadn't written all that down as it must seem as though I'm making a perfect heel and a cad out of him, when he's not at all — it's really *me*."

A male client with an "alcoholic problem" shows the oral nature of his underlying conflict with his guilt-laden oral dependency needs and his inability to express anger. "She's a wonderful wife (it's his guilt that makes her seem so wonderful). My God! She's as good a wife as any man (he, himself) could ever find. A fellow couldn't ask (particularly if he feels as underserving as he does) for a better wife than she is. I can't blame *her* at all for anything that I've done. It's all my own doing. My drinking and running around (a reference to his attempts to meet his oral needs) is my *own* fault. Sure, it would be easy if I could blame *her*, and tell you that *she* was driving me to drink, but it wouldn't be right. I've hurt her too many times in the past to believe that *she's* the cause of my problems. She's only given me back what I deserve and *nothing* more. I know what I have to do. I have to simply *stop* drinking (i.e., "simply *stop* trying to satisfy my oral needs"). When I get to drinking, I start getting angry. *I've got to do it myself.* (This is the most frequently heard statement of the guilt-laden emotionally uncomfortable person, no matter what his reality problem might be!) I'll try to be back next week, but I don't see what good my coming here does." He *didn't* come back, and after a futile try at abstinence, he began to drink again, attempting to seek relief in alcohol from the effects of his guilt.

When their unconscious guilt is self-felt, they may describe themselves as having a "nasty mouth," further implying that they've got to learn to keep their "big mouth out of it," appropriately presenting this self-felt oral destructive characteristic that they fear their oral incorporative needs can cause. When their unconscious guilt is projected — even if momentarily — they perceive that the therapist, in what they are metaphorically presenting, has a "big mouth." In doing so, they are on their way to reducing their unconscious guilt. Little by little, in increasing analogies, they project the guilt that prevents anger expression. This projection is a *necessity* in anger expression. (An interesting analogy can be made in the fact that many animals defecate just prior to fighting.) When the guilt is self-felt, there is a tendency to block anger expression. There *must* be first a *projection* of guilt in order for there to be an expression of anger. This is true even in cases where a person literally "runs amok." This person's guilt is projected to a great many people who take on a transference significance. The anger then is unleashed in violent form that so often is associated with their own suicide. The problem for the therapeutic listener is to get the client to *continue* his relationship with the listener, with oral dependency gratification, while at the same time accepting projected guilt and expressed anger in small enough amounts that will not terminate the relationship, be destructive, or "suicidal," to the client's position in his reality, or his position in the unreality of the therapeutic transference.

It becomes the work of the therapeutic transference to gratify these ego alien and guilt-laden dependency needs of the client, as well as to accept the previously ego alien anger, not only as a simple catharis for past self-felt injustices, but because of the conflict-resolving "here and now" of the therapeutic transference. That this is most difficult is implied in the remark: "I *can't* (i.e., "I shouldn't") get mad at him, as I'm always afraid he'll just walk out the door as I know he's had *enough*, putting up with me already!" And within the manifest content there is often a reality truth to this which should be respected. This client, in her emotional past, *has* had emotionally significant part objects and objects "walk out the door." She feels, in part, that it *is* due to her excessively felt oral dependency needs imbued with guilt and anger that has been the very cause for it. These clients realistically fear their anger, which can actually be at rage proportions, and can, as such, *be* potentially destructive to any dependency relationship that they might find themselves in. Since they would rather *not* be in such dependency relationships in the first place, they seek to cover their hostility from perceived injustices, their guilt, and most of all, their oral dependency needs.

Ironically, it is the unconscious guilt that has made them sensitive enough in deeply feeling so inadequate and inferior to perceive these injustices. It is their unconscious guilt also that makes them feel that they shouldn't express their anger, annoyance, or irritation, even when they *do* perceive an injustice. They tend, instead, to blame themselves and their oral dependency need, which they feel is grossly excessive, for the frustration. This is a reflection of that oral incorporative guilt that makes them feel that their very earliest oral frustration was *because* of the oral need. That old "If I didn't *have* this oral need, I wouldn't be frustrated" seems to be the operating unconscious principle that prevents anger expression. They chastise themselves for being so easily irritated or annoyed, remarking as one client did: "I don't care if I were married to Jesus Christ, I'd find *something* wrong even about Him!"

But it is through the emotional support afforded by oral dependency gratification that the annoyances and the irritations become issues of great conscious concern. Previously, the unconscious guilt made it such that these irritations of oral deprivation wouldn't even be consciously recognized. They would be repressed, denied, or rationalized as not originating from their true selves. They seem annoyed or irritated at *themselves* for finding themselves irritated or annoyed at others. One client rationalized his guilt-derived inability to express anger as: "I never like to point the finger of blame at anyone else for my troubles,because when I do, I've got three fingers pointing back at me!" Another client, with some knowledge of psychology, put it this way: "people who are critical of others are really pointing out their own inadequacies!" Somehow these admonitions, so well remembered when feeling excessively guilty, either become forgotten, or substituted, for ones more appropriate for anger expression when a person feels less guilty. Anger, that was at first repressed, with less guilt, becomes suppressed. And finally, with still less guilt, it is externalized.

The unacceptableness of getting angry was shown in one therapy session by a client as: "I take petty, picayune things that I should adjust to as being just a part of life, and blow them all out of proportion. I get mad over such little things, and get everyone upset for no reason. I seem to make mountains out of molehills (but enough molehills *can* make a mountain) and that's because I must be pretty immature. I got angry last week because my wife (therapist) put a jar of *crunchy* peanut butter on the table. She knows that I only eat *smooth* peanut butter, and that I just *hate* those peanuts! I felt she wasn't showing any consideration for *me* in doing that. I ranted and raved like a *mad man* about that. Only a person who has something mentally wrong would act that way. As good a wife as she's been in putting up with me, and as good a mother as she's been to my children (i.e., my oral dependency needs), I had to act like I was crazy. I must be in the right place, sitting here in a psychiatrist's office! I got all upset and mad over *peanuts*. I said things that I shouldn't have said, and now I feel guilty." (Note the metaphor "peanuts" connotes that which is so trivial, or of so little value, and yet psychodynamically the analogy that he presents here is symbolic of all his past "injustices." Because it *is* symbolic of so much, it *does* have a great significance. a significance that greatly *transcends* the reality importance. But he attempts here to *minimize* this importance by emphasizing the unimportance in reality in his opposition to the expression of anger to the therapist, because of his guilt.)

What the preceeding client presents, arises from his particular level of guilt that makes him feel that anything he might want to project his guilt and anger to is only picayune and, as such, is little cause for any anger expression. Many times the therapist will hear this same message, but in different *metaphorical* contexts as: "I don't like being around Susan (an unconscious aspect of himself) as she's so nit-picking. *Nothing* seems to please her, and she'll complain about the most insignificant things as though they were of great importance." There are a great number of possible variations of presenting in metaphor and analogy the idea of not getting angry over things of great symbolic emotional importance, but which are made to appear "petty," "picayune" or "insignificant."

It does seem so often that the little things in life do mean the most. Perhaps they do is, not only because they can be symbolic of oral need gratification, but also because they can be so symbolic of oral need frustration. It is only in reality that "peanuts" can seem so small and picayune. But in the unreality of the transference, where these "peanuts" can be equated with a multiplicity of past frustrations from a multiplicity of part object experiences, that they reach their true importance. This importance comes not from the size of a single frustration, but the accumulated *number* of them. This tendency to minimize the importance of what is symbolized in anger expression is illustrated by the guilt-laden client that states: "All Roy (latently referring to the therapist) did was take the wrong salad dressing out of the refrigerator, and I jumped all over him. Now I had no reason to do that. I went up one side of him and down the other. I was an ugly bear, and a regular shrew! I shouldn't be that way at all, as good as Roy has been to me. I've turned his hair gray. He works so hard and he has enough to put up with in his work, without me adding *more* to him. You've got to get me to *cope* with things *without* my getting angry. I should be thankful I have a husband like him. There's plenty of women (an aspect of she, herself) with children, and *no* husband at all. I have absolutely no logical reason whatsoever to be angry at him. What is wrong with me anyway that I fly off the handle so? Why can't I cope with things the way other housewives do? Why can't I be satisfied with what I've got, instead of wanting him to be perfect all the time? I know he can't be perfect — *nobody's* perfect. And I wouldn't want him perfect anyway. So I have no reason to get angry. That's my main problem. And that's what you've got to help me with."

On a reality basis, this client could not possibly accept, at least not emotionally so, with the level of guilt she has, the fact that the therapeutic listener *must* get her to do *more* of the very thing that she is so consciously *opposed* to. She must emotionally accept, in time, that she is *right* in feeling dissatisfied, and *right* in the expression of her anger. Another client, who seems as guilt-laden as the previous one, remarked: "Well, I try to watch what I say. If one says something in anger, one can't *ever* take it back. The damage is done and it's irreparable! I mean, I *know!* I've had it done to me when I was growing up. I can still remember one time when my mother was angry at me, and told me I was just *no damn good* for anything. She apologized later, but I can never forget that statement. That feeling of being *no damn good* sticks with me now no matter what I do!"

Like the meeting of the oral needs, the *frustration* of these needs is also done on a *part object basis*. When a person recalls a single incident, as the above client did, she is attempting to logically concretize in a single symbolic memory all the many unconscious perceptions of oral need rejection in her experiences with others that have occured on a part object basis. It is an unconscious concretization of these perceived part object frustrations that is the true origin of her feeling that she's *no damn good*. There can never be a single incident of the past that could possibly imbue so pervasive a feeling in any person. Instead, there must be a host of repetitive "peanut like" oral frustrations and rejections that are unconsciously perceived, eventually concretized and then "remembered" in the sub-conscious. It is because they *are* part object derived that they *must* be concretized and placed in a logical, but still metaphorical memory for that individual. When these part object frustrations are concretized and logically presented, the individual can communicate this feeling, not only to himself, but to others. It is the multiplicity of them that gives the need for a metaphorical memory, no matter how picayune it might seem the emotional significance of *one* is.

To get the guilt-laden individual to even *talk* of past frustrations would involve a latent expression of anger toward the therapist. This, because of his guilt, the individual would rather not do. When the client does talk of the past "memories" of oral need frustrations, he is, from the unreality basis of the transference, talking about unconsciously perceived, and identically equated, aspects of the therapeutic listener, himself. That the client will spontaneously bring these up, in time, is due to the subtle transference between that person and his listener. The spontaneity is directly under the influence of the transference. It involves intimately what is unconsciously being perceived in regard to the relationship *at the very moment* between the client and his listener. This spontaneity in verbalizing these "memories" will be braked by the level of unprojected unconscious guilt that will give the client the feeling "I have no right to be angry (because of my guilt) but *others* have, instead, a right to be angry at *me!*"

There should be a mention here of a frequently encountered request that is often heard when a very guilt-laden individual finds himself initially involved in a talking and listening session with a therapeutic listener. The client comes to this initial session, and then verbalizes about not only his somatic complaints, but also his interpersonal relationship difficulties, where it becomes obvious, by implication, to that listener, that this client has been orally frustrated and "mistreated" in his circumstance of life. But instead of continuing with the verbalizations, the client begins to repeatedly ask: "Get my wife (or husband) in here." The client feels, on the one hand, as though they have been "telling tales out of school." or "saying things behind her (or his) back," and wants the spouse to come in, as though to retaliate or to correct, what their own unmet needs make them feel, in part is true. They want the spouse in, because they know, on the one hand, that their oral dependency needs *have* been frustrated, and that their spouse *is* to blame. But on the other hand, they feel, because of their guilt, that perhaps they are all *wrong* and that *he* deserves a chance to present the "other side." "He might be able to tell you what *I'm* doing wrong that *makes* him act the way he does." They seem to want a confirmation of what their guilt leads them to feel — that there is no reason for their being angry, and no reason for them to be complaining and becasue they *are*, there must be something *"wrong"* with them. It is only in the very guilt-laden that one will hear the request: "Get my wife (or husband) in here!" The less guilty client can verbalize more freely. He will establish a therapeutic transference, meet his oral dependency needs that previously went unmet, express his anger, and will thereby decrease his uncomfortable level of unconscious guilt. With still lessened unconscious guilt, he can accept oral dependency need gratification from his spouse, meet more of her oral needs as well, express his anger that tends to "clear the air," and "feed" more upon other objects in his interpersonal relationship sphere. But the very guilt-laden person is confused in his ambivalence, wanting confirmation of his oral deprivation on one hand, and of his guilt on the other. He wants the therapeutic listener to somehow judge and make a decision, as though in a court of law, but where the client's own ambivalence wouldn't be able to accept a decision if one were made from any standpoint.

"Sure I'm angry — but only at myself" is also frequently heard in early verbalizations. One client metaphorically presents this as "I had to get after this one child (an unconscious aspect of she, herself) in my class (the therapeutic transference) that was getting too loud. I can't be in a classroom when children are unruly. I don't like any child to act out, as I'm afraid if I let one do it then all the children in the class will do so, and I'll never be able to handle them. I don't think this permissiveness in the classroom that's supposed to be in vogue now is good at all. Why does the principal (therapist) seem to condone this behavior?" What she is metaphorically presenting is that the child that she refers to in her manifest content is the symbolic anger-expressing aspect of herself that she is attempting to control within the "permissiveness" of the oral dependency gratifying therapeutic transference, which promotes the mobilization of her guilt, and the externalization of her anger.

Ironically, the client who may, after a few sessions, reach this point and will often view themselves as "not progressing" in regard to the original reality oriented "reason" for entering the relationship with the therapeutic listener. "I used to be so patient. I'd never get irritable and annoyed the way I do now. Nothing seems to please me. I'm not getting better, I'm getting *worse!*" Many times this feeling of the client is supported by those in her interpersonal relationship sphere that are emotionally close to her. These people have required that she *not* be so irritated or annoyed by *their* guilt projection to her. For their own emotional comfortableness, they seem to require that client to continue to accept their projected guilt and anger, and they defensively seek to keep a status quo, often telling the client she *is* worse.

These objects of the client's interpersonal relationship sphere are often referred to, in the metaphorical manifest content, as supportive of the feeling that anger expression *is* unacceptable. But when they *are* so used, though, in the manifest content, they represent the client's own perceptions of how the therapist is perceiving, in part, the anger expression, as well as their own *resistance* to anger expression. One may hear a client remark: "My husband isn't going to take much more of my fighting and arguing with him. He says that if I keep on *this* way, I had better get another psychiatrist." This client implies that the psychiatrist should not be accepting her anger expression. In her manifest content, she interestingly implies a connection between her husband and the psychiatrist — fearing she will lose her psychiatrist as she fears she will her husband in reality.

153

One housewife who, in a previous session, did express some angry feelings, attempts now to cover over these feelings. However, she seems to blame the listener, which is a continuation of therapeutically projecting guilt, for allowing her the expression of these feelings. This is presented as: "There's so much violence being shown on television now-a-days, and it just isn't right. There'll be no good come of it! It's a disgrace the way the networks (latently referring to the therapeutic transference) allow programs to have such violence. I saw a program just last week (a reference to her feeling that her anger expression in the preceeding session was excessive) in which there were four murders and two hangings in just one half hour! My God! There's enough violence in the world already without showing how it's done on television! I can't see where there's a bit of good in all that fighting and carrying on, particularly with children (her oral dependency needs) involved. What good is it anyway? Can you answer me that? (Therapist gestures.) What effect is it going to have on the children? They'll think it's a way of life! Why can't they show stories of devotion, of love, of loyality, and of respect, instead of all this fighting and violence? I was always taught that a child should *respect* their parents and not act the way some children (meaning she, herself, in part) are acting toward their parents now-a-days (a reference to what is occurring in therapy). Why, what some kids put their parents through now, I'd *never* think of doing. Yet they have to show it all on television! It seems as though the world (again referring to the therapeutic transference) is getting more and more violent (and reality-wise, she may be quite correct!) Good Lord! I haven't gotten over President Kennedy's assassination (a reference to the destructive aspect of her oral needs). I thought the world of him. Somehow I felt so close to him. I just went to pieces when he was killed. There's no one else to blame except those networks, and I want to tell *you*, it's high time they started cleaning up television!"

Sometimes there is a part object recognition that the expression of anger *is* accepted. In the following excerpt, "you" and later "father" are metaphorical for one aspect of the therapist that seem to be *accepting* of anger, while "husband" represents a perceived aspect of the therapist that is felt as *not* accepting of her anger. "I know *you* don't think I'm hateful, but my husband sure does! He thinks I'm mean and ornery. He told me jokingly one time that when he comes home for supper, he feels like tossing his hat through the door to see if it comes flying right back. He said he'd know if it were safe then for him to come in. (Laughs.) He thinks I'm an old grump. I must admit that I have been acting that way, but then it was only because the children were upset because they didn't get a chance to see him. They love to play with their father — you know, like roughhousing on the floor. I can tell he likes it as much as they do. But all that fighting is hard on me. The way I yell at him it's a wonder he stays around. I thought he'd leave the last time when the children got so loud and noisy. I don't know what I'd do if he did! But, he hasn't left yet."

There seems to be a tendency for the very guilt-laden individual to consciously see only the reflections of the "good breast" in his past and present object relationships. They deny their anger from unconscious perceptions of the "bad breast," or if the perception is more conscious, feel that they have misperceived and are grossly in error. They present, initially, trying to appear "thankful," "lucky," and "grateful" that things aren't worse, but somehow not fully convincing themselves of this position. They would prefer to place their problem as originating in a physical abnormality, rather than their interpersonal relationship sphere. When their oral needs begin to be met, the previously repressed anger is ventilated, and their added oral guilt diminishes. As the guilt begins to decrease, they now "remember," as it were, the *bad* aspects of the past that they couldn't see before. Where previously their guilt blocked a recognition of a "bad breast," either in their distant emotional past, their present, or the very "here and now" of the therapeutic transference, they now, with less guilt, begin to see it more clearly. (It isn't only, as the saying goes, that "Love — meaning intense oral need gratification — is blind," but also it is the underlying unprojected unconscious *guilt*, that is always associated with anyone's *intense* oral need that will create the blindness in seeing oral deprivation.) With lessened guilt, that initially seen "perfection" that was created by their own intensity of concentrated oral need toward an object, changes to *imperfection*, and what they first saw as perfect, now is seen as flawed. They imply a more correct recognition, that there can be no "perfect" love in reality. With decreasing guilt they can, in fact, become *most perceptive* in seeing the "bad breast," and can show no difficulty in finding it amidst a host of "good breasts" they tend now to overlook. But it is these "good breasts" upon which they are drawing oral dependency need gratification that gives them the needed feeling of being supported or "backed up." This is necessary for any guilt-free anger expression. When there were a relatively few number of unconsciously perceived "good breasts" in their interpersonal relationship sphere, including the therapeutic transference, effective anger expression wasn't possible.

A client who had previously held a passive, overly-dependent position with the therapist begins to perceive an aspect of him, which she implies, she really doesn't want to see. She has not reached the point of expressing anger, but is only one step away from it. Note that she doesn't want to recognize what she has unconsciously projected to the therapist. But she *has* seen it, and she knows she cannot deny what she has seen. "I'm sorry that I read that article in the paper last night about my car (the therapist). I thought it was the best car I ever owned. I didn't know that it had so many defects. I thought so much of it, and had been so proud of it that I just don't want to recognize that it has all those defects. But Ralph Nader (an aspect of herself) can't be wrong. Now that I do know about them, I'm going to be thinking about every one of those defects every time that I'm riding in it." She seems to imply that she'd rather not have recognized that the milk is really sour. Where previously she had been "thankful" for *any* type of milk, she now has reached a point, brought about by lessened guilt, of expecting good milk. She has projected the guilt that arises from the sour milk of the past to the therapist, and sees in him that same sour milk. But in doing so, she will make right the past, as only the unreality of the therapeutic transference can.

Often a client, when he's in this certain stage of therapy, will be heard to remark: "There's something I feel I want to bring up; something I feel I haven't told you yet, but I don't know what it is." This is a client that probably has already felt secure enough in the oral gratification from his therapeutic listener to have exposed his guilt in some metaphorical presentation. But now he is aware of something else that needs to be "told," or "brought up," yet can't seem to specify it. What this "something" is, is the anger toward the listening transference figure that is coming closer, as oral gratification is more secured, to being mobilized. That this *is* anger that is getting closer to being externalized is metaphorically confirmed by later verbalizations that begin as: "I'd like to tell him off, *but ---.*"

There is often an apparent initial reluctance to project the guilt that is so *necessary* for the expression of anger. The difficulty of continuing an oral dependency relationship with the presentation of a justification for anger expression can be metaphorically expressed in many different ways. This is illustrated in the following excerpt: "I don't know if I can continue on these tranquilizers (referring to oral dependency on the therapist) that I'm taking. The longer I stay on them, the *meaner* I seem to be getting. I've gotten now that I fly off the handle at my husband if he just looks at me cross-eyed (a self-felt exaggeration of her anger). And I know he can't possibly keep on taking it. I've never been this way, so I lay it all to those pills (oral dependency) you have me on. I feel so guilty (but only *in part*) treating him this way. (Laughs.) Really, now, he hasn't been that bad at all that he deserves the way I've been acting toward him. He asked me just the other day if you knew what you were doing in putting me on those pills. What's in them anyway that makes me so evil and ornery? He says if this is progress from your treating me, then one of us is crazy" (a projection of guilt to the therapist vs. self-felt guilt). As this client continues, the projection of guilt will be utilized more firmly, and less ambivalently so.

A similar analogy involving "pills," that metaphorically stands for the oral need gratification that leads to anger expression, is shown as: "Just the other day (a time reference to the last therapy session) I got real mad at my husband. I found myself getting angrier and angrier by the moment, just because he was sitting there eating potato chips while watching TV (referring perhaps to the therapist satisfying his oral needs in the therapy situation). I'm supposed to be on a diet (a latent reference to the *emotional* "diet" of a guilt-laden person). Every time I heard the potato chips crunch in his mouth, I felt like going over there and just grabbing that bag and dumping the contents all over him. I was never

156

like that! (Laughs.) I told him about it, and he said that he knew it was the birth control pills that I've been taking. He knows it really isn't me, and so he said he really didn't blame me. (Therapist: Good.) He wants me to continue on those pills."

The point of beginning anger expression is often presented in the manner illustrated in the preceding. What previously was tolerated in the sphere of interpersonal relationships of the client is no longer tolerated because of the lessened guilt. What the previous level of unconscious guilt made them endure before, they now find, with less guilt, that they are *less* able to tolerate the increasingly perceived injustices of oral dependency need frustration, as: "I used to get so blue and weepy after I had exploded and lost control of myself. But I don't now." For this individual, the ease in loss of control of her anger is equaled by the ease in less controlled oral gratification. This client, for instance, had been unable to reach a climax with her husband until she had reached this point of "losing control" in regard to both anger expression and oral gratification. Metaphorically referring to oral gratification, she remarked: "I've just found out what I've been missing all these years!"

Though there still may be a reluctance to express anger, there may also be an indication that the client feels, in the reality situation about which they verbalize, that *they* haven't *initiated* the expression of anger. This is shown in: "*She* (referring latently to the therapist) started it — *I* didn't want to get in the fight, but *she* was just itching to start a quarrel. She's like that. She was baiting me, and she *knew* I was in the right, and that she was in the wrong. And yet, she *purposely* provoked me. *She* started it. I wouldn't have gotten mad if *she* hadn't acted this way!"

Another client seeks to rationalize, with lessened unconscious guilt, her beginning expressions of anger. She does so in a way that is utilized by thousands of others who use this same rationalization that finds support in several "best sellers" on hypoglycemia. (And note that in these as well as the psychologically or religiously-oriented best sellers, the emphasis is on the philosophy that one need only do it *themselves* — which is what the emotionally uncomfortable and guilt-laden individual *wants* to hear!) "This hypoglycemia I found out I have is making me irritable. I've had, all along, every one of those other symptoms that was listed in this book I've been reading on hypoglycemia, except one. (But it's that one "symptom" that causes all the others!) I had the tiredness, the depression, the weakness, and even the feeling that I was going to pass out. I never thought I had the symptom of irritability, but I've sure got that now! And I've been *so* careful of what I've been eating — you know that (and she has been characterized as "eating" very little in her therapy sessions). Why I just pick at my food. Now I've got the symptom of irritability. I've gotten so that I'm irritable about everything. I told my family that it's just part of my illness, and my family doctor said I might

157

as well put up with it. My husband has been very understanding of it — a lot more than I thought he'd be, and a lot more than I am myself."

When oral dependency is firmly established, a client will begin to metaphorically "set the stage" for anger expression in manifest contents. The client begins to develop the analogies that upon verbal expression will allow anger ventilation about some reality-oriented problem in his interpersonal relationship sphere. They imply that they are "right" in the position they hold; they imply that they've been "wronged", in the past, and they acknowledge that they are now angry, but aren't quite ready to express it. Just bringing up the fact that they *are* angry represents that they are on the threshold of actual anger expression. For instance, one client, with more secured oral dependency gratification than she had before, remarked: "I don't like to talk to Mr. Rodgers about my job, as I'm afraid I'd lose control of myself, and *really* tell him off. I *need* this job, and I'd hate to be fired!" This client is already beginning to project her guilt in presenting a problem as due to somebody *other* than herself. She has reached a point where, in the reality-oriented manifest content, the stage is set for anger expression. Emotionally, the anger expression will be to the listening transference figure. This is similarly shown in the following, where there is a more direct reference to the therapist: "I'd like to tell that damn Joyce (her employer in reality, but the therapist in metaphor) off, but I'm financially (*latently*, emotionally) *dependent* on her. If I told her off, she'd probably fire me, and then I wouldn't be able to do things I like to do that I'm doing now . . . (Laughs) like seeing *you!*" How this client can tell off "Joyce," and still keep her job, will be shown in the following chapter.

CHAPTER 8

THE EXPRESSION OF ANGER IN TRANSFERENCE LANGUAGE

Not only does human communication serve to *meet* the emotional needs of an individual, but it also affords an opportunity to *express* the anger from the oral needs that must be frustrated because of reality. Because the oral needs are so early frustrated in life, there is always an inevitable secondary "need" to express anger. The individual with a large enough sphere of object relationships has enough part objects within this sphere from which to draw a continual meeting of his oral needs, as well as a dispersion in his anger expression. Within the unreality of his transference relationship, he can bite the "bad breast" while still obtaining emotional nourishment from the "good breast." He can do this because he has a *diffusion* of his oral dependency needs. It isn't that he has less of an oral dependency need, but that he has *diluted* this need within a variety of transference relationships with many objects. In an expanding world of interpersonal relationships, he has gone from the infant-primary object relationship to many object relationships.

But the individual with a *concentration* of unmet oral needs has been excessively frustrated. He will, first of all, find himself emotionally uncomfortable, and secondly will find himself involved in intense transference relationships. This will tend to set up the object, upon whom support is reluctantly drawn, as a target for the potential expression of his repressed angry feelings. It is the emotional support from that object that equates the object of the present as the symbolic frustrating object of the distant past, and allows anger ventilation for those past oral need frustrations. The emotional support is oral dependency need "feeding" that fosters transference formation and makes the object more and more emotionally significant as emotional need gratification is continued.

When a point is reached in the relationship between the client and his therapeutic listener where anger is beginning to be expressed, it is more effective for that listener to verbalize very minimally, in order to keep the relationship ongoing toward an unreality that an intense transference can give. There is a need for a formal stance on the part of the therapeutic listener, in that he is, within the unreality of the therapeutic transference, both the object from which oral dependency supplies are drawn as well as the target for expressed anger. Such an ambivalent situation is best continued when the oral support is being unconsciously perceived, and is being presented metaphorically. In similar fashion, the anger expression is best done in metaphor or analogy. If anger is directly expressed toward the therapeutic listener, the relationship may be threatened with termination.

This expression or ventilation of previously repressed anger makes the therapeutic listener more than a mere "sounding board." To imply the therapeutic listener is a "sounding board" is a failure to recognize that the listener is a highly emotionally symbolic figure to whom latent references and implications are being *continually* made. It fails to recognize the importance of the *moment* in the client's emotional life, in rectifying his emotional problems and conflicts, and emphasizes erroneously the past as though only a cathartic process is taking place. Others have erroneously attributed anger ventilation to being directed toward an "authority figure" when in fact it is due to the primal position of a symbolic mothering part object that is elevated to a position of importance through oral dependency gratification, or perceived or phantasized oral gratification. It is not then that the therapeutic listener is representative of any authority — for he may be the most permissive of therapists — but that he is being symbolically perceived with an emotional significance through his position of granting oral dependency that places him in a high position. It isn't that the hated aspect of the dictatorial and cruel parent that harshly exerted his will upon the child that the anger is directed, but that the object that is granting oral dependency has an aspect that is symbolic of the distantly past emotionally significant objects that not only attempted to meet this individual's *oral* needs, but have frustrated him as well. This despotism is distinctly an *oral* problem, though it may be presented in metaphor and analogy on a superficial reality-oriented *manifest* level as an anal problem and involving authority figures. On the more basic level, it is the oral "bad breast" of oral dependency need frustration that is the object of the anger. And note that the *fear* of punishment for partaking a forbidden pleasure is a Freudian "anal" problem on a reality level, but underneath is the guilt-fear of destructive oral incorporation in regard to pleasure. That this seems so is born out by the general paucity or complete lack of guilt, or a previous fear of punishment, on the part of those in prisons even after having been adjudged "guilty," and the prevalence of intense guilt in so many people who have no reality reason for feeling so guilty.

In just a matter of time and frequent regular sessions, the dependency gratifying therapeutic listener will invariably become the object or part object for expressed anger. As the transference deepens, or becomes more intense, the object previously perceived as orally gratifying, and so much symbolic of the "good breast," is ambivalently viewed as frustrating and symbolic of the "bad breast" as well. When this ambivalent stage is reached in the therapeutic transference, there has been a projection of guilt by the client to the therapeutic listener. This projection of guilt enables the repressed anger to be externalized. An individual must have the feeling that he is *"right,"* in order to express anger, for when guilt

160

is self-felt, this anger ventilation is not possible. When the guilt is projected, it is as though the client is saying: *"I'm* right and *he's* wrong."* The immensity of repressed anger, that, before, was so difficult to express, when guilt was self-felt, now becomes "righteous wrath" when the individual projects his guilt with conviction. He is then able to externalize his anger at the part object within the transference relationship that is now imbued with his own projected guilt. By expressing his anger, the client's guilt then diminishes. But this is best done *with* ambivalence while the client is *both* continuing to meet his oral dependency needs, and while still continuing to express his anger. Both of these are done subtly, simultaneously, and without a conscious focus on the listener.

With decreasing guilt afforded by this process, the client has less of a reluctance to express his anger as was seen in the preceeding chapter. A client metaphorically shows this in her remark: "I *have* to tell things about Barbara (a perceived guilt-imbued aspect of the therapist) — I don't *like* to do it, but it's my job. I wouldn't be doing my job if I didn't. My boss (a perceived supportive aspect of the therapist) *has* to know what's going on in the office, and he can only do so from what *I* tell him." In spite of the expressed reluctance shown here, there is a justification now in the expression of this client's anger. Where previously she had a reluctance to express anger, she now begins to ventilate. Another client shows this same initial ambivalence, and this beginning feeling of justifiable anger expression, in the following statement: "I went to Father Moore (a supportive aspect of the therapist) to help me pray for forgiveness for exposing Dad (a guilt-imbued aspect of the therapist) in front of others for being the alcoholic, tramp-chasing son-of-a-bitch he *really* is."

When the guilt is projected and metaphorically conceptualized, the expression of anger can be done while still drawing oral supplies. There is a distance that affords a safety in ensuring a continuation of oral need gratification, yet still allows the client to continue to make remarks that convey his anger to another metaphorical part object that is now being unconsciously perceived in the therapist. It seems as though the client looks into the reality of his past or present interpersonal relationships to create his metaphors and analogies, and to find the rationalizations, on a reality basis, to express his anger toward the therapeutic listener. "I thought I lied a lot until I started listening to *Mary.* I thought *I* was bad until I met *her"* represents the beginning of anger expression of a previously depressed client. "Those people that come to the house and say Dick is so nice really don't know him at all. God! If they only knew what he is like when he gets into one of his drunken stupors, where he's all over you and just smothering you with kisses. I just hate his alcoholic breath. I know a wife shouldn't say this, but I hate him near me. I wish others knew him the way I do, but no, they think he's so great and so perfect!" is a prelude of an analogy of how she is viewing, in the transference, the therapeutic listener that will allow enlargement and lead to still other anger ventilating analogies.

Support for these statements, though, must be minimally verbalized or else simply non-verbally supported, in that they frequently show ambivalence. To vigorously support such statements conveying anger expression is to disregard the other facets of this ambivalence. This then conveys to the client that the therapist is not so understanding of his client's feelings. And this misunderstanding jeopardizes oral dependency support. In other words, to vigorously support anger expression can be a frustration of oral dependency gratification, simply because the unconsciously perceived therapist is *both* the "good breast," and simultaneously the "bad breast" too. When one too actively supports the orientation toward the "bad breast" that the client is temporarily taking, the position of the "good breast" can be made too distant, hampering further anger ventilation. The therapeutic listener may then find that he has lost "therapeutic ground" in being too hasty in his approach to allow the client anger expression when the client is not ready for it. The client *himself* will set his own pace for his anger ventilation and needs little help from the therapist other than his continued listening.

Sometimes the ambivalence in anger expression seems to be not only metaphorically recognized, but then seemingly justified. This is nicely shown in the following excerpt: "I could feel the tension building up between Jack and Bill (metaphorically, unconsciously perceived aspects of therapist and client). I didn't like it, and it made me feel a little uncomfortable. I don't like to see people angry at each other. But I've come to realize that there *has* to be tension like that. Jack and Bill see things from a different point of view because of their different positions within the company. They're not paid to agree on things, but to bring up different and often opposing viewpoints. Sure, there'll be some angry words, too. The success of the business depends upon this. I've never realized that before. Now I see it's a *necessary* part of their jobs."

At other times the difficulty in the expression of anger implies so well the oral problem of expressing anger toward an object on whom one is orally dependent. This is shown in the following excerpt of a client previously characterized as passive, meek, and frequently depressed: "I'm boiling mad! It's that God-damn plumber of mine! He sent me a bill that's outrageous for what little work he's done. I'd like to tell the s.o.b. off, but what can I do when he's the only one who knows the plumbing system? With a crazy, mixed up plumbing system like I've got, you just can't have anyone working on it. Everything that goes under the floor and behind the walls he knows about. I've had him so many different times in the past that he knows, like no one else knows, where each pipe goes. I could get someone else, but I'd have to start all over again. And that would be even more expensive! And I'd hate to have sewer pipes backing up (a reference to her previous high level of guilt) like I did last year. So he's just got me where he wants me. Damn him! But I can still get mad at him. Just the thought of him gives me that same feeling of increased adrenalin I had when I first started coming here 2 years ago. I didn't know what was causing it then. I thought I was actually going crazy. It was nothing but stored up anger from people like the plumber. I know it was. It's all making sense to me now. I was angry *then,* just like I am at this God-damn plumber *now!"*

That there are so many different possible analogies that one can derive from their own particular realities in order to express their anger seems implied in the following excerpt: "Mary Sue (metaphorically, the client, herself) found out she was allergic to a lot of different things she never even suspected. Some of the things she wouldn't want to do without. She never believed that she was allergic to so many different things that could cause her trouble. She had at least 40 different tests done by Dr. Wentworth (metaphorically, the therapist). He showed her that she was allergic to more than half of them. The biggest reaction she had was to cat dander! Can you imagine that! As much as she loves that cat (i.e., the unconsciously perceived orally gratifying aspect of the therapist) of hers! She could hardly believe that the very thing she cherishes the most was the biggest cause of all the trouble she's been having the past winter. Dr. Wentworth told her that's how it usually goes with allergies. She likes him a lot. He's easy to talk to, and seems to take such a fatherly (fatherly in reality — but the "good breast" in the unreality) interest in her. Why, she even found out she was allergic to sycamore trees (a more complex metaphor for the therapist, denoting closeness). (Laughs.) I wouldn't think that anyone would be bothered by something like that. And she lives in the middle of a grove of them. (Laughs.) I hope she won't have to move." (Therapist: I certainly hope not!)

Sometimes the expression of anger by the client himself is metaphorically referred to later, as though the recognition of it comes as a surprise. This is metaphorically presented in the following excerpt: "I was really shocked when I heard Alice (Alice is metaphorical for an aspect of herself that is now capable of expressing anger) say very loudly 'Goddamn it!' I was so surprised to hear her talk that way. When she found out that the restaurant had closed (a reference to perceived oral frustration in the therapeutic transference), boy did she get angry! I would have just contented myself with waiting until another time to go out to eat, but not Alice. She's the one that's always supposed to be in control of herself, and of situations that she's in, and I'm the one that's always falling apart. Why, I'd *never* think of saying something like that to anyone else — not even silently to myself. Alice actually shocked me as she's the one, too, that has a Bible study group (a latent reference to the part object make-up of the transference), and is always reading something religious into anything anyone says. She didn't let that hold her back, though, from calling the restaurant manager one 'son-of-a-bitch' when he closed the restaurant with us standing at the door (perhaps a reference to the termination of a therapy session). I'd never think of calling a person that no matter how frustrated I felt, or no matter how much they *were* one!"

A client spontaneously brings up in a talking and listening session an episode that occurred when she brought her daughter to a surgeon for the removal of a wart (latently referring to the symbolic removal of the client's guilt): "That Doctor Green (one perceived aspect of the therapist) is so damn mean. He just can't be civil. He can't say anything without insulting a person. He's so overbearing and thinks he's so great. (But it's her transference reaction and her oral dependency that has made the therapist *seem* so "great"!) I'd just love to buy him for what he's worth and sell him for what he thinks he's worth. I'd make a fortune! (Laughs and therapist does, too.) Mary (an aspect of the client) just can't stand him. I wouldn't blame her for kicking him the way he was talking to her. He talked to her like she was a dog, like she was nothing but a bother, and as though he couldn't have cared less. But Dr. Smith (another perceived aspect of the therapist) is just the opposite (smiles warmly). He explains things out if you don't understand them. He's always so patient and understanding, and makes you feel at ease. Nothing is more important than *you,* when you're with Dr. Smith. Dr. Green is always gruff. He told Mary to shut up and quit complaining, and that she was just being a cry baby. Now, how in the hell does he know whether it's hurting her? The big boob! He asked her 'What are you, a little infant or something? I thought you were a lot bigger than this.' That made her feel terrible. I thought she was doing very well for a little girl of only ten. Now she just abhors going to see him. Everytime she goes to the surgery clinic, she hopes and prays that she'll get Dr. Smith. I try to tell her that she's got to expect a little rain now and then with the sunshine in life. I hate to say it but I think I would have been proud of Mary if she had just upped and kicked Dr. Green instead of being like me, trying to grin and bear it. I don't think a person should have to take anything like that from someone, even if he is a doctor, do you?"

Sometimes a client will metaphorically present an analogy, as though supporting an aspect of herself that is expressing anger. This is shown in the following excerpt: "Jimmy (an unconscious aspect of the client) has kept his mouth shut too long, but lately he's begun to speak out for what he feels is right. I'd like to see him do a lot more of this, but the principal (an unconsciously perceived aspect of the therapist) apparently doesn't want him to. She thinks he's too talkative, and that it's *he* that starts all the fights. But Jimmy and I (here "I" is metaphorically, a concretization of both a supportive aspect of the therapist, and a guilt-free aspect of herself) know differently. I told Jimmy that if anyone started picking on him at school to hit them right back. I don't want him taking anything off of anybody. I know what that's like from *my* childhood. (Therapist: That's right.) The principal said if she caught Jimmy fighting again, she'd expel him (that is terminate the client-therapist relationship). But why does she have to blame *him* when other kids (referring to the therapist) start the fight? He has a right to protect himself, doesn't he? Wouldn't you say a child should be able to defend himself? Why should he be a kicking dog or door mat to others? That old principal is nothing but an old witch who *never* has treated Jimmy fairly. I'd like to take Jimmy out of school so he wouldn't have to put up with the old bag!" (Therapist: I hope he doesn't back down to her.)

Even when oral need gratification is metaphorically presented as being acknowledged, anger can still be expressed in the same analogy. This is illustrated in the following: "I just can't stand Dad's housekeeper ("Dad" is she herself in metaphor, and the "housekeeper" is the therapist). I know what she is up to! She would like nothing better than to be *Mrs.* Ruark! (Therapist: To be *Mrs.* Ruark?) Yes! She has it all figured out. I've been onto her ever since she came to Dad for a job. But if I have anything to do with it, she'll *never* become Mrs. Ruark, and she won't get a red cent of his estate either. I've noticed little things that she'll do to make him more comfortable. Things that I think go beyond her job as a housekeeper. She's trying to be a wife on the sly. Just little things at a time — nothing really forward. For instance, when he sits down to eat, she has to pull *her* chair right up to *his!* She's always fixing him his favorite meals. He likes sweets, but I don't think she should be giving him so much of them. And then I've seen her fixing the collar on his shirt, or brushing away pieces of lint from his clothes. You know, like a wife does. That just makes me so mad. She's probably just after his money. He's got a large farm, and she'd just love to have it. What she's probably planning is to get him more and more dependent on her, and then when he is so, she'll tell him she's going to leave him unless he marries her. I know the type (and she does from her own past emotional experiences). All that type does is use you. So, I've been trying to fight his getting dependent on her. I will admit that it does take a load off of me to have her with him, but as far as I'm concerned it'll be over my dead body that she'll ever get *married* to him."

A panorama of inter-related, but ambivalent feelings associated with the variously perceived aspects of the therapeutic listener are succinctly expressed in the following excerpt. This forty-year-old housewife came to therapy because her husband felt that she needed "straightening out" and "maybe some shock treatment." She conveys latently her feelings about the transference situation, and unconsciously presents perceived attributes of herself, and the therapist, while analogically conceptualizing these in a dynamic verbal interplay by various metaphors that fit the reality of the analogy. "Steve" is her underweight son, and latently represents the self-felt "psychopathologic" aspect of herself, while the "pediatrician" is the benevolent, understanding and reassuring aspect of the therapist, on whom she attempts to gratify her oral needs, and who implies the relationship was not necessary as far as any pathology is concerned. "Jim" her husband, represents those unconsciously perceived "pressuring" attributes of the therapist, toward whom her hostility seems justifiably directed from a reality standpoint. "We have a problem with Steve. He's been a very poor student, and I know he doesn't want to involve himself much in school (therapy). But maybe it's just the stage he's going through in growing up. He's been content to kind of go along on his own, but everyone (i.e., perceived aspects of the therapist) is on his back. (Therapist: On his back?) They're *always* after him, though I do realize they're trying to help him. But they're going at it the wrong way (this is an unconscious perception *she* makes about the therapist's behavior in therapy, through her guilt, for the therapist verbalizes little). He hears too much: 'Don't do this, and don't do that' at school. While at home, he gets: 'Have you washed your face?' 'Have you brushed your teeth?' 'Have you done all your homework?' 'And have you done your chores?' He's sensitive, so that these questions hurt and seem to imply he's *not* doing what he's supposed to. (Therapist: I see.) I will admit he is at times immature and a little thoughtless, and it does bother me that he's like that. But he *could* grow out of it if they would just leave him alone. Jim is always picking on him (implying a perceived condemning aspect of the therapist). For instance, he says he doesn't eat enough, but who can eat when they're always being put down? Everyone is always running him down in the family. Even his brothers and sisters (other perceived aspects of the therapist) do it. I have to admit that I've done it too (and she has been self-debasing). But I know from my own childhood that it's not good for Steve. Jim wants him to be much more active, much more aggressive and to eat more. I think he's trying to make him what he himself wanted to be as a boy. (Note that she may be quite correct in the reality of this analogy, but it is more important for the reader to recognize what she is expressing *latently* to the unconsciously perceived therapist at the moment.) Jim will get upset about things that Steve does that I consider just normal for a boy in his stage of development. Jim even insisted that he go to the pediatrician (i.e., the therapist as a "psychiatrist," or one who "treats psychopathology"), but I can tell you Steve sure didn't want to go (and neither did this client!). He cried because it made him feel he was *sick* in some way. The pediatrician just said to leave him alone. 'He's getting enough of the food that he needs, even though he's just picking at it. He'll take what he needs. Stop hounding him. He's going to have to develop at his own pace.' The pediatrician also mentioned that each one of us is an individual, and that no two people are exactly alike, so that we can't be judging one boy against another. He said that it isn't fair to compare Steve to how his father was at that age or perhaps how he would have *liked* to have been. To do so just isn't fair to the boy and that's what makes *me* so mad. (Therapist: I see.) Even though Steve didn't want to go to the pediatrician, I think that it did help him and that it's still helping, in that it showed Jim that Steve wasn't really as bad as Jim thought he was. I only wish the pediatrician could have talked directly to Jim. I don't see why *I* have to be the one to take Steve in, when I can see so well now that *Jim* has played a big role in Steve's problem of not eating enough.''

Another client, who unwillingly has accepted a gratification of her oral needs, now begins to project different aspects of herself within the therapeutic transference. She is a "witch" that ought to be locked up on one hand, while on the other hand, as "Nancy," representing a part of herself that does accept the gratification of her oral needs, she is causing a "scene on the beach," implying that the oral gratification is associated with guilt. "I've got a real problem with this neighbor, Mrs. Lock (a denied unacceptable guilt-laden aspect of herself that is being projected). She tries to get to see anybody every time they go by her door. I think she's just *starved* for attention. I hate to be around this type of *dependent* person. Nobody likes her (and this client previously hated herself). She's ready to hang on *anybody* if they'd let her. But if anybody *does* let her, then she's *mad* at them the very next day. She's either the greatest of friends with a person, or the greatest of enemies. No in-betweens. It's always one way or the other. If you're foolish enough to be her friend one day, then watch out, you'll be her worst enemy the next! (Note the appropriateness of this analogy to the therapeutic transference process.) She must sit and watch for me, because as soon as I go out the door to go visit, she has to come out, and then I can't get rid of her (i.e., because "Mrs. Lock" is still so much a part of herself). I hate to have anyone see her with me. And to think how I used to believe she was so nice and so concerned about other people (and this client previously tried to live up to superhuman standards of nicety in regard to others). Lately, I've been trying to avoid her just as much as possible, as I don't want to have anything to do with her. I don't like the way she clings to people, and then runs them down later. She's a regular two-faced witch! One day she'll go out of her way to get the children to play with her, and the next day they can't do anything right for her and she doesn't want them near her. She'll scream at them at the top of her voice. She's so bad she ought to be seeing you regularly. But she won't (and neither will this client). (Pause.) Well, let's see now what else is new? — Oh, yes, Ralph and Nancy (i.e., the therapist and the client herself) were seen smooching on the sand. I understand they caused a scene on the beach and someone at the hotel complained. (Laughs.) I don't mind them going together, as I think they make a nice pair, but Nancy can go *too far*, you know."

What is taking place between the part objects of both client and therapist within the therapeutic transference is metaphorically presented by a young secretary in the following excerpt: "Boy, am I mad! I've never been so mad in my entire life! It started out in the office the other day, when my boss (an unconsciously perceived aspect of the therapist) asked why I hadn't got those insurance forms out. He said: 'They should have been completed a week ago!' I turned right around to him and said: 'Look, Mr. Nelson, I'm going as fast as I can. I've only got two hands!' I've *never* spoken that way to him before in my life! I don't know what happened to me. It seemed as though it just slipped right out. It surprised him when I said it. I thought he'd fire me on the spot, but he just smiled and said: 'Okay, Okay! I've got the message!' (Laughs.) Before, I would have kept my mouth shut and then gone in the back room and cried for a few minutes. But right after he and I had that run in, then in came this client with her little boy (another unconsciously perceived aspect of the therapist) whom I dearly love. He's the sweetest thing! (Smiles warmly at therapist.) I mean, I just love him and I could sit and hold him all day. He knows it too. (Laughs warmly.) He came running over and crawled right up in my lap. He gave me a great big kiss, a big grin, and then he hugged me. Well, Betty (a perceived unaccepting aspect of the therapist) saw all this. I could see she didn't like it. I just ignored her, but then she had to say: 'You shouldn't be so friendly . . . that can only lead to trouble.' Now that just made me angry again, and without even thinking I said: 'What's wrong with it, and what's it to *you* anyway?' I was ready for a fight. So Betty said: 'Well, what if all the other children (all the other unmet and guilt-laden oral dependency needs that could be satisfied by the therapist) want to crawl up in your lap? How's the work going to get done? And the way you let him play with your typewriter (metaphorical for her oral dependency needs and *not* sexual, as many analysts would interpret this), he'll wreck it!' I was so mad that I went in and told Lois (the chief secretary, but latently, an unconsciously perceived, more accepting aspect of the therapist). Well, Lois said: 'I know you've got to work with Betty, but you've got a right to express yourself too. I'm glad to see you're sticking up for yourself for once.' (Therapist: nods approvingly.) I was so uncontrollably mad. It seems as though I lack the patience I use to have. I use to put up with stuff like this; now I don't. I must be getting *worse,* not better! (Laughts.) This Betty reminds me of another girl (referring again to the therapist) I used to have to work with in the past, that would go around and tell others how bad I was behind my back . . . you know . . . that I wasn't a good typist and that I didn't know my job. It was because of her that I went into a shell, got depressed and finally lost my job. She used to make me feel I was only an inch high. Betty is just like her. I can see a resemblance between the two that I couldn't see before. It's so plain to me now. But now I won't take it. I'll stand up now and fight. You'd better believe it! I'll fight her tooth and claw! Anytime this boy comes in to see me, he's going to have a special place in *my* lap, and he can play with my typewriter all he wants!"

A forty-two-year-old food inspector who frequently had been depressed in the past, and subject to incapacitating episodes of anxiety as well as recurrent headaches, angrily remarked in his twentieth session: "I went to see a doctor (latent reference to therapist) a week or so ago about my headaches, and he said it might be my blood pressure because of the tension and anxiety of my job (i.e., therapy) I told him I had the easiest job in the world, and that I wasn't worried about a thing that I knew of. But he told me that I still could have high blood pressure, causing the headaches, because of *subtle* factors in my work. I've thought about that a lot during the past week. Perhaps in the past (when his guilt was at a higher level) I tended to overlook some factors in my work that I can see more plainly now. I do have to call attention to things on the production line if they aren't being processed right. That's my job. That's what I'm supposed to do. But it's not easy to do when I'm caught between the company on one side and the government on the other (metaphorically, the oral dilemma). And I will say it *does* kind of make me mad when I have to keep telling a certain foreman (an unconsciously perceived aspect of the therapist) what's wrong, just because he's so damn interested in keeping the production lines open, and everything going on schedule. I've let him get by with substandard things in the past that I know I shouldn't have. I'd do it just to be nice to him. But that's not my job. Why should I be nice to him? I don't owe that guy a damn thing. I don't work for him or the company. Uncle Sam (i.e., the therapist) is backing me up and Uncle Sam pays me too. I've been noticing lately this foreman has been itching for a fight. He's been asking for one and, by God, he's going to get one, if that's what he wants (note the projection of the "spoiling for a fight," in anger expression of his, *to* the therapist). He doesn't listen to half of the things I say, and he acts at times as though he doesn't give a damn whether I'm there or not. I can see now that it's my *job* to get angry now and then, when the food on the line isn't meeting the U.S. Government standards."

A friendly, always smiling bank official, who was also referred for therapy because of recurrent headaches that were unrelieved by the medication of his family doctor, shows his ability to express his previously repressed and defensively denied anger to the therapist in the following excerpt: "I seem to be doing a lot better. But things aren't quite right yet. I've still got those pressure headaches. They're not as frequent as before, but they're just as uncomfortable when I do have them. (Therapist: "I bet they can be very uncomfortable.") Yes, they can. A person (specifically, the therapist) can't understand how uncomfortable they really are unless they've had them themselves. (Therapist: "That's right.") They feel as though the top of my head is ready to blow right off. It's a sensation of a pressure building up in my head. I've been trying to figure out these headaches of mine. Before, I couldn't relate them to anything. I was always feeling that there was absolutely no rhyme or reason to them. I just couldn't see that they were due to anything but a physical abnormality. You know, like a blood vessel anomaly or maybe an atypical form of migraine. Before I started coming here, I even felt they might be due to a brain tumor. (Laughs.) But I've finally come to the conclusion they have something to do with my work and with my boss. (Therapist: Your boss?) Yes, my boss. The headaches seem to come *only* when I'm around him. I *never* have that pressure unless I'm around him. It's funny how I couldn't see the connection before. Last week I had a spell right after I noticed he was on me a little. It's tension right on the back of my head. Right here. (Puts hand on back of head.) He's the type of person that wants everyone afraid of him. He's got to have it that way. It must meet some type of need on his part. When he's there in the morning, it's 'Here I am — let's get *going*, everyone!' Just like *he* is necessary for us to do *our* jobs. We get more done when he's *not* there! He's domineering and has no diplomacy or tact whatsoever — just blares right out with things that are best not said, or at least said with some tact. He's the one that ought to be sitting here (points to his chair) in this place (a projection of *his* guilt to the therapist). But, oh no! He'd have to have *that* chair (points to therapist's chair). I'm beginning to see him for what he really is now. He'll tell someone in the office to get busy on one thing, and before they can be finished with that, he's off on something else. And that confuses the hell out of everyone (i.e., "me"). Even his secretary (the client again in metaphor) doesn't know if he's coming or going. He's always confusing her with what he's trying to do. And that puts pressure on me because I have to keep smiling and humoring him. He says he wants an office where everyone (specifically, the client) is happy. He likes to emphasize what he calls "togetherness," but what he really wants is a togetherness of everyone bowing down to all his little whims and making him the focus of their attention. How can there be any real togetherness when he wants the whole office to revolve around him? (Note that this is a manifestation of how the transference of the client emotionally imbues the therapeutic listener with an epitome of emotional significance, which is then *resented* by the client. This same phenomenon that is so often seen latently in client-therapist relationships shows itself as well in other interpersonal relationships.) I'd like to tell the damn bastard to go to hell! (Laughs.) The old son-of-a-bitch! (Therapist: "Yaa.") I've been smiling at him for 10 years now (12 sessions to be exact) and that's just about long enough. From now on, I'll tell him where to head in. (Therapist: "Good.") I can feel that pressure right now on the back of my head. (Puts hand on top of head.) Just my talking about him has brought it on."

Many times the anger is only tokenly expressed, with a metaphorical presentation of the dilemma this poses, when dependency gratification is insecure. This is shown in the following: "I don't know how much longer I can put up with Mr. Donaldson. He really thinks he's a king-pin, a 'Mr. Perfect,' and a 'know it all.' (His perceptions of greatness and perfection in the therapist are derived from his *own* transference — this is similar to a client's feeling of increasing emotional closeness or an emotional moving in, brought about by the transference, and then interpreted as originating with the therapist, feeling then that the therapist is "seductive.") He thinks he's the greatest thing going on the face of the earth, but I *know* he's not even qualifed to do the work he's doing — or trying to give the the impression he's doing, and on top of that, I know what he's really like. I caught him out with a girl (the previously guilt-laden but now projected aspect of *himself* that gets "caught" in dependency) once when he was supposed to have been working. He was driving along with this pretty young thing (a projected aspect of himself) sitting right there next to him with his arm around her. (Therapist: How about that!) He's the one that likes to put up the formal 'high and mighty' front in the office. And she's got the *worst* reputation in the whole county! I've known her for a long time and she's *worse* than worthless! She'd go with anything wearing pants (implying this projected guilt-laden aspect of him-

170

self is just this orally hungry — but note how the analogy is appropriately presented in a reality-oriented sexual context.) There he was riding around with her like a couple of teenagers in love. The way he acted when he saw me made me laugh. (Laughs.) I don't think he wanted anyone to know he was making out with her. You know, he was supposed to be checking on the highway construction. He's paid to do this, not make love. But he's not fooling anyone. No sir! Any man (latently, the therapist) that goes around with the type of person (meaning the client himself) I've caught him with can't be worth much himself! It means he's just that low-down and common *himself*. (Therapist: Yaa.) Well, that's the way he is. (Pause.) He makes me so mad at times (I'd just love to tell him off right to his face. And if I did, I probably wouldn't have all this stomach pain and those pains in the back of my head. But I can't tell him what I really think of him, because I've got my job to consider. (Therapist: Sure.) If I told him that I thought he was nothing but a pompous ass, or even a son-of-a-bitch, well, you know, that would finish me as far as my job is concerned. (Note how tenuous he feels his dependency position is in regard to the therapeutic transference at this point. With continuing oral dependency gratification within the therapeutic transference, his dependency position will be more secured. This will be mirrored by first, an ease in anger expression, and later by more stable emotionally gratifying relationships in his interpersonal sphere. This ensures a better position to express anger for any perceived frustrations of his oral dependency needs and will lead to a position beyond, where, because his oral dependency needs *are* being diffusely met, there will be *less* of a need to *express* any anger.) He could dismiss me and there wouldn't be a damn thing that I could do about it, at this point. I can't go out and find another job that pays me (i.e. gives oral gratification) like this one does. That's the fearful type of working relationship I have with him. (Therapist: That puts you in sort of a dilemma.) Yes it does! It's just like you and your secretary (a less latent metaphor for the client, but with different connotations, in that there is less guilt implied). She's *got* to be nice to you because if she wasn't, you'd fire her, wouldn't you? (Here the client seems to be testing how far he can go with the expression of his anger.) I mean, you wouldn't want her telling *you* off, would you? (Therapist: Well, I'd want her to feel free to express her feelings toward me.) Sure, but you know what I mean." (Therapist: I understand.)

Another client who had tried to get up with the therapist in between therapy sessions remarked in her following session: "I was mad as hell at Bill (her divorced husband, and a metaphorical aspect of the therapist, toward which she has perceived an oral need frustration) because he didn't call me last week when I tried to get up with him. I had promised Stefanie (her daughter, and the metaphorical aspect of herself equated with her dependency needs) she could talk with her father. She got to crying and then that upset me. I got so mad at Bill when he didn't call that I swear I could have killed him. It didn't bother *me* (the aspect of herself, that denies oral dependency) one single bit whether he called

171

or not, but Stefanie *did* want to say a few words to him. She wanted to hear his voice because, after all, he still is her father (father in reality, but the unattainable "good breast" on the implied *oral* level) and the very least he could have done was to have called her. (Therapist: That's not asking too much!) No it isn't! I finally thought to myself 'Well, the hell with you.' So Stefanie and I went over to my neighbor's house (a perceived supportive aspect of the therapeutic transference). We had a pretty good time. (Smiles warmly.) I chatted all evening with the neighbor. She's easy to talk to as she's gone through the same thing herself. (The therapist hasn't, but through her perception of his understanding she views him as such, and conceptualizes this in the analogy.) Stefanie played with her child (an unconsciously perceived aspect of the therapist that the client feels is *mutually* dependent in the therapy situation). They're both the same age and they have so much in common. (Therapist: That's good.) Yes, it is! It's good she can get her mind off her father."

In the following excerpt, a client shows ambivalence in her expression of anger toward the therapist, rationalizing that the therapist never tells her *she's* any good. With the level of guilt she has at this point, she, *herself*, feels she's *not* any good and wouldn't be able to accept a verbalization as truthful that she was. She utilizes the metaphor "Bill" (her son in reality) to conceptualize an aspect of herself that she apparently doesn't know whether to support, or to condemn. In her requesting the therapist's opinion, she is asking for verbal confirmation for what she emotionally feels, but only *in part*, in regard to anger expression. It isn't really necessary for the therapist to give any verbal confirmation, for through the simple act of his listening, oral dependency support is conveyed, including the support for anger expression. (This "simple" listening process will not only promote transference formation and oral dependency need gratification, but will also support the expression of anger which ironically becomes *necessary because* of that very transference. It is the transference itself that will invariably put anger and a need to express it into any emotionally intense relationship. The more intense a transference relationship becomes, the greater is the need for anger expression.)

"Randall's father (initially "Randall's father" is the therapist, and she herself is "Randall") never told him he was any good in his life. That's the basis of his inferiority complex. Randall could *never* do anything that his father (i.e. the therapist) would say he did a good job, and that he was pleased with him. His father was always running him down and still does it. I think that's the whole problem. It's made him feel so inadequate and inferior. But he's (note how the connotation of the metaphor shifts now for "Randall" here becomes the therapist) doing the same thing with Bill (she herself). Bill worked so hard the other day to get his father to notice him. At his age, he needs attention from his father. He cleaned up the entire yard and at the end of the day, he asked me if his father had noticed what he had done. I told him: 'Well, I really haven't had a chance to talk with him to find out whether he's noticed it or not.' Well then, Bill went and asked his father himself, and that damn Randall said: 'I didn't see anything different. It looks the same to me.' That really made me mad. I want to tell you it made me see red (rolls up fist and squints angrily at therapist). Sometimes I feel like just knocking him in the head with a piece of wood. Maybe that would put some sense into him. But I really don't think it would do any good because it's all too late! He's got Bill hating him now. Bill is *despising* him and actually *wishing* he'd die! I dislike to say it, but I *know* it's true. But I don't know whether to put Bill *down* for talking that way about his father, or to try to give him some *support,* knowing that he's right. What do you think I should do?" (Therapist: Well, how do you feel about it?)

Referred for "psychotherapy" after a suicidal gesture, a woman who was also recovering from a cancer operation demonstrates that a client can always find *something* about the reality of the therapist, or the therapy situation toward which her guilt can be projected, and anger expressed. Sometimes, going well beyond the reality of the transference situation, what the client unconsciously utilizes as a justification for the expression of their anger toward the therapeutic listener is often either a projection of an aspect of themselves, or a product of their own transference. This is then attributed as arising not from themselves, but from the therapist. In her twenty-first session, a client angrily remarks: "Well, Joe (i.e., therapist) is still as complacent as he ever was. (Therapist: Oh?) He knows that I nearly died from this cancer (a reference to her past self-felt feeling of overwhelming oral guilt) but it apparently doesn't seem to bother him any. Sometimes I wonder if he isn't hoping that something *will* happen to me so he can just get rid of me. But *he* married me and I think he's got an obligation to me. (Therapist: Yes, he does!) I resent his just sitting there without showing much feeling at all about it one way or the other. Sure, he provides me with the bare necessities of life but I think I should be getting more than that. I *need* him, for instance, to help me at meal times (a reference to the emotional "feeding" of the therapeutic transference). He just sits there with his nose in a paper (perhaps a thinly disguised reference to the therapist taking notes) and says: 'Oh, Marlene (the client's teenage daughter, but latently, an unconscious aspect of herself that she feels, because of her guilt, is supposed to "do it alone") can take care of it.' But Marlene *can't* do it. She's tried, but it didn't work out at all. She's got her school work and she's flunking two courses (a reference to how the client feels, *in part,* about how she is doing in therapy). *He's* got to help, but he gives me the impression of 'Now, dear, don't bother me — go off by yourself — you're just too much of a bother to me' (a feeling engendered from the reality of the distant past, but now transferred to the unreality of the therapeutic transference situation — as well as probably all her interpersonal relationships). Yet he still wants meal times right by the clock (her sessions are regularly at 2 p.m. on Wednesdays). They can't be even five or ten minutes late or else he'll get all upset and

173

make some snide remark as though I purposefully planned the meal late. There's a certain time for meals with him and that's it. That's something I had told to me just as soon as we got married. This was a pretty hard adjustment for me to make. I want *you* to know that. When I was growing up, this type of neurotic regularity of meal times of his was unheard of (a latent reference to unconsciously perceived aspects of the emotional "feeding" earlier in the therapeutic transference). Lots of times, we'd even skip a meal (i.e. when her guilt was that excessive, the oral need gratification in the therapeutic transference was "skipped" — but note too that this also reflects her distant emotional past). But not my husband. He still insists on it. Come 6 p.m. and the food has to hit the platter. It doesn't make any difference to him if it takes time for me to get ready for a meal, and particularly for a good meal when I feel so hungry. That doesn't seem to bother him at all. Not a bit! He wants his meals right by the clock regardless of what is being served. He's so damn clock-conscious about having meals right on time that it just spoils my meal. I can't enjoy a meal as I'd like to under these conditions, and he knows how important it is for me to eat after that weight loss I had. Then, even before I finish, he's finished, gotten up from the table and gone. You know — he does his usual disappearing act. Now what can I do about that? (Therapist: Gestures.) I can't come right out and tell him that I don't like his behavior at meal times. I can't just tell him I don't see enough of him in between meals. I couldn't do that. And he wouldn't change anyway (Pause.) But I shouldn't be wanting to change him. (Note the presence of her guilt here that makes her anger expression ambivalent and implies the self-felt feeling her needs are *excessive*.) It *is* my job to be ready for meal times as a housewife. I really can't blame him since he does provide for the children (i.e. her oral needs). I shouldn't be as angry as I am about it all. But I just can't get close to him, and I'm sick and tired of being put off. I tried to get him to talk yesterday evening (i.e. last week in therapy), but he just doesn't want to say anything. He shuns me like he doesn't want to have anything to do with me. I can't talk things over with him. He won't talk — won't say anything. And to make matters worse, he thinks I talk too much (i.e. *she* unconsciously perceives the *therapist* feels that her oral needs are excessive). What am I to do? He's my husband, but in order for me to get to him during the week I almost have to make an appointment. I shouldn't have to have an appointment to see my own husband, should I? (Pause.) Well, I'm just sick and tired of it, as it shouldn't be that way! Just last week I told him to go to the doctor and have his hearing checked because I actually thought he had a hearing loss. It never seemed as though he was hearing anything I was saying. He did go, but they told me there was nothing wrong with his ears. Maybe it's the way I talk. Don't I talk plain enough? (Pause.) Now I want you to stop me if you think I talk too much."

Many times the first awareness, for an unknowledgeable therapist of a transference language, that the listener has become a focal point in the latent communications of a client-therapist relationship — whether he wanted to or not — comes about in the session following one that the therapist, himself, has cancelled. Perhaps it is that the anger expressed seems less disguised, or perhaps because of possible guilt feelings on the part of the therapist that the recognition is often suddenly made. But once the therapist *does* make this observation, he should have no difficulty in reasoning that the same process, the same phenomenon and the same latent and subtle interaction of unconsciously perceived parts will continue. For instance, one client remarked in her first session following the therapist's vacation: "I've been working real hard at the office (therapy) right along. *You* know how hard I've been working. But Clarence (her husband, a teacher — and the therapist in metaphor) was out of school. It didn't seem to bother him that I was working and he wasn't. But do you think I could get him to stay home with the children (i.e., her oral dependency needs)? Well, I guess not! He apparently has no respect for me and the only reason he stays with me is for the money I can bring to him. He left the children at home by themselves while he went off somewhere. Now I don't think a child ten years old is big enough to stay by himself, do you? (Here she seeks support from the therapist while simultaneously expressing anger at him.) I actually *pleaded* with Clarence to stay home with the children. I said: '*Please,* Clarence, don't leave them. They *need* you. They *need* somebody to care for them. *Please,* Clarence! *Please* stay with them!' (Pause.) But the son-of-a-bitch went off anyway!"

This is again shown in an excerpt of a client following a therapist-cancelled session. Here the ability of the client to express anger to the therapist for previously abandoning them shows *more* strength than those that might have simply discontinued. "I was sick this whole Christmas vacation with the flu (reality-wise perhaps she *did* have the flu, but in the language of the transference "flu" is a metaphor for her feelings of uncomfortableness from being abandoned). I want you to know I was absolutely miserable. I felt especially depressed because this is the time people are supposed to be happy and enjoying their families. But I just lay there in bed and thought how nobody loves me. I thought of how nobody seems to give a damn how uncomfortable I am, or whether I live or die. Peter (her husband, and the therapist in metaphor) had gone off somewhere, God only knows where. And there I was sick in bed trying to take care of the children (her oral dependency needs) myself! I felt like killing myself just to fix Peter in hopes he'd have the guilty feeling that *he* caused it. I was even *hating* this neighbor (another unconsciously perceived aspect of the therapist) of mine who had gone to Florida, as *nice* as she's been to me. I kept thinking of her lying on the warm beach in Florida, living it up and getting all tan while I was sick in a cold, God-forsaken and lonely house with three children, who wouldn't leave me alone. And then Peter came back wanting me to act as though nothing at all happened."

Once the phenomenon of transference language is recognized, one can easily follow the ventilation of anger in a client. This is shown in the case of a thirty-five-year-old lawyer, who angrily describes the unconsciously conceptualized aspects of the therapist and the therapeutic transference through the use of an analogy involving his work situation. "Henry," in the reality of the manifest level, is an associate that he recently hired to help him do the added work that he believes has caused him to become depressed. In the unreality of the therapeutic transference "Henry" is an unconsciously perceived aspect of the therapist upon which he is attempting to draw oral dependency need gratification. Though actually frustrated by his own guilt in this gratification, he blames the therapist. When he projects guilt to this metaphorical aspect of the therapist, the client is able to ventilate his anger. Another aspect of the therapist that is perceived as more supportive and having less projected guilt is that of his wife. This allows different facets of his ambivalence to be expressed so that more of his problems in the part object oriented orality can be exposed and presented for an emotional resolution. A manifest content that utilizes more and more different metaphors and analogies is indicative of *progress* in regard to decreasing the unconscious guilt while continuing to draw oral dependency gratification. In other words, a multiplicity of "good breasts" are being unconsciously perceived in the transference relationship and a multiplicity of targets for anger. Simultaneously, the reality of the interpersonal relationship sphere that provides the metaphors and analogies reflects this same dilution of oral dependency, and dispersion of anger. The metaphor of "Henry" allows an expression of anger, while the metaphor of his "wife" can convey his perceptions of oral gratification and present the problems that this can bring at this particular level of guilt. Such manifest content can be infinitely enlarged, allowing every possible facet of his ambivalence an expression. Yet this can be done with a distance that can be controlled by the client in that he is spontaneously verbalizing and therefore sets the emotional distance in regard to either oral dependency gratification or anger expression. The therapist, in his many variations of his transference role can support the client at whatever distance, simply through listening. Here in his eighteenth session he remarks: "Well, things are going good and bad. First of all, I think my wife is understanding me now much more than she ever has before. I didn't think she was capable of this. She knows I'm moody, but she seems to accept me more. She's been patient with me, and that's what I've needed most. We've done a lot more talking to each other lately than we have ever done in all the past years of marriage. She's been a big help to me and I appreciate her. (Therapist: smiles.) But I'm kind of worried about Henry. His attitude is bad, and all he does is sit there and watch me. I'd like to see a little activity on his part for a change. I hate to keep going over things with him that I think he ought to know already. He's paid enough to know it all. I dislike going over every case in detail with him before he can take any load off of me. I get so aggrevated with him at times for

176

not seeing things on his own, or going to the law books (psychiatry books?) and looking them up ahead of time instead of asking *me*. He waits until *I* bring them up, and that's not really helping me at all. I could actually do the work myself in *less* time, and at *less* expense, if I *didn't* have Henry trying to help me! I have to take time out to spend time with him to show him what a certain law problem is. So I end up paying *him* for *my* time. (Therapist: That doesn't seem right.) It isn't! What aggrevates me the most is having to stop and explain things to him. I keep hoping that it's going to be easier on me in the long run, because once he gets it, he's going to have the chance then to lighten the load for me. In the meantime, it's making me damn mad at times, while at other times it's damn depressing! I had planned to get much more work done than what I'm getting done now (note it's his guilt that makes him feel he should have accomplished more than he has). I'm even *further* behind in my work *because* of him. And that doesn't make much business sense since it was getting behind in my work that made me *depressed* (note the apparent transferring of the problem a client had prior to seeking professional help *into* the therapeutic situation). He's not as fast as I am. In fact, he's pretty damn slow. I can see problems that I just can't put into words. It takes time to explain it all out to Henry, and then I don't think he gets half the things I try to explain. I have a tendency anyway to want to do the thing myself, rather than take the time and effort to explain it to others. I think the whole problem, at this time, is whether I can accept the fact that I've got to show him what the problems are, and how I want them to be worked through, in order that he can help me *later*, as we go along."

In a following session, this same client continued to ventilate hostility toward "Henry." "I think I'm going to have to light a fire under Henry. He's just too damn slow for me. He just sat there all day yesterday and watched me work. It gripes me because I can see so much work that has to be done. But he won't go out of his way to look for it. No sir! He just sits there and waits for *me* to point it out. He's not taking any responsibility whatsoever, or any worry off of me, and that's what I really wanted a partner for. (Therapist: Sure.) At this point he's just collecting his money from me. That's all! And lately he's been telling me about all the money he could be making by working with somebody else as a full partner. He doesn't know it, but at this point I'm considering letting him go. (But "Henry" does know!) If he thinks he can make more headway with someone else, then he can go get someone else. (Therapist: That's right!) I get tired of leading him around by the nose. He's got no initiative — no push — and if he doesn't get on the stick, he not only won't be a full partner with me, but he (points finger emphatically at therapist) won't even be associated with me! And I get tired of his getting up and going home right at four p.m. every single working day. Now that really gripes the hell right out of me because there's so much work to be done. He knows it. Yet it doesn't seem to bother him a bit! Come quitting time and he just ups and leaves. I'm used to working on a problem until it's done, and done

177

right! I've always been that way (a direct manifestation of his guilt) — at least when I wasn't depressed (i.e., when his guilt increased still further). I guess Henry can't be hurried up. But I'm mad about it and I'll tell him so!"

Still later on in this same session, this client implied a perceived *supportive* aspect of the therapist in his metaphor of a "younger person" in his analogy of "playing basketball." Again, this represents a sign of progress in the broadening of his manifest content orientation, which is indicative of less guilt. This is also reflective of his widening interpersonal relationship sphere, which previously had been so restricted because of hypertrophied unconscious guilt. "I try to play a little basketball (a reference to the "enjoyment" of oral gratification in his therapy sessions) now each week because I think it helps me to keep trim and fit. I feel better if I'm able to exercise myself this way. It's a good way to relax and get my mind off my practice worries. I think it's also a good habit to get into. (Therapist: Yes, it is.) I've met a young fellow whom I've been shooting baskets with, and although he's quite green, he has shown some real spunk and some interest in the legal field. I think I could train him and use him part time in the office. I couldn't use him full time, but just part time at this point. He wants to come to work with me, and I've been quite impressed with the way he catches on. He's fast. We do a lot of talking together when we're playing. It wouldn't worry me a bit now if Henry said: 'I've had it, and I'm going to quit!' because now I know he can be replaced with someone that I myself can train (Note that this implies, on a reality level, that a trained lawyer isn't necesscary and on the latent level, that a trained *psychiatrist* isn't either!) and like a lot better."

Several sessions later, the therapist was unable to keep a scheduled appointment because of a psychiatric meeting out of town. The client was informed two weeks in advance of the session to be skipped. During the session in which he was told of the planned absence of the therapist, he implied that it would be good for the therapist to get away from his practice, but *latently* implying it would be good for him to get away from the client's guilt. In the next session, this guilt is projected. There is anger expression now, which continues the process of diminishing the guilt, counter-acting the effect of being abandoned by the therapist which, if anger couldn't have been expressed, would have *increased* the guilt. "That God-damn Henry had the gall to ask for time off. He wants to take his children (perhaps referring to the therapist's own oral needs and the psychiatric meetings) to a ball game. Now I'm not against his enjoying his children (i.e. meeting his oral needs) but I don't want it done when he's supposed to be working for me. He hasn't done a damn thing except sit there and read from my library (perhaps a latent reference to the therapist sitting and taking notes from the client). He hasn't done anything that I know of that deserves any time off. If anything, he ought to be working overtime! I have a feeling, that gets stronger each week, that I'd be better off right now if I hadn't ever *met* him, let alone *hired* him to *help* me! I'm going to let him go off to his damn ball game, but I intend to tell

178

him I don't like it one single bit when he returns." At the close of this session, during which there was considerable projection of guilt to the therapist and ventilation of anger within a metaphorical guise, the client asked: "Now let me see, you're going to be gone next week? (Therapist: That's right, but I'll be back the following week, and we'll continue as usual.) Well, I hope you have a nice trip. You deserve it for all you have to put up with in your practice."

In the session following the skipped one, the client began with: I'm slipping right back into the same depressive symptoms that I had when I first came here. I'm just not interested in my work anymore, and I'm down on myself. But I've been doing some thinking, and I think I know what the problem is. I came home the other day and there was nobody there. Just an empty house. My wife had to go somewhere and left me. Though she had told me ahead of time, I still didn't like it. I didn't think I'd miss her as much as I did. It aggravated me that she left me just when it seemed as though we were closer together in the marriage than we ever had been. She knew how much I needed her, particularly when the practice load is so great. And yet she went and left me. (Pause.) My problem isn't just my job. It also concerns my wife. I've always had the feeling in the past that no one ever had time for me, that I wasn't important to anyone, and that I didn't have the recognition that I really needed. I thought, though, that she could see by this time that by giving me a little bit of attention, and by setting aside a little time each day for me, that this is what makes the difference in how I feel. She was beginning to do it. It was showing itself sexually too. She was beginning to take the initiative for the first time, and this is what I've always wanted. I could never have told her to do this, just like I can't *tell* her to show me attention now. She's got to do it on her own. When some men get their sexual needs met outside of marriage, it's because the wife doesn't make them feel that they're important enough at home. It just made me mad for her to go and leave the home empty. I'd like to go out and find some other woman to meet my needs!" (Note that this "some other woman" can still be found in the same therapeutic listener, provided that there isn't too much of the perceived frustrating "wife" that would terminate the relationship!)

One might raise the question here of whether the client's expressions of anger should be interpreted to him. If the therapist should do so, he is, first of all, introjecting a manifest content of his own. Though this manifest content may be quite reality-oriented, it will still convey an unconscious latent content of the *therapist's* reflecting *his* transference reaction to his client. (This is termed the *counter-transference* in classical psychoanalysis, but essentially is no different than any other transference reaction.) Secondly, the therapist would be making an intellectual attempt to logically *rationalize* a process that is rooted in the primary process illogic of the transference. And, thirdly, to do so usually will threaten the client's oral dependency with exposure, hampering further projections of guilt to the therapist that are necessary for anger ventilation. A good

179

example of a therapist, attempting to emphasize reality to his client, at the expense of what is occurring therapeutically in regard to the unreality of the transference is where Beier,[1] in a paragraph entitled: "Call To Reality" mentions that it is sometimes advantageous to correct a client's misconceptions of reality, and uses the following example:

"Patient: 'I was riding on Launer and was coming to State Street and the othe- car just ran into me. This blind bastard of a driver ...'
Therapist: 'Isn't there a stop sign at Launer Street?' "

What Beier apparently fails to see is the unreality of the transference, where, for this client there certainly *was* a "stop sign" to the expression of his anger — one that his therapist erected!

1. Beier, E.G.: "The Silent Language of Psychotherapy" — Aldine Publishing Company, 1966 Chicago page 81.

CHAPTER 9

THE ORAL DILEMMA

It is not a "simple" psychodynamic process, by any means, for one individual to listen to another, and the longer the listening is, the more complex becomes the process. Even before an individual begins to verbalize, one can suspicion that there is a transference effect that is already in operation. A person doesn't simply talk to *anyone*, particularly about things of a personal nature, unless this person is of *some* emotional significance. For the more emotionally *comfortable* person, there may be a very small significance initially assigned to the listener. But if the person is emotionally *uncomfortable*, the listener will have a greater emotional significance. The person sought out for help, in whatever professional reality role he might have, is often a ready-made transference figure, because he *is* sought out for help, and often with desperation. Whether the professional listener is a medical man, a member of the clergy, an analyst, a counselor or a confidant, there is an emotional significance that has already been assigned to this individual even before any verbalization takes place. Emotional uncomfortableness drives a person to seek out the "good breast." Regardless of the reality role that the helper may have, the initial visit by the person seeking help will unavoidably entail the transference phenomenon. It is this transference, within the reality of the listener's role, that will emotionally endow the person sought out for help as someone "specially" able to alleviate the uncomfortableness, even if this person is a proven quack or charlatan to someone else.

The transference at this point isn't usually ambivalent, for the person sought out, in whatever reality-oriented involvement there might be, has the characteristic of hopefully being able to bring about some type of relief from the rationalized underlying oral conflict. The transference isn't ambivalent in that the object is initially being viewed unconsciously as the *good breast*. But as this transference is continued, it will *become* ambivalent by the process of listening. The more the transference figure meets the oral dependency needs of the person that has come for help, the more quickly he will attain an ambivalently-held position.

Any individual that is emotionally uncomfortable has an increased level of unconscious guilt. In most cases, the added unconscious guilt has been of very recent origin, and prompts the individual to seek some type of relief in some type of reality involvement with someone else, that he *logically* sees, as being hopefully capable of relieving this uncomfortableness. When he begins to verbalize his difficulties as he sees them to this someone else, he begins subtly to gratify his oral dependency needs from this individual. Because he has an increased level of unconscious guilt, he must also have ungratified oral dependency needs that will create a potential for an intense transference situation. He will also have, behind his guilt, repressed anger. The unconscious guilt has arisen from the repressed anger from past and present frustrations of his oral dependency needs. It is this emotionality that is carried into the transference, and becomes directly associated with the transference figure.

When an individual does involve himself in verbalization with a transference figure, he begins to draw oral dependency supplies. But the unconscious guilt will tend to block oral gratification and will block the expression of anger unless the guilt can be projected. When the individual projects this guilt to a therapeutic listener, he usually does so "piece-meal," latently, and on a perceived part object basis. He may talk of a "friend" that has let him down, but in describing this relationship, he mirrors the transference relationship of the *moment* between himself and his listener. As he continues to verbalize, drawing oral support and projecting guilt, the previously repressed anger is externalized, and his more recently added unconscious guilt is diminished to a more comfortable level. Once the individual has decreased this recently added unconscious guilt, he will tend to emotionally resist continuing deeper into the transference relationship, and will usually discontinue.

In order to decrease the personality *core* guilt, it is necessary to involve the individual longer in this transference relationship. This will always be in the face of resistance from the core guilt. This resistance to emotional closeness beyond a certain point (which comes as a part of the personality), will be supported by the ego defenses that make up that personality. Some personalities carry more "chronic" uncomfortableness than others. This is so because they have more of this personality core guilt. An individual, after having initially involved himself with a therapeutic listener, may continue just long enough to remove the more recently *added* guilt, and then discontinue, or he may ambivalently continue the involvement, held by intense oral need gratification, and resisted by his guilt.

Personalities not only differ in the degree of uncomfortableness that they usually have, but also, correspondingly differ in the amount of *distance* that they tend to keep in their interpersonal relationships. The personality core guilt tends to put a block against sustained emotional closeness beyond a certain point which is determined by their unconscious guilt. The unconscious guilt gives the individual a tendency to resist further an intensity of oral dependency gratification, and a further externalization of anger that would diminish the personality core guilt. Everyone then functions with a certian level of emotional uncomfortableness, and a certain level of unmet oral needs, repressed anger and guilt.

182

There is a dilemma that comes about because of this guilt, wherein the more orally *hungry* a person is to have his needs met, the more *fearful* he is of *having* them met. The oral incorporative guilt first seen in infancy becomes more prominent, the more the individual finds himself, later in life, frustrated in oral dependency gratification and repressing anger. His increased unconscious guilt taints each interpersonal relationship, and will become a major problem in the therapeutic transference relationship as well.

Burnham, Gladstone and Gibson[1] describe a "need-fear dilemma" as characteristic of "schizophrenia." The presentation of this simply illustrates the intense conflict of the emotionally uncomfortable person with unmet oral needs on one hand, and an unconscious guilt on the other, that makes the very object on whom oral dependency is sought as threatening. However, it is erroneous to limit this *fear of emotional closeness* to any special group, particularly as nebulous a one as "schizophrenia." It is a universal fear. Closeness is only more *intensely* feared when there are *more* oral dependency needs that are going ungratified, where there is *more* repressed anger, and where there is *more* of the manifestations of the unconscious guilt. These individuals, though they tend to attempt to *avoid* becoming emotionally involved with someone else, often *do* become involved because of the pressure of their unmet oral needs. They very quickly make the object on whom oral dependency is sought — or the object toward which oral dependency is to be *avoided* — a *transference figure*. Into this transference relationship then will come a pressure to express the underlying hostility toward this object, when the guilt is projected toward that object. When the unconscious guilt is *self-felt*, the individual avoids closeness for fear of *contaminating* others. When the guilt is *projected*, the individual avoids closeness for fear of *being contaminated*. In either position, the unconscious guilt puts a block to emotional closeness.

The oral dilemma is characterized by ambivalence. This is not a simple bipolar ambivalence, but a constantly shifting multifaceted one, so that no matter what the client verbally expresses, or even thinks to himself, is immediately negated. What is presented as a thought seems always opposed by a different facet of this ambivalence, which when consciously recognized is again opposed by still another facet. One aspect of the ambivalence may make the person feel as though they *deserve* to have something they don't have, latently symbolizing their unmet oral need gratification, but then, on the other hand their guilt makes them feel that they *don't* deserve this. No position that they can take will be comforting to them. Nothing that they can either do, or say, can be *totally* acceptable to them.

The oscillating ambivalence derived from guilt, on one hand, and the unmet oral dependency needs on the other, places the person in a *dilemma* that makes it difficult for another person to deal with. This other person can't support *any* position that the former has just verbalized, in that his ambivalence is so shifting that he seems alienated by his own verbalizations. Many times simply rephrasing, or even repeating what the person has just said, is either immediately qualified by the other person or denied outright.

When a lay-person perceives this ambivalence in another, they recognize that the other is "mixed up." They see that the individual is indecisive, that he can't take a definite stand on any issue, and that he appears to see too many different, but equally valued, sides of a question, such that he can never take a definite direction for a course of action, or even the conclusion of a thought. People that have an extreme of emotional uncomfortableness in particular show this intense ambivalence. They often present themselves as two or more "sides." Many times an individual will come for professional help fearful that they have a "split personality" or that they might be "schizophrenic" when they can perceive within themselves so many different "me's." The descriptive terms commonly applied to these individuals convey this perceived ambivalence. The term "batty," implies a likeness between the individual's constantly shifting thoughts going off in different directions, and the erratic flight of the bat. These people are sometimes described as "squirrely," again equating their inability to "think straight" and the characteristic of a panicked squirrel suddenly changing his course of direction. When the term "nutty" is applied, it probably is referring to the difficulty in getting at the "meat" of what the person is trying to convey because of his ambivalence. In a similar way, this metaphor is used in the phrase "It's a tough nut to crack." The individual himself may feel "mixed up", not knowing with any conviction what he really wants or what he doesn't want. It is interesting to note that the term "going to pieces" implies the increased level of ambivalence from unmet oral needs and opposing guilt that causes an ego to collapse.

The *intra*psychic ambivalence can be projected so that the person may feel that it isn't *he* that is "mixed up," but that *someone* else is. A projection of their unconscious guilt creates an *inter*personal ambivalence, such that they view the actions and the verbalizations of others as "mixed up." Their objects may cease to be oral need gratifying, and they perceive, instead, criticisms, condemnations or put-downs. Even the actions that with less unconscious guilt can be easily perceived by others as oral need gratifying, are twisted around in their thinking and perceived instead as oral need frustrating. When this is so, there is a "snowballing" of the unconscious guilt, such that the sphere of interpersonal relationships that *might* have been oral need gratifying shrinks, and becomes, instead, orally *frustrating*. The individual then becomes more *hungry*, in regard to his oral needs, and more *angry* underneath that his needs haven't been met. And because he has a high enough level of unconscious core guilt, this anger, from this recent oral frustration, is repressed, and is added to the *total* guilt, increasing it still further. With increased guilt, the oral dilemma is intensified making it most difficult, emotionally, for the person to get the help he seeks.

184

When a client first enters a professional therapeutic listening relationship, he does so bringing this oral dilemma with him. Initially the therapeutic listener can often do little more than simply listen to the presentation of the oral dilemma in that any verbalization on his part may be viewed as "misunderstanding" of what the individual is ambivalently presenting. The level of unconscious guilt makes the client hyper-sensitive, and too quick to interpret a latent meaning behind anything verbalized that signifies that they are what their unconscious guilt and immense oral needs make them feel they are. Neither should the therapeutic listener lend support, verbally or otherwise, to the hopelessness of the "no solution" dilemma that the client is presenting. No verbal confirmation or no reiteration is best in that any might reinforce the client's conceptualization that within the facets of reality no answer is possible for his emotional problems. The therapeutic listener should only listen, and let the client present, in metaphor and analogy, his oral dilemma. In doing so, the listener gratifies the client's oral dependency needs. This, after all, is the first step in eventually externalizing the repressed anger that is necessary in diminishing the guilt that *produced* the oral dilemma. When the unconscious guilt diminishes, ambivalence diminishes as well. This can be best accomplished with a minimum of verbalization on the part of the listener during this initial stage. This initial stage may be termed the "presentation of the oral dilemma".

Until the clients can reach this point of diminished guilt, their verbalizations will reflect their underlying oscillating ambivalence. If they are introspective — as self-felt guilt tends to make an individual — they will frequently attempt to intellectualize or rationalize their emotional difficulties, but then frustratingly remark: *"I don't know,"* implying that they then doubt what they had just tried to conclude. An example of this is: "I feel so guilty about being mercenary. But he *owes* me money and he *ought* to pay me. And I should *tell* him so! (Frustrated sighing.) But *I don't know*. His friendship is worth *more* than money. I shouldn't accept his money. (Pause.) But I'm not rich. *I* need the money more than *he* does, and he *knows* that. (Sighs.)But then why should I let money come between he and I? I *just don't know*. (Cries.) He's got plenty of money," etc.

Another client demonstrates her ambivalence with: "I need to be *strong-minded* — my whole problem is that I'm *not* this way, and I *need* to be. (Thoughtful pause.) But I don't want to be *bull-headed* either — nobody wants a bull-headed individual around. (Pause.) But then no one likes a weak-minded, wishy-washy person either. (Frustrated sighing.) I don't want to be bull-headed and I don't want to be wishy-washy. (Cries.) I just don't know how to act around others."

Still another client remarked: "I just don't know if I'm doing right (always a manifestation of self-felt unconscious guilt). I try to telephone people, but then I wonder if I call them too much, I'm afraid they'll think I'm bothering them. I don't want to be a bother to people I like. But then, I wonder if I don't call them enough, they might think I'm angry at them. And I don't want them to feel that

185

way. (Frustrated sighing.) I just don't know if I'm calling them too much (cries) or not enough."

This same ambivalence from the *need* on one hand, and the *guilt* on the other, is invariably brought into the therapeutic transference. Even in direct references, the ambivalence will often show itself. For instance, if, in answer to a client asking: "Are you writing all that about me?" the therapist had replied: *"Yes,"* the client would immediately have preferred, because of his *guilt*, that it be about someone else. However, if the therapist had replied: *"No,"* then the client would have immediately preferred, because of his unmet oral *need*, that it be about him. And, because of the intensity of the relationship with such an emotionally significant transference figure, *either* position that the therapist might have taken, is perceived as *not* orally gratifying, and upsetting to the client. What is more orally supportive to the client is an ambiguous gesture denoting "I'm listening," or a "How do *you* feel about it?" reply.

One client who was very guilt-laden came to her session remarking: "Johnny beat me up last night just because I said something at the supper table that I shouldn't have. He grabbed me around the throat, knocked me to the floor, and strangled me until I nearly passed out — I tried to call you, but I couldn't reach you." She implies her ambivalence in her admission that she had tried to call the *therapist*. Had she felt less guilty, she would have called the police, and sworn out a warrant for her husband's arrest. With the level of guilt that she has, she feels, in part, that she *deserves* the beating that she got. Another part feels she *doesn't*. But she would be at a loss to say what she really wanted to hear from the therapist. If she had reached the therapist, she would have only presented this ambibalence. One would alienate this person if one took a firm stand and verbalized it to her. What is most supportive is to simply *listen* to her verbalize her ambivalence. In doing so, one meets some of her oral dependency needs, and allows some expression of her anger in a way that lets her set the emotional distance in regard to both.

The oral dilemma that implies a "no logical solution" is frequently shown in people that have severe "psychosomatic complaints," and who go from one doctor to another. What they present is a metaphorical stalemate of guilt-blocked oral gratification, guilt-blocked anger, and a "need" to suffer. They often give the impression they don't really want to feel better, and that they deserve or even enjoy being in the misery they feel. They focus on their "physical problem" as "this constant pain in my shoulder," verbalizing continually on this as a presentation of the oral dilemma. They don't blame anyone for their pain. They imply the cause of their pain is unknown. They imply that nothing helps at all, and with the amount of guilt they have, nothing in reality *will* help. They haven't reached the point of decreasing ambivalence which comes about when a person talks of *object* relationships, metaphorically representing an externalization and a dispersion of their intrapsychic ambivalence. Demanding a *somatic* treatment

186

for their "shoulder pain" protects them against oral gratification and anger expression, both of which are blocked by guilt. "The pain is driving me *crazy!*" seems so metaphorically appropriate for what the intense oral dilemma can do.

Metaphors and analogies of a medical orientation conceptualize the emotional uncomfortableness in some psychosomatic problems that symbolize the guilt-blocked oral needs. There is no medicine, no surgery, and no therapy, quackery or even religion that can break a most severe stalemate unless, in some way, the guilt can be decreased. The more severe the oral dilemma, the more likely the person will end up hospitalized for one reality reason or another. The less severe oral dilemma can be "talked out"; the more severe dilemma seems to demand a *somatic* resolution. (It is interesting to note, for instance, that "schizophrenics" are said to respond best to "drug therapy" rather than to any psychotherapy.) A client, beginning to resolve his dilemma with anger expression, remarked: "I'm just starving for food. (Oral need gratification.) But everytime I eat anything, I get that pain in my stomach. I've come to the conclusion that if I didn't have to eat (i.e. "if I didn't have oral needs") I'd be alright. The very foods I crave the most cause me the most pain. I've got now where I can't eat a single thing. And that damn medicine doesn't help at all. I've tried every medicine in the book, and not one has helped. I don't see why, when a doctor can't help a patient, that he, instead of *admitting* his failure, just turns him over to a *psychiatrist!*"

Before a client reaches this point of rationalizing the previous oral dilemma, he will metaphorically present this dilemma as a word picture which seems logically impossible to resolve. They may present a situation within the family where they are caught in a "no solution" arrangement, between for instance, their children and their husbands, or their parents and their children. No matter what course of action imaginable they might make, they are easily seen as the "loser." They may present an oral dilemma, metaphorically presented in regard to any type of interpersonal relationship or situation that symbolically conveys this entrapping oral dilemma between the oral needs necessary for life, and the death deserving guilt on the other hand. They might remark: "I can't live any longer with my husband, but he won't let me move out or else he'll take the children away from me," or "I feel guilty if I don't go and stay with my daughter when she's having a baby, and I feel guilty if I leave my husband alone." And "I'd run away from home to get away from my mother, but I'd miss my father so. I can't live with my mother, and I can't live away from my father."

Other metaphorical examples of the stalemate of guilt-blocked oral dependency needs are given in the following excerpts. "There's nothing that I enjoy more than working in flowers. But with my allergy now I can't even be in the same room with a flower before I get to sneezing and wheezing." "The only girlfriend I have is Stella, but my husband won't let her come to the house. In fact, he blames *her* for the marriage difficulties *we're* having." "I feel so lonely, yet I can't stand to have someone around me." "I'd like to leave my husband, but how can I

187

support the children on my own." "I just love to sit out in the sun and talk with others at the beach, but with this skin condition I've got now, I can't even go outdoors, and nobody wants to sit indoors with me this time of the year." "I'm bored and depressed at home by myself, but when I go out, I get panicky and all upset." "It's a shame to feel as sick as I do, and not to be able to take the medicine (oral need gratification) that's supposed to cure a person of what I have."

These people are *rationalizing* the unconscious oral dilemma that makes them feel so depressingly that there is *no solution* in reality. The initial phase of the therapeutic transference involves the metaphorical presentation of the "no solution" oral dilemma. This is all the more reason for the therapeutic listener to simply listen at this point, in that the oral dilemma is not possible to be resolved on a reality oriented basis. People with less of an emotional problem don't get into such severe oral dilemmas, and the solution to their problems lend themselves to logical advice and counsel. There is no realistic or *logical* solution to any of the problems of *intense* orality. These problems demand a *part object* unreality for their solution. For instance, there can be no logical solution at all for an emotionally uncomfortable person that presents himself complaining that he essentially *hates* the very person that he *loves*. Or a person that wants so desperately to be *free* of anyone, while on the other hand, wants to be *inseparably bound* to someone else. Or the person that desperately wants someone close, and who simultaneously also doesn't want an invasion in any way of their privacy by another person. Or finally the person that doesn't want to *live*, but doesn't want to *die* either.

This dilemma of *wanting* one's oral dependency needs met, but then not being able to *accept* gratification because of the guilt is an expression of the *oral anhedonia*, or a fear of anything pleasurable. This oral anhedonia gives another reason that the therapeutic listener cannot be vigorous in his emotional support while the client is in an oral dilemma. Oral dependency gratification represents hedonia, and at this point it is unacceptable to the client. The therapist, even in passive listening, will activate some resistance of the client to a continuation in the transference relationship because the relationship *is* pleasurable. The client may very well know that he is getting very little, if any, pleasure in life, and may angrily resent this. But he still cannot accept pleasure in anything without it immediately mobilizing the guilt, making him feel that if he were to continue to experience pleasure, then there will be some painful price to pay — just as he had in the past. The oral dilemma becomes a *need* for the "good breast" and a simultaneous *fear* of it — the "need fear" dilemma.

In metaphorically verbalizing this oral dilemma to a therapeutic listener, the client, through the transference phenomenon, will soon make the listener, himself, the most important part of this dilemma. In other words, the oral dilemma that brought the client to a professional in the first place becomes an integral part of the therapeutic transference. The *emotional* resolution of this dilemma is the goal of the therapeutic listener. The therapeutic listener must realize that the reality of any manifest content is superficial to the more important underlying emotional unreality. What is then continued to be expressed as a *reality* dilemma, is a metaphorical concretization that mirrors the *identical* emotional problem with the unreality of the therapeutic transference!

The oral dilemma becomes the *major* concern of the client in his relationship with the therapist. What was expressed as a reality dilemma in the initial visit becomes metaphorical for the developing oral dilemma with the therapist. The reality situation from which the client came was characterized as being insolvable, and so the therapeutic transference, likewise, becomes unconsciously perceived the same way. By believing that neither other people in their reality situation *can* change, nor *should* change, implies they seek some type of "magical" change within *themselves* to remove the troublesome oral dependency need. After presenting the oral dilemma and then latently transferring it into the therapeutic transference what they propose as the *only* answer is the "magical change." There sometimes is a direct admission of this problem with the therapist, such as: "I feel better when I see you, but my family, in knowing I see a psychiatrist, now views me as having two heads or that I'm about to run amok." This "what *helps*, makes matters *worse*" implication is typical of any metaphorically presented perceptions by the client of any attempt of the therapist to remove the dilemma.

As the therapeutic transference continues, one can easily see the dilemma of treatment in regard to this oral dilemma as: "Sure, Ralph (latently, the therapist) is nice to me now — he's doing things *now* he's never done before in the past — but that's just it — he never *did* them, back *then*, when I needed him the *most*! He's just trying to make up for what he didn't do in the past, and it makes me *depressed* now, where before I just accepted it." One cannot simply intellectualize this dilemma to the client to explain to her that she has transferred her emotional problem to the therapist. This would jeopardize the unconscious process that will allow her to ventilate her anger and will decrease the troublesome unconscious guilt. However, it is not just the therapist that will allow her to continue, but the level of her unconscious guilt as well as it's *"set"* (or the certain *individualistic* way this guilt manifests itself). The level and "set" of the guilt may very well terminate the relationship, regardless of what the therapist may do, or not do.

As an example of this dilemma in the therapeutic transference, a client remarked: "I just don't feel like saying anything today. (Long pause and then the therapist asks: "Are you a little angry!") Well, yes I am. I'm peeved at Frank (therapist in metaphor). He's concerned because I don't talk to him enough. But people get tired of hearing complaints all the time, so I just keep it to myself. (Long pause, with the therapist finally remarking: "You seem a little thoughtful") You remind me of Frank! He's always wanting to know what's on my mind. I wish he'd just leave me alone. I don't know what he expects of me. I wish he could just accept me the way I am, but he can't seem to do that. He has to try to change me. Why should I change? (Angrily.) Why do I have to be the one to always change? Why doesn't *he* change?"

Many clients come to therapy seemingly seeking that magical solution for their oral dilemma. They seek an unrealistic "help" in becoming "independent." They want help in repressing their anger, and help in denying their oral dependency needs. Viewing the therapist as having some God-like power, they want him to *magically* remove their guilt, *without* gratifying their oral needs or ventilating their anger. Though they came for relief from their oral dilemma in their reality world of interpersonal relationships, they quickly find themselves facing the same thing in their relationship with the therapeutic listener that they had hoped to avoid. The same emotional problems that brought them to the therapeutic transference become the same emotional problems of the therapeutic transference relationship. As a solution to the oral dilemma, the clients often convey the impression that they are seeking not to be so emotionally involved and entangled with others. They seem most unaccepting of the only way that a person can really *be* independent of such intense emotionality; and that is by being, *first*, intensely involved with *one*, long enough, so that one *can* move on to a greater number of part objects on whom emotional supplies can be drawn. In such a position, no *one* part object has any *great* emotional significance. But one must reach this point by *first* going through an *intense* emotional process with *one* object, just as the emotionally comfortable individual did in his earlier formative years. If an individual *didn't* satisfactorily go through this emotionally intense involvement with one object that leads to the drawing of oral support from many part objects, then any attempt to take a short-cut, and go directly to a multiplicity of part objects for oral support is immediately made impossible at this first attempt. Because of the intensity and concentration of unmet needs, he will make any single part object chosen too emotionally significant. In other words, the intensity and the concentration of the denied unmet oral needs that one was hoping to spread out on many part objects will raise an object to an emotionally uncomfortable significance that one was hoping to avoid. The emotionally uncomfortable person always seeks to avoid this intensity, and searches instead for a magical *removal* of his guilt-laden oral needs. He chides himself that he hasn't learned to "keep his big mouth shut." He fails to see that by doing so his oral needs only increase in size, until they seem as though they are a "bottomless pit." This predisposes any object, or part object, to the potential of an intense, uncomfortable emotionality. The client has a dilemma of being that "*hungry*" for oral dependency gratification, but also having an accompanying need to "*bite*" whatever might approach for that satisfaction. These people constantly resist reaching a certain level of intensity in oral dependency gratification that is necessary for them to attain this point of "independency" that they so des-

190

parately desire. This desire for "independency" is motivated by guilt. If unconscious guilt does decrease by involvement in what the client would rather *not* be involved in, the desire for "independency" decreases. The person that *desires* "independency" is therefore an emotionally uncomfortable person, or, at least, is *potentially* one. It is often *impossible* for him to see any value whatsoever in verbalizing, on a regular basis, to a therapeutic listener in a relationship that is so characterized by the very *dependency* they seek to avoid. Their unconscious guilt makes them feel as though they're not making progress, that they're not presenting "significant" material, or when they do project their guilt, that the therapist isn't doing something that he *ought* to be doing, so that they can make the progress toward "independency" that they feel they *should* be making at this point. One client in metaphorically presenting with a religious orientation a recognition of this oral dilemma and its solution remarked: "I've been reading this book where one can reach emotional comfortableness by 'letting *go*, and letting *God.*' It says that one doesn't *have* to work at it, and that God will take care of *everything* in his own way. But how can a person *let* God do it, if one *can't* let go?"

The "snowballing" effect of the depression-engendering "no solution" dilemma of intense orality is shown in a client *wanting* her oral dependency needs met, and simultaneously being *too guilty* and underserving to accept any gratification of them. This makes her increasingly angry for not having the needs met, then even *more* desirous and more desperately needful of oral dependency support, but even more guilty because of the increased repressed anger. This ambivalence — a *hungry fear* of oral incorporation — in regard to her needs, guilt and anger is shown in analogy with the following: "I'm ashamed for anyone to see my living room (a concretization of both her "shameful" guilt and the paucity of dependency need gratification). I'm actually ashamed to have anyone come in, and see the furniture the way it is. The couch (she, herself) is tattered and torn. The sharp springs coming through are too dangerous for anybody to be around. I'd like to throw the damn thing out, as it isn't any good to anyone, and it's an eye sore. Why can't I have a living room like other people have? I've seen what theirs are like, and there's no comparison with mine. Mine is gloomy, dark and depressing. It depresses anybody to even be near it. But what I can't understand is that people with lesser positions than my husband's (a projection of blame to the therapist of her own ambivalent orality) have better living rooms. Why is it that I have so little, and what little I *do* have is so poor and shabby? My husband (i.e. therapist) can go out and buy himself a camera or a boat trailer, and last spring he bought himself a riding lawn mower. But *I* can't even get new drapes for the living room, for which I've been waiting for fourteen years (according to the husband she never *would* accept the money for the drapes). (Cries.) But I shouldn't be this way. I'm just a fussy, cranky, old nagging wife that should be *thankful* for what I do have (once again the implied: "My needs are too excessive and I don't deserve more than I have."). My husband doesn't drink, and he's home every night. He works hard and has done so much for me already. So why can't I enjoy what I have instead of being self-centered and thinking all the time of myself. I *hate* the way I am (i.e., "I hate my oral needs"). I'm just being selfish and immature in wanting what other people have. (Continues to cry.) I'm only angry at myself for acting this way. And you've got to help me." (Here is the *paradox* of orality of wanting "help" in how *not* to be helped.)

This same *intra*psychic ambivalence brought about by the triad of oral needs, anger and guilt, is shown in the following excerpt: "I've got a cleaning lady (therapist) now, and I feel awfully guilty about it. She comes in once a week (therapy is once a week) and goes over the whole house (her problems in orality?) but it's something *I* should be doing myself. I shouldn't have to pay someone $10 a day (the therapy session is $15; however when the client uses $10 in the manifest content she is utilizing a reality-oriented and factual metaphor to convey in the latent reference a reference to the the therapy session) to do my work. I do feel very guilty about it. My husband (again the therapist with differently perceived attributes) is working very hard, and I'm not doing anything. I'm just sitting back, and he's not going to take this very much longer. Oh, he *says* he doesn't mind. He says he wants me to have *some* help each week, but I can't see it. I should *make* myself do it, for *other* people have to do it themselves — why can't I? I have *no* right to complain at all. I have no *reason* to be depressed. I know my husband isn't home as much as I'd like to have him. That's his job! There are many husbands that aren't home for months, so I shouldn't complain. I don't have one legitimate reason to complain (for *any* reason will be falsified by her *guilt*). I *hate* myself, for I'm a fussy old shrew that has it easy and has no right to complain to her husband, but ought to be *made* to get off her fat duff, and do her *own* housework without relying on others. You know I could actually get to *liking* this way of life if I were to let myself. But then things would be even *worse*! I don't want to be lazier and more good-for-nothing than I already am. And I certainly don't want to be a drug addict. My husband has enough trouble with me. I don't think anything could be worse than being a drug addict or an alcoholic. (The metaphorically expressed fear of her *own* self-felt exaggerated dependency needs.) I've got to get straightened out, but I don't think *you* can help me. I've got to do it *myself*! I've just got to grab hold of myself and tell myself that I've just got to shape up and quit this feeling sorry for myself. I've got to stop being self-centered, selfish and immature. I'm a grown woman, and I don't need to be waited on hand and foot. I think I'd feel better if I were more active, if I were doing things myself, and if I were off this medicine. Do you know what I mean? Are you sure you've got the right approach to my problem in wanting me to let others (i.e., the therapist) help me?"

"I just can't accept that my headaches are all emotional, particularly when I've been told in the past by so many different specialists that I've got an atypical case of migraine that just can't be treated. How can I be mentally ill when Dr. Jackson said from the tests he's made that I had a vascular problem? (Therapist: Who said you were mentally ill?) Well, I *must* be mentally ill, or else I wouldn't be sitting in a psychiatrist's office! Why would a doctor send me to a psychiatrist if I wasn't mentally ill? (Therapist somewhat angrily: I don't see people who are mentally ill! If anyone is mentally ill, they have to see somebody else. Mrs. Brown, I am not a member of the hospital staff and I don't see any psychiatric emergencies. Have you seen anyone that looks mentally ill in my waiting room?) Well, no, they all seem normal to me, but I don't know how crazy they are. I'm not a *psychiatrist*. How can I tell? I'm just all confused. (Long pause.) Maybe you could ask me some questions. (Therapist: Whatever comes to mind, I'm interested in.) Well, *nothing* comes to mind! (Long pause.) I still have a headache and now I've just got a sour stomach as well. I'm sending my mother (the perceived supportive aspect of the therapist) home today. I can't expect her to be with me indefinitely. I'll make out without her. I've done it before, plenty of times. John (still another aspect of the therapist) has gotten disgusted with me. He thinks I should be feeling better by now. He gets tired of me talking about my problems and he doesn't want to hear them anymore. He means well, but he isn't as understanding as he could be. (Therapist somewhat apologetically: He gets that way at times.) Yes he does. (Laughs and therapist smiles.) John told me I *was* going to get the groceries, (i.e. increased oral gratification) and I told him I wasn't going to be pushed. I'm not ready to go grocery shopping. I told him that I'd get the groceries when I *felt* like it, and not before. (Therapist: I'm glad you were able to express yourself.) I know I should go after the groceries, but I can remember in the past when I had to go alone, when I was so sick I should have been in bed. He didn't seem to care then. I don't want to get groceries too, because I'm afraid my first husband will be there in the store at the same time (Note what this metaphorically implies in regard to the transference.) I know it sounds silly, but he mistreated me, so that I'm afraid now that I might run into him. He's the one that ought to be here in a psychiatrist's office, but he'd never see one. He'd easily tell someone else to go, but he'd never go himself. I've got to leave what's in the past alone . . . forget it and go on. This isn't like me to be so depressed. I've always been so independent, so strong and always doing things for others. I want to get that strength back, as there's so much to be done in the house — so much cleaning to do. That's what I like to do when I'm feeling good — not dwelling on the past. I used to pride myself on how clean I kept the house, though I never was quite satisfied with how it was..."

"This whole thing isn't working out at all (i.e., "therapy isn't helping"). I'd like to end the marriage for all I'm getting out of it. I'm not blaming Barbara (therapist) . . . don't get me wrong . . . Well, yes I *am*, in a way. But it's *my* fault too (i.e., "It is *my* fault for having the oral needs".), and I know it is. Here's an example of what I mean. I was sitting at the table (a reference to the oral gratification of therapy) drinking a cup of coffee, and having a piece of toast, and she was busy running the vacuum cleaner all around the family room (a latent reference to his guilt), cleaning up, but not bothering with me. Just acted as if I wasn't even there. That made me mad. Sure, I'm glad she tries to keep things cleaned up. That's her job. But I wanted her to sit down beside me, and have a cup of coffee *with* me, and maybe *share* a piece of toast. But she didn't . . . no, she didn't. She kept right on running that vacuum cleaner (a reference to his feeling that the therapist is concerned only with his *guilt*) all around, and I was feeling miserable. I mean, I was *really* feeling miserable, as I wanted her *beside* me. 'To hell with the dirt' (i.e., "my guilt"). I felt, right then and there, I wanted *her* (i.e. "I wanted my oral needs met") and the more she ran the cleaner around, the madder I got. I was saying to myself: 'Goddamn you! I don't *want you* near me! I don't want you around me because of the Goddamn way you've treated me in the *past* . . . just exactly like the way you're treating me right *now*. I can get along without you. I don't need you!' But I was feeling miserably depressed because I was mad at *myself* for *wanting* her. Yet I know she has her work to do, and can't be bothered with *me* acting so infantile. I was mad at *myself* for needing her to sit down beside me. I even thought of taking a gun and solving the problem that way, once and for all. I could have done it, as I was mad enough at myself and at her to do it. Whenever I've thought of suicide in the past, I'd always chicken out because I didn't want Barbara to be hurt . . . she's been hurt *enough* by me. I've put her through plenty already without putting that added shame on her. But when I was sitting at the table, I came the closest I've ever come to suicide. I thought: 'I'll get a gun and kill myself, and that will fix her. Then she'll know how badly she's treated me, and I'd be able to end the misery I've just caused myself.' But then I couldn't hurt her anymore than I've already hurt her. I've hurt her enough. So I got out a bottle of whiskey instead and drank until I fell asleep just to forget it all (a very popular solution to oral problems for the older generations). I'd like to get away from it all. Maybe it's because Barbara and I are so incompatible. I shouldn't have gotten married in the first place. She should have married someone else. She'd have been much better off."

"I'm a wreck. I've been running here and there, trying to get a thousand different things done that *have* to be done, and I just can't take it any longer. (Breaks down and cries.) Frank (i.e. the therapist) expects me to do too much. (Perhaps he does in reality, but it's her own guilt that puts the pressure on her to be continually accomplishing things in an anhedonic way that she resents.) He expects me to be here one minute, and there another. I wish he'd just leave me alone. (Continues to cry.) And the children (her burdensome oral needs). . .I have to pick them up from school, take them to piano lessons, bring them back from their lessons, take them for haircuts and then to scout meetings. I get the groceries, clean the house, which is a never ending job, and weed the garden, which one can never get ahead of. I never have a chance to rest. I'm supposed to go to Millie's (therapist with different connotation) for coffee. I told her I didn't want to go, and that I've got too much that *has* to be done to be having coffee, but she insists I go. And then I've got to do this program (i.e. therapy) on Christian giving for the church. I can't get out of it, and why I ever got involved in the church is beyond me. They're all a bunch of hypocrites there anyway! I've just been at the end of my rope for the past week. I can't keep this pace up, and I know I'll end up in the hospital. That's the only place I'll get some rest . . . or else in my grave. And I can't take those pills of yours (Mellaril 10 mg, but latently, oral dependency) They slow me down. I can't be slowed down. I have to be speeded up to get all the things done I've *got* to get done. I've quit taking those pills. Give me some other kind of pill. (Therapist: Some other kind of pill?) Yes, give me something else that doesn't slow me down. (Pause.) Well, if you don't give me something, I'm going to go to Dr. Allison (another aspect of the therapist) to get them, as he'll give me something that will help. I won't go to that damn Dr. Frankling (still another aspect of the therapist). That stupid quack ought to leave town. Anybody's a fool (a reference to an aspect of herself) that would go to him. Doctors! Bah! I thought they're supposed to *help* a person instead of making them worse! And that reminds me, I can't come in this Thursday, and I don't know whether I'm going to be here next Monday either. I've got to go to the church conference meeting (a reference to a perceived more distant aspect of the therapist) in Detroit. How can I be there, and be here at the same time (only in an unreality as the transference is this possible)? (Therapist: I feel it more important to be here.) Tell that to the Methodist Church."

The following is illustrative of *both* the *intra*personal and the *inter*personal ambivalence of a client. This client at one time expressed her anger in metaphor when the therapist *didn't* phone her when she didn't show for a scheduled appointment. This seemed to imply to her that the therapist didn't care for her (because of her oral incorporative guilt). In another session, she again expressed anger to the therapist following a skipped session, this time, because the therapist *did* call. This seemed now to imply to her that he was just a money grubber who was only interested in what he could get out of her. It is her unconscious guilt that makes her feel, no matter what the circumstances of reality are, the therapist couldn't *possibly* be interested in *her*, nor *should* he be. "I've always had this bronchitis as far back as I can remember, and I *hate* going to the clinic (therapy) for the treatment I know I need. I only go as a last resort, but when I started coughing up black stuff, I thought I'd better get down there fast. At the clinic nobody wants to get Dr. Eller (therapist) as he never tells anyone anything. But a patient can't simply choose the doctor he wants. He gets whatever doctor (referring to aspects of the therapist) is right there at the moment (and that's the way it is in the transference!) Usually it's Dr. Eller. He'll never say what the problem is, and I'm always left in the dark as to what's wrong and what his treatment program is going to be. Well, with my luck I *got* him. As soon as I got into his office, I started coughing like I was going to die, but he acted like he couldn't have cared less. Finally he said: 'Well, what's wrong with you?' That's for *him* to find out and tell *me*! He could have seen what the trouble was with all my coughing, and he could have read the chart as it was lying right in front of him, but he didn't take the time to read it over (if he *did*, she would probably have been angry that her guilt was exposed). He kept asking me what the trouble was. I didn't like that. I wanted *him to tell me*. He finally got out his stethoscope and listened all over my chest, but never said a word. Just kept listening and listening (a reference to the therapist "listening" to the client). Never told me how I was doing; never told me what I *should* do, and what I *shouldn't* do; never said anything (a safe course in dealing with this much ambivalence). Finally he put his stethoscope back in the bag (therapy session completed) and just said: 'I'll see you next week.' Now if that didn't make me mad. I'm telling you! (Hostilely.) It's a damn waste of time! Why didn't he tell me what was wrong, or what to expect, or what to do (with her degree of anger, her exquisite sensitiveness in regard to her guilt, and her reality-distorting ambivalence, the therapist would quickly alienate himself if he did so). He did tell me to cut out my smoking (this may be a reference to her "smoking" anger; or perhaps a reference to *her* feeling the *therapist feels* her oral needs are excessive). Now I don't think he's treating me right, do you? Do you *actually* think that's the way to treat a patient? I wish I had Dr. Sager (a differently perceived aspect of therapist) instead. He's not there as much. Everyone likes him. (Smiles warmly.) He's very understanding, kind and considerate. He's exactly the opposite from Dr. Eller. But I don't have any right to complain about Dr. Eller, as I wouldn't like it if someone came in and told *me* how to clean *my* house." (Note here how ambivalent she is in wanting, and *not wanting*, to be told what to do, in regard to therapy.)

"I feel so depressed. (Sighs.) Bob (her husband, but here, an unconsciously perceived aspect of the therapist) and I (*one aspect* of herself) are not hitting it off together. (Pause.) It's all my fault (i.e., "*my* fault for having the oral needs in the first place"). Last night he wanted to have sexual relations with me (a latent autistic reference to the pressure of the emotional closeness of therapy, that her own oral needs create) and he *was* in a real loving mood. But I just froze right up. I wouldn't let him even touch me. I could easily have gotten hysterical if he persisted, but he didn't (Therapist: He didn't force himself on you.) No, he didn't, but I don't know what I'm good for. (Cries.) I just didn't want him near me, and I actually felt repulsed by him. I was repulsed, because all this while, I've gone *wanting* him to show me love, and I *do* crave a lot of affection, and *need* it more than the average person. But he's never been affectionate in the past, when I *wanted* him to be. Now when he tries to make love to me, I think of all the times he's treated me so poorly in the past. . .the times when I needed affection, and he wouldn't give it to me, or I wanted him and he wasn't there. The marriage just hasn't been what I hoped it would be (i.e. free of guilt-blocked oral needs).

196

But maybe I'm wanting too much from it. He told me that if I was thinking the marriage was going to be one big, long honeymoon, I was a dreamer. He said my idea of a marriage was to lock ourselves up in a bedroom (a latent reference to the aspects of the therapeutic transference that are free of guilt and anger) together, and exclude the rest of the world (referring to the guilt-laden and angry aspects of the transference relationship). But I know that wouldn't be very realistic, nor fair to him. It really isn't what I would want either. I mean it *is* (note the ambivalence here of her oral needs on one hand, and her guilt on the other), but I would want *him* happy too, and I know he *couldn't* be (Cries.) I don't know what I want. I don't want him unhappy, and I'm making him so. He knows how mixed up I am. (Wipes away tears.) I told him how in the past, when he was loving me, that I felt he must have had someone else in mind. Then *I'd* get *mad* thinking he was wishing it wasn't me. I know I'm all mixed up inside. I know that what I *do* want, just isn't possible (i.e. a gratification of an immensity of guilt-blocked oral needs) and I know what I *don't* want. I did know the other night (a reference to therapy) I didn't want him close to me, when he wanted to be, because I was so mad *he wasn't* close to me in the *past!* That sounds crazy, But I can't help it. (Pause.) I can't do anything right it seems. (Cries.) I've always felt, even as a child, I was a no-good daughter, and that *I* was the cause of my mother's drinking, and her unhappy marriage (i.e. once again, "my oral needs destroy"). I'm a poor excuse for a mother to my children, and I'm a lousy wife. (Wipes away tears.) I'm too idealistic. I'm asking too much of the marriage. I've wanted Bob to be understanding with me, but how can he be with my being as mixed up as I am? I guess I've wanted Bob to be a lot of things to me, which, in a way, he is. But in another way he isn't! And *this* is what makes me depressed. (Not only is she ambivalent about knowing what she wants, but she is ambivalent in knowing what the cause of her depression is. Previously, she was implying she was angry at herself for having oral dependency needs, but now oscillates from this position of *self-felt* guilt to one of *projected* guilt, but then seems to have a partial recognition of this ambivalence.) Yet, I know that the very things I *want* him to be to me, *conflict* with other things I want him to be. For instance, I want him to be stable, serious, always dependable and, above all, respectable. And yet I want him, at the very same time, to be a carefree, full-of-fun, and a devil-may-care playboy too! I know the trouble is with me. I simply want what I can't have. I've recognized I need to be *loved*, and yet I do things just wanting to be *hurt* as though I have a *need* to be hurt or treated poorly (i.e., "to assuage my guilt"). I wonder, if, because I have so many mixed-up feelings, I wouldn't be better off without him (i.e. "without gratifying my oral needs"). I don't think I should have gotten married in the first place (this is just a variant of: "I should have never been born"). The other night I was taking a shower (a symbolic reference to removing guilt in anticipation of meeting her oral needs) and Bob showed no concern for me whatsoever. He just went to bed without waiting up for me. He shut off the bedroom light (perhaps a reference to terminating a therapy session, or a reference to her perceptions of the therapist withdrawing when she seeks oral gratification, which arise when she projects the blocking of this gratification by her own guilt to the therapist.) I came in later and stumbled in the dark trying to get into bed with him. I was so mad then I could have killed him for not seeming to *care* about me. But then I don't really know if I was mad at *him* because he turned the light off and . . . well . . . rejected me . . . or whether I was mad at *myself* because I haven't learned to walk in the dark alone without stumbling (i.e., "I haven't learned to go through life without needing others").

"I just don't know about Bud. (therapist) His work is getting him down. His hair has turned a little gray on the sides. He hardly says anything anymore to me, and whenever he's with me he's usually half asleep. He never listens to what I say. I don't blame him though with the long hours he has to keep to pay all the bills we have . . . particularly doctor bills. My coming here doesn't help, but only makes it worse. The children (her oral needs) are always running to the doctor for this and that, and there seems to be no end to it all. Besides his regular job at the plant, he's trying to get the ground ploughed and a crop in that we're going to need, or else we just won't make it this year. It's so discouraging! (Therapist: Discouraging?) Yes. He has to tend to the chicken house each morning, adjusting the windows for the proper ventilation and letting that smothering nitrogen gas from the chicken manure (a reference to her guilt) out. Besides that, he has to fill the chicken house feed hoppers. I wish we didn't have those damn chickens (her oral needs). I know that's more than enough for any man right there, but then he has to slop the hogs as well (another analogy of the therapist meeting her oral needs). It's no wonder he hasn't felt in the mood for sexual intercourse! (i.e. a closer emotional involvement with more oral need gratification.) He's too tired for sex because of his jobs. (Pause.) Is it time to go? I thought I detected a 'Gee, how am I going to get rid of you' look. (Pause.) Well, I don't have a happy husband on my hands. He's working too hard and he's getting tired of putting out as much work as he does, and having so very little to show for it. That's bound to be discouraging. You know that. I don't want to ask him, or bother him with my needs when I know how his job drains him of his strength. He has a lot of plain unpleasantness in his job that no one else seems to want to contend with. I've often suggested to him that he change his work, and get away from what he has to put up with now. There's no pleasure in his work for him (a projection of her own oral anhedonia to the therapist). I'm reluctant to ask him to help with anything around the house as he has too much on him to handle already. I have to go easy on him . . . after all he is the bread winner (note the symbolic orality). And too, I must be pretty boring company for him when he comes home. It must be depressing for him to come home to me in the condition I'm in. I'm a depressing depressed person. I don't go anywhere! I don't do anything, and I don't have a single thing to say that's interesting to him. I'm just a *worry* to him that he'd be better off not having. (Cries.) When I look at myself, I don't like what I see (the distorting ego-alien *guilt, anger* and *oral* needs). I really don't think he would have tried raising hogs this year if he didn't need the money, but he's *so* up against it. He can't have the vacation I know he needs because of *my* coming down here twice a week for therapy."

NOTES

1. Burnham, D.L., Gladstone, A.I., Gibson, R. W.: Schizophrenia and the Need-Fear Dilemna, Internat. Univ. Press, New York, 1969.

CHAPTER 10

RESISTANCE TO THE THERAPEUTIC PROCESS

Resistance is the tendency to withdraw from an emotional involvement of a therapeutic nature. It is *emotional* in origin and *not* intellectual, deriving itself from the unconscious guilt. Whether the guilt is more recently added, or whether it is part of the core personality guilt, it creates a resistance toward a continuation of an emotional involvement that could lead to a multiplicity of part objects from which to draw oral supplies and to express anger. It is this resistance that makes the gratification of the oral dependency needs, and the ventilation of the repressed anger, within a therapeutic transference, most difficult for the emotionally uncomfortable person. In those people who *are* emotionally uncomfortable, their personality core guilt offers a resistance that will tend to block the necessary emotional involvement that would tend to diminish this guilt. Even in those clients that may initially involve themselves quite readily in a therapeutic process, one will very quickly recognize how difficult it is for these individuals to continue in this process at *regularly* scheduled intervals.

Most frequently, a client will enter a therapeutic relationship when he has become emotionally uncomfortable from *added* unconscious guilt. If he is initially seen on a two or three times a week basis, it is usually within only two or three weeks before this client is much more emotionally comfortable, having decreased the *added* unconscious guilt through a ventilation of his previously more recently added anger. The resistance toward *further* emotional involvement will show itself, though, by requests, or demands, to "stretch out" the time between appointments, or attempts to simply discontinue altogether. If a client is initially seen on a weekly basis because of the uncomfortableness of added unconscious guilt, he will usually become more comfortable within five or six sessions. This client, too, can then be expected to attempt to "stretch out" the time between appointments, or may even abruptly terminate. After having decreased the recently *added* unconscious guilt, it is most difficult to keep the client emotionally involved at an intensity that is necessary to lower the personality core guilt. It is the personality core guilt that has the tendency to *repress* anger in times of oral frustration, which will then lead to the formation of newly *added* unconscious guilt.

The tendency is for the individual with a greater amount of core personality guilt to show *more* resistance toward continuing than the individual with *less* unconscious personality core guilt, once the added unconscious guilt is removed.

What so frequently happens is that a client begins a therapeutic transference relationship on a twice a week, or once a week basis, and then after becoming emotionally comfortable will show their personality resistance by either discontinuing, or insisting that the time between their appointments be increased. This *personality resistance* can be likened to a wall that prevents others from getting any further emotionally involved with them beyond a certain distance. If there are no further episodes of increased oral frustration, or no emotional crises, they can function fairly comfortably, drawing enough oral supplies and expressing enough anger in their interpersonal relationships. But in doing so they will continue to prevent anyone from getting beyond this "wall" that surrounds them. (Kinzel[1] has interestingly shown that incarcerated prisoners have a "no-man's land" that prevents others from getting too emotionally close.)

The therapist may attempt to hold the client that is showing resistance to a regular schedule. However, the client will often either not show up for his appointment, or will cancel. If the therapist continues to hold this client's time open for him, and charges a fee whether the client comes or not, the client will sometimes use this as a good logical reason to simply discontinue. He may rationalize his resistance as: "The therapist is only interested in what he can get out of me," and will find ready support from his relatives. If the time is kept open for the reluctant client without a charge the therapist will usually find himself sitting alone, while the client, himself, sets an increased distance between the therapy appointments kept. In other words, if the therapist holds to twice a week sessions, the client will cancel with good "logical" reasons one of those sessions each week. If the therapist was attempting to keep the client on a regular once a week basis, the client will consistently cancel every other week. By increasing the time between sessions the naturally occurring process of anger ventilation and oral dependency that the client is resisting is slowed down. It is not at all helpful to attempt to bring out to the client that he is showing emotional resistance to the process, in that it will be denied, and the questioning felt as antagonistic and non-supportive. For the analysts that *do* bring resistance to the attention of their clients, and the clients *do* continue, it is only because these clients have *less* resistance, and *not* because they have any added intellectual insight.

Rationalizations that are financially oriented, even though realistically supported, are only manifestations of the *emotional* resistance. Any rationalization *should* be realistically supported. Clients that are financially *able* to be seen on a continuation of the previous regular schedule can always find *other* excuses for cancelling their appointments. Even in those clients that have insurance coverage that would pay most, if not all, their visits (as Medicare, "Champus" clients), will likewise find reasons of one sort or another for "stretching out" their time between sessions. It is interesting to see the very same emotional resistance that one sees in private practice in a free mental health clinic, where the clients will offer a multiplicity of rationalizations why they can't continue to come on the previously set regular schedule of session appointments. "I have no transportation," "I have a cold and the doctor told me to stay in," "I had to work that day," etc., are frequently heard excuses for skipped clinic appointments. And sometimes the appointment is simply "forgotten." Even in cases where a client is being seen "gratis," as with professional courtesy, the same emotional resistance will show itself and good "logical" rationalizations will be made to "stretch out" the time between these sessions.

Sometimes a client will begin on a twice a week basis, continue this way for several weeks, then decrease his appointments to once a week for several months, then go to an every other week basis, and finally, after a few more weeks, when the "wall" is reached again, to a once a month basis. By "stretching out" the time between his appointments, the client will prevent the therapeutic process from becoming emotionally intense enough to allow a ventilation of his repressed anger and lower his personality *core* guilt. When his appointments are on once a month, or on a longer interval, the client will do little, if any, to decrease the personality core guilt, and will draw upon this relationship for some added oral supplies or anger expression that is very little more than that found in any other object relationship.

If the medical therapist makes an error in keeping a client on any "tranquilizer" after the time that the resistance shows itself, the client will often end up coming for little more than "medication checks." These "medication checks" do offer some oral need support and perhaps some mild anger ventilation. There is no change, however, in the personality *core* guilt, and the personality remains essentially the same. It is better for a client that might have been started on a tranquilizer by his family physician to be kept on this tranquilizer only until he is into the therapeutic transference, and then taken off of it, when more comfortable, just prior to, or at the first sign of resistance. The longer the time between sessions, the greater is the tendency for pill-taking clients to demand *more* medication, when they experience oral deprivation or oral frustration. The added unconscious guilt reinforces the resistance from the core guilt to a closer emotional interaction. This often causes the inexperienced doctor to try different medications, or to add still more when the client complains: "The medicine isn't helping me." The guilt has increased and made more ego-alien the unmet oral needs, intensifying the oral dilemma. Many times it isn't possible to get the resisting client off of medication, in that their unconscious guilt makes them feel that they *do* have a "sickness" or a "mental abnormality" that *requires* a medication. They seem to require a conscious drug-orientation to the professional relationship to keep the emotional concern more repressed. They see little reason to come in and talk to the doctor. If they cannot get medication from the therapist with whom they are involved without coming in to see him, they will sometimes go to another that tends to use medications more freely. This type of client is often typical of having had one or more psychiatric hospitalizations. Those clients that end up

202

being pyschiatrically hospitalized do have a very high personality core guilt, with a proportionately high resistance to any emotionally-close therapeutic involvement. This high guilt gives them a preference for somatic treatments rather than any of the psychotherapies. When they are released from the hospital, they are often characterized by neither taking their medications *regularly* nor keeping *regular* appointments with their outpatient doctor. They turn to medication on an "only when I really *need* to take it" basis that is identically the same for getting professional help — "only when I really *need* to," which is, all too often, when they are considering suicide. Accepting increased dependency in the face of guilt seems equated with committing suicide and like suicide, resorted to only as a very last resort.

The therapeutic listener does not need to dispense medications for his client, and in cases where a tranquilizer may be initially beneficial, a client could better obtain this from his reality oriented family physician. The important point is that a therapeutic listener certainly doesn't *have* to be, and perhaps *shouldn't* be, a physician. For a physician to be totally involved in therapeutic listening of any type, including all the various psychotherapies and psychoanalysis, is to literally make a *sow's ear* out of a silk purse. He is wasting the medical skills which he has learned. The physician might *better* practice medicine, for which he was trained, and let others do the therapeutic listening. The psychiatrists that are interested in the medical aspects of organic illness might better go into neurology. The so-called biological psychiatrists are essentially neurologically oriented anyway, and their interests should be under that medical speciality that by rights should cover this area. And the psychiatrists that aren't neurologically oriented are practicing something that many quacks and faith-healers can do just as well, if not even better.

One client had discontinued therapy after only a few sessions, and apparently discontinued the Mellaril her family physician placed her on. She phoned her therapist several months later, when the family physician wisely refused to refill her prescription after he had referred her for psychotherapy. "I'm going to go to work and I'm getting nervous about it . . . maybe I should go back on that Mellaril." Since the "Mellaril" is, in part, a metaphor for the supportive aspect of the client-therapist transference relationship that she desired, the therapist told her that he felt it was a very good idea, and gave her an appointment to come in to see him. The therapeutic transference relationship was begun again, and this particular client was able to discontinue her reality need for medication. Had the therapist simply phoned in a prescription he would have rejected the client in her latent bid for oral dependency, and she might have phoned still later remarking: "The Mellaril doesn't seem to be enough . . . maybe I need something else." Reality-wise she means another drug, but latently she refers to oral dependency. Even if the therapist had been medicine-oriented, and unknowledgeable of transference language, he could have been expected at this point to have invited her in, in order to "get her on the right medicine." Some individuals have such high levels of resistance that they even refuse to come in to see the physician. When the physician refuses to simply phone in a refill for the medication, the client will then attempt to find a physician who *will* give them the medication without the threat of any emotional involvement.

The client that shows a resistance to a certain schedule of regularly kept sessions, and stretches out his appointments with longer intervals, eventually will reach a point with this new schedule where the personality core guilt will offer resistance again. The client invariably demands his intervals between sessions be increased still further. Eventually the therapeutic transference is so weakened, and of so little an emotional threat because of the time interval between the sessions, that the client will go for months and even years, coming in for the oral dependency this allows at the emotional distance their high level of personality core guilt demands. Their very frequently occurring *added* unconscious guilt only reinforces their belief that they "need" to continue "because I'm mentally ill," or "I don't want to have to be psychiatrically hospitalized again."

It is most essential for the professional listener to realize that the therapeutic transference can lower not only the recently added unconscious guilt, but also the core personality guilt. But the client must be kept involved on a regular schedule of interaction at an intense enough level without skipping sessions or stretching out his appointment schedule. Whether sessions are a half hour, or one hour, or whether the schedule is twice a week, once a week, or every other week, the therapeutic transference will naturally progress — faster when seen more frequently, and slower when seen less frequently. In a matter of time the unconscious guilt can be so decreased that the oral dependency needs are met in a multiplicity of part objects within the interpersonal relationship sphere. The therapist eventually becomes *reduced* in symbolic emotional significance to a level that is no more than that with any other object. This eventual lessening of the intensity of the therapeutic transference depends upon regularly kept sessions. But this is most difficult for any client to do, when one realizes that what is most feared by any adult human is oral dependency, especially when it is intense, prolonged, and so threatening to the unconscious ego defenses that were developed to avoid this very thing.

If a client has to ask how long he must continue then he indicates, by his very asking, not only his resistance, but that he is not ready emotionally to discontinue. For a client involved in an intense therapeutic transference this question of "How long must I continue" is always an unconscious, and often a conscious issue. It is an issue that can't be answered by the therapist with any helpful logic, in that the client, who may *fear* that it could go on "for years and years!" ambivalently and unconsciously *desires* that it *does* go on for *years*. Neither should the therapist imply in answer to such a question that his client *has* a "need" to continue. In doing so he would be implying an oral rejection connoting that the therapist *does* see something "wrong," or "abnormal," about the client that he "needs" to continue. And, reality-wise, the client can often too easily "prove" by discontinuing that he can easily get along without his therapeutic listener. It isn't necessary to answer the question of "How long do I continue?" with other than an "It's all right to continue." The person who is more emotionally comfortable in life is still feeding upon the symbolic "good breast," but not from any one object. He does so from a multiplicity of "good breasts," and perceives as well a multiplicity of "bad breasts." The therapeutic transference should be continued until it *fades* in emotional significance in a multiplicity of these other much less intense transferences of the client's interpersonal relationship sphere that are allowed to be created by the reduction in the level of the unconscious guilt. At this point, discontinuing is no longer an issue, either consciously or unconsciously. The metaphorical, or transference language of this person will indicate that he has little uncomfortable guilt, either self-felt or projected, that he is not prone to be adding unconscious guilt, and that he is diffusely involved in his interpersonal relationships, drawing oral dependency needs from a great many objects. This client shows very little resistance to involvement with the therapist, but he *also* shows very little resistance to any *other* object relationship. It is because of this that the therapist eventually takes a position like the biological "good" mother . . . not really left behind, but orally incorporated and reflected into many ongoing object relationships.

But well before this point is reached, most clients will be actively engaged in trying to resist further emotional involvement with the therapist on the previously set regular sessions. Clients will come for several weeks, or several months, and will become emotionally more comfortable than they have been in a long time. They will often then decide to take a vacation, which their diminished unconscious guilt now allows them to do. But when they return from vacation, and finding out they can function without therapy, they often never return for a continuation of any therapeutic transference to lower the personality core guilt. Clients will involve themselves, though, with others as their interpersonal relationship sphere increases. They are more comfortable in relating to others because of their diminished guilt, and so become more readily involved in taking college courses, in bowling, in working or being involved in anything that effectively interferes with a continuation of their emotional involvement with their therapist. One client who had become much less guilt-laden from her involvement in a therapeutic transference told her therapist: "I'm going to take up flying (metaphorically symbolic of increased oral need gratification). It's something that I've always *wanted* to do, but always felt in the past that I *shouldn't*. (Therapist: It sounds like fun.) I'm really looking forward to flying!" It is in the next session that the therapist is duly informed that the only time her flying lessons can be scheduled is not only during the time that her therapy sessions are now, but during the time that her therapy sessions could *possibly* be scheduled as well. "I never know ahead of time when a plane is available." She would deny any implication in the fact that the only time the plane is available is at whatever time her therapy is scheduled.

These involvements seem unconsciously determined to specifically interfere, or completely preclude the possibility of being further involved in a therapeutic transference to lower intensely defended core guilt. Business trips, vacations, or moves to a distance city seem to necessitate that the appointments, if they aren't completely discontinued, be "stretched out." The client has all of reality to support his emotional resistance, while the therapist has only the illogical arguments of an unreality which, because they aren't reality-oriented, wouldn't be acceptable anyway to the client.

To tell a person to involve himself in a rather unrealistic and highly illogic process as the therapeutic transference is not very convincing, and can be easily refuted by reality. Because the unconscious of a person *is* unconscious, it is most difficult for clients to understand that their emotional problems are part object oriented, and involve so much the past. Reality-wise, they are uncomfortable in the *present* about present reality problems. To them, what is past is past. Why should they involve themselves, they ask, with anything that essentially deals with "water long gone over the dam?" The client can't be convinced that one always sees the present in the light of the past. The person in his own mind, or his own consciousness, *knows*, or *thinks* he knows, what his emotional difficulty is. Certainly, he believes, it has *nothing* to do with his therapeutic listener. His unconscious part object concretizations and condensations when projected into his conscious are such that they appear to *him* to be logical and realistic as ultimate explanations. It is these things that he is interested in, and not an illogical relationship with a listener, who, from a reality point of view, should mean *nothing* to him. Furthermore, with the recently past instability of his ego functioning when he was emotionally uncomfortable, he is more concerned, now, with hanging onto reality. The unrealness of those previously repressed feelings that seemed so ego-alien were *enough* to contend with, he feels, without courting *more* unreality when he doesn't really *need* to now.

Frequently, a client who was referred for psychotherapy comes long enough to eliminate added unconscious guilt, but then schedules a "needed" surgical operation that is well supported by a surgeon or gynecologist. These clients will often rationalize their previous emotional uncomfortableness as having been *caused* by their surgical or gynecological problem. They then discontinue the therapeutic transference when they involve themselves in the reality of medicine as so many other people do in handling the orality of their personality core guilt. Clients will discontinue when they "find out" their emotional problems were really due to something an allergist, or an ENT man, or an internist can "help" them with. And these professionals can offer the facts of reality for their emotional involvement with the client, while the therapeutic listener can't. If the analysts describe an "escape into health" to avoid the therapeutic transference, then this represents an "escape into sickness" — a medical or surgical *reality-supported* sickness or problem — which is still an escape from the emotionality of the transference.

Those individuals with the greatest need for involvement with a therapeutic listener will have the greatest *resistance* to becoming involved because of their guilt. It then seems ironic that those that are able to endure in some type of *continued* talking and listening process are often those with *less* of a need to *be* so involved. The continued involvement in a talking and listening process is an *emotional* one. It has very little to do with one's ability to intellectualize either a need for continuing a relationship, or the disadvantages for discontinuing it. Neither is any knowledge of psychological or psychoanalytic principles of any benefit. Clients who are psychologically "trained" or "educated" show just as much emotional resistance to continuing as anybody else. The main problem in therapeutic listening becomes how to keep the client involved on a regularly scheduled basis. So much of a person's ability to be involved depends upon, first, the amount of unconscious guilt that he has, and secondly, the "set" of his personality core guilt in relation to being involved with a particular reality orientation

In other words, an individual might involve himself in a talking and listening process with a psychiatrist, or any therapeutic listener, and continue in this relationship even though he might have *less* guilt than another individual who is either unable to go to a professional for help, or else discontinues after an initial visit when "getting professional help" concretizes too well, or focuses too sharply, his unconscious guilt. If seeing a professional too much threatens the ego defenses one has established for handling repressed anger, denied oral dependency needs, and guilt, then continuing will be emotionally difficult for this person, if not impossible. This is particularly so in those people who have adopted defenses that involve somatic symptom complaints and seem to require a medical orientation to their relationship.

The resistance to involvement in a therapeutic transference is sometimes even shown *before* the person has even made an initial contact with the professional. The appointment is made, but then is not kept. The individual simply doesn't show up, or he calls to cancel the appointment, remarking it isn't convenient for him to come at this time, implying he is not presently involved in an emotional crisis to such a degree that he is unable to function. How ambivalent they are about seeking help, and how prone they are to emotional crises, is shown when shortly after cancelling the initial appointment, or after not having shown up for one, they will sometimes call again and make another appointment, and may fail to show up for this as well. Many times they will come late for the initial appointment, but then show their ambivalence by standing in the doorway at the close of the session, attempting to gratify their oral needs after the session is over. Sometimes a client will appear for an initial appointment with no apparent intention of continuing any further. These clients seek to elicit a confirmation from the therapist that they don't "need" to come, when their own guilt makes them feel they do. Whether the initial session is the known last one for the client, or whether any particular session is known by the client to be his last, the therapist is usually impressed how emotionally close the client will get at that time. The client seems to be able to allow closeness he might not have been able to do otherwise in simply knowing he won't be seeing the therapist again.

Ironically, many clients come to therapy seemingly seeking help on how *not* to need help. They seek an unrealistic "help" in becoming "independent," in repressing their anger and in wanting the therapist as if with some detached and distant God-like power to magically remove their guilt without gratifying their pressing unmet oral dependency needs, nor ventilating their anger. All too soon, they verbalize in metaphor the dilemma of finding themselves, because of the transference, involved in the very same problems of orality with the therapist that they had hoped to extricate themselves from when they sought professional help. The same tendency to find someone to help in their quest for "independency" that brought them to the therapist causes them to leave the therapist to look *elsewhere* for this "help" in being "independent."

For those clients that *do* make it beyond an initial appointment, emotional resistance is soon shown when they come late for their scheduled session. Their initial verbalizations as they come in late metaphorically conceptualize their resistance, as: "I'm sorry I'm late . . . I couldn't get the children (referring to her guilt-laden oral dependency needs) ready in time," or "I think I hit just about every red light I could possibly get in coming here," or "Boy, did I have a difficult time making it here . . . all the traffic seemed to be going the other way," and "There was so much fog on the road I could hardly find my way to your office." One can easily "read" the metaphorical implications in remarks as: "I couldn't get the car started this morning," and "I thought my appointment was a half hour from now, and that I was coming *early* instead of being late!" At times the resistance seems to be projected, as though originating in the therapist. This is illustrated by remarks as: "I'm late because my baby sitter (i.e., the therapist) didn't show up on time," and "Bonnie (the client's girlfriend, and the therapist in metaphor) tried to keep me from coming today."

Clients that do come regularly may find themselves with an apparent "need" to remain silent. Unlike long comfortable thoughtful pauses, or the "silent treatment" of the angry person, these silences are, instead, reflections of emotional resistance. The client seems to be saying through his silence: "I'm not going to say anything because I don't want you to know how guilty I really am, how angry and violent I can be, or how hungry I am." For the very guilt-laden individual any verbalization at all, and particularly to a transference figure, can become a threat to their tenuously controlled anger and their guilt-laden oral needs. They show a fear of their own feelings because they seem so illogical and so alien to the reality of their situation in life. They may have already implied that "they have no reason in the world to be depressed, when I have so much to be thankful for," or "no reason whatsoever for being as angry as I know I am." Any concern of theirs for their unmet oral dependency needs is felt as: "I'm just being self-centered and being selfish. . .I should be thinking of *others,* and not myself." The "I have no reason to feel the way I do . . . so orally hungry and so angry," prompts the silence that they hope can keep their secret feelings hidden. If they were to talk at all . . . even of the most seemingly benign and most unrelated subject, they would be immediately involved in meeting their guilt-laden oral needs through communicative processes, and would be threatening the defenses that keep their anger repressed. Afraid that they might unleash a "Pandora's Box" of uncontrollable feelings, they verbalize little more than "name, rank and serial number."

The therapeutic listener should recognize and respect the client's "need" for silence. It allows the client to set a comfortable emotional distance not only between himself and what is so ego-alien about his feelings, but also between himself and the unconsciously perceived parts of the therapist. It isn't necessary for the therapist to get the client to talk. He'll do so in time, when he feels *comfortable* enough to do so. Even as the client sits through a long silence without the therapist making an effort to get the client to verbalize the therapeutic transference *is* continuing. It is still in effect, and can actually be deepening as long as the client *comes* to therapy sessions *regularly* and remains emotionally involved. It isn't necessary to be always *verbally* involved. It is the *emotional* involvement that is of primal importance. This emotional involvement is always more important than anything that is ever verbalized. (God, for instance, speaks very little to those that are emotionally involved with Him.)

If the therapist, himself, is uncomfortable in long silences of resistance, he may tend to "push" the client toward verbalizing. This may tend to drive the client away, and may even lead to a termination of the relationship. To move in on an emotionally uncomfortable client, or to uncover emotional feelings too rapidly and too prematurely, may exacerbate the resistance of the client. This may lead to his discontinuing, where he might not have, had the therapist been more patient and more accepting of his silence. At other times, the therapist's intolerance of silence may provoke an interestingly appropriate transference language as in the excerpt of a seventeen-year-old high school girl in her twelfth weekly session of psychotherapy, who remarked, following a long pause in which the therapist, several times, had said "You appear thoughtful": "Well, that's it. I've said it all. I don't have anything more to say. (Long pause.) Everything has come to a screeching halt. (Long pause with the therapist eventually asking "How have things been this past week?") I haven't *seen* anyone, or *done* anything different, than what I told you last week! (Long pause with the therapist finally asking "How are things going in school?") Boring! Real boring! Especially the

Spanish class! God, how I detest that class and when I'm in it, I just can't wait until I get out of it! (Pause.) I've made up my mind I'm dropping that course. At first I thought I'd like Spanish, but I've gotten so now that I just hate it — I hate every moment I'm there and I can hardly wait till the end of the hour. I've developed a purple passion for the teacher (laughs anxiously) that thinks she's a buddy of mine. Maybe it's because I don't like the way she's always checking on me. (Pause.) I'm tired of people like that who are always checking on me, and trying to find out what I'm doing. She's just like my mother — always checking — 'Where have you been, Mary, and what have you been up to?' I feel like telling her 'For God's sake, leave me alone!'"

Long silences are often followed by remarks as: "Can't you *tell* me what's wrong?" or "Don't you have some *advice* for me to follow?" and "Why don't you *summarize* my problem?" One client presents, in analogy, his unconscious perception of the therapist's tolerating the long pauses as: "I can't think of anything to say. (Long uncomfortable pause.) What do you want me to talk about? (Therapist: "Anything that comes to mind.") Well, honestly now, the only thing that comes to mind is that girl (therapist) in my art class that I'm kind of interested in. I'm attracted to her and I've tried talking to her, but it seems as though she can only give me a curt 'hello.' I'd like *her* to talk (as a form of his resistance) but she won't. She gives me the brush off like I was some kind of leper. You know, like I had some contagious disease. (Pause.) It's like she has to keep her distance from me all the time. I try to talk to her, but she just won't open up. I don't know whether she thinks that if she said more than 'good morning' to me, that I might fling her down and rape her. I'd like to ask her for a date, but I can't do it when she acts this way to me. (Pause.) Now, what the hell does that have to do with the problem that brings me here?"

In the following excerpt, there is a metaphorical reference to the therapist's listening silence, and the client's resistance to continued involvement. "I can't stand having my mother (therapist) hanging around me and never saying anything. If I were smart I'd put her away in a nursing home. (Long pause.) I told her the other day, 'Mother' . . . I'm telling my mother now . . . 'I've *got* to get away from you! How can I have fun when you're always around checking on me? How can I do what others are doing when you're always around me?' Do you know what she said? (Long pause.) Do you know what she said? (Pause.) Well, *do* you? (Therapist: What? — What did she say?) Nothing!! She said *nothing*, just like she always does!"

Another client with an unwillingness to verbalize freely shows resistance that arises from his guilt in the following: "I don't like going over to Mrs. Chase's (a guilt-laden aspect of himself that he has projected to the therapist). She can't talk about anything that's nice. She's got to start talking about people and implying things about them that aren't true. (Therapist: "Things that aren't true?")

Well, I don't want to talk about it! I hate her! She's always making up *lies!* She twists things around right in front of me. You know how much I enjoy Andrew and Elaine (the guilt free interaction of an aspect of himself and the therapist). They like to go around with each other, but it isn't for *sex!* But Mrs. Chase has to make it dirty. She has to twist it around so that they're involved *more* than what they really are. According to her, they're always in bed together. Sure, I know that they share the same apartment when they come down to the beach here. It's just for the weekend. But they don't back home. Maybe they do live in the same building, but he's on the 8th floor, and she's on the 6th floor. They simply aren't as dirtily involved as Mrs. Chase would like to have them. I hate to disappoint her! The nosey old biddy! Maybe it's wishful thinking on her part, but I happen to know otherwise. She's nothing but an evil and dirty-minded old busy-body!''

The unconscious guilt that makes a client feel so inadequate may also make that client feel that he is doing an *inadequate* job in therapy, and can lead to a withdrawal from therapy, or a long depressing silence. Not only has the guilt made him feel that he is a failure *before* coming into therapy, but then, after he has become involved, the feeling of failure is now transferred into therapy. The client feels he has "failed" in this relationship too. This is sometimes· expressed directly as: "I feel I should be *better* by now," or "I don't see where I've made *any* progress." What progress they would like to see is a feeling *better* in their present oral-need frustrating situation in reality, with a more effective *denial* of their unmet oral needs. They don't see the hoped for "progress" in magically removing their repressed anger and their unmet oral needs that guilt leads them to feel they shouldn't have. They don't see any "progress" either in removing the uncomfortable manifestations of their guilt. Sometimes this is expressed denoting that it is a projection of only an aspect of their ambivalence as: "My *husband* feels I should be better by now." This latently implies that it is the *therapist* who is metaphorically presented as "my husband," not *she,* who is expecting her to be doing "better" than she is.

The unconscious guilt, if it doesn't promote silence, will tend to make the individual feel that whatever he is presentaing as verbalizations is "trivia," "nonsense," or "drivel." When a person is so guilt-laden in the initial phase of their therapeutic involvement, they will frequently comment on their verbalizations as "I have a feeling I'm not telling you what *you* want to know," or "I have a feeling that what I'm telling you is trite and insignificant," or "I have a feeling that I'm just repeating myself, that I'm just making a fool of myself and that I'm being too irrelevant." No matter what the verbalization might concern, unconscious guilt makes the individual feel that he is wasting his, as well as the therapist's, time, that he's not getting down to the "real problem," that nothing is being solved, and that no progress is being made. Just as the guilt was the main problem in the client's interpersonal relationship sphere, it becomes the main problem in the therapeutic transference.

That there can be two sides to this unconscious guilt is shown in the following exchange: "I just sit here and babble away about *nothing!* (Therapist: "I never felt you babbled away about *nothing.*") Oh? (Suddenly appears anxious.) Well, I see I have to *watch* what I say!" This seems to imply that the guilt makes the client feel, on one hand, that what he is saying is emotionally insignificant, or "no good," but on the other hand, he is afraid that what he is saying *may be* too revealing, and again "no good." He fears it may mean something that he would prefer to keep hid, that he is "tipping his cards," that the therapist might "draw the wrong conclusion," or that it is somehow "misleading."

The "set" of the unconscious guilt may be so great, as mentioned before, that clients cannot continue a therapeutic transference relationship. In their mind, the clients' going to see a clergyman, a psychologist, a counselor or psychiatrist is "proof" to them of their unconscious guilt, which may be manifested in self-felt "sinfullness," inadequacies, inferiorities or unacceptableness. Each visit then represents to them something which is an oral need rejection, another "put down," or is simply *oral need frustrating.* Their involvement focuses for them on the "fact" that there *is* something "wrong" with them, or something "abnormal" or "different" that they feel has prompted this "need" to see a professional. These clients do not get emotionally comfortable in as short a time as the clients referred to in the beginning of this chapter do. Some may even appear to *worsen,* or to show manifestations of *increasing* guilt, the more they are involved with a professional. This is the basis of the saying "Psychiatry can't help everyone." It is because psychiatry, for some, is too much an *oral rejection* and too indicative of their guilt.

Sometimes the emotional involvement with a professional is avoided because their verbalizations seem rationalized in the clients' mind as being somehow "unfaithful" to their spouses. They feel as though they are being "untrue" to their spouses, or that they're "two-timing" them, if they involve themselves with their therapist, where they engage in a "hidden pleasure" made *forbidden* by their guilt. They don't like "saying things behind his back" and would rather the spouse be present with them. There is a *realistic* guilt in the emotional "affair" of the client with the therapist. As one client, who talked of her husband's "indiscretions" — and latently her *own* with the therapist — "I'd rather John be involved *sexually,* than to be *emotionally* involved like he is." The therapeutic transference is actually less likened to prostitution, and more like "having an affair," but the client's projected guilt makes it seem like the former, and self-felt guilt like the latter. Either way makes for resistance.

But if the "set" of their guilt is such that going to a professional listener focuses or concentrates this guilt in the act of seeking help, then the individual often seems to get *worse* by continued involvement. The individual is already orally

212

frustrated enough, but if he perceives his visits to the listener as another oral need frustration, he becomes even more uncomfortable. He may seek then to avoid a relationship that threatens his defenses against his guilt-laden oral needs and his repressed anger. For these clients involvement with a psychotherapy-oriented psychiatrist definitely *does* worsen their emotional condition. Both they, as well as their spouses, would rather the orientation be medical, or surgical, but *not* psychotherapeutic. If they do see a psychiatrist, they often demand a time-limited psychiatric intervention that is *medically* oriented toward drugs, hospitalizations, and shock treatment.

At times, a client may involve herself long enough to reach a level of emotional comfortableness, but rather than continue, seeks to have someone else take her place in therapy. "I wish you'd see Mrs. Johnson because *she* sure needs to come. The way she's been acting it's a wonder that someone hasn't caught her with a net and locked her up." This client is metaphorically presenting an unconscious aspect of *herself* in describing "Mrs. Johnson's need for therapy." These clients project their guilt, deny it within themselves, and seek to disengage themselves from the relationship with the therapist. And yet, through "Mrs. Johnson," they can fantasize continuing the involvement. Other times, instead of projecting their guilt, they *seem* to project their *oral needs*. They want the therapist to see a "very close" or "dear friend" of theirs, which does not appear to have as much projected guilt as it does an oral pleasure which they themselves feel too guilty to continue in. They seem to imply that they *want* to continue on with a relationship with the therapist, but with some *distance*. By wanting to sub⁻ stitute a friend, they can vicariously go to the therapist, and still keep in touch with him through the friend. Many times, a client will discontinue after only a few sessions, but then several weeks or so later will send in a friend or a relative to the therapist, as though they still want to have a relationship with the therapist, but at a distance, and by proxy. This "therapy by proxy" is seen, for instance, in the woman, who very obviously is emotionally uncomfortable, but makes an appointment with a psychiatrist for her three year old son, and wants to be "in on his evaluation," so that she can hopefully do what any client in a therapeutic transference does, but with the focus on her *son* and *not* on herself.

The resistance from the unconscious guilt of a client can be metaphorically attributed, at times, to someone else. This may be shown as: "My *parents* don't want me going with *Kathy*." Here, "parents" represents a concretization of one aspect of the *client* that resists the emotional involvement with the therapist, and too, unconsciously perceived aspects of the *therapist* that the client feels doesn't want him to continue. "Bill thinks I'm not getting any better, so he wants me to see another doctor" represents more of the same resistance attributed to someone else in reality, and the therapist in metaphor. It might have been expressed as: "I don't understand what's going on in algebra, and the teacher wants me to drop the course." The "teacher" here is metaphorical, as "Bill" is, in the preceeding example. Both are metaphorical for projected *aspects* of the part make-up of the client's unconscious.

Sometimes a client will discontinue, feeling that the therapist *wanted* to get rid of them, without realizing that this feeling they attributed to the therapist was a projection of their *own* guilt and resistance to further involvement. This often isn't expressed directly, but metaphorically as: "I used to think *I* was the only person in the company with the feeling of wanting to leave. But recently I've found out that there are *others* on the management level that share my views."

Difficulty in communicating is often projected to the therapist, but usually in a metaphorical manner. "I just can't talk with John — I don't know what it is about him, but we just can't communicate." Though this client could be truthfully stating a *fact* about her husband, at the same time she is presenting in this spontaneous remark how she *perceives* the therapist within the transference. "I have given up talking with Bill — it's like he's put a wall between us — I just can't get through to him." When the resistance is projected to the therapist, communication for the client becomes difficult, and a continuation of the relationship is resisted. Here, in the following, guilt is projected, even though the client is implying that oral need gratification has been perceived: "I just don't like working in the department where I am. Betty's husband (therapist in metaphor) is always trying to get me alone in a corner to talk with me. He's actually been trying to "make out" with me, and I don't know what gives him the idea I'm *that* type of girl. *I* certainly haven't given it to him. Sure, I talk to him but that's all. I'm not leading him on, at least I hope I haven't. But to think *he* can make out with *me!* Who does he think he is anyway? (Therapist: Yaaa.) I just don't understand, as Betty (an aspect of the client) must know about it. She's right there too. And he knows that she kids around with all the men (other aspects of the therapist) in the department. Where is this world going to? I'd like to transfer out of the department if I can, as I don't want to get involved in anything like that!"

As another variation of this projected resistance to oral need gratification that comes about from unconscious guilt consider the following excerpt: "I can't do *anything* without my father (therapist) thinking I'm having an *affair* with some man. All I have to do is look at a man and somehow he finds out and starts accusing me of running around. I might as well do it as get accused of it like that. And with the past he has, I just don't see how he can talk about anybody. I've actually seen him following me (and this, in reality, is a *fact,* but at the same time, she is *still* projecting her guilt to the therapist) whenever I go out in the evening. The other night I saw him come up behind me in the car, so I really took him on a wild goose chase. I drove up and down all the rural roads I knew, as though I was going to meet a secret lover someplace. I don't know where it was that I finally shook him off. Whenever I see him he'll ask questions about what I've been up to, trying to check up on me. He's always been that way. Going to visit him is like going to

214

see a parole officer. Isn't he a great father? My mother (therapist) was the same way too, when I was growing up. She was always suspecting the worse from me. I guess I didn't disappoint her too many times!"

To illustrate again how projected guilt can be present as resistance, even when oral need gratification is being perceived, take the following excerpt: "He thinks you can *buy* love — he give me things (metaphorical for perceived oral dependency gratifying behavior on the part of the therapist) and then expects me to forget the past, and be loving to him. I don't see why he can't understand that what he's done to me in the past I've *forgiven*, but I won't ever *forget*, and that love from him, now, has an *opposite* effect on me."

A different presentation of this resistance, due to projected guilt, is shown in the following, where there is a perception of oral need gratification: "Nothing makes me more mad, than when I'm washing a floor in an old pair of shorts, feeling so dirty and grubby (i.e., so guilt-laden) and in he comes and says: 'Let's go somewhere together.' I say: 'I can't go looking like this!' and then he'll say: 'You look alright to me' (for she is, reality-wise, a very attractive woman) it just makes me so mad! He tells me I look *good*, when I know darn well I don't!"

Similar to this is the following excerpt: "I've been working over at the college in the Registrar's office, and now I've got some Chinese professor (the therapist, with certain implied negative characteristics) giving me the eye. I didn't really notice it until this past week when he started coming into the office on an almost daily basis. He is always giving me a great big warm smile. People are beginning to ask: 'What's with you and Professor Chin anyway?' I say: 'It beats me. I don't know why he thinks I'm interested in him!' In fact, I've been avoiding him now as much as possible. If I see him coming, I'll run the other way. I don't want any of that stuff. Oh, sure, I kid around at work. I enjoy working there, but people will think I'm there for all the wrong reasons. This Professor Chin has me scared. I don't know what his motive is — I don't know whether he's after me to make love with him, or maybe he's out to kill me. Anyway, I don't like it!"

Many times the unconscious perception of the "good breast" seems to prompt a retreat from the therapeutic transference. It is as though the individual is overwhelmed by the availability of the "good breast" that it provokes a withdrawal or even a panic, so that they discontinue. The suddeness of the termination of the therapeutic transference may seem difficult to understand when the initial stage of therapy appears to be going so well. For instance, a client will begin an involvement and, after only a few sessions, will appear to be intensely gratifying their oral dependency needs. Their emotional warmth, their frequent smiling, and the ease by which they relate to the therapist indicates they view him as the "good breast" and are actively drawing emotional support from him. Where previously they were entangled in emotional turmoil in their interpersonal relationships, they metaphorically imply they are much more comfortable, and that their interpersonal relationships are much less chaotic than they had been. But just

215

when the therapist feels his client is in the midst of the "honeymoon" stage of a therapeutic transference, the client abruptly cancels without making a new appointment, or else he simply doesn't show again for any further sessions.

These clients that *suddenly* discontinue, when they appear to have been so actively "feeding" from the "good breast," demonstrate by their sudden termination that they have a marked fear of oral dependency. They have past histories of rather severe emotional deprivation that go back to earliest childhood. They have always tried to function under a facade of "independency." This fear of oral dependency becomes a panic when exposed to an overwhelming unconscious perception of the "good breast." Perhaps it is because their past attempts at gratifying their oral needs were so *disastrous* that they are so reluctant to involve themselves again with an intensely gratifying oral dependency relationship. The unconscious perceptions of the "good breast" itself apparently threaten their facade of "independency," and they immediately withdraw with no reasons given to either themselves or their therapist, and with *no evidence* of any anger expression. One client, who previously was extremely unhappy, came for only two sessions before she gave blatant evidence she was unconsciously perceiving the therapist as the "good breast." At the close of this session, she stated: "I think I'm coming here for the *wrong* reasons." She then expressed her fear that "this might go on forever," implying the immensity of her ego-alien oral dependency needs that were being uncovered emotionally in the relationship. Rather than continue with such a close involvement with the immensely perceived "good breast," she abruptly discontinued.

The type of client that abruptly terminates the therapeutic transference after only a few sessions, when apparently they are unconsciously perceiving the "good breast," is likened to the familiar person that will get emotionally close to another person, and then suddenly back away for no apparent logical reason when a continued closeness is expected. A young woman may feel as though she has found the "perfect mate" in her fiance, set a wedding date, but then suddenly call off the ceremony just before it is to take place. This erroneously termed "homosexual panic" is frequently seen when emotional closeness precipitates a *panic* from the unconsciously perceived immense "good breast" in another person. Just when the therapist feels he has an "excellent" therapy client that is actively "feeding" within the therapeutic relationship, he suddenly finds that his "excellent client" has discontinued.

They discontinue because the intense gratification of their oral dependency needs is so symbolic of all the past emotional difficulties that they have had when they intensely sought in the past to have their oral needs met. They have engendered an unconscious feeling that they will have to pay a price for intense oral need gratification. In order to prevent a repetition of what they have gone through in the past, when they attempted to "feed" from the "good breast," they seek to *avoid* it. They seem to liken their attraction to the "good breast" to the

216

moth's attraction to the fatal flame, and therefore seek to put distance between it and themselves.

The price they feel is to be paid for oral gratification is metaphorically presented in the following excerpt: "Well, I went out to a bingo party last week (a reference to the orally gratifying aspects of the preceeding therapy session) and I really enjoyed it. I don't think I've had as much fun in years! I laughed and carried on like I didn't have a care in the world! But I'm not going to do it again. This was the first time that Skip (her husband, but perhaps metaphorical for her own guilt, projected to the therapist, which kept her in a rather schizoid and anhedonic existence) has ever let me go out. I know I'm going to end up *paying* for the fun I had. He's going to be throwing this up to me that I went out without him, so I'll be expecting to be left alone, just like I have so many times in the past. It's his excuse now for *me* to be left alone with the children (her unmet dependency needs), while he goes out. Rather than put up with that I'm going to *skip* the next bingo party." Whether she ever went back to any more bingo parties is not known, but she never came back for any further sessions.

One can see the resistance to oral need gratification in metaphorical statements as: "I'm afraid to take a drink for fear I'll become an alcoholic," or "I was afraid that if I started eating those donuts I wouldn't stop," and "I'm going to stop taking that tranquilizer my doctor gave me, as things have been going so well that I'd never be able to get off it." One recently divorced client, who withdrew from interpersonal relationships because of her fear of "diarrhea" (which appropriately symbolized her increased unconscious guilt with very interesting implications when she feared — and unconsciously wished, in part — "it might even get on others") recognized her intense need for others, which she then later sexualized. She analyzed her situation as: "If I didn't have this diarrhea and lack of self-confidence holding me back, I know I'd be a *sex maniac!* I never realized it before, but I think my whole problem is that I'm *starved* for sex!" Like the client whose father was an alcoholic (and who probably emotionally deprived his family), and *fears* alcohol, and the obese client who was "starved" emotionally as a child, this client fears there will be no control on her sexual appetite if she but let herself go. The alcohol, the food, and the sex are *metaphorical* for the immensity of the oral needs that they fear will result in *disaster* if they give in to any gratification in the therapeutic transference.

There is an element of *realistic* truth in what they do fear. The immensity of their unmet oral needs *is* that great that if it *wasn't* for their guilt, in checking an uncontrolled gratification, that a disaster in reality *could* result. Their unconscious emotional fear is well rationalized on a reality basis. Yet it is their guilt, as we have seen in previous chapters, that will effectively block any uncontrolled gratification of any perceived "good breast." An individual with less guilt doesn't have this immensity of unmet oral needs. With less guilt, there is less of an intensity and concentration of unmet oral needs. And wherever there *is* such an intensity of unmet oral needs in an individual, there will always be an appropriate level of guilt that would prevent any *sustained* unlimited oral dependency gratification.

This individual with an immensity of unmet oral needs basically fears any "addiction" to the "good breast." This will be metaphorically rationalized as "bad," and often in a way that is supported by reality. One can give good "logical" reasons for *not* drinking, for *not* over-eating, or for *not* having sex in an *uncontrolled* fashion. But these reality-supported rationalizations metaphorically stand for the illogic emotional resistance to the "addiction" on the unconsciously perceived "good breast." The problems of reality, in regard to any addiction, are utilized as manifest content to express their guilt-derived resistance to the emotional "addiction" to the "good breast." This addiction is *necessary,* at least in part, for the therapeutic transference to continue to its finality in a diffusion of a multiplicity of "good breasts" in a wide sphere of interpersonal relationships. It is at this point that addiction is no longer an issue. Verbalizations about any addiction within the manifest content of a therapeutic transference always refer to the *emotional* resistance to a continued involvement with the therapist.

Ironically, it sometimes seems as though these clients do better, and continue longer, when the therapeutic listener is not unconsciously viewed so much as so great a "good breast." A more ambivalently perceived therapeutic listener, or perhaps a lesser viewed "good breast," seems to lead for this type of client to a longer and a more beneficial therapeutic relationship than one in which the listener is viewed so totally as an immense "good breast." But it is the *immensity* of the unmet oral needs of the client that will tend to *make* the listener a proportionately immense envisioned "good breast," as well as informality on the part of the listener. It is often hard for a therapist to maintain a necessary formal position with a client that so actively "feeds" initially in the therapeutic relationship, and to curb his tendency to emotionally "move in" when perhaps it *is* so gratifying for *him* to have a client "feed" so readily. But he will shortly learn from the client's sudden termination that too much of the "good breast" can provoke an equally immense resistance to an further involvement.

A client will sometimes discontinue therapy after metaphorically presenting the problem of medication, as so often is the case with those with an alcoholic problem, to the therapist as: "I can't see substituting one addiction for another." Reality-wise, they are referring to the continued use of the tranquilizer, or to the client-therapist relationship, but latently they are referring to the fear of being "addicted" to the "good breast" of the therapeutic transference. "I know what my problem is . . . have to give up _____" (and one can fill in the blank with anything that is symbolic of pleasure, or oral need gratification.) I have to lick this thing *alone,*" is always an ominous statement that can be heard in regard to a resistance that will terminate the therapeutic transference. They fear addiction, and make an issue of "crutches" as being "bad." They fail to see the philosophy being presented here that the *more* crutches a person has in life, the better he is able to stand. With a great many crutches shoring up an individual, an individual is secure. One's security is derived from this shoring.

These individuals will often admit they *do* lack an emotionally gratifying relationship with their God. To feel that the therapist is a "crutch" one can better do without is to symbolically imply, in part, that God too, is but a crutch, and that one should seek Him only in times of need. (It is a natural "solution" to the shortcomings of being human that the powerful oral need gratifying aspects of part object relationships eventually do become concretized in religion.) They admit that their faith gives little security, that they don't and can't trust Him, and that they don't have the feeling He is always with them. In fact, one guilt-laden individual felt God had it in for him! With their independent facade, they have an artificial "need to stand alone." In spite of their past experiences, they don't seem to be able to understand that no man can ever stand alone for long. When they have fallen in the past, they blame their having leaned on others as the *cause,* rather than their not having leaned *enough.* They see only that the answer to the future is for them *not* to lean at all. With this, they hope *not* to repeat what they have gone through so many times before. Like the person that turns to God only in times of crises, this person too will only stay with professional help long enough to get "over" the emotional crisis, and then discontinue. He lacks the strength that the person has who *continues* with relationships that are orally gratifying. (And it was the former's guilt that made him feel it was *"leaning,"* rather than a *mutual* dependency.) To gratify their oral dependency needs is to them a *weakness* to be avoided, and that to stand alone is erroneously felt to be a "show of strength," when it is exactly the opposite . . . a show of emotional *weakness.* And yet they have reality to support their convictions — prized stories of people they believe have "stood alone" in the face of deprivation. The therapeutic listener could only give those illogical "reasons" that are part object and timelessness oriented — and simply "don't make sense" either to clients, or to their relatives — for continuing the therapeutic involvement. The client who has been entangled in past emotional conflicts has reality on his side, when he says: "If I can *keep* people at a distance, I'll do all right," but the emotional unreality of orality will make this a most difficult task. When a teenaged client remarks: "I'm not ready to go steady," she implies this need for distance from the "good breast" of the therapist that another client may put as: "I get uneasy if I'm around other than a stranger . . . maybe because I know that familiarity breeds contempt."

Where some clients seem to discontinue when they perceive *too much* of the "good breast," others seem to discontinue when they don't *continue* to view *enough* of the "good breast." These individuals seem characterized by past interpersonal relationships in which they are *intensely* involved with someone, but only for a short period of time, before discontinuing the relationship completely.

219

Just prior to this complete discontinuation, they become involved in still another intense relationship, where again an *immense* "good breast" is viewed. The intensity of their unmet oral dependency needs gives them the tendency to initially perceived such an *immense* "good breast." The oral need, like the unconscious guilt, can effect or distort perceptions of objects in the interpersonal relationship sphere. The intense need of the individual creates the perception of the immense "good breast," and their unconscious guilt, when projected, will later tend to counter this perception. They seem to view the object as an irresistable "love," that, at first, seems to them to be so immeasurably beautiful and perfect. Their daily life becomes altered while their emotionality centers around the object which often has the same intensity of concentrated unmet oral needs. It is this intensity of oral need which makes the object appear so attractive. The superceding intense, and often passionate "love" that they always are looking for begins to fade because of the accompanying guilt and anger that invariably is brought into the realationship, along with the unmet oral needs. Their intense relationships, which initially seem to be likened to a "honeymoon" (whether they are homosexually or heterosexually oriented) are always doomed to failure by the projection of guilt. Guilt in individuals who can show their "love" so easily is likewise so easily projected, so that the object that was previously viewed as an immense "good breast" is viewed as a much lesser one. They disengage from this relationship when they don't perceive, as before, the same degree of "need" in the other . . . a perception that is distorted by their own projected guilt. However in projecting their guilt, and ventilating their anger so readily, they do become comfortable enough to become closely involved with another object relationship, again viewing this relationship as an immense "good breast." Personality core guilt never has a chance to be reduced, but any added unconscious guilt is easily projected to the previous object they were involved with, and with anger ventilation, decreased.

If these persons become referred for therapy, they present themselves tearfully verbalizing: "I guess I've always hoped for *too much*. I should realize by this time my dreams can *never* come true. (More crying.) All I've ever wanted in life is just to find someone that will love and cherish *me* as much as *I* would love and cherish them." One can hear the evidence of what their guilt has done in shrinking their perceptions of the immense "good breast" by additionally adding: "Every person I ever find to love so *deeply*, ends up letting me down (and their guilt will make them invariably perceive this let-down when it is projected to the object). Why can't I find someone that will love me, not because they *have* to love me, or because they *should* love me, but because they sincerely *want* to love me?" But this perception can never be sustained because of the quickness to project an immensity of guilt upon the object from which they are attempting to draw an immensity of oral dependency need gratification!

220

Clients who quickly perceive the therapist as an immense "good breast" will very shortly discontinue when they project their guilt to him. With this projected guilt, they don't perceive the same degree of intensity of unmet oral need in the therapist that they saw at first, and perceive it, instead, in still another intense emotional relationship outside of therapy. This repeats again the same cycle in their object relationships that has been operative since earliest childhood. The same repetitive behavior seen in their past object relationships is unavoidably reenacted with their therapist. Even though their emotional feelings are usually conveyed in metaphor and analogy to the therapist, they end up asking (latently implying the therapist): "Why is it I always end up getting involved with the *wrong* person?" The "sugar teat" that they are continually searching for always seems to go sour from their own projected guilt. After leaving one object relationship, and intellectualizing that they will *"Never* get so involved again," it is only a short period of time when they inadvertently discover another "sugar teat." This new object, to them, is the essence of perfection, and totally unlike, they feel, to any past object relationship. But it is because their projected guilt to those *previous* objects makes them appear so unlike this *present* one. And the cycle begins to repeat itself. It becomes a functioning pattern of emotional behavior that adequately handles their recurring problem of added unconscious guilt, but their personality core guilt remains the same. It is as though the perception of such an immense "sugar teat" in the earliest stages of the therapeutic relationship always seems to doom that relationship to an early demise. Transference language that conveys a perception of an *immense* "sugar teat" in the therapeutic listener, is an ominous sign, heralding an early termination.

The therapeutic listener should not find himself in a dilemma trying to tell a client that they shouldn't be so emotionally involved with *one* object. Even though, in reality, this *is* true, one would be, first of all, implying a rejection of the client within the transference relationship, and would secondly be ignoring the pressure of the emotional problem from the client's intensity of unmet oral needs. One can't simply tell this type of client to go out and make a lot of friends, to join many different groups and to get emotionally involved with a lot of different people in order to *diffuse* their oral dependency gratification, and to provide a diffuse array of part objects for their anger ventilation. The client must *emotionally* reach this point *first* with one object, before they then are able to do this. Again, the popularity of the religiously or psychologically oriented "self-help" books that erroneously imply that it can be done intellectually, or logically, is derived from that manifestation of the oral problem — the need to be "independent," and to "do it one's self." But it must be emotionally done with at least one other object, and under an appropriate reality-oriented manifest content for that person. If this type of client is referred for therapeutic listening, the frequency of the sessions should be more prolonged, even though the client, when viewing the immense "sugar teat," seems more than willing to come much more frequently. The therapeutic relationship for this type of client can be sustained longer with the therapist, himself, "stretching out" the time between appointments. In other words, where the client may emotionally appear to be *wanting* to be seen regularly more often, the therapist "stretches out" the time between sessions to a less frequent, but still regularly occurring appointment time. Whatever the manifest content being utilized, it can be maintained such that one can reduce, in time, the personality core guilt at this slower pace. But the therapist will always be competing with the extra-therapy "good breasts" the client will be perceiving. If the therapeutic listener can provide some oral dependency gratification, and if he can continue to keep the client emotionally involved on a regular basis, he will also provide an opportunity for metaphorical anger ventilation necessary to reduce the core guilt. The difficulty that sometimes arises for the therapist is in setting too distant a time between sessions, so that the client finds, in his object relationship, not just a "good breast," but a "sugar teat" that then may preclude further involvement with the therapist. This is a risk the therapist takes. He does have a *better* chance to retain the client in an on-going therapeutic relationship if he *isn't* viewed as such an immense "good breast," and can possibly retain him, even if he is temporarily involved with a "sugar teat" type of object relationship outside of therapy.

Resistance that arises from perceptions of the "bad breast" has already been illustrated in the previous chapter on "The Expression Of Anger In Transference Language." If these perceptions are not *immense,* the therapeutic relationship can continue. (Remember that it takes some perception of the "bad breast" to make the relationship *therapeutic.)* However, some clients will perceive an immense "bad breast" in the therapist. They project too quickly, and too immensely, their guilt to the therapist, so that the therapeutic relationship is terminated. The therapist becomes a dumping ground for their recently added unconscious guilt, and no source of oral support at all. At times, this anger is expressed directly in their last session over something they consciously perceive the therapist did, or didn't do, that the client felt he should have done, or shouldn't have done. Rather than continue to ventilate their anger toward him, in much lesser amounts, either directly or indirectly, utilizing metaphorical language, they unload it *all at once* and *discontinue.* This anger that is unloaded so abruptly is the repressed anger behind the more recently *added* unconscious guilt. Its ventilation then allows the person to function comfortably, and often function exceptionally well, utilizing their high level of personality core guilt as an *asset.* But, in a matter of time, this asset will gradually become a *liability* when it allows *added* unconscious guilt to form. The individual then must find another object to dump this guilt upon.

Clients will not only discontinue with an immense expression of anger, but will sometimes discontinue *rather* than express anger either directly or indirectly to the therapist, when they have reached a point of unconsciously viewing the "bad breast." When their unconscious perceptions tend to make the therapist an immense "bad breast," the therapeutic transference is terminated. When they consciously recognize the therapist as "bad," they ventilate their anger within other object relationships, utilizing a manifest content oriented about their abandoned "no good" therapist. These object relationships are also transference relationships, so that their anger is latently being expressed to the person who listens to them. Their verbalized experience with the therapist is simply manifest content, but it was the therapist who assisted them into a position to be *able* to express anger.

As illustrations of this resistance arising from an apparent reluctance, or even fear of anger expression to the therapist, the following excerpts are given. "I'm worried because I can see a little of Tom (her first husband whom she divorced) in Bill (her present husband), and I don't like my seeing this. I can see it more and more, where I couldn't before. I think I need to get away from Bill." (She didn't, but she *did* quit her therapist.) That there is no reason, the client feels, to be angry with the therapeutic listener, is metaphorically shown in the following excerpt: "That Joanie (she, herself) was beginning to act terrible! She was acting like Jesus Christ, Himself, couldn't please her. I didn't like that one single bit and told her that I wouldn't stand for it. I told her to go upstairs and sit in her room, and not see anyone for a while. I think that's what she needs more than anything else." (And she too discontinued, but then reinvolved herself a few weeks later.)

The people who discontinue from a fear of anger expression still have a high enough unconscious level of unprojected guilt, such that they seem to feel: "I shouldn't see the faults in others, when I feel so fault-ridden myself." This is metaphorically shown by one client as: "Well, some people (an aspect of herself) blame my uncle (therapist) for the accident. They say it was *his* fault that my father died, for not having the boat in a safer condition. They would like to sue him, and drag it all out in the open. But I try to stay out of it. What's past is past, and I don't like to hold any animosity toward anyone!" These people don't want to express any anger. They often fear, realistically, that to express anger seriously weakens the ego controls against the hidden rage within. As one client put it: "I'm afraid if I lost my temper, they'd lock me up," implying perhaps the derivation of the word "mad" to mean "insane" or "crazy." They dislike the expression of *any* anger, not only in others, but even the thoughts of it within themselves, and unconsciously fear that a continuation of the dependency relationship with the therapist will lead to some expression of anger. So they discontinue.

It is interesting to note that these individuals that fear any anger expression often live in family situations involving people that do not tolerate the expression of anger as a means of hiding their own. These clients will often make remarks in therapy metaphorically referring to their relationship with the therapist as: "My husband (i.e. the therapist) is against anyone getting angry. He believes it's immature, and he won't tolerate it."

Another client metaphorically conveys her perception of the therapist's intolerance to anger expression as: "I've been hateful lately, and my husband can't take much more of it. I've been yelling and screaming like a banshee for no reason whatsoever. I know it's due to my uterus and all the trouble I go through with that (this represents a manifestation of less guilt, as before she felt she was "crazy" when she was first referred, but now she blames her uncomfortableness not quite to someone else, but to her uterus). It makes me such a hateful thing, and a holy terror to be around. It's not fair to put my husband through all this. He wants me to have a hysterectomy. Doctor Green told me that I ought to have one, but I've always been too afraid before (now with *less* guilt, she is *less* afraid). I don't see why I should go through all this swelling, cramping and irritability when I could be free of it. It would make it so much easier on my husband too, if I got rid of it. I can't go around feeling I could knock everybody down I run into. I think I should see Dr. Green." And she did see Dr. Green, and did have a hysterectomy. And she never returned to the therapist.

Very often a therapeutic relationship is resisted with skipped sessions, and frequently terminated, *as an expression of anger* toward the therapist. Many times the anger isn't directly expressed, but it can be determined that there was anger involved from the transference language given, and by reconstructing events prior to discontinuing. For instance, one client came a half hour late for her half hour appointment. Because the therapist wouldn't see her during someone else's scheduled time, she angrily discontinued, remarking to the nurse: "Well, if I'm not *that* important to him, let's forget it all!" This client had been brought to the point, by transference involvement, of being orally supported enough to be *able* to express anger. But rather than continue the relationship, it is discontinued. The *act of discontinuing* the relationship is an expression of anger that the client couldn't do and still continue the relationship. Similar to the client that seems especially close to the therapist, knowing it is their last session (perhaps because they are moving to a different area), this client expresses anger that they couldn't do otherwise, knowing that they're not coming back. This may be helpful in lowering the added unconscious guilt, but does nothing toward lowering the personality core guilt.

Many times the resistance toward a continuation of a transference relationship is *projected* as being derived from someone else in their manifest content, and latently *implied* that it is derived from the therapist, as: "My husband doesn't want me to bowl on the team," or a little more directly, "My sister says that I ought to quit this psychotherapy as it couldn't possibly help me." What they refer to in their manifest content may very well be true in reality, since it represents a *conscious* perception. However, because they bring it up spontaneously within the client-therapist relationship, it represents an aspect of an *unconscious* perception of the therapeutic transference relationship. *They* themselves, *in part*, don't want to continue.

Resistance to therapeutic involvement, sometimes, is *totally* from a relative, and will effectively terminate a relationship that would have been very easily handled had not this resistance been introjected. This is especially shown in dealing with young children or teenagers who may show very little, or no resistance to the therapeutic transference, but their mothers or fathers, because of *their* oral problems, provide the resistance. Take for instance, the mother of the teenager that angrily tells the social worker that her daughter only goes with "trash!" One can be sure that it'll only be a few sessions later that this guilt-projecting mother will be threatened by her daughter's lessened dependency on her, and her lessened "need" to accept the mother's projected guilt and anger. At this point she will also feel the therapist is "trash" and will actively undermine the daughter's relationship with him. One mother that was so worried about her daughter's delinquent behavior, fearing (unconsciously wishing) her daughter "might have her throat cut by that type she goes with" or that she'll be involved in a car accident, "and get herself killed," remarked: "She's been such a *disappointment* to me (implying she wasn't as "perfect" as her guilt demanded that her daughter be to cover the self-felt imperfection in herself). She's made me a nervous wreck." This is the mother that will often say "She's always wanted *more* attention than I could give," as though blaming the child for an "abnormal" need, but inadvertently indicating that she, herself, doesn't have the capacity to give the daughter what she really needs . . . a consistent meeting of her oral needs. When she calls to cancel her daughter's appointments, she'll add: "She's got to learn that she can't have someone to go running to cry to, or to hold her hand all her life — *I* never did!" This guilt-projecting parent *needs* to retain the daughter as a target for her projected guilt and "needs" the daughter for her own dependency. She realistically fears that with therapeutic support the daughter would be less guilt-laden, and as such, less willing to accept her mother's projected guilt. What the mother really wanted in taking her daughter to a psychiatrist was only *confirmation* that her daughter was what her projected guilt made her appear to be. Resistance in the daughter's therapeutic transference is first from the parents, even before it has a chance, later, to come from the teenaged client herself. If the child were smaller, the resistance would be totally from the parents.

When the client has resisted involvement by not coming to a session, they will sometimes metaphorically present this as though blaming the *therapist* for "going away" when it was the *client* that didn't keep the appointment. Reality-wise, the client "goes away," but she unconsciously perceives it as the *therapist* going away. "My husband (therapist) had to go away last week, so I didn't get to see much of him. I thought when he left 'good riddance,' but then I got to missing him. It was good to see him (smiles warmly at therapist) when he finally returned home. Now I'm afraid he won't be going away again." Similar to this is the client that says: "The marriage is breaking up (he's breaking it up with his guilt, but blames his wife (therapist) for not showing him that she loves him) so there's no reason for me to come anymore."

When a client has begun a transference relationship with a manifest content that is oreinted toward symptoms or somatic complaints, his resistance toward a continuation may show itself as an "escape into health." These clients present a logical case that they can see no reason for continuing the involvement when they feel "fine." Even though the person is asymptomatic, there can still be evident a high level of unconscious guilt. They can be feeling "perfectly fine," but the potential for emotional difficulties comes from their unconscious *core* guilt that makes them want to seek an emotional distance from an oral need gratifying object. "Everything is fine — I'm feeling wonderful. (Long pause.) I was thinking about asking whether these sessions could be made every other week (if they are on a weekly basis)." This individual has less core guilt than the one that discontinues completely, remarking: "If I get sick again, I'll give you a call." They leave, implying that they have been "sick," meaning that there's been something "wrong" with them, instead of staying long enough to feel that their uncomfortableness is due to others. When they leave, they also do so with the implication of: "I hope I never have to see *you* again!" The need to hopefully say "goodbye forever" reflects the level of unconscious *core* guilt that can make a continuation of oral dependency from the therapist most difficult. And when they do leave, the emotionally uncomfortable unconscious *added* guilt has been removed, leaving personality core guilt, which without the added guilt, can be a distinct asset, in some reality situations. These clients, at this point, can well substantiate that they *are* doing very well, and can see absolutely no *logical* reason for continuing.

Simply discontinuing, or "stretching out" the sessions, is not the simple answer for some clients with a high level of core guilt. There must be a continual *denial* of any uncomfortableness produced by additional guilt. This is illustrated in the following excerpt where a woman that had previously come somatizing to the therapist did well when seen on a regular basis, but then "stretched out" her appointments by cancelling to a once a month basis. She presented at her first monthly session with some reluctance, remarking that things were continuing to go well, but "Mrs. Smith (she herself) kind of upset me a little this past month. She comes over and tries to talk to me about all her complaints. I don't want to hear it. I told her I just didn't have time for her." What she doesn't have time for is an unconscious aspect of herself that represents the denied emotional uncomfortableness in regard to the unmet oral dependency needs, while she outwardly presents as: "Continuing to feel just fine." This is very similar to the client who complains at her monthly session: "I don't like anyone getting into the attic as I've got everything put away and neatly boxed up. Nothing gets me more upset than to have either *John* (therapist), or *the kids* (her needs), trying to rummage through those boxes."

Sometimes there isn't a complete "escape into health," but a rationalization that though they are feeling somewhat uncomfortable, it is *less* so than before, it is *impossible* to "cure," and it's *"something* I'm going to have to live with." This is an indication that they are discontinuing the relationship, implying that the therapist is no help (a subtle expression of their anger), that they are wasting their time, effort and money, and that it (implying guilt-blocked oral needs) is an inseperable part of their life they might as well accept.

Similar to the "escape into health" is the client that first comes for a marriage problem. They discontinue as soon as the marriage is on an even keel, even though they seem to have a conscious awareness that the marriage has always been characterized by emotional turmoil, and that this is the first time that the marriage is going smoothly. They still discontinue the relationship as a manifestation of their emotional resistance with the therapist as though they are leaving because they have a "happy marriage." This is the "escape into a happy marriage" and is representative of the resistance rationalized as "I don't *need* to come, so I *won't.*"

Unlike the client who "escapes into health" is the much more difficultly handled and guilt-laden client that seems always to function with a large personality core guilt. With an immense build up of added guilt, this client seems to seek psychiatric hospitalization and even shock treamtment. What they present is, literally, an "escape into *mental illness.*" They frequently fall into the hands of the psychiatrists that help *make* the illusion of "mental illness." These clients have such guilt-laden oral dependency needs that an involvement in an oral need gratifying relationship seems to *worsen* their emotional state. They come feeling they *are* "sick," and their relatives *also* feel they are "sick" too. Both the clients and their relatives demand a *medical* treatment to "make him right." They least of all desire, and would least of all respond to, *talking* about their problems. They feel the basis of the emotional uncomfortableness lies in some deranged microphysiology, neuroanatomy, or some hither-to undiscovered neurological abnormality that is making them depressed. They defensively and steadfastly emphasize they have "no reason in the world" to be depressed. The emotionally significant objects with whom they live are described as "so good to me" when it is their own guilt that makes the relatives seem "so good." They frequently emphasize "He'd do *anything* in the world if I just *asked"* — but their core guilt makes them individuals that would be least likely to ask anything of anyone. Their spouses don't expect to be "asked" and do expect "independency" of them. To others, the relatives may appear as dominating, guilt-projecting people who would not tolerate, just as the client himself doesn't, that there might be even a question of a problem in their interpersonal relationships. They have an obvious "need to get away from it all" that may show itself as suicidal ruminations. Their guilt prevents them from taking a vacation to accomplish this "getting away," as a less guilty person would, or to visit relatives living in another area. The hospital conveniently provides the opportunity that so many others utilize under a guise of any illness, to get "treatment" for their "mental illness," their "nervous breakdown," or their "depressions." If they aren't initially tranquilized to the point of being sedated, they may find themselves having "shock treatment." Shock treatment causes them to have an acute brain syndrome to a point where they can then accept oral dependency gratification, which they couldn't do before, with lessened volition on their part. These are clients who show the most resistance to any emotionally-close oral need gratifying relationship with a therapeutic listener. After their shock treatment and psychiatric hospitalization, they frequently resume the emotional distance that provides them with a minimum of oral need gratification, and little, if any, effective anger expression to reduce their core personality guilt. So they begin accruing the added guilt all over, and the psychiatrists that provided this "treatment" iatrogenically produce the "mental illness" that the client wanted confirmed.

An "iatrogenic" termination that arises from the client's resistance is one in which the client doesn't pay for his therapeutic listening session. For instance, a client with a marriage problem and a husband that's left her begins therapy depressed, but who responds very quickly to the therapeutic transference. After removing her added unconscious guilt within a few weeks of twice a week sessions, she shows a desire to continue her warm friendly relationship with the therapist while ventilating her anger, verbalizing in the manifest content about her husband, but latently about a perceived aspect of the therapist. Therapy appears to be going very well, but the *therapist* terminates therapy after the client doesn't pay for her sessions while remarking: "Send the bill to my damn husband . . . that should fix him!" This is a means of expressing anger to a *therapist* in private practice that is least likely to be acceptable for any length of time as well as a good logical "test," to see how much the therapist cares, *in reality,* for her. Another client, who previously felt self-debasing and undeserving of anything pleasurable, was latently encouraged by the therapist to express anger and accept oral gratification. She reached a point just before the therapist terminated her of taking the money her husband gave her for the therapist's fee and spending it on herself before coming to the session, remarking: "I don't care *what* my husband thinks — that's *his* problem, not mine!"

Resistance to the therapeutic process always presents illuminating transference language interaction. One client that didn't come for his appointment, after previously showing metaphorical evidence of resistance in the preceeding session, remarked on entering: "I didn't come last time because I had a bad case of the flu. (A bad case of resistance!) (Therapist: I hope you're over it now.) Yes (smiling sheepishly). I think I'm over it." Another client, who "stretched out" her appointments to an every other week basis, and who always presented her own unconscious resistance as coming from her *husband,* was not seen for a month when the therapist was on vacation. Upon his return, she remarked at the

228

beginning of the session: "My insurance (her oral need) will now allow me to come every week, so I was wondering if maybe we could try it weekly. (Therapist: You know how Frank is. He'll hit the ceiling if he found out you were coming once a week. You'll be lucky if Frank lets you keep on coming every other week!) You're right! Knowing how Frank is, I shouldn't have even asked. Let's stick to every other week!"

Interesting dynamics in regard to the underlying unconscious guilt also become quite evident when a client resists. One woman, whose often chaotic home-life presented very variable levels of oral gratification, was involved on a once a week basis for therapeutic listening. When her guilt *increased* from circumstances within the family situation, she would show considerably *more* resistance to coming regularly, and would be more symbolically "closed mouthed" and more self-debasing. At these levels of increased guilt, it would be most difficult for her to accept a weekly appointment, and she would stretch out her appointments to every other week. When she showed evidence of lessened unconscious guilt, she would readily accept appointments on a weekly basis. Thus the *better* she felt, the *more frequently* she came.

Resistance remains the main problem in any therapeutic listening. A process that seems so simple and so easily executed is made most complex and most difficult by this resistance. After all, as one client put it, "no one likes anyone messing around with their guilt."

1. Kinzel, A. F.: "Body-buffer Zone in Violent Prisoners," presented at Amer. Psychiat. Assoc. Annual Meeting May 8, 1969.

CHAPTER 11

THE ORALITY IN SEXUALITY

Perhaps no subject has been of greater human interest as a manifest content subject than that of sexuality. However, it is important for the therapeutic listener to recognize that sexually oriented verbalization is *only* manifest content and that underneath lies the same orality that can be found within any other manifest content. But because there are social taboos in regard to sex, and because sexuality is so much of a reality concern in anyone's personal and intimate life, this particular manifest content deserves special consideration. It is a subject that is frequently suppressed, or purposefully avoided as a topic of conversation. At other times, it is often made light of, ridiculed or joked about. Yet it is an area of behavior where one's emotionality is usually most intense. One's own sex life is a subject that is often consciously guarded, secretively hid, and sometimes denied, because it *is* so emotionally laden. Since reality puts a premium on the intellectual, and views the emotional as a detriment, the conscious seems wary of this emotionally laden subject. But more than being a major part of one's *reality*, sexuality often concretizes the nebulous part object oriented orality, which is the basis of human emotions, into an understandable whole object oriented concern.

When an individual is emotionally uncomfortable, he may naturally attribute his uncomfortableness as arising from the *sexual* area of his reality. His emotionality, on a whole object basis, is probably most intense in this area because of transference factors that have made his sexual object so emotionally *significant*. He may tend at first to hide or to deny this area as the *conscious* cause for his resentments, his self-felt rejections, his inadequacies or his guilt. But he will usually admit to his therapeutic listener, in time, that his sex life has not measured up to his expectations, as either his fault, his partner's, or a combination of both. The sexual sphere of his interpersonal relationships is consciously taken as the very basis of his emotional uncomfortableness. When he finally *does* talk of sexual matters, he conveys the feeling that he's now talking about a rock-bottom subject as far as his emotional life is concerned.

One client, who for several sessions had been talking of her problems teaching school, became more reticent during one session, and finally remarked: "you've probably noted that I haven't been entirely honest with you about my problems. I've been *hiding* my real problem all along. I just wasn't able to talk about it when

I first came to see you. I know I've *got* to tell you, if you're going to help me. It's about my sex life..."

One can go no deeper *in reality* than the whole object analogy one unconsciously presents for their underlying orality. If one were to go any deeper, they would leave the reality of whole object perceptions, and would enter the realm of an unreality, of illogic, of part objects, of primary process cognition and of disregarded time. Sex is a whole object subject; it involves a biological need and the realistic problems in gratifying that need. What one verbalizes in his manifest content as a frustrating problem may be true in regard to reality, but what he simultaneously implies on a deeper oral level between himself and his listener is also true. Manifest contents *should* make sense on the reality level. Manifest contents *do* make sense when a person, for instance, explains his unhappiness as due to being frustrated in his sexual needs. His sexual problems concretize, in reality, whatever else his emotional problems might be. When one talks of sexual need, one is talking about a biological, reality-oriented need that his listener can readily comprehend. To talk of the oral need is to talk of an emotional need that is derived from a part object unreality. It is too unreal and too nebulous to logically understand. The sexual need, on the other hand, is very real, and implications in regard to this need are very understandable. Even though it is the problems that lie deep to the conscious that have caused the sexual difficulties, the individual can't *logically* talk about them.

Since one's sexually oriented interpersonal relationships are so much of a reality concern, an individual's oral problems will often more clearly show themselves in this particular sphere. The guilt-derived feeling, for instance, of inferiority, may be concretized in a sexually-oriented conscious thought. A woman who feels inadequate, or unacceptable to her mate, may unconsciously focus her feelings of inferiority as due to a sexual characteristic, such as the size or shape of her breasts. A male may concretize his feelings of inferiority, inadequacy, or unacceptableness, in the size or shape of his penis. These feelings of sexual inadequacy are the reflections of an unconscious inadequacy that arise from the part object derived unconscious guilt. Through an unconscious function of the ego, the feeling of inadequacy becomes *concretized* in a reality-oriented presentation that the person, himself, intellectually understands as the very etiology of the feeling. He may then present this to others as part of an appropriate manifest content, as a statement of his emotional uncomfortableness and a plea for help in resolving it.

Sexual relationships, on their most basic reality level, are simple biologic acts that are shared in common with the acts of the other mammals. This biologic act, and the physiology associated with it, is no more complicated on a physical level than the physiology of, say, the digestive system. The reproductive system is no more *biologically* important than any other system. Man, as an animal, has a biologic characteristic of reproducing his kind as do all species of living things.

231

However, there *is* more to the sexual act in the human than a simple biologic reproducing of the species. What is *added* to this natural biologic function in man involves the emotionality that the underlying *orality* gives to sexuality. The emotional aspects of this orality become an inseperable part of this biologic act in humans.

It is the same oral need — the need to feel that one is unique, or *special* above anyone else to at least someone else that often becomes the major part of an ongoing sexual relationship. In most cases, what makes a sexual relationship so *gratifying* involves *less* of the biologic factors of that relationship than the oral aspects. And, what makes a sexual relationship so *frustrating* involves again less of the biologic factors than the oral aspects. In an on-going sexual relationship, it is these *oral* aspects that are of primal importance. All that is above and beyond the simple animalistic sexual act involves that same orality that has been shown as the major *unconscious* concern of all humans in the motivation for any behavior. The primary intense pleasure of the infant at the "good breast" becomes concretized in the intense pleasure of the sexual act. The desire for this pleasure reflects the original desire, and the *need*, for the "good breast." An An aversion of sexual pleasure reflects the oral anhedonia, or that oral fear of pleasure that comes about with guilt, when one has been exposed too much to the "bad breast." The illogical "my oral needs destroy" can be made understandably logical in reality when applied to the cautions, warnings, and taboos of uncontrolled sexual gratification. It is still this orality, and not the biologic sexuality, that one deals with in regard to the conflicts of sexuality on a reality basis. But this orality must remain in the latent content of communication and in unconscious thought.

There is no necessity that the oral needs be met in a sexualized interpersonal relationship. For many people they aren't. But when the oral needs *are* so sexualized, they do imbue sexuality with an exaggerated importance just as is done in anything to which a concentration of oral need gratification is closely associated. The problems of orality, for instance, are frequently reflected in many people, not to the reproductive system, or to sexual concerns, but to the digestive system, creating problems in eating. The oral problem may then show itself symbolized in gastric distress and bowel difficulties, as well as the pre-occupations with diets, dietary taboos, special foods and food fads.

It *is* possible to have one's concentrated oral needs met, not in the sexual sphere, but within a business, a profession, an organization or a group. The transference phenomenon may show itself more prominent in a group of these interpersonal relationships, than in one's sexually associated relationships. The object in reality of one's intense desire doesn't need to be a sexual object. For instance, the majority of religions, where emotionality is often most intense, have an object that is not sexually desired, but *orally* desired. People can go through life, if not denying, certainly minimizing sexuality. Many people do go through life denying themselves all types of pleasure, and they may specifically deny themselves sexual pleasure. But a denial of any type of pleasure *isn't* the displaced denial of *sexual* pleasure, as the analysts would propose. It is instead, a manifestation of the denied *oral* pleasure.

Many people mistakenly interpret the oral need for closeness when perceived in another individual as *sexual* seductiveness. The individual, himself, may also erroneously conclude that it is a sexual end-point that he is desiring in his expressed seductiveness. Sexually suggestive expressions of warm and loving feelings that are oral on their basic level, may be a way of relating to others for some individuals. This is particularly shown in those that are promiscuous.

The need for emotional closeness is *not* of a sexual origin, but has as its basis the oral need. Note that the oral need for emotional closeness can be turned into a fear by oral guilt. This fear of emotional closeness may reach a panic level when it activates the fear of the hidden immensity of self-felt destructive oral needs, when it threatens the ego defenses that withhold the immensity of repressed anger and violence, and when it uncovers the sense of contamination from the guilt. But to call this panic a "homosexual panic" is grossly misleading!

The basic human need has often been erroneously presented as the sexual need, even in psychiatry. Reich, an early disciple of Freud, propounded that as a reason that human beings became emotionally uncomfortable was because of "sexual starvation." He knew that those that *were* emotionally uncomfortable usually had an "unfulfilling sex life," and falsely concluded that *this* was the fundamental problem. To rectify the inability to achieve an orgasm became the goal of treatment. Freud too had failed to see that it was the unmet *oral need* that was basic in the emotionally uncomfortable, and not the frustrated sexual need, which was only a manifestation of the former. He sexualized the oral need to be important, to be recognized, or to "stand out," concretizing it as the penis. In the male dominated Victorian Age, he theorized a "penis envy" for the same sought-after oral needs of women. This theory of penis envy, interestingly enough, is denounced by Women's Lib today, who apparently take it as a very oral put down.

The fear of castration that Freud presented as a "basic" male fear is, from an *oral* standpoint, the dread of having one's oral dependency "cut off". That, of course, is by no means limited to males. It is the fear of being orally deprived, catastrophically, at a stage in psychological development where dependency needs are concentrated on relatively few objects who are perceived, ambivalently, in granting this dependency gratification. Freud's proposed death wishes are only manifestations of the wish for oral incorporation to destroy the "bad breast." The entire oedipal stage, as described by Freud and others, can be seen as a *whole* object, *sex*-oriented explanation for oral problems seeking a resolution. The ambivalence toward the primary object is eventually resolved not in simply loving one parent and hating the other, as proposed in Freudian theory, but by an increasing sphere of object relationships, in which some part objects are "hated" when guilt is projected to them, and some "loved" when they are particularly perceived as orally gratifying. What Freud did in his oedipal theory was to sexualize the oral need, and to explain, on a whole object basis, what actually occurs on a part object b sis, first within the family, and later in the entire interpersonal relationship sphere.

Analysts have always had difficulty in justifying a castration fear and penis envy in regard to the female in that it relegates the female to an inferior position to the male. For the female to want recognition, to want a position of importance, or to want to "stand out," is hardly to want to possess a penis, as a male, but rather an equality *with* the male. Emotionality is most fundamentally asexual in that emotional feelings, fears and wishes are deeper than anything sexual. If there *is* a sexual aspect, it is *added*, like the icing on a cake, to the basic *oral* emotionality. The explanation of psychodynamics doesn't require sexuality as its focal point. If, for instance, a woman is described as a *castrating* person, it implies an appropriateness only in regard to a male. This woman who apparently projects her guilt to a man, "cutting him down," belittling him, and frustrating him in his oral need gratification, could also do this to another female, if this female had a vulnerable dependency relationship with her. Anyone can be orally depriving to anyone else who is orally dependent on that person. Further, what is perhaps more true is that anyone can be, *in part*, orally depriving while continuing to meet the other's oral dependency needs, *in part*. At this level, sexual terms as "castrating" are most inappropriate.

Undue focus on sexuality is further shown by the analysts who propose that sexual need gratification can be symbolically displaced in an occupational endeavor. They imply, for instance, that the anhedonic "old maid" school teacher gains a symbolic satisfaction of her sexual needs in her teaching. Seeing this as only displaced sexual need gratification prevents the recognition that oral need gratification and oral guilt are primarily involved. Similarly, analysts have implied that the essentials of a "happy marriage" involve "having a good sex life." What is actually entailed in a good marriage is *good orality*, of which the sexual relationship is just one manifestation.

Psychiatry has always listened carefully to a sexualized manifest content or to its innuendos or implied connations. Psychiatry, and particularly psychoanalysis, has often "read into," or heard erroneously "between the lines" messages of a sexual nature. It apparently has always attuned its listening ear to the frequency of sex. To do so, though, represents a type of *selective* listening which places an unwarranted importance to this particular manifest content at the expense of other manifest contents that may imply the same underlying orality as well.

Unfortunately, psychiatry has had great difficulty in recognizing this primal position of orality in the levels of described psychological development. Freud discovered his "phallic" or "oedipal" stage first in a Victorian era of suppressed

234

sexuality. He then progressed later to describe his "anal" stage. But he had very little to say about his oral phase of psychological development. These later stages are not readily understandable except in terms of rescue and survival attempts from the oral need and oral dangers. In stripping off levels of so called "psychopathology," like the skins of an onion, one usually will find the source of any emotional problem lying well within orality, and *not* sexuality. The building of a psychoanalytic understanding of human behavior should most *logically* begin not at the top with the sexual facade — though this may be most readily observable — but with the foundation. It is this that supports all the rest. It is well to remember that the cracks in any facade are usually due to stresses in the foundation. To accept sexuality as basic, as is done in Freudian theory, is to disregard its oral foundation. And any psychoanalytic approach to orality from the reality-oriented sexual level can only distort the emotional importance of this orality, while giving sexuality a focus that can be falsely accepted as the ultimate concern of the unconscious.

Take for instance the psychoanalytic explanation of the Don Juan Syndrome. The "Don Juan" is a male that shows a compulsion for sexual conquests, and is characteristically involved in one sexual affair after the other. The analysts theorize that his problem is that he is a *latent homosexual* and that he defensively proves he isn't by his heterosexual over activity. Contrastingly, we are presenting this individual as having an *oral* problem with a sexual manifestation. His guilt-derived feelings of inferiority and inadequacy are compensated with sexual gains. It is as though he is saying to himself: "I am not inferior, as my unconscious guilt makes me feel I am, because I can seduce all these women." The basic problem, then, isn't sexual at all, but derives itself, instead, from the unconscious guilt arising from part object oral frustrations with a repression of the resulting anger. It is no more sexual in its *origin* than the person who compensates *his* feelings of inadequacy with educational gains, or someone else who compensates these same basic feelings with one financial fortune after the other. The attempt to prove oneself superior in a particular endeavor, the direction of which is conditioned in one's earlier life, is *not* compensatory for *sexual* inadequacy, but for the feelings of inadequacy derived from unconscious guilt. Analysts err, for instance, in postulating that the individual that buys himself an expensive and showy car is compensating for basic feeling of *sexual* inadequacy, rather than the guilt-derived inadequacy. If this individual admits to sexual inadequacy, or even impotence, then this too is only a *manifestation* of the guilt-derived feeling of inadequacy that can show itself in *any* area of his life's activities.

In each of the "higher" levels of psychological development, as elaborated by Freud, the orality can now be seen as always playing the motivating role in the level's psychodynamics. As a resolution to oral problems, one recognizes that in the Freudian "anal stage," there is a price that one must pay for pleasure. The "reality principle" is learned at the expense of oral gratification, where the issue becomes *not* whether to be orally frustrated or not, but *how much* to be orally frustrated. One learns he has to conform to others and to his society, in order to have his oral needs continually met. It is a necessity of his reality that he learns through orally frustrating experiences certain "do's and don'ts." Not to do so can create even greater orally frustrating experiences. Obligations and responsibilities for continuing to receive oral dependency need gratification, and for avoiding future oral frustration are learned early in what Freud has called "the anal stage." Freud concretized guilt as symbolic of feces. Freud emphasized reality too concretely, as he did with sex, when he theorized the unconscious was concerned with bowel elimination. But what he emphasized was metaphorical and analogous to the orality underneath. One learns to handle their part object derived oral guilt, symbolically keeping it in its place, hiding it, regulating its disposal, assuaging it, projecting it and maintaining a facade of orderliness and cleanliness. Reality demands that the anger and guilt be kept tightly repressed by the psychological sphincters of the ego, and that it not be freely eliminated. The unconscious is concerned with this unconscious guilt and anger, not the reality problem of bowel elimination, though it may provide the metaphors and analogies for the former.

A rather myopic view of unconscious behavior is created by psychoanalysts, who are so sexually oriented that they can only see the oedipal, or the sexual aspects of symbols. They seem too quick to identify these symbols as fundamentally "phallic," rather than the more important part object derived orality beneath. What is so pervasively *oral* in unconscious human behavior is viewed instead as *sexual*, when the oral need is sexualized. Even the liking to have one's arm stroked has been theorized by the sexually-oriented psychoanalysts as being equated with masturbation. To be so sexually focused blinds them to a deeper oral interpretation that may involve an expression of caring, and that may be more appropriately equated instead with the tactile perceptions of oral need gratification of infancy. Support for this can be seen in the show of affection by people toward their mammalian pets where to postulate a masturbation basis in petting them is most ridiculous. Whenever a sexual etiology is presented for either human behavior or symbolism, one loses sight of the primal position of orality.

When the analysts attempt to assign a specific whole object meaning to a symbol, they invariably choose a sexual meaning. For instance, the "flag pole' and the "church steeple," as well as anything that is more long than it is broad, or that is standing upright, has been consistently viewed by the psychoanalysts as rpresenting phallic symbols. More importantly, they represent the "upward" symbols of "special" importance, and of "outstanding" recognition that focus the attention on a complexly abstract condensation of *orality*. The symbols embody *oral* significance, and *not* sexual.

As just another example, the snake, for instance, has long been interpreted in the phobias and dreams of people as representing a "phallic" symbol from a classical psychoanalytic standpoint. An interpretation such as this is at the expense of an understanding of the underlying orality that may have, for instance, a representation of the unexpected and feared symbolism of the guilt-derived and death-deserving aspect of orality that may suddenly show itself.

The undue focus on sexuality by psychiatry, and particularly by psychoanalysis, leads to a distortion of the primal position of orality, and a skewing of explained psychodynamics. What happened *sexually* to a child has been given momentous importance by psychoanalysis in the etiology of the emotionally uncomfortable adult. A single experience of a sexual nature is sought out by the analyst, or presented by his client, or perhaps mutually "discovered" by both, as the very *cause* of a later emotional problem. This search for the childhood experience that can "trigger a neurosis," erroneously implies that a single experience *can* be productive of emotional uncomfortableness later in life, rather than the part object accumulations of oral frustrations over a period of time. As another example, incestuous wishes and taboos have been presented in psychoanalysis as a major concern for the unconscious in the origin of guilt. Again, this is but a whole object sexualized explanation of that emotional taboo of oral dependency, the forbidden feeding from the "good breast" that everyone has to a certain degree, depending upon the amount of his personality core guilt.

Childhood experiences of a sexual nature are certainly more *logically* understood as a psychological trauma than anything oral. For instance, the sexual crimes, and particularly sexual assaults on children, are considered the more heinous of crimes, and are often punishable more severely than that of manslaughter. What makes any sexual crime so intolerable is what it symbolizes in regard to the implied orality. It is these same oral factors that have made the punishment for rape, up until recently, equal to the punishment for murder. If people were as much concerned for the "crimes" against childhood oral deprivation as they have been about sexual crimes, perhaps there would be less emotional uncomfortableness — and probably less crime. But like people in general who seek a logical origin, psychiatrists have been unable to get beyond a theory of sexual whole object primacy in postulating the psychodynamics of what makes a person emotionally uncomfortable.

Psychiatry has, for too long, taken as it's *reference point* for basic human feelings an orientation that is sexual. We have terms such as "sexual" versus "non-sexual"; or "pregenital" and "genital" to describe human needs, and "pseudohomosexual," "latent homosexual," "homosexual," and "heterosexual" to describe human relationships. This reality orientation toward sexual gender prevents a recognition of the transferential part object perceived relationships that are as basically *sexless* as the unconscious is. There is no sex in orality unless it is added as a superficiality from reality. The "good breast," like the "bad breast," is sexless. Maleness and femaleness have little bearing on the ability to give or to receive oral gratification. The oral need, unlike the sexual need, has no

237

climax, nor does it wane with age. Only in reality need there be a finality as in the climax, or the biologic end of life. The oral need, on the other hand, is insatiably on-going, and must be continually gratified to a particular degree for a comfortable existence. To the degree the oral needs *are* satisfied determines how comfortable a person is in his emotional life. It certainly isn't the degree a person satisfies his sexual need. But reference points do require something concrete, and anything as nebulous as orality can quickly lose its importance to sexuality from a *reality* standpoint.

The intellectualization of psychodynamics, no matter how scientifically correct, and no matter how applicable to the individual and his emotional problem as he sees it, still remains a part of the *manifest content*. The oral emotional involvement between two or more people with a part object interaction can progress, *regardless* of the orientation of that manifest content. A sexual problem whose roots lie within orality may very well *be* resolved within a sexual orientation. But it may also be resolved within some *other* type of orientation. For instance, take the man who may be experienceing a sexual problem with his wife. He may change his job, or perhaps both he and his wife may join a church. As a direct result, the sexual problem decreases or even disappears. Not only was the sexual problem resolved without being made a focus of concern, but more importantly, the unrecognized oral problem was resolved as well.

It is because sexuality lends itself so well to metaphorical frameworks and analogies that so many people rationalize their emotional difficulties this way. To them, their problem *is* sexual, and they attempt to seek definitive answers to these specific problems. Their verbalizations will focus on logical, realistic and "understandable" questions and dilemmas that they feel their sexual need produces. What a person presents as his problem in reality is always analogous to his oral problem. When, for instance, a person becomes acutely anxious that masturbation might cause him "mental illness," he is utilizing a problem in his reality to present the underlying oral problem. The emotional difficulties are brought about by a decrease in the gratification of his oral needs, an increase in his repressed anger, and the subsequent increase in his guilt. This guilt will make him feel that he is "abnormal" and that anything pleasurable is bad. The masturbation may also reflect a resulting tendency to defensively withdraw from interpersonal involvements, and to seek to meet his own needs. If the masturbation does represent more of this withdrawal, it *can* be indicative of "mental illness", meaning emotional uncomfortableness. This person's anxiety then, may be quite appropriate, and to brush off his anxious concern about masturbation as simply a result of a "silly old wives' tale," or inadequate sexual education, would be most misunderstanding of his emotioanl problem.

The sexual needs are an undeniable part of being human. Yet, they metaphorically represent in any manifest content the oral needs, which are even *more* of an undeniable part of being human. The sexual need is the metaphorical

238

representation of the oral need when used in a manifest content. The oral guilt that is so difficult to explain seems so well conveyed when placed in a metaphorical framework oriented toward sexuality. Because a person is often reluctant to talk about such an intimate and personal part of his life that the guilt of sexuality lends itself so well to expressing that emotional resistance of orality, we saw in Chapter Ten.

When a person is able to talk about *something* which he has kept as a guilt-laden secret to himself, he has reached, through oral dependency gratification and an externalization of his anger, a point of *decreased* unconscious guilt. It is *not*, as some would think, that when one *is* able to talk about some guilt-laden subjects openly with his therapist that the guilt *then* becomes less frightening and incapacitating. To be sexually oriented in studying the unconscious motivations of human communication produces not only this "cart before the horse" type of error, but a "blind spot" to what is psychodynamically occurring in the "here and now" of the *immediate* transference relationship. When a client *can* talk about something very guilt-laden, it is *because* he has simply become *less* guilty! The emotional resolvement necessary to do this in regard to his underlying orality is the reason that he can *now* talk about something which he previously felt too guilty to do. Even though his *conscious* concern and the therapist's may be sexual, it can provide a metaphorical framework that can still be effective in attaining a degree of emotional comfortableness.

The client's unconscious attempt to concretize or conceptualize, realistically, the feeling of his guilt, and to place this in a reality-oriented framework can involve such sexualized metaphors and analogies as masturbation, abortions, premarital and extra-marital affairs, and unwanted pregnancies. Sexual dilemmas are often presented as a result of an attempt to satisfy their guilt-laden oral needs where the implied moral is an: "I shouldn't have tried to gratify my needs." The client may consciously believe her guilt or dilemma to be sexual in origin, and attribute it to a particular incident. This sexualization is convenient in conveying the feelings in an understandable way not only to oneself, but to the listener as well, for it is reality oriented on a secondary process, or logical level for something which is too illogic, and too irrational on the unconscious part object level to be appropriately expressed.

The feelings of inferiority and of inadequacy are erroneously concluded, even by analysts, to be of sexual origin rather than to be *oral* in etiology. *Sexual* inadequacy is only one of the mutiplicity of ways in reality that inadequacy from unconscious oral guilt can be manifested. To explain all these other non-sexual manifestations as displaced sexual inadequacy is just one more example of the psychoanalytic error in explaining psychodynamics with a superficial *sexual* orientation.

For other individuals, oral guilt might be metaphorically expressed in *non-sexual* "embarrassing" metaphors or analogies, as remembered acts of hate, selfishness,

239

self-centeredness, thievery, disrespect, callousness, losses of self-control and self-indulgences, and behavior that they feel have hurt deeply someone they love. Sexual guilt isn't as popular as it used to be. Many in the younger generation seem to show little guilt in their blatant sexual behavior, and show little or no respect for Victorian mores or taboos. However, they still have an unconscious. This unconscious must be concerned then with something *other* than a sexual orientation as previously thought. And if they do feel guilty, they do so with some other reality orientation than sexual. In today's culture, we are witnessing a vast disinhibition of sexual behavior which had been previously suppressed. Nudity in entertainment, the acceptance of pornography in serious literature, and the acceptance of what had previously been termed sexual deviations as the normal sexual behavior is all a part of the "now generation." Sexual satisfaction is being presented as just a simple body appetite that should be sated, without guilt, in much the same way as any other hunger. Such a general acceptance of sexuality has caused the reality manifestations of the oral guilt to shift. Clients who might have previously presented attributing their guilt to a sexual act are more likely to present now feeling guilty that they can't perform sexually as much as they believe they should. Or else, the manifestation of their oral guilt has shifted to a non-sexual presentation. One woman who seemed to have little else to realistically feel guilty about attributed her massive oral guilt to picking her nose — "Nobody knows what a *terrible* habit I have, and I've never told anyone except you."

One can speculate that if it were not for the reality of a metaphorical and concretized presentation of a person's oral guilt there would be some other manifest content metaphor or analogy chosen from reality to act as the "peg" to hang their "hat" of guilt. This perhaps explains why a client will cling tenaciously to what they feel or believe in their conscious is the origin of their guilt. It is simply because the guilt is *there*, and *needs* a rational explaining. Someone else, who doesn't have as much unconscious guilt, has little guilt over exactly the same act. It is quite possible too, for one person with an *equal* amount of unconscious guilt to feel guilty over a specific sexual act, while the second person, with the same history of the act feels no guilt whatsoever in this regard, but feels guilty instead in some other reality-oriented concretization. There is no universally accepted reality-oriented peg upon which to hang the unreality oriented hat of the unconscious guilt. Each person has a hat of guilt, and each human being can usually find, in his own individualistically *conditioned* way, a suitable reality-oriented peg for that hat.

In other words, one feels guilty simply because they have unconscious guilt, and because they haven't projected it, they therefore *must* feel guilty. Whatever reason can be offered for the guilt is a rationalization that is done so within a reality oriented framework. Guilt is ubiquitous in humans, and as such, it can present itself in many varied metaphorical ways. But sometimes a person must go to the very extremes of logic (and beyond, if guilt-laden enough) to find something he can be realistically guilty about on a level equated with how he unconsciously feels. For instance, a Negro boy attributed his guilt to the following: "I haven't told you this before, but I've been so ashamed to bring it up. I know that you'd eventually find it out, as we continue, so I'm going to tell you now. It might seem as though I'm a 'man-about-town,' as I have many girlfriends chasing after me, and I'm a college student and a basketball player. People probably think I'm pretty suave, but I've hidden the fact that I've *never* had sexual relations before! (Appears very embarrassed.) I feel very guilty about this, as I'm 20 years old and will be 21 next month. If anybody knew this, they'd know for sure I was *abnormal*. Most fellows my age have been having sexual relations for at least the past 6 years! I'm afraid that they'd think there was something *wrong* with me — like I was a homosexual or maybe that I'm sexually impotent — because I haven't had sexual relations."

The feeling that sex is "dirty" comes about from the unconscious feeling that oral dependency gratification or pleasure is "dirty." This nebulous oral guilt has been concretized, and given a sexualized orientation. Why sex becomes "dirty" or repulsive for one person, and not so for another who may have the same degree of underlying oral guilt, and who may even revel in sex, must involve the same unconscious processes that compartmentalize one phobia for one individual, and a different phobia for still another individual. Sex becomes "dirty" to an individual in the same way a person may develop a phobia, say to dogs, and who may simply and "logically" attempt to explain his phobia as due to "having been bitten at the age of two by a dog." Complex conditioning processes channel, focus and determine the direction guilt, fear, pleasure or any of the emotions will manifest themselves in certain situations of reality. The past experiences, the unconscious associations and the manifest behavior are often "explained," or accepted by the client as due to specific things, isolated situations and certain episodes of his past reality. He really *has* to turn to reality for his explanations, because the unreality of his unconscious motivations are so part object oriented. It is not possible to present, either to one's self, or to another, the part object oral derivations of his emotional uncomfortableness. It is because the conscious is under the influence of secondary process cognition that such emotional problems *must* be presented in a "logical" and reality oriented way. Explanations will then involve "wholes" and totalities for the nebulous part object experiences, feelings and fears of the primary process oriented unconscious.

Masters and Johnson have taken sexuality out from behind the taboos of society and culture, and have scientifically studied sex as a biologic act. They propose that sexual expression is in the same category as the natural bodily functions of alimentation, respiration, and bowel and bladder activity, and as such, should be treated more openly than it has in the past. To propose this *does* appropriately emphasize sexuality's proper position in *reality*. But in doing so, they erroneously conclude though that sexually oriented uncomfortableness is *basically* due to a *sexual* problem, rather than to the underlying part object derived orality behind any sexual problem.

This erroneous conclusion gives acceptance to surgery, then, to people who have concretized their emotional problems as a "transexual" one. One can fail to see the same orality in these individuals who seek to change their sexual identity, as in other individuals who seek some other magical type of solution. They hope to "change" themselves with a single act of reality from being dissatisfied with themselves — from feeling "different" or from being blocked in the gratification of their emotional needs. Being guilt-laden like any other person with an oral problem, to this degree, they feel they *have* to live a "role," and that they are not able to be "me" — whatever they feel that real "me" is. They, like anyone else with many unmet oral needs, feel they are "missing something." But the transexual feels he *"knows"* what that "missing something" is, where, as we saw before, other people are simply aware that something is missing from their emotional lives, but haven't been able to concretize it as the transexual has. Where suicide is so often the solution for those with guilt-blocked emotional needs, the transexual similarly seeks a "death" of his being, and a "re-birth," in just the same way the depressed and suicidal person often seeks a new life in death, and an escape from the misery his guilt has given him in his present life. Or in the same way a person becomes "changed" through a deeply religious experience.

The oral ambivalence that makes an individual wonder *who* he is, or *how* he should act, or *why* he acts or feels a certain way, seems magically resolved when an individual can put a label on himself. The emotionally uncomfortable person *always* has an identity problem because of his ambivalence. He may feel more comfortable in labelling himself an "alcoholic," a "homosexual," "schizophrenic," or a "transexual." A sexual identity problem is a reflection of this oral ambivalence. The "transexual" blames his guilt blocked oral needs on the "fact" that he is really of the opposite sex. He provides a sexual rationalization of his oral problem, and offers a solution to it. "If I were only of the opposite sex, I would then be happy!" This sexual orientation of an oral problem should be no more important than what any person verbally presents with an immensity of unmet oral needs. It is the same old "I can't get my oral needs met because . . . " where one just fills in a logical reality-oriented reason. Listening to the manifest content of the sexually frustrated person coming for professional help in regard to their emotional problems, one will hear the same orality with the same oral dilemmas, and the same oral guilt. The woman, who complains: "I didn't even know I had a clitoris or could reach an orgasm" implies, and will give evidence in her later verbalizations about her past and present that she didn't really know she could be *orally* satisfied either.

One can't reassure a person, and by this reassurance remove his guilt. The guilt is there because there is repressed anger from unmet oral dependency needs. It may be possible to shift the guilt's "set" or its presentation in reality. In other words, one may change the "peg" of reality guilt for some other realistically appropriate peg to then hang the hat of unconscious guilt. But the unconscious guilt can only be decreased by an *externalization* of the underlying repressed anger. It is erroneous then to believe that one can, through sexual education, per se, remove a feeling of guilt.

How erroneously one can interpret the feelings of guilt by accepting the reality-oriented manifest content as the etiologic cause is well shown in a recent issue of *Medical World News* (March 2, 1972, page 42):

"Leaders in sex education, such as Drs. Lief, Money, and Wardell Pomeroy of the original Kinsey research group, have worked for years to broaden understanding and tolerance of the remarkably wide range of sexual expression and behavior. To the physician, this may involve acquiring increased knowledge in order to allay the painful and mostly needless anxieties of patients about what is 'normal' and 'abnormal'!

Dr. Holmes cites the case history of a 15 year old girl, a 'model child', who was deeply fond of her steady boy friend but refrained from having intercourse. During a petting session, the girl in a totally instinctive act performed fellatio on her friend. Guiltily worried, she first consulted an older girl, who assured her that the act was 'perverted' and that she should see a doctor. Summoning all her courage, the girl went to her lifelong family physician and blurted out the story. The doctor gravely concurred that such behavior was abnormal and that she should see a psychiatrist. The girl instead went home and killed herself.

Another suffering, but luckier, youngster was encountered by Dr. Crist. In the examining room, the teen-age girl wept that she was bad. 'I masturbate,' she said. Dr. Crist was able to reassure her gently that research studies indicate about 90% of boys and 65% of girls masturbate, that it is thus very normal, and that medical experts regard masturbation as a healthy release of tension."

If a person believes he feels guilty because of masturbation, no amount of reassurance can remove the guilt *unless* through the process of reassurance there is opportunity for anger externalization. It is possible that through sexual education the guilt may shift, in the same degree, from a sexual orientation to some other type of orientation. But reassurance, per se, is worthless if it is considered only on its manifest content value. To tell a beautiful girl who has an intensity of unconscious guilt that manifests itself as a distorted sexual self-image, and makes her feel that she is an "ugly old witch," she is *beautiful* will only make her feel "You don't understand my problem." She will continue to feel unattractive to others until her unconscious guilt can be decreased. Reassurance, though, is a part of a manifest content that may convey an opportunity through its latent content to meet the oral needs of the guilt-laden individual, and afford an opportunity to ventilate his repressed anger. In such a case, reassurance can be helpful. but the reason that it *is* so is because any acceptable manifest content can be helpful, if it is *appropriate* to what is being presented as the concretized manifestation of the underlying problem in orality for that individual.

243

As an example where reassurance wasn't helpful, a high school girl presented herself to a psychiatrist admitting: "I associate masturbation with babies." She also related that she was fearful that she was pregnant as a result of a session of "heavy petting" with her boyfriend, who had ejaculated on her underclothes. Rather than to understand the degree of guilt in this girl, and her latent reference to her wish for, and fear of, oral need gratification, the psychiatrist emotionally rejected her. In his "setting her straight," he met *his* needs, not hers (for *he* was the one talking, and she was the one listening). He simply "reassured" her by verbalizing at great length on the physiology and anatomy of the female and male reproductive system, and methods of birth control. He indicated to her how "ridiculous" her fear was in reality.

What the above psychiatrist failed to understand most was the amount of unmet oral needs behind this degree of guilt the girl showed. Unfortunately, he did not feel it was necessary for her to come back. But she did, some two months later, pregnant and more guilty, feeling an "outcast" to her friends and family. In spite of her new-found knowledge of sexual matters, she was in a position she *feared* she would be in (and perhaps unconsciously *wished*) when she first consulted the psychiatrist.

Perhaps there is involved a wish for a "magical solution" for some in believing that a program in sexual education could have prevented her difficulties. Some people can no more "solve" their sexual problems by becoming "educated" in sexual knowledge than one does in "solving" their psychological problems by reading books on psychology. For some, orality is too much a part of sex to be simply solved by sex education. Emotional problems *do* become less severe if there *is* an element of oral need gratification and guilt reduction associated with remedying a lack of "sexual know-how," utilizing this manifest content as a guise for emotional therapeutic action.

The worthlessness of advice or counsel except as an effective manifest content applies as aptly in sexual matters as it does in any other aspect of reality. Good advice and good counsel *should* be logical, factual and reality-oriented. But when a person is emotionally uncomfortable, he is so with *an ambivalence* that is brought about by his unmet oral dependency needs, his guilt and his repressed anger. This ambivalence isn't resolved by intellectualization except when it is a manifest content to a latent emotional resolution. The *more* emotionally uncomfortable a person is, the *less* likely that this individual will accept any "logical, factual and reality-oriented" solution to his uncomfortableness. The reason that this is so is because of the multiplicity of ambivalent feelings associated with what he is perceiving in his reality in relation to his needs, his guilt, and his anger. In order to become more comfortable, he must have *less guilt*, so that he can *perceive* oral gratification. But to reach this point requires anger expression and guilt projection.

244

Take for instance the individual who discovers that his wife is unfaithful. She may be repentant, but he becomes emotionally upset. In his emotionally uncomfortable state, he is orally frustrated, hurt and feels orally deprived. He is angry, resentful and vindictive. He is acutely in need of added oral gratification. He may feel, *in part*,he has been the cause of her unfaithfulness. He may feel, in part, he *hasn't* been. He may feel, in part, that *she* is totally to blame, etc. His problem at this point is emotional, and involves orality. Biologically, she can just as easily meet his sexual needs as before. It becomes most obvious his problem isn't a sexual one at all, though it has a sexual orientation. In such a state, he can neither accept "logical" advice that he should *leave* his wife, nor can he accept "logical" advice to *stay* with her. Whatever reasons that might be rationalized intellectualy either way would be unacceptable on a whole object basis. If he comes to a therapeutic listener, he may initially present as wanting advice or counsel. This is logical, but really isn't so. He really wants a *resolution* to his emotional problem. In verbalizing his problem, he will become involved in a process that will lead in time to *his* making the decision, if one is necessary, for what is "logically" best, but only when he is more emotionally comfortable.

To illustrate an example of the complex orality behind a manifest content of a sexual nature, consider a young house wife who had been referred for psychotherapy because of "frigidity" with her husband. The excerpt presented here is from her twenty-seventh session with a therapeutic listener: "Phil (a certain perceived aspect of the therapist) came by the house yesterday (a latent reference to an aspect of the previous session) which really surprised me, as I didn't expect him. All the time he was there, I kept thinking to myself: '*Why* did you have to come when I look so grubby and dirty?' I had been cleaning up the bathroom (a reference to her guilt) and I must have looked a *mess*! I didn't even have a chance to run a comb through my hair, and didn't have a bit of make-up on. I felt so 'icky' with him around. But he said I looked nice, and when he found out I was alone, he gave me a little kiss (smiles warmly). He talked some of his job. He's working as an undercover man with the drug problem (the problem of her guilt-laden oral dependency). You know we have a terrible problem with drugs around here. It's a thankless job he has as, first of all, some of the kids (certain aspects of the client) themselves will put up such a fight if they're caught on drugs. They want to be on the stuff and they don't care about the consequences. And now even the parents (certain aspect of the therapist) will back the kids up. I just can't see how any parent could tolerate his child taking dope (the oral dependency needs made unacceptable by her guilt). But I guess some do. I know one thing, I'd (here the "I" is metaphorical for only *one* aspect of her) never let mine! And I don't want to catch anyone (specifically referring to an aspect of the therapist) trying to *slip* dope to my children. In fact, I've been cautioning them about watching what they eat or drink, and to be on the alert that someone (i.e., the therapist) might try to put some in their food. Phil knows the drug problem real well. I guess he's

245

a specialist in that. A policeman's job is a hard one though, and I know it's getting to him. He hates to be the mean cop with the kids because he does like them. Yet he has a job to do. Somebody has to make sure kids aren't taking drugs. Someone must stop them if they are, and Phil is the one. It's a dangerous job too, because you never can tell when you'll run into the violent type (an aspect of herself). I worry about Phil and his work because of that reason. That's a risk he says he has to take in his profession. I can tell that his work gets to him, because he's an entirely different man when he's off duty. He asked me how things were going, and I told him. Then he made a few advances to me. He could see how I tensed up the minute he came near me. He asked if I were afraid he was going to rape me. I told him 'of course not' but I knew he wanted to make love to me. I've been keeping away from him all summer. I've purposely avoided running into him I don't know how many times. I told him I wasn't afraid of *him*, but my *own* feelings. (Note that she refers to the intensity of her unmet oral dependency needs.) I've never had an affair (*both* bragging and complaining). I had a very strict upbringing and we weren't supposed to talk about certain things. My mother never told me about sex and maybe that's why I've been so frigid with my husband. But then maybe she did, and I didn't listen. I've been afraid of sex and I don't know why. Phil seems to bring that fear out in me. I've never met anyone that could shake me up the way he does. I can feel my heart beating when he's near me. But why should he do that to me? My husband (a differently perceived aspect of the therapist) and I have been getting along so much better this past summer. He's been much more attentive to me; and has played more with the children (her oral dependency needs, but without the guilt that was conveyed in the metaphor of "dope" and "drugs") than he's ever had. Somehow I feel closer to him than I have in a long time. But I'm just not *happy*. Yet I *should* be. Bob is a good husband. He's dependable. He's faithful and I can trust him. I can't ask for a better husband (and with her level of unconscious guilt, she implies she *should* be satisfied with the level of oral gratification, metaphorically conveyed in "Bob," and contrasted with the higher level of oral gratification conveyed in "Phil off duty"). I shouldn't be interested in Phil at all. I've heard what others (i.e., latently she, herself) have said about him. I'm quite familiar with how he'll chase anything in a skirt, and that he's had one affair right after the other. I know he's been seen with that Diane Green (a very guilt-laden aspect of herself) and she's got a terrible reputation. I ought to know what Phil is like, if he'd go around with someone like Diane. But what I *know* and what I *feel* are two different things. What I feel isn't logical. If I were logical about the whole thing, I'd tell Phil to get out of my life, and stay out! I'd tell him I'm satisfied with the good husband I have. (Pause.) But I feel so *much* for Phil. Somehow he does something to me. When I'm with him, I'm the happiest I ever have been. (Smiles warmly.) I told Phil this, and he said: "Well, what are you waiting for?' I told him that I was *afraid* of the consequences and that I wouldn't be able to face my children, knowing that I would be what I've always despised (i.e., one who gratifies her guilt-laden oral needs) and what I want my girls to despise as well. Y et I *wanted* him to make love to me, even as I was saying it. (Cries.) I wanted him to say: 'Oh forget about all that and just live for the moment.' I love him so much, and yet, there's no *reason* why I should. I know he'd marry me, but I wouldn't want to hurt his wife (this is still metaphorical for the *therapist* and not the client, for it implies that "my needs destroy" feeling.) She's very nice, and I do like her. I couldn't ever bring myself to hurt anyone like her. (Pause.) I'm not so sure I'd want to be married to Phil anyway. I've heard that marriage spoils many a good relationship (referring to anger expression in any emotionally close and pro-longed transference relationship). Maybe I don't want to see him as realistically as I would if I were married to him. Perhaps I'd rather continue to see him in a way I know isn't realistic. I just don't know. (Cries.) Why does he mix me all up? Why does he have this effect on me? There must be something *wrong* with *me* to feel so mixed up about him. Can't you help me? (Therapist: Gestures non-commitantly.) I could see he was confused by my action and that he wasn't go-ing to make any more advances. He told me he wasn't going to force me into anything I didn't want. He said that he knew that I could always reach him if I really wanted him. I felt like telling him then that I *did* want his love so very much, but I was *afraid* that if I did let him love me, he might find out what I'm really like. I felt somehow I might be a let-down for him. Do you know what I mean? (Therapist again gestures as above.) I feel as though I'm a *poor substitute* for what he thinks I am. What is it within me that makes me *feel* that way? What is it that makes me *desire* Phil beyond all reason? And why is it that I can't go ahead and *have* an affair, like I know other people do, instead of sitting here crying and feeling sorry for myself in some psychiatrist's office?''

In handling the above client, the therapeutic listener has, first of all, structured a once a week session that is characterized by being client-centered in the manifest content. The therapist takes a formal stance, verbalizing minimally, and only when appropriate to offer some verbal support. He predominately listens, knowing that the therapeutic transference will resolve this woman's emo-tional problems in time. And as long as the therapist can *continue* to be "Phil," in part, the Phil of reality will be less and less a problem to her. Already she has alluded to a betterment in her marriage. A sexual affair with the Phil in reality is no answer to her emotional problems. At this point in her transference relation-ship there is no *one* thing she wants to *hear* from her therapist. There is no logical advice that would be acceptable to her because of her ambivalence. With as many different "parts" that are apparent here, she emotionally wants only the feeling that the therapeutic listener is staying by her — but not too close and not too distant. To tell her she doesn't really want a sexual (oral) relationship with Phil (therapist) would be a latent oral rejection to her — for, in part, she obviously does — and would give evidence that the therapist doesn't really understand her communication. The therapeutic listener conveys his understanding through *listening*. The therapeutic transference will eventually lower her guilt so that she'll meet her oral dependency needs in a great many part objects of her interpersonal relationship sphere, and where there will never be again an object, as the Phil in reality, that can have such an emotional impact on her.

It is interesting to mention another irony in all this. The "Phils" of reality *are* more passionate lovers and not the type that her husband is metaphorically presented as. People with emotional problems have a greater capacity for more intense, more passionate love (sexual and otherwise) — but of course, they *also* have a greater capacity for being involved in "heartbreaks" and emotional turmoil as well. The person whose oral needs are met in a multiplicity of part objects *can't* be so intensely "happy" as the orally deprived person, who, in his search for his emotional solutions may find temporary intense happiness — and may find intense unhappiness as well! This fact that the orally deprived person *can* be such a *successful* lover in reality is consistent with all outstanding success in reality. It has a basis in uncomfortable orality. What makes a person outstanding, what motivates him to higher achievement and recognition is the *same* orality that simultaneously makes him uncomfortable. It is only within the whole object orientation that reality demands that "success" and "mental illness" can seem so *unrelated!*

CHAPTER 12

THE ORALITY IN SEXUALLY-ORIENTED MANIFEST CONTENT

In the preceeding chapter sexuality was emphasized as a problem of reality and not a major concern for the unconscious. But as a problem of reality, sexuality can convey, in metaphor and analogy, the underlying oral problems that lead to sexual difficulties. These difficulties represent a whole object orientation with an appropriate timeliness for the deeper oral problems that are part object derived, and which fuse, with a disregard for time, the distant and more recently emotional past with the emotional *immediate* present, seeking to resolve in the moment of the present all those emotional problems of the past that *logically* ought not to be of any concern.

The error in believing that sexuality *is* a concern of the unconscious may be derived from the fact that it frequently occurs in the manifest content of dreams. If the dream in its totality is an unconscious process (as opposed to communication, which has an unconscious latent content and a *conscious* manifest content), then one might conclude there is an unconscious concern with sexuality. The error, made by earlier psychoanalysts, is assuming that the unconscious must be *basically* concerned with sexuality. It must be remembered though that the manifest content of the dream, like the manifest content of language, tends to be *reality* oriented. Issues, conflicts, and problems of reality, including sexual ones, are utilized in the manifest content to present the problems of the latent conflict that are always part object and part experience oriented. There may very well be latent implications or inuendos of a sexual nature evident in the drama presented in the dream manifest content, but the basic issues with which the *latent* content of the dream is concerned remain consistently oral.

It is interesting to go through the published studies on dream recall to see how the analysts seem quite capable of providing interpretations of dream symbols or dream analogies to anything other than that which is outright sexual, and *making* them sexual. The end-point in their analyses always seems to be sexuality. They don't seem to be able to go deeper than the sexual. It ironically becomes evident that the analysts, themselves, must have a "sexual hang-up" (and not necessarily their clients) in not being able to interpret to a deeper level. But by focusing upon, and making an issue of reality oriented sexual taboos and the often anxiety-provoking subjects of sexuality that one usually will not talk about, particularly if guilt-laden, they enhance their position in the transference and perhaps cover their own personal problems in orality.

What will be presented here in the following excerpts of manifest content is that sexuality is not a psychoanalytic end-point. What is hoped to be conveyed is firstly that in regard to any emotional problem, the roots must lie in orality, and secondly, in verbalizing this problem to a listener, the problem becomes mutually both the speaker's as well as the listener's in the unreality of a developing transference. The interaction within this unreality has the potential of resolving the difficulties of reality. Lastly, one should recognize that any other manifest content could have been used to present this orality just as easily as these sexualized manifest contents do.

Orality, as the basic issue of the language of the transference, is well illustrated by a client metaphorically presenting his unacceptable and "destroying" oral dependency needs as a *sexual* problem of his marriage. The dilemma of his unmet oral dependency needs on the one hand, and oral guilt on the other, is clearly shown in the following: "I think my marriage (a latent reference to the therapeutic transference) got off on the wrong foot because I tried to force myself on my wife (therapist) too soon. I should have seen she didn't like sex the way I do. I have an overly strong sexual drive (i.e., "my oral needs are excessive") so that I seem to need sex more than she does. It's a part of me I don't like, but there's nothing I can do about it. (Pause.) I understand some people do have a greater sex drive than others, isn't that right? (Therapist: Well, how do you feel about it?) Well, I *know* it's so. Ive just read some articles that confirm what I've felt all along. This is what my problem is, and I can't see how you can help me with it. When I forced myself on her early in the marriage, I just ruined the sexual relationship. I know I've hurt her. I've often thought of taking something to cut down on my abnormally large sexual drive. I've even thought of having an operation so that I wouldn't have so much of a sexual need. It's been a very selfish sexual need on my part as I haven't really considered her, and now it's as though I'm driving her away. She doesn't want to have anything to do with sex (a projection of his emotional resistance to the therapist). She'll go for weeks without sex if I don't make advances (and he is characterized in therapy as often being "cold and distant" for weeks). I should be taking some saltpeter to cut down on my needs, for it seems to me that the more I want sexual gratification the further away I drive her. (The story of his past emotional life!) It's *because* of my sexual drive that has made her so frigid. My abnormal need for sex is just ruining her. I've finally decided that it's just a cross I have to bear and I'll never be able to be close to her again. It's too bad too, for her, because I'm like the rotten apple that spoils the bushel. Now she probably doesn't want to have anything to do with any man."

An attractive college girl with a history of anxiety attacks that began after she left home to live, schizoidly, in the dormitory, states in her tenth session of therapy: "Oh, this is very embarrassing. (Blushes.) I feel funny talking to you about this. (Pause.) I've put it off before, but I know I've got to tell you everything. (Pause.) It's about my sex life. (Pause.) If you were a woman, I think I'd be able to talk about my problem easier with you. (But her unconscious guilt makes it difficult for her to talk to *anyone* — male *or* female.) But I've *got* to talk with someone if this is my problem. (Therapist: I know it's not easy for you.) It sure isn't. (Pause.) Although I'm seventeen and not married . . . well (Pause) . . . I'm taking birth control pills (a latent reference to therapeutic transference and its potential for emotional closeness). You must think I'm terrible. I've never had sexual relations before, but I've met this boy (the therapist, in metaphor) that I think an awful lot of. I've always believed in waiting until a girl gets married before having sex. That's the way I grew up. (Therapist: Sure.) I was told that over and over (a metaphorical presentation of "my oral needs destroy"). I started taking these pills about two months ago (she also began therapy approximately this time) just in case I did get intimate. I haven't been as yet, but *he* wants me to be. I'm going to keep on with the pills because I have been much more comfortable with my periods (guilt). I used to have such terrible cramps, and I really was in such misery. But now I'm feeling a lot better. I talked with Dad (another perceived aspect of the therapist) about sex (perhaps a reference to her ability now to "air" her guilt, which is being concretized as "sexual"). I was really surprised to find him so open-minded. I didn't think he'd ever talk with me about a subject like that. But he did. And afterwards, he came over and gave me a hug. He even kissed me. (This is a metaphorical concretization of a perceived aspect of the emotional closeness of the therapeutic transference.) This is the *first* time that I *ever* remember him being *that* accepting of me. ((Smiles warmly.) It did a lot for me just knowing I could talk with him about problems like that. That's what seemed to bother me the most in the past . . . my not being able to talk over personal things — like sex (i.e. "my guilt-laden oral needs"). I didn't want to tell mother (the therapist again, but viewed with a *different* set of attributes as contrasted to those conveyed in the metaphors of "Dad," and "this boy"), as I know for *sure*, she'd get mad at me. She doesn't understand like Dad does. I have talked a lot more with her recently than I ever have in the past. But I haven't mentioned sex. I can't talk to her about sex. That's a taboo subject with her. I'd *never* tell her I was on the pill, and was going to keep on. She wouldn't think it was a good idea at all. She said she didn't ever want me to do anything bad. She's always suspiscioning the worst in me. I told her I wasn't any 'Chris Duncan' (but she is, *in part*, what 'Chris Duncan' metaphorically *stands* for!) and *she's* on birth control pills. *She* wants to have sex (a guilt-free gratification of her oral needs) with *any* boy she likes. She just has to *look* at them and if she likes them (seductively smiles at therapist) she'll try to get them into bed!"

251

The implication that to satisfy one's oral dependency needs is not in one's best interest can be metaphorically illustrated in a variety of ways, but particularly in regard to the reality of sexuality A seventy year old male in supportive psychotherapy describes, on the manifest content level, his feelings toward his nineteen year old part-time secretary, Nancy Lee. He had hired her the summer before, but his wife had insisted that he not have her in his employ this summer after she became aware of his developing fondness for her. "Well, I got to see Nancy Lee (the therapist, in part) again. You don't *know* what I have to go through (latently implying his guilt in attempting to satisfy his oral needs) in order to get to see her. A few weeks ago, I told myself that I just wasn't going to see her anymore (and he didn't show up for his therapy session either). Why should an attractive nineteen year old girl like that go along with some old duffer like me? (Implying the therapist could do better than involving himself with this client.) My wife (a concretized guilt-laden aspect of both himself, *and* a perceived aspect of the therapist that he feels is against oral dependency gratification) thinks she's just interested in my money. But she's told me that she's not, and she's shown that to me in different ways. She'll often spontaneously give me a little kiss on my cheek if we're standing close, so I know she's not interested in my money. She wouldn't have to do things like that. Yet she won't hesitate to ask for my car (a reference to the therapist's fee?) and I let her have it, though my better judgement says I shouldn't. I don't know what it is about that girl, but she sures gives me the feeling that life is worth living. That's a feeling I didn't have before I met her. I felt like ending it all then. She's given me a new lease on life. When I'm around her, I feel the best I've felt in years. I do like being with her, but I know it's not right (i.e., "because of my guilt"). What if I should get her pregnant (a latent reference to the client's rather exaggerated self-felt destructive oral dependency needs), then I would ruin her for the rest of her life. It's not fair to her. But then she's pretty sure of herself. She's shown me that she can handle both herself and me too. She doesn't seem afraid of me at all. (Smiles and therapist returns it.) But maybe she doesn't know how I really am. If she only knew how much I desired her, she wouldn't have anything to do with me (referring to the self-felt destructiveness of his dependency needs). I had told myself a couple of months ago that I was going to break off with Nancy Lee because my wife (another perceived aspect of the therapist) doesn't want me around her. I've been married too long to my wife to hurt her with something as foolish and childish as this. I've been acting like a love-sick school boy, and I know I ought to act my age. But then Nancy Lee *insists* on seeing me, and she won't let anything come between us. How do I handle a predicament like this anyway?"

A wife who had entered therapy two months previously when she felt guilty over not loving her husband as she felt she should stated: "Last week, Ronald (the therapist, in metaphor) and I had another one of our talks that I dread having. We talked for three hours — at least it seemed that long to me, but maybe it wasn't (a therapy session is a half hour). As usual, we didn't accommmplish anything. Not a damn thing! These talks always end up the same way. They don't solve anything! The problem is, according to him — and I guess he's right — I just don't appreciate sex (i.e., oral gratification) or else maybe it's because I feel I'm not worthy of his love and can't accept him. The same old coals are being raked over time and time again. Nothing is getting solved and I don't know why he continues with the marriage. It's the same old mess (her guilt) we're wallowing in. He tells me how comfortable he *could* be and how comfortable he *was*, until I committed adultery (implying "it's my oral *needs* that caused all this trouble") and how he's only staying with me now, just to hold the marriage together for the children's sake. But he's been committing adultery for years (though this, in one aspect, represents a *projection* of her guilt to the therapist; it also implies another aspect of *unprojected* guilt, for it infers that the therapist has been involving himself with someone he *shouldn't* — namely, *she* herself). I guess that's all right in a way, as it's been my fault that I haven't been the wife I should be. If I could just quit trying to fight back, or wanting things different than they are, I'd be the type of wife I should be. If I could just accept things as they are, be appreciative and go on, I'd be all right. But he always gets me so emotionally upset and then I get to crying. (Cries.) I know he doesn't want to see me depressed and crying all the time. It's no wonder we don't have sex! He wants me to love him because a wife is *supposed* to do this. It's something I *should* do, if I were a *good* wife. (Pause.) I got him upset last week when I told him I wished there was some way I could just give up sex (i.e. "my troublesome oral needs"). I wouldn't have to *love* anybody, or wouldn't *need* anybody. I wouldn't be getting into such a damn turmoil. Well, I could tell, he sure didn't like that! Sex (oral need gratification) is a big thing with him. According to him, it's what makes the world go round and nothing else. (Her *latent* implication is correct.) I'm supposed to love him. I'm supposed to turn on like a light switch whenever he crawls into bed with me (a latent reference to the timing of her therapy sessions) and get all sexually aroused (i.e., orally hungry). Whenever he's around it produces the opposite effect and I get frigid. Then I end up actually *hating* him. I can't forget all those times he's let me down in the past — the times he's hurt me with the things he's done and how he left me alone (just as the emotionally significant objects, and part objects of her distant past did). I can't stand his figuring up from my last period just when I'm supposed to need sex (another reference to the *scheduled* therapy sessions). He's read all those books on sex (perhaps she implies psychiatry books, which unfortunately would be an erroneous implication in regard to *orality*!) and he's supposed to know all about it. (Laughs.) He even wants to write one himself, but I'm afraid he'd put *me* in it (Pause.) I wouldn't care one bit if sex hadn't even been invented! It just makes for all the trouble in this world. It's the sexual problem that's the real problem with Ronald and me. I think if he could leave the sex out of our marriage, everything would be all right. I swear — its the only thing he ever thinks of! Whenever I'm with him, there he is, ready to give me what *he* thinks I need. I know he's a man, and sex is the most important thing to him. But I don't want it — and especially from him! But it's *my* fault, now, for not *forgetting* the past, and just going on. When I do have sex with him, I just play a role. Maybe what I need to do is to go to some type of acting school so I can play his game, and then I'll make him happy (laughs — then becomes serious). No priest, no minister, no marriage counselor, or no doctor is ever going to solve that sexual problem in our marriage between Ronald and me. We've got to do it ourselves (latently implying herself and the therapist) and nobody can help us. And right now, I don't see how in the world it's possible. (Thoughtful pause.) How can *you* help a sexual problem between Ronald and me?"

A client who had previously been depressed when first seen eighty-five sessions earlier, and who had required a brief psychiatric hospitalization, had been recently showing an elevation in her mood from the continued oral support and anger ventilation of therapy, frequently laughing and appearing cheerful. "I'm still worried underneath, though I feel outwardly happy, and more like being with people. I *like* that feeling of being happy, but I'm *afraid* of it. Do you understand? (Therapist: What do you mean?) Before, I'd have that feeling like I didn't belong — that I just wasn't acceptable to anyone, in any place. I'd have that 'way-out' feeling like I was a million miles from everyone else, or that I was "numb" all over (a denial of her emotional feelings). Maybe that was wishful thinking in one way (and she is correct), but I also know it was mighty uncomfortable. Now I laugh. I'm beginning to enjoy people (a latent reference to increased oral gratification with the therapist). I'm more cheerful. But I'm still worried underneath it all. (Therapist: Worried?) Yes, I'm afraid of what will happen next. That's the way its always been for me in life. As soon as I'm enjoying life (i.e., gratifying my oral needs) then, wham! The very *worst* comes about. Lately, I've been noticing I'm interested again in sex. My husband (the therapist) thinks that's a good sign, but he doesn't know that I've found other men (other perceived aspects of the therapist) sexually attractive. For instance there's this new serviceman (a specially perceived aspect of the therapist) for the oil heater that I've just met. I like to sit and talk with him when he comes. I know I shouldn't but I tell myself 'Why should I live in a shell?' We kid and carry on, but that's *just* how I got in trouble before. That's *exactly* how my trouble began in the past. It was with some damn serviceman (therapist) the last time. That was the television repair man I've told you about. (Therapist: I recall.) I wrecked his marriage but good. And it certainly didn't help mine any. I'm still having that mess thrown up in my face by my husband to this very day. I'll never be able to live that down, and I'll be taking that guilt with me right to the grave. But then I know that *other* women are doing it (a rationalization for her apparent decreased guilt). So why shouldn't I? (Pause.) But tell me, am I headed in the wrong direction again if I'm feeling this good? I mean laughing and enjoying people the way

I am. Is this all leading to another sex hang-up? I want to hear it from you, because I can't help but feel I'm going in the wrong direction again. I *know* it's the wrong direction because I'm enjoying it too much. Whenever I enjoy anything . . . well . . . there's always hell to pay later."

Here, a college student, who entered therapy for incapacitating feelings of inadequacy and insecurity that arose following several circumstances in his reality that were oral need frustrating, states: "Ed (an unconsciously perceived aspect of the therapist) and I were in the Variety store (metaphorical for the therapeutic transference) at the beach last week, and I got to talking with a girl (another aspect of the therapist) at the check-out counter. Somehow we got to small talking, and then I found out she was going to State University too. You know how it is when two people get to talking and they find out they've got something in common. (Therapist: Sure.) I didn't put any emphasis on it, and I know if either *I* had, or *she* had, it would have frightened *me* off. We talked for a while about the school and some of the courses we both had taken. She's a very attractive girl with a real nice personality. After we left the store, Ed asked if I could tell that she was attracted toward me. 'Couldn't you tell she liked you?' he said. I said 'No, I didn't!' But then his remark made me mad. It made me mad that he was *analyzing* me. I told him I was tired of his butting his nose into my private life. I was *really* mad at him and I told him so. We argued awhile and he said that was my trouble that I didn't know, or couldn't tell, when a girl liked me. He said: 'You're always thinking no girl could ever like you, when you can't even see when a girl *obviously* does!' So, just to prove him wrong, I went right back in the store, right up to the counter, and asked her for a date that evening. That's not like me at all, but then being mad isn't either! (Therapist: Mmhmm.) She said: 'I'd love to go out with you.' I was half hoping she'd say no. I hated to think that Ed was right once again, and I told him so. But I was really surprised that a girl as beautiful as she is would want to go out with the likes of me. I always thought that the only girl that would go out with me would be some fat, ugly dog of a girl. I have to admit that Ed was the origin of this wonderful relationship. I'll give the devil his due. If it wasn't for Ed, I wouldn't be going with her now. Sue and I have had several dates already, and she's ideal. There's nothing I don't like about her. I mean anyone would feel proud to be seen with her. (Therapist: I'm glad you met her.) Ed seems to know just when to be forceful and when to be quiet. It's because of him that I've changed in my outlook on life and my lousy self-image. I use to feel how can a girl possibly see any beauty or goodness in me! I used to think I was a latent homosexual or something going around with Ed. Maybe I am, but I must be getting *bisexual* at this point. (Laughs and therapist smiles.) Sue is doing a lot for my self-confidence. Because of my relationship with *her*, I feel more normal, more of what I think a college boy ought to feel like. Yet, if it wasn't for my relationship with Ed, I wouldn't have found Sue."

255

There is a latent *sexual* connotation that this part-time secretary makes in her manifest content in the following remarks about a fellow employee, "Timmy." But, more basically fundamental than anything sexual is her *latent* concern for the explosive destructive potential of emotional closeness from oral dependency gratification. This closeness she ambivalently wants and simultaneously doesn't want — with an unconscious part object cognition of the *therapist* from a part object make-up of *herself* that both *fears* the closeness and *wishes* for it, too, at the very same time. She fears her own self-felt devouring oral needs, and her immense repressed anger and hidden guilt that she feels might be "discovered" in too close of an emotional togetherness. She attempts here to regain a more comfortable distant position with the therapist with "Boy, I had some panicky feelings this past week when Timmy came into the office and closed the door behind him. Wow! Was I panic stricken! I could never tell you what it was like! He started talking about our sexual relationship that I'd rather forget ever happened! I felt I was sitting on a wide open keg of dynamite and that *he* was playing with fire. I don't know whether I was afraid of *him*, or my *own* feelings. I mean something *terrible* could have happened! (Laughs.) I felt like running out! That *always* makes me uncomfortable when I'm shut in a room with someone, especially *him!* I felt like saying: 'Why do you have to shut the door after you — can't you leave it open?' (Laughs.) He's a nice boy all right and I *do* like him. But he's looking for a *wife*, and I'm not looking for a husband. I've got one husband (reality-wise, she's seperated from her husband) that I'm trying to get rid of, and I don't want another one. Timmy said he wanted to take me to the movies to see 'Gone With The Wind' — (Laughs.) That's me! I ought to just go off with the wind right now! He assured me it would be a strictly platonic relationship, but I'm afraid that if I get involved with him that it's going to lead to something that I won't be able to handle (a latent reference to the immensity of her unmet oral needs, which she fears). Sex is dynamite! (But even more so is oral dependency!) I've caused my husband enough trouble, and I wouldn't want to be hurting anyone else. Now that my husband (a guilt-imbued aspect of the therapist) has left the scene for a while, I don't have that bother, but I wish that Timmy would understand that I *don't* want to get into the same situation I just got out of. Do you understand that? (Therapist: I understand.) I don't want to be rushed by him. I'm just *not* looking for another husband, but I don't mind him as a *friend* — *just* a friend and not a lover! He's going to have to keep his *distance*."

A young housewife who was first seen for intractable headaches, on one hand is openly seductive in therapy, but on the other hand, expresses her hostile feelings toward the therapist by her remarks concerning her husband, "Jim." "I'm trying to get up enough courage to take the big step. I'm going to leave Jim and the sooner the better. But I'm somewhat dependent on him (superficially, she means a "financial" dependency on her husband, but *latently* she implies an *oral* dependency on the therapist.) and unless I can find something better, I'll just

256

abide my time with him. I guess I'm outgrowing him. He's too routine; he's too predictable; he's too much of what a good little American husband should be, and that makes me sick of him. I wish he wasn't so damn faithful, but would go out and find himself a mistress (here "mistress" refers to a guilt-free aspect of *herself* that she desires would meet the *therapist's* oral needs). We're just abiding our time together with no yelling, no screaming and no name calling like we use to do. We're discussing things back and forth like two civilized people. But I still don't want him to even touch me, and I make sure he keeps his distance. We haven't had sexual relations for two months now. (And she has remained cold and distant in her therapy session.) But I've got needs like any woman has that are going to be met one way or another! Sex is that important to me. (Therapist: Sure.) I'll tell *you*, but I wouldn't tell my husband, that I'm *ready* for an affair. I have a feeling he knows I am too! (Pause and then laughs.) I don't think he really knows what he wants to do with me."

A housewife who had seen many different doctors for persistent abdominal pain had undergone several laporatomies by two different surgeons, and finally, an operation to "free up the adhesions" from the previous surgeries before being referred for therapy. In one of her sessions, she remarked: "I feel like hell this morning. I feel like the devil himself, so watch out! Phil (an unconsciously perceived aspect of the therapist) is ready to send me packing to my mother's (again a reference to the therapist) for a couple of weeks (cries) and I don't want to go. I hate going to my mother's because of the way she makes over me. I guess a part me *wants* to go, because I haven't been for so long I can hardly remember the last time. Yet another part of me knows darn well Phil is just trying to get *rid* of me and that makes me angry! He told me: 'I can't go on living with you another week and hearing you complain about your damn side aching.' (Most of this client's manifest orientation has been toward her physical complaints.) He says that he can't stand living with an *invalid*. Well, I want to tell *you*, I don't like that part of me either that's an invalid. Do *you* think I get pleasure out of my side giving me pain all the time and preventing me from having any fun in life? He said: 'Laura, this business can't go much longer and that's it!' One part of me was really mad at Phil for his being so misunderstanding, but another part of me knows that he's *right*. I can understand his feeling the way he does. But can I help it if my ovaries (a metaphorical presentation of her unmet oral dependency needs) are hurting all the time? I'm no fun to live with, I do know that. I know I should have had them out in the last surgery. I'm a mess to be around and it's a wonder he hasn't kicked me out a long time ago. But I don't know what to do about it. Nobody (specifically meaning the therapist) has given *me* any answers! I've gone from one doctor to the other, and they haven't helped one single bit (implying: "You haven't either!"). I've tried every medicine in the book (a reference to her past attempts to meet her oral needs) and then some, and I *still* have this pain in my side. He accuses me of getting this pain in my side more intensely everytime he

257

wants to take me to bed. But my gynecologist (another perceived aspect of the therapist viewed as more understanding) has told me that sexual relations *will* increase the pain from that cyst on my ovary. My husband won't let me have an operation. (Perhaps another husband would, particularly when hospital insurance that won't cover talking and listening sessions such as this, will cover surgery, which when accompanied by the hospitalization does afford a subtle emotional resolution to the underlying oral problems that this woman has. It is just this type of underlying oral problem in patients that *demand* surgery, that one can blame, along *with* the surgeons, the excessive surgery in this country.) He says it's an *excuse* for not having sex with him. Well, I'm *not* interested in sexual relations (i.e., more oral need gratification) because of this pain in my side. This really upsets Phil. I wish he had ovaries (guilt-laden needs) like mine and then he'd understand what I'm going through. (Therapist: That's right!) Phil says I *should* be interested in sexual intercourse if I'm a normal woman. The ladies' magazines say I should be interested in sex if I'm normal. All the doctors say I should be interested in sex. Everyone says I should be interested in sex if I'm a normal woman. There should be no reason in the world why I *shouldn't* be interested in what makes the world go round. But I'm *not*! I absolutely *can't* enjoy sex. So I'm not normal! I must be some type of freak . . . at least Phil thinks I am. He doesn't think I'm any better at all in this regard, even after over one year of therapy. It has been that long, hasn't it? (It hasn't, but she perceives it to be this long.) He's been *wanting* me to see another psychiatrist for some time now because he doesn't see any progress at all that's been made. But I feel before I see *another* psychiatrist, I should *quit* psychiatry altogether and get the operation I need (i.e., "to magically remove my guilt"). Phil can't figure me out and he's given up on me. He thinks it all goes back to my hating men . . . or maybe he thinks it's because I hated my mother! (Laughs.) You know I've got a *psychiatrist* (a less veiled anology) at home that I have to live with! (Therapist: And they're not always easy to live with!) You can say that again!"

A young, depressed housewife was referred for therapy for uncontrollable crying spells, after her husband, who now was satisfying his oral needs in a very successful business, was becoming less and less emotionally involved with her. Because of her personality core guilt, she was unable to fill the emotional void left by her husband, and began to accrue an added level of unconscious guilt. In one session, she remarked: "Dwight (an aspect of herself in metaphor) said he wasn't coming in to talk to the nurse (an unconsciously perceived aspect of the therapist) because he didn't see any sense to it. He says it's a big waste of time as he doesn't believe in psychiatrists. (This is probably true in reality, but *she*, ambivalently, feels the same.) In fact, he thought it was a big joke. But he said he didn't mind if *I* went. He wants me to go and to get straightened out (note that one part of her feels she shouldn't be involved, but another part does). He's not against my going if it's going to help me (i.e., "make me independent" or "remove my oral needs"). He has seen some progress as I don't cry like I did. I'm not as depressed, and I'm sleeping a lot better. It must be that green and black capsule (i.e., "my dependency on you") I'm on. It has helped me so I'll keep on with it, at least for the time being. I'm not ready to give it up yet. But Dwight (now "Dwight" appears to be a metaphor for an unconsciously perceived aspect of the therapist as well as a resisting aspect of herself) doesn't want me to get dependent on it. I'd like to cut down on it just as soon as possible. You said it wasn't addicting, didn't you? (Therapist: It's alright to continue on it.) I don't like taking medicine. And he doesn't want me to continue here any longer than is absolutely necessary. He knows that some women (meaning she, herself, in part) will take going to the doctor, and use it like a toy. He doesn't want me to get that way. (Therapist: I see.) He certainly doesn't want me to get like this one woman (an aspect of the client herself) we both know. Her husband (latently, the therapist) is busy at the office, and working hard all day, and all she does is sit around home feeling sorry for herself, and dwelling on how hard she thinks she has it. She's always trying to get sympathy and attention from anybody who'd be foolish enough to give it to her. It's her own fault she's turned to drinking and running with men. (A latent reference to her guilt-laden oral gratification from the therapist.) She has only herself to blame for that (i.e., "it's her *own* fault for having oral needs"). I've heard too, she's tried to commit suicide several times (and this client has considered this, too). It's a shame she feels this way as she has so much to live for, and so much to be thankful for. (It's the guilt that makes her feel she *should* be thankful for the paucity in oral gratification she actually has.) It's a *disgrace* that a woman that has as much as she has should be making demands on her husband (it is a "disgrace", she feels, to be demanding *more*, when she herself feels so *less deserving* because of her guilt), the way she does and taking dope (a reference to the green and black capsule, and latently, oral gratification). She was just coming to the doctor simply to *talk*, because the doctor would *listen* to her troubles . . . most of which were imagined. She was using *him* to run to everytime she felt lonely. She was actually using him as a *crutch* or some type of an escape (the often heard *fear* of "escapes" is derived from the unconscious guilt that makes a person feel he ought not elude the oral deprivation his guilt makes him feel he deserves), and it got to be a regular habit. A crutch is something my husband certainly doesn't want me to have. She's old enough to be taking care of *herself* instead of wanting someone (i.e., the therapist) sitting right there beside her, holding her hand all the time. Dwight can't stand her, and I don't blame him. But I'm not here just to talk about *her* (laughs). Get *me* straightened out. (i.e., "remove my dependency need") Dwight and I have been talking more, and I think it has helped. (Pause.) I asked him what he wanted from the marriage and he said he wanted to love, and in turn to *be* loved and to have a good sex life. He puts a lot of emphasis on the sex life, and his ideas are pretty liberal. (Smiles coyly at therapist.) In fact, he's *very* liberal! (Smiles coyly, again, at therapist.)

259

He told me when we were first married that he expected to have his freedom whenever it was necessary. He wants to be able to go out with the boys for kind of a breather from me (the "me" is the guilt-laden aspect of herself), and he told me he wanted to have sex with some other woman whenever he felt like it. I told him I understood. But he said that I could have an affair *too* with anyone I wanted to, as long as I didn't get *emotionally* involved. I've had a couple of affairs in the past. (Latent references to the guilt of oral need gratifying aspects of the transference.) I met a hair-dresser (the therapist as perhaps one who professionally improves one's appearance) and he gave me a ride home one evening, but on the way we stopped off at *his* house for a drink. We got to talking, and it seemed the more we talked the more we got involved sexually. I knew *he* wasn't really getting involved *emotionally*. But I just can't do it that way. I found that out! (Pause.) *I* can't be as cold as *Dwight* can be. He seduced a girl (the perceived oral need gratifying aspect of the therapist) in a night class he was teaching. He wasn't really attracted to her. He just wanted to use her sexually, and there wasn't any emotional involvement on his part. He can be that way. Now there might have been on *her* part. There probably was — women are like that, you know — but there wasn't any on *his* part I'm sure. So I've come to the conclusion that I can't have an affair (therapy). If I do, I *would* be emotionally involved, and that's Dwight's only taboo for me! (Pause.) I've been pursued (smiles coyly) many times in the past. I've had fellows ask if they could buy me a drink. (Pause.) I can remember this one fellow (a differently perceived aspect of the therapist) who just wouldn't leave me alone. He was always singling me out to go after as a conquest. He actually gave me the feeling of being attacked. He'd try to get me in a corner whenever he could. I made sure I wouldn't get in a corner! I finally had to tell him outright, and in no uncertain terms, that I *wasn't* going to be any further involved with him. I think he got the message as he hasn't made any advances since. (Therapist: He understands how you feel.) I hope so. (Pause.) But I don't think sex is the only big thing in Dwight's life. It's his *business* (an aspect of the therapeutic transference but perceived as having little to do with her.) too. His main interests lie with his business, and I shouldn't make a lot of demands on him. I understand that now. I'm going to try to be a lot more busy. There's a course at the college on Spanish (another perceived aspect of the transference) that I want to take. I've always wanted to take Spanish as I felt it would help me in my travels to meet people . . . you know, to communicate with others. It would certainly come in handy in the future, but then I found out the course meets in the mornings (and so does therapy), so I don't see how I'll be able to take the course if I'm coming here (the reality presentation of the need-fear dilemma). I'm disappointed in a way (in a very ambivalent way). But I've got to get interested in something *myself*. I thought I'd take up knitting (i.e., "I'll just deny my oral needs"). Oh, yes, before I go I should tell you I won't be able to come here this Friday."

260

How little sexuality's role is in other than the manifest content is illustrated by the following excerpt of a young housewife, who previously had led an almost schizoid and anhedonic life, with little emotional closeness with her husband, her parents or anyone else. After a year of involvement in a therapeutic transference, she began to involve herself with her next door neighbor, Phyllis, going to coffees together, attending art classes two evenings a week, and then going out for a drink and a late snack at a nearby restaurant following the class. Her husband resented these "nights out" of his wife's, and likewise, resented his wife's continued involvement in a therapeutic transference alliance with the therapist, when he could no longer see a "need" for her continuing. However with her increased self-confidence and self-esteem from her decreased unconscious guilt, the client defended her "right" to this freedom — and continued to associate herself with both Phyllis and the therapist. The reality of her husband's reluctance to condone her involvement with Phyllis when spontaneously brought up by her in her therapy sessions metaphorically conceptualized her own resistance to continuing the therapeutic relationship. In this session, she presents remarking: "I've got a problem that I wish you'd help me with. Lenny (an aspect of the therapist that is perceived as blocking her oral needs) thinks I'm getting too involved with Phyllis (a perceived aspect of the therapist that has less associated guilt) and he doesn't like it. He resents my going out with her twice a week (and therapy sessions are twice a week). I can understand how he feels (i.e., "because of my guilt"). But I don't see that we're doing anything really wrong (a reflection of her decreased guilt). We only sit and talk. We're not on the make. I like Phyllis. She's just lots of fun to be with. (Note that she perceives an aspect of the therapist, as symbolized by "Lenny", that *she* feels *doesn't* want a closer emotional involvement with her, and an aspect denoted by Phyllis that *does*.) She laughs and carries on so. We talk about anything. (Laughs.) It can be any subject at all that we're talking about, but we'll get to laughing and enjoying ourselves like a couple of school girls (note the disregard of any implied homosexuality that *might* have been implied if she felt more guilty or had the "set" of her guilt been different). I've never met a person with whom I've had so much fun. She enjoys people. But I know she's involved with someone (this "someone" is she, herself, in relation to an aspect of the therapist conveying *oral* guilt) she shouldn't be. But I really don't blame her when she's got a husband (the therapist, in metaphor) like hers. He's going around with some old whore (a guilt-laden aspect of herself). Lenny doesn't know about Phyllis' affair. At least I don't think he does. But he suspicions what she's like. He hasn't condemned Phyllis specifically for anything as yet. He tolerates her (as though implying one perceived aspect of the therapist "tolerates" an aspect of the client) but he doesn't like *my* seeing her so much. But then I don't think Lenny has any right to talk. One of his friends, Skip (a perceived aspect of the therapist that is latently likened to "Phyllis", but different in that there is an implied *acceptance* by the therapist) drinks too much and he

261

runs women all the time. He tries to go to bed with any woman he meets. He's going with this one girl now that's got the worst reputation in town. This girl (an aspect of she herself) I just can't stand. I don't like to be around her if I can help it, and neither does anyone else. But I don't like Lenny associating himself with Skip either, and I've told Lenny so, yet they can always manage to get together. So I don't see why I can't see Phyllis. (Here she shows the increased gain in oral need gratification afforded by decreased guilt from the therapist, as well as from Phyllis, and the increasing sphere of interpersonal relationships in reality.) Do you think it's *wrong* for me to see Phyllis? (Therapist: Well, how do you feel about it?) I don't think it is, but Lenny seems to think so. (Therapist: Lenny thinks so?)"

Note that had the therapist replied in the above: "Why don't you take this up with Lenny?" it might have been perceived as a rejection by the client, as an implied desire of the therapist to terminate her ventilation of feelings — even though "Lenny" is also latently the therapist. Reality-wise it is of interest to note too, that the therapist's nurse, who was seeing the client's husband on a weekly basis for "progress reports," was actively supporting him in the meeting of *his* oral needs, while also accepting his anger. He was emotionally supported enough that he did take a more active role, afforded by a reduction in his guilt, than his usual guilt-laden passivity, in regard to his wife. He insisted then that she be home, which he *could* do now with his own decreased guilt, before twelve on her evenings out with Phyllis. This, though it initially led to some arguments, led also to a closer marriage relationship, more expression of emotions, more sexual relations and more mutual enjoyment in doing things *together* which previously they did not do. The client's oral difficulties which were initially expressed as psychosomatic complaints, now became expressed in interpersonal relationship problems that were slowly resolved to a mutual satisfaction, through the aid of their respective transference relationships with therapist and nurse.

The concern with sexuality, homosexuality (whether overt or latent), as well as sexual identity problems (again whether latent or overt) are all problems of *reality* in that they are *whole* object oriented. Take for instance the distraught college boy who remarks in his fifth session: "I'm bothered by sex. I've been keeping this a secret. (Pause.) I don't know if I'm a homosexual or a heterosexual. In other words, I wonder if my sexual desire is for boys or girls! I just can't tell. I feel sexually inhibited with *both* (implying he can't comfortably be emotionally close to any human, regardless of sex). I do desire several girls (guilt-laden perceptions of the orally gratifying therapist) I know, and yet I'm aware of a desire for several boys (metaphorically similar to "girls"). I know this is abnormal. (With as much unconscious guilt this boy has that is focused in sexuality it wouldn't be reassuring at all to tell him he must then be a "bisexual!") It's terrible! My desires will send me to hell! I'm not fit because of my abnormal desires latently referring to his guilt-laden oral needs) to be around *anyone!* I've

262

even thought of committing suicide, but that's against the Church, and I'd go to hell for sure. (This is wishful thinking! He would probably be sent to heaven, particularly in view of his anhedonic and almost saintly existence, and this would be a more *intolerable* situation for him, because of his guilt, than a guilt-assuaging hell!) I wouldn't want to bring *that* disgrace on my family. I feel I'm in a living hell now. I can't love either sex (implying simply he cannot love) and I curse my sexual needs (the cursed oral dependency) because of it. I'm so frustrated! I would rather love *girls*, but I think my desire for them is just a *cover-up* for latent homosexual desires I've always been afraid to face. When I'm around boys, I feel so much a 'phoney,' a 'fake' and a 'faggot.' And for this reason I can't be comfortable with them either. They don't accept me, as they know I'm a misfit or some type of queer. I've met this one boy (therapist) that I'm finding myself attracted to more and more. But he's a homosexual (a projection of his guilt to the therapist) and I *shouldn't* be involved with him. He's really a hustler and I know he's hustling me for what he can get out of me. He's not interested in what I want. I want to be *totally* loved and to be given a chance to return this love. (This love, that he so desperately desires, must always be found in an *unreality*, and never a reality!) I want to be the most important thing in his life, and he in mine. I want him to desperately need me. (Pause.) But in a way I don't want to *desperately* need him — do you understand? I seem all mixed up and I'm getting more so the longer I see you."

Still another client who unconsciously felt that her dependency needs were also abnormal alluded to her underlying oral guilt in her twenty-second session under a superficial guise of a "homosexual" concern: "I need reassurance (she means reassurance in the manifest content, but latently and emotionally she is asking for increased oral dependency gratification) that I'm not abnormal in some way. When I was fifteen, I had a real close girlfriend (this is a metaphorical presentation of her guilt-laden oral needs) that I thought a great deal of. In fact, I think I really *loved* her. I felt very guilty about it and still do. *Lately,* I haven't been able to get it out of my mind (because *lately* her guilt has increased). Of course, there never was any *sexual* activity, but I wonder if people might *think* I'm *homosexual* because of the relationship. I'm *sure* everyone knew about it." (Note that there is no more of a homosexual problem here than if she loved her mother, a child, a pet, or even God, since each of these could be rationalized as a guilt-laden "abnormal" relationship. The problem is essentially *oral* and involves the feeling one obtained through a past *conditioning* process on a part object basis, that to love — i.e., basically, to satisfy one's oral needs — is "bad." A few sessions later, she projects this sexualized guilt to the therapist as though he, now, is the "abnormal" one.) "I'm getting tired of Jimmy Jolsen (a perceived aspect of the therapist) and I want to drop him." (Therapist: You want to drop him?) "Yes, I do. I guess I just don't want to be around a person like I've learned he is. He's not what I'm looking for at all. I don't see how I ever got hung up with him.

(Laughs.) He's served his purpose when he came along, as it was right when I needed a boyfriend, but I'm going to drop him now. I've been doing some thinking about my relationship with him. There's something not right in it. He's actually more like a girl to me. I can talk to him like I can't talk to any other man — you know, about personal things. That helps me a lot, but people talk about him. I didn't know they did. Some even say he's a queer. (Note that she seeks to discontinue by putting distance between herself and her projected guilt — continuing with Jimmy implies a "guilt by association," which she prefers to avoid). It's all over town. Everyone knows he's a queer. My God! It never even entered my mind when I first met him. He seemed so normal and our sexual relationship was great! But I can see it all now when I stop and consider what he's really like. It's a shame (sighs). I don't hold it against him for I guess it's his mother's (a projection of *her* guilt) fault."

Similar to the above is the following excerpt: "I'm worse than I *ever* was all because of Dick (latently referring to the therapist). I might as well drop him as it's been one miserable hell that I've gone through ever since I ran into him. He's caused me an awful lot of uncomfortableness, I want you to know. Even *more* than I ever had when I didn't have a friend in the world. I was better off *before* I met him. I'll admit I was pretty sick before I met him, when I was considering suicide, but he's making me so damn uncomfortable now that I don't see any reason to keep on with him. It's not worth it, so I don't see any reason to come back here to see you. (Therapist: Shrugs.) He's made me an outright homosexual (a projection of his guilt to the therapist) and I'd be a hell of a lot better off if I ended my relationship with him right now, *this very minute*! Don't you? At least before I wasn't sure I was a homosexual. I know how society feels about homosexuals. They're misfits! They're queers! They're abnormal and odd! Everybody (i.e., both he and the therapist) knows that! People (i.e., the therapist) shun them. Nobody (therapist) wants to be around somebody like me. I'd never have anything to do before with a homosexual. You know that. The very thought of anything homosexual used to send me into a panic! I came here because I was afraid I might be a homosexual since I felt so uneasy around girls. I knew they didn't like something about me (a latent reference to his unconscious guilt) and I knew boys didn't like me either. What I was afraid of has been uncovered here. I would have been better off just staying away from people and not really knowing what I found out I am. Then I had to go and meet Dick. My God! What have I gotten into! I've come to you for help with this problem, and I'm not getting any better. You know that. I know, as well as you do, that psychiatry can't help homosexuals. They just *can't* be helped. That's all there is to it. There's no hope for them. It's a curse of God! I can't live with him and can't live without him (the oral need-fear dilemma). It's hell! Why, I'd gladly take up alcohol, or maybe even drugs, for the problem I've got now. An alcoholic or a drug addict is far more accepted by society than a damn homosexual! Just what do you do for a homo-sexual anyway?"

One teenaged girl who felt her problem was a "homosexual one" and who was apparently accepting this was brought in for therapy by her distraught mother, who remarked: "If she were pregnant, I might have been able to accept it, but her being a confirmed *homosexual* I just can't tolerate!" This girl involved her-self long enough in therapeutic transference that she eventually *did* involve her-self emotionally with males before discontinuing. But her emotional problems didn't end here, for she was brought back, six months later, by her very dis-traught mother again, who now was seeking a "therapeutic abortion" for her daughter.

The problems of sexuality are always entangled with the underlying problems of orality. It's always the orality that makes sexuality so uncomfortable. For instance, when a husband learns that his wife has been sexually unfaithful to him, he may show feelings of being very angry, hurt, depressed, inadequate, guilty or any combination of emotions, depending upon the presentation of his underlying orality to the unconsciously perceived oral aspects of what he has made signifi-cant in the past of the sexual relationship. He may even be very happy, or he may not have any emotion at all, but the basic reasons *still* for whatever behavior he shows involve orality in regard to the characterization of the sexual relationship between him and his wife. It is certainly *not* that his wife can no longer gratify his biologic sexual needs per se that leads to his emotionality after learning of his wife's indiscretion. The *motivation* for her unfaithfulness is also basically *oral* in origin, and the distraught husband must reorient himself *emotionally* — not intellectually — to the perceived change in the oral significance that underlies the sexual relationship, for he no longer may feel that he is someone "special" to his wife — and she, in turn, may have felt this way about him. It is interesting to note that this aspect of oral "specialness" is symbolically sexulized in the rationale for chastity for some. And when virginity isn't of importance, as it doesn't seem to be in this age, it is simply that it doesn't represent its previously held *oral* significance.

The elucidation of sexual problems, like the intellectualization of psycho-dynamics, no matter how scientifically correct and applicable to the individual, still remains a part of the manifest content and not the latent content. The emo-tional involvement between client and therapeutic listener can progress regard-less of the orientation that the manifest content might take. An emotionally un-comfortable person, though, will form within his own conscious mind his rea-sons for being uncomfortable. His conscious memories and his consciously con-ceptualized ideas become a reality-oriented frame-work that may demand a logical reality-oriented solution. What has been illustrated in this chapter is just one type of specific manifest content. Other than sexually oriented ones will be considered in the next chapter.

265

CHAPTER 13

THE IMPORTANCE OF THE MANIFEST CONTENT

The manifest content of verbalized communication has an importance that should be appreciated by the therapeutic listener. Although it carries the latent content by implication through metaphorical and analogic meanings, the manifest content must be recognized as representing the *end product* of a complex, unconscious ego process. This process is able to take what is being unconsciously perceived at the moment and in a fraction of a moment, construct a set of interlocking metaphors and analogies that will convey the appropriate latent meaning. How these metaphors and analogies are determined must be similar to the way that a phobia develops, or why a particular memory may stand out in one's mind. The metaphorical presentation of the manifest content is made even more complex when it is considered to be on-going, inter-reactive and highly dynamic. When another individual is interacting with this person, his manifest content will often show an ability to easily translate what is unconsciously being perceived on a part object basis to a whole object and reality-oriented manifest content.

The unconscious development of a dynamic manifest content that is interacting with the manifest content of the listener must be an ego function that is similar to the dream elaboration. We know that through the process of dream elaboration, the *drama*, or the interaction of the figures of a dream, is produced. The production of a dream drama by the unconscious ego is called "dream work". In a similar way, there must also be an unconscious ego function that can produce a manifest content in communication with remarkable swiftness and with even *more* complexity, because of it now involving an *inter*psychic process rather than an intrapsychic one, as was the case in the dream drama. The production of the metaphorical manifest content to convey the latent content by the unconscious ego can be called "language work." This "language work" of the unconscious ego is truly awesome. A recognition of it shifts the emphasis, in verbalized communications, from the manifest content to the latent content, which then appears as primal. The manifest content, even though reality-oriented, has a secondary importance to the latent content. The importance of the manifest content lies in its being reality-oriented.

The development of a manifest content between two or more emotionally involved people involves a culmination of a conditioning process that will allow certain subject matters to be utilized. People can communicate when they perceive that there is something in common that they share, or something in common that each is interested in, or that they might have similarly experienced. Since there are a great number of reality subjects for possibilities, there must be a complex process that makes for certain subjects to be more susceptible to usage in certain individuals for manifest content presentation. It has been said that the symbolization of the dream is often taken from the preceeding day's activities. So, too, the manifest content of communication may, more than likely, involve the more recently past activities of the individual. Like the dream too, there is no limit to what may be symbolically presented in the manifest content. Past, present or future can be appropriate for presenting the latent content in symbolic metaphors and analogies.

It is important to recognize that any manifest content theoretically has the potential of presenting an individual's emotional problems, of meeting his oral dependency needs, of ventilating his anger and thereby diminishing his guilt. The verbal interactions of an individual's interpersonal relationship sphere allow him in a great number of different manifest content subject matters that might be utilized to meet his needs and express his anger. With each of the objects of his interpersonal relationship sphere he will draw, in his communicative interaction, oral support from the unconsciously perceived part objects, and will utilize other part objects for the expression of his anger. The object relationships of these part objects are often utilized for manifest content material.

The more guilt-laden individual lacks a freedom in his interpersonal relationship sphere that the less guilty person has. He has to contend with an intensity of his guilt-laden oral dependency needs, and must struggle with a retention of anger when transference factors in his interpersonal relationships become too emotionally apparent. When this person's guilt increases to an emotionally uncomfortable level, he may attempt to seek help for this uncomfortableness.

Because of the "set" of his oral dependency gratification, of anger expression or the "set" of his guilt, as well as circumstances of fate, certain professionals may be sought out before others. He may be an individual that becasue of the circumstances of his interpersonal relationship involvement either gets referred to, or seeks out on his own, a clergyman for help with his problems. He may, with a different set of interpersonal relationship involvements, values and influences, find himself self-directed or referred to a marriage counselor, his family physician, a nurse, a social worker, a chiropractor or any other professional for the alleviation of his emotional uncomfortableness. Depending on what reality-role the professional he seeks has, he can embark on very divergent courses in reality that can greatly alter his life.

The road in reality that the professional will lead him down can be so very different from what another professional with a different reality-role may take him down. How whimsically he can find himself on a certain road can be illustrated by the emotionally uncomfortable person that goes to his physician and

267

is told he has a small duodenal ulcer. The physician may then refer him to an internist for treatment. He may refer him to a surgeon for treatment. Or he may refer him to a psychiatrist or a clinical psychologist for treatment. Each of these professionals to whom he might have been referred has an entirely different treatment program, an entirely different manifest content and an entirely different pattern of interaction in reality. And, interestingly enough, his chances for removing his ulcer problem is just about the same for each one of these professionals. Each one, in his professional role, can produce the same *emotional* result. But regardless of the role that this professional might have, what the individual is seeking in the unreality of his emotional world is a diminution of his unconscious guilt to a more comfortable level. He can find this when his oral needs are met and his anger ventilated regardless of whatever reality role he might be involved in. He can even reach the same point of emotional comfortableness with a quack, a shaman, or a charlatan, or may even reach it through shifts in his object relationships without seeing a "professional" of any kind.

The uncomfortable individual may seek out or be directed toward some form of "psychotherapy" or psychoanalysis. One can speculate that what any psychotherapist or analyst is actually accomplishing on the latent level, behind whatever the nature of the manifest content might be, is a meeting of the client's oral needs, and a ventilation of his anger, such that his unconscious guilt can diminish, and he can become more emotionally comfortable. This all is done though, within a reality-oriented setting that the therapist *himself* must be convinced is effective in bringing about a change. If that person with an ulcer reaches a point of emotional comfortableness with a psychotherapist, then reality-wise, psychotherapy "produced" the result. If he was involved with an analyst, then it was psychoanalysis that "cured" him. If he had been involved with a counselor, then it was the "counselling" that was effective. The manifest content between different therapists, analysts and counselors, that this person with an ulcer might have been involved with, may be extremely divergent and most dissimilar with each other. This is particularly so when one suspicions that there are as many forms of therapy, analysis and counselling as there are therapists, analysts and counselors.

What is emotionally accomplished in any psychotherapeutic, psychoanalytic or counselling endeavor, is somewhat similar to what occurs in *any* interpersonal relationship. The emotionality involved in a *therapeutic* transference tends to be more concentrated in that there is more of a concentration of oral dependency needs being met. Wherever there is a concentration of oral dependency needs being met, there will always be a concentration of emotions, and the object on whom the dependency supplies are being drawn will be an emotionally significant figure. Transferences do occur in all interpersonal relationships, but where there is a concentration of oral dependency need gratification from one figure, that figure will be involved, by necessity, in *more* emotionality. The latent content of the communication of this relationship will be more emotionally intense than the latent content of a casual object relationship. Though their manifest contents may seem similar, the manifest content of a client with his psychotherapist, or any client with his therapeutic listener, will convey a more emotionally-laden latent content than perhaps the manifest content he would have if he were talking to someone over the back yard fence.

The individual that talks over the back yard fence is less likely to be *regularly* involved in a *continuing* relationship of oral support. or to be so *intensely* involved. But whatever type of psychotherapy, analysis or counselling is utilized. there will be a particular type of reality setting, expectation and role playing on the part of the therapist, and a particular type of manifest content that is acceptable. Each client learns, by a conditioning process, what is expected of him in fitting into the reality of the relationship. What is involved *emotionally* though, remains the same just as it does in any interpersonal relationship

This is so even in cases of behavior therapy. This type of therapy has been shown to be often effective, for instance, in phobias. The behavior therapists have been successful in removing a phobia by gradually getting the individual to be-*recondidtioned*, on a step by step basis, toward accepting the thing or situation he previously had been phobic of. They explain the effectiveness of this treatment on a reconditioning process. When they do remove a phobia, it isn't just that another phobia is formed to takes its place or that the phobic reaction shifts to another object or situation. The phobia can be removed and the client is totally *more* emotionally comfortable than he was before.

According to the communication theory of transference language, the phobic individual is involved in a communicative and transference interaction with his behavior therapist. Behind the reality of their manifest content interaction is the emotionally resolving interactive latent content. The client is able to meet his oral dependency needs; he is able to ventilate some anger and he is thereby able to slowly decrease the unconscious guilt that had manifested itself in the phobia. When the guilt begins to decrease, the phobia likewise begins to decrease as an emotional problem. But it is erroneous to assume that this all was accomplished by a simple reconditioning process. It is logical and reality oriented to assume that it is. But it is only because of the *decrease* in the unconscious guilt that the phobia can be removed. When the unconscious guilt is decreased to a certain level, there is no need for a phobia.

When the unconscious guilt increases for a person, the emotional problem may manifest itself not as a phobia, but, for instance, as a marriage problem. With increased unconscious guilt, the individual may be unable to perceive oral gratification in the marriage relationship, and both he and his wife may be projecting their guilt and expressing their anger toward each other. Each spouse becomes more of a recognizable *frustrating* object than an emotionally gratifying one. They may become too emotionally involved with each other and have less part objects in their interpersonal relationship sphere from which to draw oral support, or to spread the expression of their anger. Both partners may then elect to seek together a professional for "marriage counselling." Though they might state that they want "advice," they really want an opportunity to gain emotional support from a transference figure, and to ventilate their anger. Regardless of what is recommended by a marriage counselor, what eventually does bring about a more gratifying relationship between the two is a *diminution* of their unconscious guilt. When this is accomplished, they might feel that they have "worked things out" together. What they actually have done is due to a *transference* situation that is set up between each one and the counselor. Within this therapeutic transference, they each gain a gratification of their oral needs and a ventilation of their anger. The manifest content may seem to focus on the other spouse, but the *latent* content will involve the marriage counselor. It is *from* him that the oral support is drawn, and it is *to* him that the anger is expressed. But again their manifest content *is* important in that it gives a *reason* for involvement.

It is not always possible, or at times even practical, to see both marriage partners in a "marriage" problem. One partner may refuse to be involved, so only one comes. It is possible for a marriage counselor to work with this one person, though both husband and wife may not see at first how it is possible to resolve a marriage difficulty without the other partner being present. Their difficulty in seeing this is often more a manifestation of their emotional resistance than a practical problem. The manifest content of the person that does come is oriented toward the reality of the marriage problems. As this person begins to gratify oral dependency needs from the marriage counselor, a therapeutic transference is formed with a ventilation of anger and an eventual diminution of the unconscious guilt to a more comfortable level. With decreased unconscious guilt, the individual is now able to meet more of the spouse's needs. With decreased guilt, the individual can expand his sphere of interpersonal relationships, providing more part objects for supplying oral needs and expressing anger that will take the emotional "pressure" off the spouse. This is not to imply that this person that did come by himself for professional help was the *more* emotionally uncomfortable. Most frequently, he is less emotionally uncomfortable and has less unconscious guilt, while his spouse with more guilt has more resistance to any transference involvement.

Very frequently, a client will come into a therapeutic transference relationship depressed, with a manifest content oriented toward somatic complaints. In time, with emotional support and oral dependency more secured, this person begins to ventilate anger. It then becomes apparent that the manifest content is being oriented toward a marriage problem that had been suppressed. With a previous higher level of unconscious guilt, this person blamed herself for her lethargy, her depression and her fatigue, and might have sought a physical basis for her headaches and her gastric distress. With less guilt, the marriage problem begins to unfold. This is not to say though, that the fundamental problem is a marriage problem. A marriage problem undoubtedly does exist — but it exists in reality. It is only natural that the manifest content be oriented to such reality problems. But in this marriage problem there is an unreality in that the marriage difficulty reflects difficulties in the interpersonal relationship sphere of the distant emotional past. It culminates the emotional problems of the past, symbolizing them and concretizing them into an understandable dilemma. It is this unreality that is transferred into the relationship of this person with his therapist. The fundamental problem is an *emotional* one that will involve, the more the relationship is continued, the client and his *therapist*, and *not* the client and his spouse. Verbalization of the marriage problem is a simple manifest content for resolving the emotional problem between the client and his therapeutic listener. The fundamental emotional problem becomes a "marriage problem" between client and therapist that is latent, subtle, part object oriented and hidden within the reality oriented manifest content. However, this manifest content oriented toward marriage problems works just as well for this particular emotionally uncomfortable client as some other manifest content works for another emotionally uncomfortable client. The importance of the manifest content is individually determined. The fundamental problem for anyone that is emotionally uncomfortable is always an increased level of unconscious guilt. This unconscious guilt, if the emotional uncomfortableness is recent, is due to the *added* unconscious guilt from the more recently and more additionally frustrated oral dependency needs, and the repression of the resulting anger. We have already seen that the tendency toward repression of the anger is due to the personality core guilt. When the added guilt is additional to the core guilt, there will be an even *greater* tendency for a person to *repress* his anger.

Depression has been described as the most common "psychiatric" symptom according to a panel of "experts" convened by The American Psychiatric Association to handle press queries after Senator Eagleton's medical history was revealed. They estimated that every year doctors treat some 4,000,000 to 8,000,000 Americans for it, and 250,000 require hospitalization. One may very well suspicion there is more depression than this, and may even go so far as to suspicion that *everyone* may feel a degree of depression at times. We may not call this "depression" but instead call it being "low," "kind of blue," maybe just "pessimistic" or not being very "hopeful," about a specific thing. This depression comes about when the unconscious guilt is *self-felt*. However, when the unconscious guilt is *projected*, as though: "*I'm* not to blame, *he* is," the person isn't depressed. If there were a large amount of guilt projected, the individual might be labelled a "paranoid." But everyone projects a certain amount of their unconscious guilt, and some more than others. We don't have to call this "being paranoid" either. But when a person who might have been depressed in a marriage projects his guilt to his spouse, there may then develop a "marriage problem." The spouse becomes the object of this projected unconscious

271

guilt, and marriage turmoil, separations or divorces are the result. If depression if the "most common psychiatric symptom" of emotional uncomfortableness (according to The American Psychiatric Association) then
"marriage difficulties" must certainly be a "psychiatric symptom" too. The high rate of marriage separations and divorces, to say nothing of marriage turmoil, is some indication of the prevalence of *guilt projection*.

The marriage partner is usually a very emotionally significant object that represents a transference figure for the part objects of the emotional past of the spouse. The more transference figures an individual has, the more emotionally comfortable he is. Marriage difficulties often result when the individual has been emotionally involved for *too long* with *too few*. When his oral needs are perceived as increasingly frustrated, and he increasingly represses his anger, he will have more unconscious guilt to handle. At this point, marriage difficulties may arise.

Here is an excerpt from a client involved in "marriage counselling" with a therapeutic listener that illustrates this particular type of manifest content: "I don't know why I continue with this marriage (therapy) — we're not getting anywhere, and I can't see where there's been any progress at all. It seems as though I can't do *anything* right to please him (a manifestation of her guilt affecting her perceptions of her husband in reality, implying the emotionally significant objects of her past, and the *therapist* in the "here and now" unreality of the transference). He just can't seem to accept me the way I am (but it is she, herself, that can't accept her self-felt inadequacies and inferiority from *her* guilt — as well as her husband's projected inadequacies and inferiorities from *his guilt*). I just don't know what to do. (Very long pause.) He won't even talk to me now. (Therapist: He won't talk to you?) Well not if he can really help it. He never asks me any questions, and says that I should just accept him, trust him and have faith in him. But how can I do that when he's *hurt* me so many times in the past? (Therapist: He's hurt you in the past?) Yes, he has — but then, I don't know — maybe it's *my* fault. (Note that the client is not ready at this point to ventilate her anger, because her oral dependency gratification is not secured enough with the therapist.) I've come to the conclusion that I'd be better off if I just lived by myself. I think it was a big mistake for us to have gotten married."

In the following excerpt, a client relates the difficulty that he is having with his wife: "I've talked with Mary (his mother-in-law, but an unconsciously perceived aspect of the therapist in metaphor) in regard to my marriage. (Therapist: Mhmm.) I didn't want to do this, as she's such a nosey busy-body, but I felt that she might as well know that I'm having problems in the marriage with Diane (the perceived orally frustrating aspect of the therapist), than find it out from someone else (a denied aspect of himself, the therapist, or a concretization of both). I didn't want her to think that everything was all rosy between Diane and me, because they're sure as hell not! But it was a waste of time talking with Mary. I started telling her about all the problems we've been having for the past seven years and have kept quiet about. Yet all she would say, if she said anything, was 'I'm listening, Frank — I'm listening.' There wasn't any real support there that I wanted — just 'Mhmm,' 'Mhmm,' 'Sure Frank,' 'Sure.' I just didn't get from her a 'yes' or 'no' or anything. Only an 'I'm listening.' She just wasn't committing herself either way. I thought I married *into* the family, but I can see I've been an *outsider* all along! I was raised in a family that was real close (but it's his unconscious guilt that made him feel the family was "close"). But my marriage isn't that way at all, and hasn't been since the honeymoon, which sure didn't last very long (and neither did the initial "honeymoon" relationship with his therapeutic listener). I get the feeling that *she* doesn't care whether the marriage succeeds or not (a projection of *his* ambivalence). Maybe I'm asking too much in wanting it to continue. Perhaps I ought to face up to the fact that she's going to leave me in time anyway (and his guilt makes him feel she should). Mary didn't make a single concrete suggestion one way or the other, and that's what makes me mad."

It is not that one form of manifest content is any better than any other. They all seem to work, in their own particular ways, for certain people who require for acceptance certain logic and understandable frameworks for reality oriented interaction with the therapist in his reality-role. One has to intellectualize their unconscious emotional "reasons" for being emotionally uncomfortable, for coming to see a particular professional person in the first place, and then must rationalize their emotional "reasons" for continuing to become even more emotionally involved with this professional. But it is not possible for any one particular form of psychotherapy, psychoanalysis, or counselling to be perfectly acceptable to all people with emotional uncomfortableness. People tend to have a great variation in their predispositions for a logical reality-oriented framework of manifest content, and for seeking out certain people for help. As an extreme example, the depressed "backwoods" Nigerian in a grass hut who believes he is dying (whether he is or not in reality) *can* feel emotionally better from the ministrations of the local witch doctor. He wouldn't understand or accept the manifest content or the "logical" structure expected during a session with a Park Avenue analyst. On the other hand, the depressed New York executive who has been experiencing chest pains that indicate to him that he is going to die *can* become emotionally more comfortable from the visits with a Park Avenue analyst. But he wouldn't from the visits of a witch doctor. For each individual there is a certain range of possible acceptable metaphorical presentations of their part object derived emotional uncomfortabless. Certain other metaphorical presentations would be totally unacceptable to them, but may be highly effective for some other person. Because this is so, it is interesting to note that many practitioners — professionals, cultists, or quacks — erroneously conclude that *their* technique, *their* method or *their* format is the *only* way to emotional comfortableness.

People can find solutions to their unconscious emotional problems in an unreality that is subtle between them and their therapeutic listener, regardless of what the manifest content orients itself to in reality, and regardless of the professional's role in that perceived reality. In other words, the manifest content may be oriented toward a reality of devils, demons and evil or good spirits, and may have very appropriate accompanying rituals that enhance the subtle transference phenomenon that will bring emotional comfortableness. The reality may involve pains and discomforts no medical specialist can find a basis for. With others, their manifest contents and interpersonal interaction with cerain other "specialists" do offer relief. Millions of dollars a year are spent by Americans in involvements with people the American Medical Association calls "quacks." But it is incorrect to conclude that these people don't acquire a higher level of emotional comfortableness in doing so.

The manifest content of a client may also involve accepted psychological or psychoanalytic theories that involve an educated understanding of the workings of the unconscious ego. But still, one manifest content is not any better than another manifest content, if it is a *client-acceptable* manifest content that is being utilized. The manifest content that works *best* for an individual is simply one that can diminish his unconscious guilt in a sustained emotional relationship that affords oral gratification and a ventilation of anger. The frills and trappings of the "specialist's" role only support, and give a reality credulance to the manifest content.

It is most erroneous, also, to believe, for instance, that psychoanalysis can make a person more emotionally comfortable through "insights." Emotional uncomfortableness has to be resolved through an *emotional* process. Intellectualization may help in those individuals that tend to be introspective, self-reflective or self-examining simply because it's part of a client-acceptable manifest content. But it isn't the intellectual knowledge that brings about the comfortableness, but a diminution of the unconscious guilt to a point that the client's interpersonal relationship sphere begins to enlarge such that he can draw his oral dependency support from a great many different part objects, and has enough suitable part objects toward which to express his anger. For certain individuals a psychoanalytically oriented manifest content can work very well. (For others, just as emotionally uncomfortable, an involvement with a quack or charlatan can be equally as effective, and sometimes better, in that it avoids the implication there is something "wrong" or "abnormal" with one's mind.) The analyst may remain silent, or verbalize very minimally, while the client is in an ambivalent stage. As the client becomes more comfortable, and begins to project his guilt and express his anger, the analyst may support the presented whole object psychodynamic explanations, or through careful questioning, support further introspection of whole object dynamics. These explanations and dynamics can be acceptable to the client, but they still represent only manifest content. Whatever is unconscious cannot be made conscious by any intellectualization. One can never make their unconscious *conscious* no matter how much analyzing they might do. (In fact the

274

person *best* able to bring his unconscious out in the open is on the back wards of the state hospital!) The more one is reality oriented, the less likely material of his unconscious will be getting into his conscious.

Psychoanalytic introspection is one form of a manifest content that an emotionally uncomfortable person may use. The person utilizing this manifest content may see "progress" in the logic of his explanations and feels more emotionally comfortable as this manifest content is continued within a transference relationship. His "insights," at this point, and his tendency to use less suppression are intellectualized manifestations of his decreased guilt and his increased emotional comfortableness. Almost any whole object explanation a client makes is fitting because of the multiplicity of "parts" any person has available to do so. (This is no different than what is involved in horoscope analyses of one's personality and similarly done by the psychologists.) Any characterization in analysis client may make is true, *in part*. But to say that the client is more comfortable *because* he has an awareness now of these psychoanalytic explanations is evidence again of that "cart before the horse" type of thinking.

Trying to change the primary process oriented emotional feelings by intellectual endeavors can be likened to the psychiatrically hospitalized patient who believed he was dead (as perhaps a denial of his guilt-laden oral need and his repressed anger, as well as a reflection of how his guilt makes him feel he deserves to be). His doctor was so frustrated in his attempts to convince the patient he wasn't dead that the doctor finally asked the patient 'Do dead men bleed?' When the patient replied that it was his belief they didn't, the doctor stuck him on the hand with a small scalpel blade. As the blood trickled down his hand, the astonished patient exclaimed: 'By God! Dead men *do* bleed!' Though not always as bizarre as this patient's belief, clients in psychoanalysis will often initially adhere to rather unrealistic beliefs about themselves, others or about an aspect of reality. These beliefs will change, in time, to more realistic beliefs as they become more comfortable. But the reason the beliefs *do* become more realistic is not due to anything in the manifest content, but due to the client becoming *more* emotionally comfortable. Yet the manifest content *is* important in that it is the effective *matrix* for the latent content interaction within the therapeutic transference.

Cultisms and the various forms of quackery may represent frequently used manifest contents for transferential interaction. The popularity of quackery and the different varieties of cults should be evidence enough that they must have *some* emotional appeal to people who frequently find themselves rejected in their attempts to get comfortable in more scientifically oriented interactions. Some manifest contents can be more scientifically oriented than others, but this only makes them more suitable for the more scientifically oriented individual, and *less* suitable for the less scientifically oriented, or less "learned" individual. The manifest content that is totally unscientific and totally without a factual basis may work very effectively in bringing about emotional comfortableness for many

275

people, regardless of how either the American Medical Association or the U.S. Post Office feels about the cult. After-all, quackery and "faith-healing" is very closely akin to psychotherapy in principle.. Many forms of psychotherapy seem to boder on what some people might term "quackery" or worse.

There are recognized forms of "psychotherapy" that one could label "disso-cial," "harmful" or "obscene," but someone else can find "higly rewarding." Nude group therapy marathons, group-therapist sex play, and sex-oriented inter-actions between client and therapist have become increasingly popular and psychologically "justified" by scientific explanations. Physically abusive "anger-releasing" group sessions are also scientifically explained and accepted by many as "therapeutic." Whether one labels these as "psychotherapy" or "quackery" makes little difference to the person who recognizes *all* interpersonal relation-ships are transferential, and therefore *all* have the potential of becoming emo-tionally gratifying, of involving anger expression, and of producing a higher level of emotional comfortableness. The whole world of interpersonal relation-ship interaction can be called "therapeutic". But like the medical axiom "One man's medicine is another man's poison," each person must find his own means and his own involvements in reality for being "therapeutically treated."

Psychiatry, religion and quackery do involve *more* of an unreality than reality. Each of these may seem very necessary for certain people for workable manifest contents and interpersonal relationship involvement. They each can produce emotionally comfortable results by the same underlying transferential means. Certain individuals cannot accept psychotherapy or psychoanalysis, just as some individuals can't accept religion, but they may, for instance, accept a form of quackery or some other form of emotional interaction. What is different is only that the manifest content is oriented in a different way. One can argue that if the manifest content works then it is a good one. If the end result is having a higher level of emotional comfortableness, then one manifest content is as good as another, regardless of the reality of it all.

It is erroneous to place a special importance to dream interpretation as a man-ifest content. It is important to recognize that, although the dream is made up of a latent content and a manifest content, that *dream recall* is something else, as has been emphasized. Dream recall is what one *remembers* of the manifest content of a dream. When a person *tells* this dream recall to someone else, this telling of their dream becomes a part of a manifest content of a *transference* situation, and therefore comes under the transference phenomenon. Dream recall, as such, is no different than any other type of recall. For certain individuals, it may have a spe-cial meaning in that it conveys better their emotionality, just as *any* manifest con-tent has this *personal* importance. To say that "the manifest dream content pro-vides cogent symbolic metaphors for the analytic dialogue" is to grossly disregard that *any* manifest content of *any* recall, or of anything verbalized for that matter, also contains symbolic metaphors as well. Sometimes it seems as though some

276

analysts can only understand what is being conveyed when it is done so as a dream recall. Anything else that is verbalized during an analytic session is frequently relegated to some secondary importance to the dream oriented manifest content. It would be most limiting to say, as some dream analysts do, "that a unique language develops for the client and the analyst through the experience of understanding the feelings attached to manifest dream symbols." There is, instead, a "unique language" — a *latent transference language* — that develops between *any* two people involved in an emotionally close relationship through an empathic understanding of feelings attached to the symbols of *any* manifest content. How the same orally oriented latent concern that focuses upon a transferential listener is carried in dream oriented manifest content, consider the following excerpts.

"I had a dream last night, but I can't make much sense out of it. (Pause.) I was at an office that somehow was familiar, but I couldn't place exactly where it was, and there were some people that I didn't want to be there (a concretization of unconsciously perceived unacceptable and guilt-laden aspects of herself, as well as unacceptable aspects of the therapist). It was like an office party that I was looking forward to going to (i.e., looking forward to getting her dependency needs met), but at the same time these *other* people (guilt-laden aspects of herself, or the therapist) were uninvited, and made it so that I couldn't enjoy the party. Then, later that night, I had this other dream where I was at a different office, and was using the bathroom (latently referring to therapy as a place to rid oneself of guilt), but I couldn't get the door to lock, and somebody (i.e., the therapist) kept trying to open up the door. Then somehow it finally ended with my having completed going to the bathroom, and then finding out that the flush wouldn't work."

"I can't remember everything about this dream, but I do know it concerns a boy (the therapist in metaphor) I used to like way back when I was in elementary school. I guess I've always liked him, and I still see him occasionally even now . . . (Laughs.) Maybe not enough. (Smiles coyly.) In this dream, there was also a girl (an aspect of herself) I knew in elementary school that Bob (therapist with other connotations) liked. Both the girl and the boy are now married to each other. They're a real nice couple together. In fact, they've been married (metaphorical for a part object relationship between client and therapist) for some time now (104 therapy sessions) and get along real well together . (Smiles warmly.) I wish Bob and I (The "I" here is metaphorical for one unconscious aspect of herself and is consciously recognized on a whole object basis) could get along as well as they do — we're always fighting! In the dream, the girl was trying to tell the boy a certain 'something,' because she wanted him to *know* this 'something,' but yet, at the same time, was *afraid* to tell it for *fear* he would know how she felt. (Laughs.) It's all mixed up. (And orality is!) It doesn't make much sense. I guess dreams aren't supposed to. I don't know what it was she was trying to tell, but if I did know, you can be sure I'd tell you."

"I had this dream last night . . . I dreamed of a pig. (The therapist in metaphor.) It was a great big pig with a whole bunch of little pigs (her oral dependency needs). Those sows like that can be pretty mean. I know — I've seen them when I was growing up (a reference to her oral deprivation when she was growing up as well as early perceptions of the therapeutic transference). They only think about themselves. They're not good mothers and this one kept stepping on her little pigs trying to kill them. Yet the little pigs were trying to get fed. They were running here and there trying to get milk, but she kept rolling back and forth in dirty old mud (her projected guilt) so that they couldn't get to her. She'd snap at them too. I've seen some pretty bad bites from a big sow like that . . . they don't want anyone to bother them. I don't know why I dreamed that dream unless it's because I've been eating (a reference to the oral gratification in therapy) something I shouldn't. I've heard it's what you sometimes eat that can cause nightmares like that!"

"I dreamed this odd dream last night. It had something to do with my father (i.e. therapist) and my finding a big gallon jar of pills (oral dependency gratification) like the type he kept in his office. Doctors used to give their own pills to their patients, you know, instead of their having to go to a druggist (the therapist as a less accessible "specialist" in oral dependency gratification) to get them as they do now. I guess doctors (other aspects of the therapist that she perceives as not wanting to be "bothered" with meeting her oral needs) don't want to be bothered with dispensing pills — and I don't blame them. It's an age of specialization now. In the dream, I was afraid of the pills. My father was offering me the pills and saying 'Go ahead, take some.' There was such a large amount of them that it frightened me. I knew I wasn't supposed to go near those pills, so I couldn't understand why he was offering me some now. I was afraid of this big jar of pills — afraid some hungry child (she, herself, in part) might find them (the fear associated with "my oral needs destroy") and then my father would be in trouble if the child took them."

"I dreamed that I had this trouble in my ear, but I couldn't find out what it was. Nobody could help me, but it was driving me out of my mind. I kept trying to get help for it, but no one thought there was anything wrong . . . they kept saying I was in perfect health. Yet I knew I wasn't. Then I went to Dr. Jones (therapist) and he looked into the ear, and said: 'I see the problem' and I felt good."

"I had this very vivid and recurring dream about this old alcoholic woman (an unconscious aspect of herself) while you were away. She had a very sad early childhood, which might have explained her alcoholism, but she married a person (therapist) who was a nice husband. She never could get off the bottle, though, until she met this old blind man. She befriended him and then moved right in to live with him. I guess he met some of her needs because she began drinking less and was going to church regularly. (Pause and then laughs.) I have a feeling I'm saying more than I care to. (Pause.) What am I saying anyway? (Therapist: What do *you* feel you've said?) Well, maybe I'm that old alcoholic woman in my dream . . . I hope I'm not! (Therapist, very spontaneously: Well, you haven't been living with an old blind man that I know of.) Well . . . (Long serious pause.) Oh my! (Laughs heartily.) Perhaps there's hope for his blindness after all!"

Because of her guilt, one client often felt she was going over the allotted time limit of the therapy session, was partaking too much of therapy, and was detaining the therapist, whom she felt would rather be rid of her. Many times she would anxiously remark: "Is my time up?" or "Oh, I must be running over," and "Are you sure you're not keeping me too long." It should be noted that she knew the therapist had been a teacher before going into medicine. "The dream I had last night was a very frustrating one — I dreamed I was in class, and I was being given a test by the teacher (therapist) I don't recall what he looked like. He seemed somehow familiar, yet his face was blank. (Pause.) I felt I had to put something on the paper before the time was up, and I *did* know the answers. It was very important to me to put it all down, even if it were all jumbled up and didn't make sense. But I felt so *pressured* that the time was running out, and that the teacher would be saying any moment 'Time is up — pass in your paper' that I couldn't get any of the answers out. It was terribly frustrating, and I just couldn't get out what I wanted to say. Now I can't remember what it was that I wanted to put down on the paper in the dream."

In the following excerpt from a therapy session, a woman seems to imply she has been afraid "to go up a certain road" in therapy . . . perhaps the "road" of continued oral dependency need gratification. After being frightened, she latently implies a surprise that this road didn't end in the destruction of either herself or the therapist that she had expected. "I had an odd dream last night, in which I was riding in a car with my mother. As a little girl, I always liked to go riding with my mother. But I didn't want her to go up a certain road, because somehow I was afraid. Yet I don't know what I was really afraid about. She wanted to take me some where that seemed way up — dangerously high. I can remember high cliffs and steep overlooks, where the road wound around mountains, which gave fantastic overall views. I could see the road winding below where we had been, but not the road ahead. That's what frightened me, and how high up we were. I kept telling her to go back, go back, but she kept right on going. Then suddenly we crashed through the railing on a high cliff, but instead of plunging down to our deaths, it was the funniest thing — yet so *illogical* — there was a parachute (laughs) and we just floated down very quietly and landed just ever so softly on a deserted beach that was all quiet and beautiful — like a paradise. (Smiles warmly at therapist.) And we were alone together."

Another therapy oriented dream recall implies the fascinating interconnection between the dream and the transference phenomenon. "I had my first dream about psychoanalysis last night. (Therapist: Mhmm.) I guess I should tell you about it, although you only had a 'walk-on' part. (Laughs anxiously.) I dreamed I was in an office — not this one — it was a *big* office with things in it that were very familiar to me from my past. But the walls were like these here. You were there, and you ushered me in, and said it was alright for me to be there. (Therapist: Sure.) Then you left. I don't know where *you* went, but instead, a little boy (he, himself, in part) came in and sat in a chair, like this one, while he talked about his past. He told about how his mother (one perceived aspect of the therapist) always scolded him, how his father (another perceived aspect of the therapist) belittled him, and made him feel so inferior. He told about his older sister (still another perceived aspect of the therapist) and how she seemed to get all the attention and the love in the family, and how he seemed to get little or none at all. It was odd, because when he talked about his mother, she was there in the room. And when he talked of his father, his father was there too. I could even see his sister, picking on him, just as he described it. Everything he talked about was right there in the room so vivid and so understandably clear."

Another very frequent manifest content that seems to be utilized by those that are emotionally uncomfortable involves what might be termed "medically oriented" manifest contents. A person might feel emotionally uncomfortable, and because he *is* uncomfortable, he might tend to view this uncomfortableness as a "sickness" or "ill health," or feel as though there is "something medically wrong with me." Denying the *emotional* basis of his uncomfortableness, it is only natural that he attempt to give it a *medical* etiology. This implies then that what is necessary for the person to do is to find what is "physically" causing the difficulty by going to the "right" doctor and getting on the "right" medicine. This represents the search for the "magical solution" for the underlying orality a person would rather not recognize. Emotional uncomfortableness does, after all, have it's origin with *physical* uncomfortableness in the earliest stages of life. When the infant wasn't physiologically fed, there was both an emotional need as well as an accompanying physiological one that produced an emotional uncomfortableness. The emotional went hand-in-hand with the physical. It isn't then that certain people are simply translating their emotional uncomfortableness into somatic complaints, but that they are utilizing a particular manifest content that is most appropriate for them for conveying their problem, and their hoped for solution to it. The manifest content orientation may involve, for instance, distress with their stomach, inability to walk, back pain, etc. These manifest content orientations are no different than the manifest content that is oriented toward whatever one might like to talk about with a someone else that would listen. What has been called "the field of psychosomatics" is an artifically isolated "field" of manifest content and is no more important than any other manifest content.

The physician is someone that one calls upon to remove uncomfortableness. He is trained to remove a physical uncomfortableness. Unfortunately, it is not always possible to differentiate uncomfortableness into physical or emotional because those that are physically uncomfortable are emotionally uncomfortable as well.

We have already noted that a physical discomfort or a pain represents a frustration of the oral needs as a reflection of that first physical discomfort when one wasn't fed in infancy. Perhaps this is one of the reasons that psychiatry has become a part of the medical profession. But psychiatry is really more akin to quackery than it is to medicine. (Particularly when one removes from psychiatry what should "by rights" be claimed by neurology.) The medical specialist is one that orients himself to reality. He *shouldn't* be involving himself with unrealities. When an individual comes to him with stomach pain, it is important for him to think of all the different *physical* reasons for stomach pain and not to concern himself with the possibilities of emotional origins. If he does so, he may miss the stomach cancer. A person with chest pains *should* be evaluated by a physician who puts the *emphasis* on physical medicine. One also knows that physicians can be wrong in their conclusions. Medical science isn't such that *all* illnesses and diseases can be detected. There are numerous cases where people have been adjudged "physically healthy," when in fact they did have a fatal process that they always felt they had. We know too, that there is no such thing as having "no physical illness" anyway, in that any human being has degrees of ill health. And one need not be reminded that each person is invariably involved in an aging process that will terminate in death as well.

Since it is not really possible to rule out physical illness, manifest contents that are centered about somatic complaints work very well for certain emotionally uncomfortable individuals. These individuals often come from situations where other members of their interpersonal relationship spheres are "hospital", "doctor" or "symptom" oriented. They utilize visits to the doctor, or hospitalizations, to manipulate other members. They can go into the hospital and can avoid the uncomfortable interpersonal relationships of home, and at the same time get their oral needs met, perhaps ventilate a little anger and hope that their unconscious guilt can be magically removed by some medical or even a surgical ritual. It is probable that a majority of patients in any general hospital are there mainly for emotional reasons. Some people feel that well over 80% of the people that visit a general practitioner do primarily for emotional reasons. This is not to say that the person in the hospital, or in the physician's office, doesn't have a physical problem. He may very well have one, but it is the *emotional* underlay that is making him so uncomfortable.

Whatever manifest content orientation is being utilized in a therapeutic transference, it is important for the therapeutic listener to stay within the confines of that orientation if he is to keep the client involved with him. A client will usually tend to involve himself with someone that professionally will support his manifest content orientation. However, it is more *difficult* for the therapist to understand the meanings of the metaphors and analogies if the manifest content involves a reality that the therapist is not familiar with. For instance, the client might talk of a very technical matter, or of certain fields of science, the literature or the arts, that the therapist is not at all familiar with. This makes it very difficult for the therapist to understand what is being latently implied in the given metaphors and analogies of the manifest content. It is much easier for the therapist to lend support, as well as to understand what is being metaphorically conveyed, if he knows something of the subject of which the client speaks. He seems to convey a knowledgeable interest in his questioning and paraphrasing that is oral need gratifying to the client. For instance, if a client talks of a particular place in Southern California, and the therapist has been there, this type of manifest content can be much more orally gratifying than for instance, one that involves nuclear physics where the therapist might not have even had a single course in physics. But this knowledge of the reality of the manifest content isn't a *necessity*, by any means, for the transference phenomenon will make the *listening* therapist "all things" in time. Through the transference phenomenon the therapeutic listener, regardless of his technical background, will be viewed as omniscient. Even though a client can be an authority in a certain highly technical field, he will view, in time, the therapist as even more wise and knowing than himself.

Very frequently, a client will go through an entire course of "psychotherapy," where no more is said than "good morning" and "let's continue next time." The client will draw oral need gratification. He will express his anger in time , and will decrease his guilt, while he, himself, maintains the "appropriate-for-him" manifest content in the presence of a transference figure who seems to listen. This, in a way, may be likened to the rather successful "silence of God," for the transference, as we have seen before, makes the therapist something of a *superhuman* being to his client. No matter what is being expressed in the manifest content, the client will feel, in part, that the therapist understands. No interpretations of psychodynamics, or of any aspects of reality are necessary — and they apparently aren't used by God either, who rarely seems to break His silence of late, except in some rather suspicious and poorly substantiated circumstances. The client completes his course of psychotherapy when his unconscious guilt has decreased to such a point that his oral dependency needs are *diffusely* met, and the once transferential therapist is reduced in importance to a simple object relationship.

Even though man has commonly shared emotional needs and conflicts that undoubtedly have remained the same through thousands of years, there is and has been a great diversification of his religions and faiths. A particular religion or faith may work well for one individual, but not for another. This is analogous to the manifest contents involved in professional listening where one individual may tend to resolve his emotioanl uncomfortableness with one and not another. One individual may find "help" with a chiropractor, someone else might resolve their uncomfortableness in astrology, someone else through hospitalization, and still another in psychoanalysis or psychotherapy. They all meet their oral needs; they ventilate their anger and project their guilt until they finally can diminish their unconscious guilt to a more emotionally comfortable level. They are fortunate if they can continue the relationship to keep this guilt at a comfortable level. The therapeutic listeners with a religiously-oriented reality role probably successfully handle the greatest share of emotional uncomfortableness in the world. This particular manifest content works well and should perhaps be utilized even more than it is. What is implied in "Man does not live by bread alone" reflects the emotional state with which each human must live, where there is a need for more than the physiological hunger of the breast's milk. It takes more than the *reality* of that milk to sustain a human.

In summary, there is an importance to the manifest content of any transferential interaction in that it provides a reason for involvement. The goal of the emotionally uncomfortable person is to involve himself intensely enough in a manifest content orientation until he can *diminish* his unconscious guilt and draw his oral dependency gratification from a multiplicity of sources.

CHAPTER 14

MANIFESTATIONS OF DECREASED UNCONSCIOUS GUILT IN COMMUNICATIONS

As the unconscious guilt is decreased through a continued meeting of the oral needs and an externalization of the previously repressed anger, there will be manifestations of this in both the latent and the manifest contents. As the guilt decreases, there are more metaphorical presentations that indicate an increase in self-confidence, self-esteem, body-image and self-image. The individual no longer sees himself so unacceptable, either to himself or to others. Whatever before that was metaphorically presented to consciously rationalize the previous high level of unconscious guilt, either now no longer is an issue and is simply not mentioned, or else is rationalized in a way that denotes acceptance. That this depends completely on the level of the unconscious guilt is shown in a client who rationalized the guilt-derived feeling that there was something wrong with her by the fact that she had to see a psychiatrist. "There must be something *wrong* with me or else I wouldn't be sitting in a psychiatrist's office." (Therapist: Yes, but I always see the wrong person.) "Yes, I'm the *wrong* one — I've *always* been wrong — it seems as though I can't do anything right." What had meant to be supportive of the client, and in fact quite truthful from a reality point of view, was perceived by the client as a simple statement of the fact that there *was* something "wrong" with *her*, After the emotional process of meeting this client's oral dependency needs on a part object basis, as well as accepting her projected guilt and externalizing her anger, her guilt decreased such that she was able to later remark: "People seem to accept me the way I am."

What, again, had meant to be supportive by enthusiastic therapist that should have listened when he verbalized was interpreted by a depressed client as an oral rejection because of the level of her unconscious guilt. "I guess you are what you make *yourself*. I mean I'm *uncomfortable* so I guess I've made *myself* uncomfortable (Therapist: Well, some people sure seem to *help* to make others uncomfortable!) Yes, I know. (Begins to cry.) I *always* seem to make others uncomfortable." This client steadfastly denied any interpersonal relationships involvement in her depression, but would often complain of her inability to sleep. Her husband was described initially as: "I wouldn't change him for the world," but with the oral gratification of the therapeutic transference, the client later admitted he "snores and tosses and turns all night long." Where she had been afraid she might awaken her husband with her insomnia and would lie awake trying to remain still, she could now remark with less guilt: "I'm sleeping a little better as I give my husband (therapist) a little *poke* (a reference to anger expression) when he gets to snoring too loud. It doesn't bother him a bit as he sleeps right through it." When she was no longer depressed and had removed her added unconscious guilt, she remarked: "I'm not depressed because I've *finally* been sleeping the whole night through!"

The manifestations of a reduction in the unconscious guilt for another client was expressed as: "I've kind of got interested in genealogy after reading a book on the family. I've learned that I'm actually related to Queen Elizabeth of England through my grandmother's second cousin. Can you imagine that! I've got royal blood in me." While still another client, reaching this same stage in the therapeutic involvement, and who previously felt depressed, unimportant and worthless remarked: "I never told you this, but I'm a direct descendant of Abraham Lincoln on my father's side. I had forgotten all that until my great aunt told me about it just the other day. She likes to recall that her grandmother played as a girl with Lincoln's children on the White House lawn." Just as family relationships or situations might have previously been used to denote the generalized feeling of unacceptableness derived from a higher level of unconscious guilt, the *decreased* unconscious guilt may be metaphorically manifested in a similar fashion as above.

One client entered a course of therapeutic listening rationalizing his feelings of inferiority and unacceptableness to others as being due to the fact he was an unwanted child, and that he had been born out of wedlock. "I'm nothing but a damned *bastard!* I've always *been* a bastard, and I'll always *be* one! Nothing can ever change that. You can't and I can't. And no matter where I go, or no matter whom I'm with, this unescapable fact is always on my mind." After his unconscious guilt had decreased to a more comfortable level, he presented at on session with a list of well-known successful men in history, and their accomplishments who apparently were also bastards by parentage. What had previously been perceived as evidence of his self-felt worthlessness (which was due to his guilt) was now being perceived as a special mark of recognition that conveyed he felt something in common with these *successful* men aside from being born out of wedlock.

A housewife, who previously, because of her high personality core guilt, was an obsessive compulsive and perfectionist, became depressed when the more recently added guilt made her perceive that she wasn't working hard *enough,* and that she wasn't accomplishing all she felt she *ought* to accomplish. The level of her unconscious guilt made her also perceive the house was always "filthy and a mess — a regular pig pen," as though implying metaphorically her guilt-laden oral needs. Although she had a larger family to care for than her three sisters, she had previously been the one to clean her aged mother's house. Even in doing this, she perceived, because of the level of guilt, that this wasn't being appreciated, and more importantly, that she was *less* accepted by her mother than her three sisters, who rarely if ever, helped with the mother's housework. By involvement in regular therapeutic listening sessions she was able to decrease the added guilt and remove her depression. And by continuing further she became less obsessive, less perfectionistic, and less prone to do her mother's housework. Ironically, at this point, she began to perceive that her mother appreciated her more than before, and even more than her sisters, who were compelled to help with their mother's work.

Perceptions of a person's interpersonal relationship sphere change dramatically when the unconscious guilt is decreased. When guilt-laden, they may complain they can never meet people "half way." It is their guilt that compels them to go a perceived "¾ of the way" for others, which they then resent. They will present this as being *expected* of them by others. With less guilt, they are able to express anger, and may appear that they are now demanding that others go "¾ of the way" for them. With still less guilt, both they and others have a more "half way" meeting in their interpersonal relationship interacting. Where previously they seemed to be obligated by their guilt to accept guilt-assuaging positions in their interpersonal relationship sphere, they can now, with less guilt, remove themselves from situations in which they were previously bound. Where before they depressingly felt they weren't doing a good enough job for a perceived tyrannical employer, they feel, with less guilt, confident enough to change the situation, or in leaving and getting a better job. Where before they had struggled to *cope* with a guilt-projecting spouse or parent, they become free enough, with lessened guilt, to change or leave such situations. Sometimes with reality-oriented insight they'll conclude: "I never realized it before, but the reason I was depressed was because I was in a *depressing* situation!," or "The reason I was in a turmoil when I first came here was because I was *living* in a turmoil. I guess I couldn't see it then, and thought it was all me!" These are individuals who, when guilt-laden, began their therapeutic listening sessions with: "I want to be able to handle emotional crises *without* getting all upset. (It was their high level of guilt that made them perceive their anger and frustrated oral needs, as ego-alien and unacceptable to others.) Other people can do it, so *I* ought to be able to!" They sought to be able to *cope* with situations that when scrutinized *shouldn't* have been coped with. When their guilt decreases, they might remark: "I think I handled that crisis last week very well. Sure, I got upset, but I had good *reason* to be. I think I handled it a lot better than most people would have."

Since there is a need to rationalize, in consciousness, a reason that this apparent level of diminished unconscious guilt wasn't held before, the previous difficulty may be expressed as originating from some other person. This is shown in the following, where the previously anhedonic unconscious guilt is now projected to the husband. She implies that she is comfortable enough at this time to enjoy pleasurable activities, that she is capable of expressing her anger, and that she is accepting of oral gratification. "I've decided I'm going to go to the hockey game, and no one is going to stop me. My husband has always been a stay-at-home, and he's always expected me to do the same. So I'm going to leave him at home, and I'm going up with my bridge club instead. We're all going to hoop it up and holler, and have a real good time. I'm not going to take the children (metaphorical for her guilt-laden oral needs) either. If I did, I'd just be spending my time in the bathroom with them. You could be sure that just at the most exciting time, one of them would have to go to the bathroom. Nothing is going to prevent me from having fun tomorrow night."

It is the unconscious guilt at a high enough level that can be the emotional basis for anhedonia and puritanical morals. "Sure, I could go out and live it up, but I have my conscious to live with, and I know that I'm accountable to the Man upstairs." The feeling of obligation and of responsibility are manifestations of this guilt-derived anhedonia that diminishes when the unconscious guilt decreases. When there is less guilt, a client will communicate that for some reason of reality, their duties, responsibilities and obligations are lessened. They seem more able to make decisions, and more able to take decisive action. Before they seemed continually caught between their oral needs on one hand, with a desire for pleasure, and the guilt on the other hand. "Am I being *too* forward with my friends?" "Or maybe I'm not being forward *enough*?" This ambivalence decreases as the guilt decreases and more of the oral needs are met.

Where previously they might have felt "I don't fit in anywhere," they metaphorically now present that they *are* acceptable in situations that do imply an oral dependency need gratification. This too reflects an increasing sphere of interpersonal relationships made up of part objects that are being utilized for oral need gratification as well as for expressed anger. The increase in the interpersonal relationship sphere is directly proportional to the level of unconscious guilt. When the guilt was at a higher level, there was a tendency to withdraw when these object relationships were perceived as frustrating, as a reflection of the unconscious guilt. When a person feels "I'm so stupid," his interpersonal relationships are not gratifying. In order to decrease the guilt, he will project this to others in order to externalize his anger. He must then go through a stage that shifts from *"I'm* stupid," to *"He's* stupid." There may very well be a reality basis for this latter position that is supported by others in the expanding interpersonal relationship sphere. When the unconscious guilt diminishes still further from the ventilation of anger, the person may eventually feel: "I'm not stupid, and neither are other people."

Another way of putting the above final stage is in the popular analogy of transactional psychology: "I'm okay — you're okay." When the client metaphorically presents that he is feeling "I'm *not* okay," he is reflecting the first position of the unconscious guilt. This can create difficulties in the interpersonal relationship sphere and communication problems. These problems are even more intense when there is enough guilt to *project*, as well as to be self-felt. He then feels *"I'm* not okay, and *you're* not okay either." But with less guilt, and with emotional support in the projecting of the guilt and the externalizing of the anger one can reach a point of feeling "I'm okay, but *you're* not okay." With still less guilt, one eventually reaches the position of *"I'm* okay, and *you're* okay" that is most conducive to fostering interpersonal relationships that are oral need gratifying.

Instead of a reference to one's self or to others, there may be metaphorical representations involving inanimate objects which can imply the same decrease in guilt. For instance, one client in beginning therapy remarked, describing herself in analogy: "I hate to have anyone come to my house as it's such a disgrace. One can't even use the front door as the hinges are out of line, and the door knob doesn't work. The door won't hold back any storm as rain or snow comes right in under the door. The furniture is old and shabby. I'm afraid to let anyone sit down on the couch as the springs are coming through the cushion and may hurt someone." This same client, with decreased guilt, later remarked: "Well, I've finally had the front door fixed up, and my new furniture really looks nice. I'm having my neighbors over tomorrow night for cocktails, and I'm looking forward to it." Though this woman rationalized her previous inability to have the neighbors over as due to the condition of her house, the real reason was the uncomfortable level of her unconscious guilt. Had this client in her more guilt-laden state had a workable front door and new furniture, she still would not have invited the neighbors over, and would have rationalized this in some other metaphorical way. And had later the circumstances of reality been other than her repairing the front door and having received a new set of furniture, she would have used other analogies to represent the decreased unconscious guilt, and the resulting ability to feel comfortable with other people.

The therapeutic listener rapidly becomes accustomed to understanding metaphorical representations and analogies for the shifting levels of unconscious guilt, not only in the manifest content and the reality of the interpersonal relationships, but what is implied on the latent level that indicates an increased ability to draw oral need gratification from within the therapeutic transference, and to express anger. There is more freedom in interpersonal relationships as the unconscious guilt decreases and since the manifest content is drawn from reality, there is a factual basis for what is metaphorically expressed. But on the latent level, in regard to the client-therapist relationship, there is evidence that more part objects are being perceived in the therapist that are orally gratifying, and more part objects that are being used for anger expression. For instance, the previously depressed client that later felt that no one in town was good enough for him to socialize with, eventually reaches a point where he *does* find someone in his reality who is orally gratifying. 'I've finally found out there is someone else in this town with a higher I.Q. than 80!" While another client, who previously rationalized her inability to expand her interpersonal relationship sphere as: "I don't want anyone to know that I'm seeing a psychiatrist, and have some type of mental problem," now can remark: "It's reassuring to know that others have problems like mine, and that they've seen a psychiatrist too."

When clients state that they are unable to express their feelings, they are unconsciously referring to the inability to meet their oral dependency needs, and the inability to express angry feelings that is due to their guilt. When their guilt diminishes, they not only present metaphorical representations of gratifying previously unmet oral dependency needs, but of expressing previously repressed anger as well. This is shown in: "I used to be afraid to meet anyone for fear that somehow I wouldn't be acceptable to them. I'd try to put up different fronts, attempting to do or say what I felt I ought to do or say, and then ending up creating the opposite impression. I was always taking insults off of other people, and trying to adjust to certain situations that now I know I shouldn't have even bothered trying to adjust to. I felt then that I *had* to cope with everything. Well, I've been thinking that this country became free and independent because it *didn't* adjust to its situation back in 1775. One can still be friends, like England and the United States (latently referring to herself and the therapist), even when one (meaning herself) stands up for what they feel is right. That's like my relationship with Eleanor (a perceived aspect of the therapist). I don't really feel that I *need* her. It's not that type of relationship anymore. I'm involved with her now because I *like* being involved with her. I don't *have* to be with her. We have such good times together, talking about this and that, and going places together. She enjoys me too. It's a two way street. We have a good relationship because I can tell her off without her getting all upset. That's the type of friendship we have."

An individual's inability to involve themselves in interpersonal relationships is often rationalized with some reality oriented shame or guilt. They feel as though they are guilty of something in reality, and avoid others for fear that they might find out about their "secret." Many times a client, after just a few sessions of talking and listening, will remark: "I never told you this before, but — ," and then will go on to tell of a guilt-laden secret that previously with a higher level of guilt they couldn't tell. With *less* guilt the "secret" doesn't seem as guilt-laden as before. A client might remark: "I know I'm going to have to talk about my sexual problem. I've been hiding it all along, and I can't hide it any longer. I know that if I'm going to get better, I'm going to have to tell you *everything*." She then goes on to *expose* her guilt, which is metaphorical for the unconscious guilt that is *less* now, in that she *is* able to talk about it. When an individual is able to talk about their guilt, in whatever reality context it has been concretized, they are able to do so simply because the unconscious guilt has diminished that much. Eventually a client might feel, as their unconscious guilt becomes less, "Why should I feel guilty about sex? Everyone else is doing it! Why should I continue to feel I'm such a damn sinner, when people are out doing *worse* than I've ever done!" This client had previously rationalized her unconscious guilt as a sexual indiscretion, and no amount of reassurance could allay her feeling of guilt: "I don't care what Kinsey said was normal for the average woman! *I* have to live with *myself*, and *I feel guilty* about it!"

Metaphorical manifestations of decreased guilt may involve a manifest content involving food. A woman that had previously put herself on a very strict diet, now, with less guilt can remark: "I don't think it would hurt at all if I took a small pudding once or twice a week." Previously, she would not allow herself such a luxury as pudding, which is metaphorical for increased oral gratification from the therapist, but with decreased guilt, she can now do so. This "eating" more is symbolic of one's "feeding" more in interpersonal relationships. One doesn't seem to get laden down with that ugly "fat" of guilt as before. Sometimes this "eating more and getting less fat" feeling is projected to someone else as: "I don't see how Peggy (a metaphorical part of herself) can eat as much as she does, and not get fat! She's been visiting me for the past week, and I admire her ability to relax and take things easy. I (another metaphorical part of herself) have to push myself continually, and I have to constantly watch what I eat. She doesn't push herself, and she's always eating something. She's continually snacking away. Everytime I look at her, she's got something in her mouth, and yet she doesn't gain any weight. I look like a big fat slob! She's a nice trim 105 pounds, and not even on a diet. How can she do that anyway? If I ate what she eats in one day, I'd be big as a balloon!"

This need to "push" oneself brings up the subject of work. The individual that is overwhelmed by his unconscious guilt, and his guilt-derived feelings of worthlessness, is often unable to work at all. He may be completely incapacitated, and in a depressed state. However, if enough guilt can be removed such that he is able to function, one can often see that he has an apparent "need" to work from his personality core guilt. These people seem to feel as though they are lazy, worthless and useless unless they *are* pushing themselves with continual work. Even when they do so, the unconscious guilt often makes them feel that they have to accomplish even more. In spite of the work they do, they feel they could work *harder*. No amount of work can give the feeling of satisfaction, for their level of guilt will always give them a feeling of self-dissatisfaction. (Note that if the work were difficult enough, it might be guilt-assuaging, and that many people seem to seek this as a solution for their increased guilt.)

The manifestations of decreased guilt may be oriented to dream recall that indicates that there is now an acceptance of anger expression, and an acceptance of oral need gratification. The verbalizations involving dream recall in the manifest content often reflect the stage that the client is in in regard to the therapeutic transference. (This implies, perhaps, a link between the transference phenomenon and the dreaming phenomenon.) At first, dreams tend to be manifestations of the guilt, or of the potential anger, violence, or destructiveness that the individual fears. This may shift with decreasing unconscious guilt to dreams of expressing uncontrolled anger, and finally to dreams that convey the expression of anger that is non-destructive and justified. One's pleasant or "sweet dreams" that are recalled imply oral gratification that is less blocked by guilt, and stand in contrast to the "nightmares" of increased guilt. When one's guilt is at a high enough level, one's dreams *and* one's transferences are "nightmares." When the guilt is decreased enough, one's dreams and one's transferences become more pleasant.

The level of one's unconscious guilt markedly affects the perceptions that an individual makes. "People accept me" is a perception that comes with less guilt, while with more guilt this perception can become: "People *don't* accept me." With less guilt a person may remark: "People look at me, and are envious," while with a previous higher level of guilt this person felt: "People look at me and are critical." Sometimes these perceptions seem to fit poorly with reality. For instance, one client, early in therapy, remarked: "I do an awful lot of talking," when actually she did very little talking in her sessions, but her guilt made her feel that what little she did say was excessive. Later with less unconscious guilt, she remarked: "I do an awful lot of listening in my work," when she was actually more verbal than she was previously.

Perceptions within the therapy situation shift when there has been a reduction in the unconscious guilt. For instance, even the perception of the therapist as a listener can change. A client, who, earlier in her therapeutic listening sessions, remarked: "You are a very good listener . . . in fact you're *too* good of a listener," implying in this her "need" to hide both her guilt-laden dependency needs and her anger. Several months later and with decreased guilt, she remarked: "You're *not* listening to me!" now implying an acceptance of oral gratification and of anger expression even beyond that which she unconsciously perceives the therapist of offering.

Another client had initially expressed concern that the therapist wasn't always available to her, although he was seeing her on a twice a week basis: "You're never around when I need you (very anxiously) . . . How can I reach you in between these sessions?" By maintaining regular sessions, she later, when her guilt had decreased, remarked: "Well, here we are again! My God! I was just here. (Laughs.) I can't get rid of you!" This is similar to the client that, when guilt-laden early in her therapeutic listening sessions, would often remark: "I know you're going to drop me when you find out what I'm really like." When a little less guilt-laden and more actively feeding in the therapeutic transference, she would now remark: "I'm afraid you're going to keep me coming here forever!"

It's the guilt-laden client that will remark: "What I tell you just doesn't seem significant. I have the feeling that I'm not telling you what is important!" What this person wants to communicate is the ambivalence of wanting and needing so desperately the therapist, while *not* wanting and preferring *not* to need him at the very same time. But with less guilt, and with the ambivalence having been expressed metaphorically in the analogies of her manifest content, she can now remark: "Somehow I feel that this is significant material I'm bringing up now. Somehow it's important, and I know I'm on the right track!"

In the manifest content of the above excerpts, the therapist is referred to as a consciously perceived whole object. Within any *latent* content, the therapist is always *part* object perceived. How this part object perception can also shift, with decreased guilt, is illustrated in the following, where the client is a graduate student who previously had feelings of severe depression, inferiority and inadequacy from his self-felt guilt. "The sociology department (a reference to the therapist and the therapy situation) is so damn passive. It really gripes me to think of what little they do for the graduate student. They simply provide the setting, and the student *himself* has to do all the work, mapping out his own program, and setting his own goals. The department won't even help when a curriculum problem is presented by the student. It's a kind of '*You* work it out . . . it's *your* problems' attitude that makes me so mad. I'm beginning to see things a lot different than I did before about that department. And to think how I thought it was the very best department in the whole University. But now I can see those little flaws in it I couldn't see before. And one of them is it's passivity. (Long thoughtful pause.) I got a warning ticket last week for reckless driving (a reference to the previous expression of anger). I really deserved it too. I didn't have the car under control like I should have had, and furthermore, I was bucking traffic going the other way. I've got to watch myself more. Lately, I've gotten so I yell and scream with a gay abandon when anything makes me mad. If I'm at a light and the driver (the therapist) in front hasn't started moving, I'll give him a blast on the horn, and yell: 'Come on you bastard! Get going!' (Laughs.) I was *never* like that before (Laughs again.) It's going to graduate school and driving in the city that's done it. I guess I'm frustrated at the school. It's not giving me all I feel it should, so I take out my frustrations on the highway rather than get expelled. But that's not right now, is it? I get mad at people whom I know I shouldn't be mad at. Instead of a warning ticket, I should have gotten a fine! It surprised me that a state trooper (another perceived aspect of the therapist) can be so tolerant!"

The perceptions of a previously self-debasing client about her "best friend" markedly change when the level of her unconscious guilt decreases. "That damn Katherine! (Therapist.) She makes me so damn mad! I'm seeing her for the first time for what she really is! I must have been *blind* before to have thought she was so great. I've decided I don't owe her a damn thing. I don't have any obligation to her, so why should I put up with what she's been dishing out to me for years. I used to take it because I felt I *needed* her. But she's never really done anything for *me*. It's always been for *her*. She's always made it *seem* as though she were doing it especially for me. I can see a lot of things now I couldn't see before. I used to be reluctant to even think anything but the very best about Katherine. Whenever I thought there was something I could criticize her about, I'd think instead there was something *wrong* about *me* . . . you know, like *I* wasn't seeing

292

her right, and that the fault was *mine*. I'd just keep my mouth shut, and she's gotten worse. Now I know I'm not the only one that sees Katherine the way I do. I was talking with Helen (a supportive aspect of the therapist) and she's beginning to see the very same thing. Helen has always known Katherine. But she can see that Katherine needs to be told off for her own good. It really irked me when Mildred (a guilt-laden aspect of herself that puts a damper on anger expression) tried to stand up for Katherine last week. *Nobody* needs to stand up for Katherine. She knows her work in the office. There's no question about that. And she can take criticism. It doesn't bother her. She's thick skinned. I've just been a fool in the past to have put up with her the way she's acted toward me. What really gets me is that Katherine is supposed to be my best friend. I guess it's true what the psychologists say about a person that's depressed. 'Always look to the person's closest friend for the cause!' Well, I'm looking, and I'm seeing what I didn't see before! (Therapist: Good.) Yes it is good (vigorously pulls several tissues from box beside chair). I shouldn't use up all your Kleenex (oral support) this way (blows nose loudly.) But why the hell shouldn't I, I pay for it!"

In the following excerpt, the client obviously perceives the therapeutic listener as being more understanding, but in the *reality* of the manifest content she indicates her relationship with her husband is *also* more oral need gratifying. "Andrew and I went to the movies the other night, and I could hardly believe it, because for the first time, he sat quietly through the whole show without asking his usual one thousand questions. He usually upsets me so that I can't even enjoy it. Before, when we'd go to a movie, he'd make me so damn mad with his questions such as 'What did she do that for?' or 'Where did she come from?,' or 'What's he in love with her for?' etc., etc. He could never follow a plot. The problem with him is that every movie he's gone to he had to think he knew the entire plot ahead of time, and when it didn't turn out the way he had it figured out, then he'd start questioning everything. That just ruined it for me. I couldn't enjoy it at all. Now he seems to have changed. We sat through our first quiet, peaceful and enjoyable movie, and I hope there's more to come."

A client who previously expressed her difficulties with her own unconscious guilt by verbalizing about her work with less guilt remarks: "Things are going much better at the store. That girl (a perceived aspect of the therapist that was previously imbued with her own projected guilt) that used to make it so difficult for the rest of us, and was continually messing things up, has finally quit. Boy, was I glad to see her go! It doesn't seem like work at all now. I actually look forward to going to work. The boss (another perceived aspect of the therapist) even said that if she was ever hired again, *he'd* quit! (laughs and therapist does too.) And I wouldn't blame him one single bit."

A previously depressed businessman, that with increased unconscious guilt could see no reason for continuing in business, remarks with less guilt: "The business has taken an up-turn. That new man (therapist) I hired has really taken a load off of me. A year ago I was ready to quit the business. I think it was the best move I ever made in taking him on as a partner. We've even thought of expanding. He's had a good psychological effect on me. I only have a 6th grade education as you know, and I can't read or spell very well. That's always made me feel inferior, and that I couldn't possibly succeed in business against people with a higher education. But now I've noticed that I can pick up a blueprint and read it faster than anyone of my engineers. I even have to explain things out to my partner, and he's a college graduate! He's good though, and he catches on fast. I like working with him, and I wish I had taken him on years ago, as I wouldn't have had to go through what I have."

Note that the client in the following excerpt perceives her son as more acceptable. Her son is metaphorical for an aspect of herself in the transference language. In her own reality, her son probably had represented her unacceptable projected guilt. With less guilt, she has less to project to her son, and can relate to him in a way that meets his oral needs. With more of his oral needs met, he has less reason to frustrate hers. (The part object interrelating between client and therapist reflects a client's object relationships outside of therapy, and vice versa.) "I went to school, and boy was I surprised. The teacher said that Jimmy is a *leader* in his class. I said: 'Are you sure you haven't got the wrong boy?' He said: 'Certainly! I couldn't believe that *my* Jimmy was who he had in mind. He was always so insecure and so bashful. He's always been withdrawn. I thought he'd be just another shrinking violet like me, but he's blossomed right out into a person that can handle himself and others too. He'll stick up for himself now, and he expresses himself so confidently. I'm so proud of him, and the teacher (therapist) said I had every right to be. I used to think I'd have to be dragging him off to see some psychiatrist, but I can see that he sure doesn't need one now (implying she, in part, doesn't either). Where before he hated school, he loves it now. And I've been noticing a big change in him at home too."

An individual whose perceptions before, when she had an increased level of guilt, were of oral need frustration, now perceives things that indicate more oral need gratification. "I'm doing a lot better in that real extate class (therapy) that I'm taking than what I thought possible. I didn't think I'd be able to understand it, and I thought for sure I'd flunk out. The other day I was the only one in the class that did a problem that the teacher put on the board. The rest of the class (the therapist with projected guilt) didn't even understand it. That really boosted my ego. I have the feeling, for the first time, that I can *do* something, and do it *well*. It's carried over at home too. I mean my cooking is tasting better while before I felt as though I couldn't even boil water. My cakes are turning out just scrumptious. I took one over to my neighbor (therapist), and she really appreciated it. She said it was one of the best she's ever had. It was one of those pineapple upside down cakes. Before I took this real estate course, I would never have tried anything so complicated as a cake like that. Cakes that were supposed to come out right side up always turned upside down for me. (Laughs.) People seem a lot more friendly than they did before. Maybe it's because I get out more, having to go to the class. I have met a lot of nice people (the orally gratifying aspects of the therapist) there. I enjoy them now, while before I'd be scared stiff to meet people. I think that this course has done a lot for me. I'd sure recommend it to others (other aspects of himself)."

What is being perceived in the following is that the individual is feeling more acceptable to others. The person is able to perceive this now because of his decreased unconscious guilt. "My boss (therapist) told me that I was doing much better in my work. I thought for a while he was going to fire me because I had reached a point where I just said 'to hell with the job.' I used to try to knock myself out to do a good job, and got nowhere. I was never satisfied with anything I did at work, and no one else was either. When it came to writing letters, for instance, I had to rewrite every other line, after crossing out every other word. I'd write a letter over and over again, and still wouldn't be able to mail it. I'd finally end up throwing it away in the waste basket. Now I say what I want to say, and that's it. I don't worry whether they'll criticize me. I feel that I'm doing my job, and I'm not going to knock myself out for them. They're just going to have to accept it. Apparently my boss has. He's never complimented me before, but the other day he came up to me and actually said 'Keep up the good work.' I could hardly believe my ears!"

Many clients will refer to the above as a type of "reverse psychology." This impression seems to come about after they had an increased level of guilt where they tried, unsuccessfully, to gain the perception they were pleasing somebody emotionally significant. Because of their unconscious guilt though, they were always perceiving, instead, a rejection. Associated with their increased guilt was an uncomfortable level of unmet oral needs, and poorly controlled anger. With the emotional support of a therapeutic transference, they become able to *express* their anger, and they do so, not only in therapy, but also in their reality situations. This ease of anger expression and decreased sensitivity to others gives them the impression that the *worse* they treat those who are emotionally significant to them in their reality, the *better* those people seemed to treat *them*. "I raised holy hell with my husband last week. I mean I thought *sure* that I would never see him again after I told him off. It seems as though it had a *reverse* effect on him. He's been treating me *better* than he's ever had! Our marriage has been going more smoothly than it has in the past. I use to treat him so nice before, and I always did things for him (this behavior was motivated by her guilt) and he never appreciated it at all (a perception blocked by her guilt). In fact, the *better* I treated him, the *worse* he'd treat me. Now, the *worse* I treat him, the *better* he treats me!"

What has happened, in this case, is that through the expression of anger which has a tendency to clear the air in any reality situation she has diminished her unconscious guilt. She no longer is as sensitive, or as obligated to please (which she had previously resented, in part) as she was before. She now is less guilt-blocked in the meeting of her oral dependency needs, and can more easily meet the oral dependency needs of others in her reality situation.

When an individual reaches a state of lessened unconscious guilt, there is a tendency, as mentioned before, to rationalize this in terms of reality. But the unconscious guilt has been diminished because of part object oral need gratification and part object anger expression. However, to convey this to one's own consciousness, as well as to others, it has to be metaphorically expressed on a whole object basis. This is shown in the following excerpt: "We've got a new minister at church, and I've had some real nice talks with him. I enjoy him very much. He's pleasant to talk to, and I've learned we have a lot in common. He's been to Europe (the therapist hasn't, but the emotional closeness in the unreality of the transference is as though there is a common bond between him and his client), and he's seen some of the places that I have. We've sat for an hour I bet, and just reminisced about those places. (Long comfortable pause.) I guess my whole trouble before, when I felt like ending it all, was that I was just too much concerned with myself. I wasn't getting out enough with people. A person needs to *communicate* with others. And I guess I wasn't doing that. If I had met that minister before, I wouldn't have needed to see a psychiatrist (an aspect of the therapist different from that implied in the "minister"). He's got me to go to church (therapy) regularly, and also to attend all the church suppers (therapy with certain special connotations). That wasn't easy to do because I could always think up reasons for not going to church before. (Smiles.) The only reason I go now is because of him. I must say there are others (other aspects of the therapist) at church I particularly despise — I remember telling you about them last time. (Pause.) I don't know why I felt so guilty about things before as I can see now that others in the church haven't been the saints I thought they were. Realizing this has helped me a lot. The minister accepts me the way I am, and this too has been a big help. He and I are planning a trip up to Washington as he's interested in stamp collecting, like I am. There's an exhibit there, and we're going to take it in together."

There is an element of anger expression in these rationalizations that attribute the level of decreased unconscious guilt to someone other than the therapist. It is as though the person is saying "it's because of *him* I feel better, and not *you.*" Yet this is, on a part object basis in the unreality of the transference, where the therapist is *both* "him" and "you" at the same time. This is shown in the following: "I'm glad I signed up for that Dale Carnegie course (therapy), as I think that's what has helped me the *most*. I was always afraid to meet people, was always unsure of myself, and lacked self-confidence. I was one scared little boy when I first started this course, but then it was like one happy family sitting around the dining room table. We'd all share our problems, and our fears, and we'd all laugh together. My apprehension and fear in meeting others gradually disappeared. I

296

could stand up and express myself with no difficulty. Before, I couldn't talk on any subject, but through this course, I can stand up now and expound on anything just as well as the next person, if not better. Even my wife (a concretization of an aspect of himself and the therapist) has noted that I'm more self-confident. She's so glad I took the course."

Other clients latently acknowledge that the therapeutic listener brought about a betterment in how they feel, but usually with the implication that he was to *blame* in the first place. For instance, one previously unhappy housewife remarked when her guilt had decreased: "My husband is finally letting me be myself. I've always wanted just to be *me*, and now for the first time, *he's* letting me!" But it was her own unconscious guilt that prevented her before from being herself. Before she felt obligated to him, and always tried to please him, and yet always resented it. Because of her high level of guilt, she could never perceive that her efforts were appreciated, but were perceived instead as ending in an oral rejection. By projecting guilt, she could express her anger and lower her guilt. With decreased guilt, her perceptions change, but what is implied is that getting better is *due* to her husband in reality, and to the *therapist* in the unreality of the therapeutic transference.

Another client rationalizes her more comfortable emotional state to alcoholic intake. Her metaphorical presentation implies the difficulties in oral dependency gratification she has had in the past, and implies an acceptance of it now with much less, although still evident, guilt. "I never used to drink at all as my family (referring to perceived aspects of the therapist) was always so against alcohol. I was always given the feeling that I was going straight to hell in a handbasket if I so much as thought of even taking a drink. My parents have gotten over that now. They don't seem to care as much, at least I haven't noticed anything from them when I do drink. I guess they've mellowed a little with age. (Smiles.) I know alcohol is a crutch, but I've come to believe that the more crutches a person has, the more comfortable he is in life. I found out the hard way that you can't go through life standing alone. I've tried that too many times in the past now. It's not practical to have just one crutch either. I guess the whole secret in life is to have as many crutches as possible so that no single one can ever let you down. My minister (therapist) told me that, and I think he's right. He's so different from other ministers (aspects of the therapist that are guilt-imbued) that tell you not to have crutches. They're against smoking and they're against having a drink or two now and then. They're even against getting together for togetherness sake. To them, one isn't supposed to depend on anything, and yet they turn around and want you to rely on God (a perceived aspect of the therapist). It doesn't say not to drink in the Bible, and wine is served at communion (a reference to certain perceived aspects of therapy.) I even read where one psychiatrist (latently, the therapist) has shown that he can successfully treat alcoholics by giving them so much alcohol a day. I bet that shocked some people (an aspect of herself) who thought

297

abstinence (oral deprivation) was the only answer! So I guess a little beer at mealtimes won't hurt at all. Perhaps I might be called an alcoholic by some people (an aspect of herself or perhaps a perceived unaccepting aspect of the therapist, or a concretization of both), yet I'm not going to quit drinking a beer at meals. It's not all that bad, and it's helped me to relax. Now do you think this is really so bad?"

Many times clients with a very uncomfortable level or unconscious guilt will involve themselves just long enough in the therapeutic transference to decrease this guilt, and then will rationalize this position in such a way that angrily implies that it was a mistake for the client to have been involved with a psychiatrist. This is illustrated in the following excerpt: "Well, I finally found out what that chest pain was coming from that caused me so much trouble in the past. Before I was referred to a psychiatrist, I saw three other doctors that just told me it was my nerves. I haven't had any of that pain for the last couple of months, but I went to another doctor just to have a checkup. Doctor Brown (a perceived aspect of the therapist that is orally gratifying) said that I had a small hiatus hernia, and *that* was the cause of my chest pain. He said it was very common among people, and he disagreed with Doctor Green (a perceived aspect of the therapist that is guilt-imbued) who implied that I was nothing but a *neurotic*, and that I was imagining all my uncomfortableness. I guess I know when I was in pain, let me tell you (points finger at therapist) *that*! I *couldn't* have been imagining it. He gave me an upper GI series, and it *definitely* snowed I had a small hiatus hernia. I saw it *myself* on the fluoroscope. *All* my chest pain could be explained on that basis. He said that it was just something that I'd have to live with, and that from time to time it would kick up a little, depending on what I eat. He told me to watch what I had to eat, and I've been doing that. I've stayed away from things that were upsetting to my stomach, and I've only been eating things that agree with me. That's made all the difference in the world. I just wish that I had met Doctor Brown *before* I met Doctor Green, who sent me here."

Hypoglycemia is a good example of frequently used metaphorical rationalizations for the difficulties that an uncomfortable level of unconscious guilt can give. A client with less unconscious guilt can now remark: "I just read a book on hypoglycemia that just fits me perfectly. It explained so well the symptoms that I was having before, as all due to hypoglycemia. I suppose you know something about that. Apparently it's a diagnosis that's not easy to make because routine blood sugars don't always show it. You have to go through some special tests. This book said that hypoglycemia tests ought to be give to *any* person who gets irritable for no reason, has angry outbursts, has difficulties in marriage or who has had suicidal tendencies. The book said that all too often, when a doctor can't find anything wrong with a person, he'll just send him to a psychiatrist as a *neurotic*. This book has really helped me to understand myself as a person with hypoglycemia and to see some of the mistakes of the medical profession. I've been doing a lot better, and feeling a lot more comfortable.

Many times a client will have the guilt-induced feeling that they are "mentally ill" or "need psychiatric help." They either seek a psychiatrist on their own, or will accept the referral to a psychiatrist from their family physician. They involve themselves in therapeutic listening just long enough to decrease the level of their unconscious guilt to a point where they no longer feel (so ambivalently) they are

eurotic," "hypochondriac," "mentally ill," or "need to see a psychiatrist." They can present now a more reality-oriented set of symptoms that some other physician can "buy" as fitting a possible organic etiology. In other words, their guilt was high enough before, and their unmet oral needs were that intense that they accepted themselves as a "psychiatric patient," or were seen as such by others. But on decreasing their guilt, they quit their therapist, feeling they, and their referring doctor were wrong, and that they *did* have a physical ailment all along. They are at a level of guilt now that many other people are at who seek out physicians for the resolution of their emotional problems. They couldn't do this when their guilt and needs were at a higher level.

Very frequently, a client will utilize a religiously oriented rationalization for their more comfortable state. For instance, one client entered therapy as a very guilt-laden individual. Her verbalizations from the beginning were oriented toward religion. She, at first, spent much of her time confessing her "sins" of self-centeredness, of being lazy, of eating too much, talking too much, drinking too much, and of not caring enough for others. As such, she felt that she was unfit to be a Christian, and no reassurance could make her feel that she *was* a Christian. As she began to decrease her guilt, she tended to orient herself toward praying for *strength* to overcome her adversaries, and no longer was so concerned about praying for *forgiveness*. She prayed for the ability to express herself, and that God be with her in all that she did. Where she first felt that the therapist was so much a Christian, she finally reached a point before discontinuing in feeling that the therapist was *less* of one, but that she herself was *more* of one.

What was previously felt so much a "sin" often is felt as *justified* when unconscious guilt decreases. For instance, one client who had marital problems sought out a therapeutic listener when he felt depressed and "sinful," attributing this incapacitating feeling to having taken money for himself that was allotted to him in his position of operating a large farm for a wealthy industrialist. When he first came, he was unsure whether he should tell his employer of his wrong doing, and take the punishment he felt he deserved. While the therapist only listened through several weeks of sessions, the client gradually began to meet his previously unmet oral needs, and to ventilate his repressed anger. He began to rationalize that his employer had treated him unfairly, had not given him the pay raises that he had been promised, and had, on several occasions, been sexually indiscrete with his wife. He justified the taking of the money as just part of the operating expenses of the farm, and felt that he owed his employer nothing. He quit his job, taking another in a distant state, and simultaneously quit therapy. Needless to say, from the latent implications, he left owing the therapist money.

Another client always felt she had to turn over her paycheck each week to her husband, who accepted this matter-of-factly, with little or no expressed appreciation. Previously, she felt as though she didn't deserve any part of her own paycheck, as a reflection of her oral anhedonia. But later, with decreased guilt, she remarked: "I've decided I'm not giving my paycheck to William. I work hard for my money, and I don't see why I have to continue to hand it all over to him. I could see he got all upset last week when I didn't hand my check over to him. 'Where's your check . . . you haven't lost it, have you?' He treats me like a five year old, and I'm getting tired of it! I fuss and fume at him, and it never seems to bother him at all. Whether I yell at him, or just give him the silent treatment, it doesn't phase him one iota. But now I've found out what really gets to him. (Smiles coyly.) I keep my check! I've found out his sensitive spot, so I'm going to hit him where it hurts. He isn't getting my paycheck this week either!" And she didn't pay for her session again either!

Rationalizations for decreased guilt often imply a guilt projection. Though there is a decrease in the amount of unconscious guilt that the ego has to handle, there is usually evident a projection of the guilt to the therapist. It's the guilt that makes a person initially say: "If I'm crying — it's *not* because of you — it's because of *me.*" When the guilt is decreased, and the anger expression is possible with guilt projection, it becomes: "If I'm crying, it's *because* of you — *you* have caused it!" In other words, the client begins therapy with the feeling: "If I'm frustrated in getting my emotional needs met, then it's *my* fault and *I* have caused it!" This is an overworked theme that one hears initially in dealing with the depressed and frustrated person having difficulties in his interpersonal relationship sphere. The client will often make remarks early in therapy as: "I don't think I would want your job — I don't see how you can stand it listening to other people's problems all day long." Or "I am so lucky to have found you — you're so helpful." This client will later remark: "Just what do you do anyway? You never give advice. You don't even prescribe pills. You just sit there and listen. (Pause.) And I'm not even sure you do that. You've got the *easiest* job in the world!"

It is interesting to note that in the course of involvement in a therapeutic transference clients will come laden with an excess of poorly controlled guilt. They imply directly or indirectly that they are so much of a *burden* on the therapist, when in actual reality they aren't at all, and often present themselves as the very opposite. They appear exceedingly nice, overly polite and especially sensitive to the needs and problems of others. They often appear "saintly," or so much the martyr to the therapist, in that they are so anhedonic, so considerate of others and so opposed to being self-centered, selfish or wanting anything for themselves. Yet they consider themselves anything, *but* "saintly," and feel instead the *therapist* is a "true saint." But these same persons who saw themselves so much a "difficult" client before, when guilt-laden, later *do* become "difficult," when they are projecting their guilt, and expressing their anger directly and indirectly to the therapist. But ironically, at this point, the clients believe they are *not* difficult, and that the therapist has it easy. The therapist is told, either directly or latently that he is no "saint" at all, that he's not even doing his job, and that he's not remembering and is probably not even listening to what is said. The therapeutic listener has a much more difficult task dealing with his clients, in *this* stage of resolvement of emotional problems, than he did initially when the clients felt, themselves, so much of a difficult burden and a problem.

Many times the therapist is never referred to *directly*, but only metaphorically. A client who metaphorically presented his developing relationship with his therapist in verbalizations about his newly found friend, "Ken," previously had remarked: "I like Ken — we share a lot in common." However, with *lessened* guilt, this became: "I've found that Ken has his faults. I can see him for what he is now." In his seeing "Ken" as not the "faultless Ken" he saw before, allows him to see *himself*, if not faultless, at least more acceptable to others, as well as to himself.

It is interesting to also note the evidence of diminished unconscious guilt in those clients involved in psychoanalysis. Psychoanalysis has been described as a body of knowledge, a method of treatment and a means of research, but what is not included in these definitions is that it is a specific orientation for manifest content. Certain individuals, because of their unconscious guilt, feel that they *ought* to see a psychoanalyst. Others with the same amount of guilt, or even with more unconscious guilt, may not feel that it is necessary to see a psychiatrist of any type. Because of past conditioning processes, and because of certain circumstances, some individuals *do* find themselves involved in a psychoanalytic process. Their unconscious guilt tends to make them self-scrutinizing. They are interested in a *self* "analysis," and in finding out about themselves, and their relationships to others. In the psychoanalytic setting, there is opportunity for intellectualizations and rationalizations that all involve a whole object orientation. What is acted out emotionally on a part object basis between client and listener, who, in this case is a psychoanalyst, is the same type of interaction that is involved in any client-listener relationship — and for that matter, any interpersonal relationship. When a client in psychoanalysis asks: "I'd like to know precisely what my problem is, and whether we are making any progress," the client is implying that he is emotionally uncomfortable, and that he is in a position to *intellectualize* his reasons for being in this state. This involves that whole object type of orientation, which, we have seen in Chapter One is erroneous. However, it does represent reality, toward which the manifest content is oriented. A resolution can be obtained within this manifest content — or any other — when part object oral need gratification is obtained, as well as anger is expressed on a part object basis.

The evidence of unconscious guilt early in psychoanalysis is shown where the client feels as though he is not doing as well as he should, or that he isn't making as much progress as he feels he should. As he continues to meet his oral dependency needs, to project his guilt and express his anger, he diminishes the unconscious guilt. He shows in his communications *more* self-acceptance, and *less* self concern. He will usually begin psychoanalysis with wanting "to straighten *himself* out." But as time goes on, and with less unconscious guilt, the orientation changes to a concern of "straightening out *others*."

The evidence of decreased unconscious guilt in a psychoanalytic setting is often manifested as reflections of self-acceptance. This can be metaphorically presented as: "My mother says I don't need to come any more — she says it's a waste of time." The client *himself*, of course, feels this way, *in part*. It was a higher guilt that made him feel before it was so *necessary* to come. It's the guilt now that will make him continue until he feels more acceptable, or that psychoanalysis is a "waste of time." When a client remarks: "I think that psychoanalysis has helped me escape the bonds and the chains of the past, so that I can live free in the present," he is metaphorically presenting in this intellectualization that he has been freed of his added unconscious guilt. Guilt is part object derived, but one will present a whole object reason for a decreased level of self-felt guilt. The psychoanalyst is *whole* object oriented. He can make this type of manifest content go for any client that either demands this or is amenable to it. The final rationalizations that reflect lessened guilt might involve such statements as: "I've martyred myself for years to make others look good, but I'm *not* going to do this any more!" or "I've decided I'm not going to worry about what other people think, but I'm going to do what *I* feel like doing!" These clients give evidence of the freedom that diminished unconscious guilt has given them. They attribute this comfortableness to the psychoanalytic process, to their "insights" and gained psychological knowledge of object relationships, without realizing that they have only externalized the previously repressed anger that was the basis for their troublesome unconscious guilt. They don't realize, too, that they have done this in an unreality of emotional support and anger ventilation on a part object basis that was made possible in their relationship with their analyst, while verbalizing on their object relations.

The unconscious guilt of a client in psychoanalysis may, at first, be manifested by a determination to keep secret their involvement with their analyst. If they have insurance that covers partly or totally the cost of psychoanalysis, clients are at first reluctant to inform the agency that they are so involved. The person who feels guilty about seeing a psychiatrist often feels just as guilty about going to a neighbor's for coffee. They can rationalize a reason for not being involved in any orally gratifying interpersonal relationships. Their guilt-laden oral needs and the manifestation of the unconscious guilt are verbalized as : "People have other things to do in the morning. They don't want to be bothered by *me*. Or "I'm not fit company to be going anywhere the way I've been feeling lately," etc. Later, with lessened guilt, they don't hesitate to let the agency know that they are involved, and they try to get reimbursed for what they feel is due them. This individual now is more likely to be likely to be going next door for coffee, and more likely to be involved in any gratifying interpersonal relationships.

These people that find themselves in a psychoanalytic orientation tend to be intellectual self-scrutinizing people, who because of past conditioning processes and the "set" of their guilt, can accept an introspective involvement. Those that unconsciously *deny* their guilt, primarily, won't be found so involved. Those that tend unconsciously to *project* their guilt won't be found either. The person that *does* see, on his own, a form of psychotherapy or psychoanalysis, feels there is something "not right," "different," perhaps "abnormal," or even "wrong" about himself or his behavior. He may feel he has some type of "hang-up," or perhaps a "neurotic tendency," if not an outright "neurosis." With an increasing degree of guilt, he may even feel he is "mentally ill." This is the same guilt-induced dissatisfaction with oneself that is seen in those that are not psychoanalytically oriented, but want to change their sexual identity through a transsexual operation. A *dissatisfaction* with themselves that comes about from their unconscious guilt, and a recognition that they are missing that "something" from life that makes it worth living, prompts seeking "help." The feeling of unacceptableness can always be rationalized in reality with an intellectual process based on the particular "set" of the guilt. One can rationalize their reasons for involving themselves in psychotherapy, but this too will manifest their unconscious guilt. For instance, one client apparently identifying, in part, with Senator Eagleton, reveals her guilt in the following: "That was a terrible thing that happened with Senator Eagleton just because people couldn't accept his sickness. I don't know why it is that people (a perceived unaccepting aspect of the therapist *and* herself) can't accept mental illness. Mental illness is an *illness* like any other one. Nobody wants an illness, but one has to *accept* it, in order to seek help for it. It's like the treatment of alcoholism in A.A., where a person has to *admit* he has an alcoholic problem, or that maybe he's an outright alcoholic. If he *doesn't* see he has a problem, then there's no hope for him. It's never easy for people to accept their illness. People didn't accept TB or veneral disease when they had it. But they do more readily now. Why can't mental illness be accepted too? There are a lot of diseases the etiology of doctors don't know. But they're working on them. Give them time. They're trying to find the cures. They did it with syphilis, so they should be able to do it with mental illness."

A person may begin the therapeutic listening process feeling they have "something akin to syphilis." Going to psychiatrist, as a *medical* specialist, is with the intention of being "cured of a sickness." It is as though they wish: "Take away this illness of intense oral need, of intense anger, and this feeling of unacceptableness that I have, but don't want, and make me *normal*." But that syphilitic-like infestation they initially felt within themselves they eventually see, when their guilt is mobilized and projected, within others. This they were previously *unable* to see when their guilt was at a higher level. In expressing their anger, they decrease their guilt, and that syphilitic-like infestation they originally perceived in themselves, and then later perceived in others, is eventually no longer perceived at all. A woman who earlier gave "proof" for her being a "psychiatric patient" with: "I *must* be abnormal, or else I wouldn't be sitting *here* in a psychiatrist's office!", much later remarked: "Good Lord! The people that *ought* to come here *don't* come!" Her husband had originally encouraged her to seek help from a psychiatrist and after introspectively analyzing herself, while meeting her oral dependency needs, and ventilating her anger toward a heavily-imbued emotional transference figure, she remarked: "Jimmy (her husband, but the therapist in metaphor) goes around thinking he's so great. Lately, I've been taking a good look at *him. He's* got a few hang-ups that I couldn't see before (laughs), in fact, he's got a *hell* of a lot of hang-ups!"

One client began her sessions of therapeutic listening firmly believing she *was* inferior. She unquestionably felt "I *am* inferior!" With *less* guilt, she came to believe that perhaps she *did* have an inferiority *complex.* This represented, then, a manifestation of *less* guilt than she had when she felt she *was* inferior. With still more guilt reduction, she became less introspective, and this was reflected in her manifest content. Her verbalizations now contained interpersonal relationship references that manifested the effective presentation of her ambivalence. These metaphorical representations indicated a drawing of more oral dependency not only from the perceived parts of the therapeutic listener, but on a reality basis, from those people in her expanding sphere of emotionally significant people. These references, too, became the metaphorical representations of targets for her expressed anger in a similar fashion. She remarked at one time: "I just read where people who are oustandingly successful are characterized as having inferiority feelings that they try to cover by seeking to be superior. I've figured out that a person that feels himself superior is just covering his deeper feelings of inferiority. Therefore, whether a person feels inferior, or whether he feels he's superior, he's still got feelings of inferiority. It must be that everybody's got *some* feelings of inferiority, whether they recognize them or not. In knowing this about others, I've concluded I've got less feelings of inferiority than what I originally thought I had!"

In the preceeding examples, levels of decreasing unconscious guilt were evident, with resulting changed perceptions of oneself, and those in the interpersonal relationship sphere. Perceptions can shift as easily as the woman whose husband committed suicide, leaving her with a deficit of oral gratification, and a loss of a target for projected guilt, and who sought "counseling" for her depression. With a high level of unprojected guilt, she would blame herself for his suicide. With a lesser amount of guilt, she was able to project it and ventilate her anger, comfortably concluding that her husband had been sick (and latently implying the therapist), and that she was not to blame. At this point, she would discontinue therapy. When depressed some few years later, she once more sought help, again blaming herself for her husband's suicide. One can readily see that a person may seek "professional help" when their added unconscious guilt prevents them from functioning as they previously did with their personality core guilt. The obsessive-compulsive, perfectionistic, conscientious and striving persons are unable to explain incapacitating depression caused by an increase in guilt. Their conception of "enjoyment" reflects their personality core guilt. What they say they "enjoy" is *work* . . . "I *love* work," even though to others, what they love may appear quite orally depriving. If this person's *added* unconscious guilt is removed, they return to a functioning that, although it may bring success in reality (and what better qualification for success is there than the love for hard work), accrues added guilt, and lays the foundation for another depression.

In a course of therapeutic listening, one can see the levels of decreasing unconscious guilt that are reflected in the metaphorical verbalizations of the client. A focus on the level of guilt rather than the *degree* of uncomfortableness of a person allows the therapeutic listener to see the *potential* uncomfortableness in a *comfortable* person. Clients that are acutely uncomfortable often begin therapy with manifest contents oriented to a *"There's something wrong with me"* feeling. They imply their needs are excessive, destructive and unacceptable to themselves and to others. There is a stalemate often presented between the oral dependency needs, on one hand, and the guilt on the other, where the client seems unable to either gratify his needs or express his anger. He seems preoccupied with the high level of his unconscious guilt, perhaps with the death-deserving manifestations of it, as hypochondriasis, or the anxiety attacks, or preoccupied with his feeling unacceptable, inadequate, inferior, etc. Metaphors and analogies are developed for this guilt which become increasingly exposed. Things that were implied as "none of your damn business" eventually become unveiled. A feeling of being accepted by the listener is enhanced that allows the client to expose still more guilt. This is countered by verbalizations that imply that the client feels more self-control is needed.

As the therapist continues to listen, there is more of a feeling of acceptance in the client, so that in the mobilization of the guilt in bringing it out, more of it is *projected* and anger ambivalently expressed. Anger expression is always only a level behind that where the client feels accepted enough to reveal the symbolic concretization of his most hidden guilt. That it isn't very far away is revealed in statements as: "I'd like to tell the damn contractor off, but I'm going to wait until the house is a little more finished!" Verbalizations as: "I'm being too *sharp* with others," give way to those like: "Mr. Howard says he likes me *better* when I talk back to him." Anger is less ambivalently expressed and more increasingly ventilated with a self-felt justification. Where, with a much higher level of guilt, anger expression was felt as being destructive, the client now implies he is even "helping" the object of his anger in "setting him straight," "getting him on the right road," and doing it "all for his own good." Anger is expressed with a complete self-acceptance as: "I don't always think Robert is right, the way I used to. Maybe it's because I'm standing more on my own two feet (actually it's because she's drawing more oral dependency need gratification!) and I like it that way. I actually think Robert does too!" With anger being expressed comfortably, while there is a continuation of an adequate gratification of the oral dependency needs, the client now has a comfortable level of unconscious guilt, and is comfortably involved in an expanding sphere of interpersonal relationships.

What the therapeutic listener hears in his therapy sessions the experienced listener will overhear in the communications of any interpersonal relationship. We are all clients, in part, and we are all therapeutic listeners. It is only human that we all require an involvement in therapeutic listening processes. It is hoped that this book has helped to clarify that need, and the obstacles to it.